The Future of Money

Through his work for The London Speaker Bureau,
Oliver Chittenden has worked as an agent to many of the world's
most inspiring individuals for the past ten years. In 2008 he wrote the
book, *Inspire: Courageous People of Our Time*, featuring many of
the UK's most celebrated heroes.

Oliver lives between London and Montelimar in southern France.

The Future of Money

Edited by Oliver Chittenden

Introduction by Vince Cable

Mixed Sources
Product group from well-managed
forests and other controlled sources
www.fsc.org Cert no. TT-COC-002139
© 1996 Forest Stewardship Council

FSC

For Emily and our future

CONTENTS

FUTURE

EDITOR'S NOTE

The Future of Money brings together a unique and varied list of high-level contributors from within politics, business, finance and academia. The aim is to provide viewpoints across different areas of expertise and from different areas of the globe in order to explain the complexities of our worldwide economy at a time when the foundations of its existence came so close to collapse, and to suggest new ways to approach this truly global problem.

Contributors were given a choice of questions to answer, divided into three sections: past, present and future. Some contributors focused their essays solely on the impact of the global recession on their own nations while others looked at how it affects the world as a whole; some wrote essays especially for this book, while others drew on pertinent, even prescient speeches or articles that were remarkably relevant to the goals of *The Future of Money*.

Whether a recipient of the Noble Peace Prize, a senior economic adviser to presidents and prime ministers, a CEO of a multinational corporation or a professor of economics at an internationally respected institution, each contributor has given their outlook on the global financial crisis without any strict guidelines, allowing them to offer an unique insight from their particular perspective.

The essence of this book is consistent with the universal acknowledgement that the effects of the financial disaster filtered rapidly across the world, needing an equally rapid and concerted effort to avert more destruction. The future of our economy and how we reform it should be decided not only by bankers and economists but rather through dialogue among experts from a variety of backgrounds and cultures.

It is my hope that these fascinating essays gathered from around the globe go some way towards explaining how the credit crisis came about at such pace and with so little warning; where the global recession is now and what is being done in the short term to battle towards recovery; what lies ahead for the future of our global economy; and how it will affect us all.

Oliver Chittenden

INTRODUCTION

What is the Future of Money? Who can see into the proverbial crystal ball to tell us whether, in five years' time, we shall be jingling yuan coins in our pockets, or euros? Whether we shall invest in the price of oil or in companies that install wind farms and solar panels? Will we have changed our attitudes to debt and to the pursuit and accumulation of wealth? Will we begin to feel more social responsibility? Will we be more responsive to the demands placed on the environment by our continued economic expansion? Will we learn to work together, across the globe, to eradicate poverty, protect our climate and prevent the boom-bust economic cycles that so far have seemed to perpetuate themselves repeatedly throughout history? Or try to struggle on with 'business as usual'?

Of course, no one has a crystal ball, though many have claimed ownership to one. One of the lessons I learnt in my years in Shell was not to attempt to forecast the future; it is more productive to think of different, plausible, challenging scenarios. What we do own is the combined wealth of knowledge of the world's finest economists, entrepreneurs, statesmen and academics, many of whom have contributed to *The Future of Money*, affording us a glimpse into their different vision of the future. Within these pages, we are invited to share their understanding of the influence of past financial arrangements on the present and on the evolution of our relationship with money – the earning, the creation, the saving, investment and borrowing of it.

The Future of Money gives us different views of how the financial crisis occurred when the constructs of our supposed wealth were exposed as little more than sleights of hand by overleveraged banks and we realised our financial system had shallow roots that were exposed by a strong gale.

We have been fortunate enough to live through one of the most successful periods in economic history, which has allowed many to be lifted out of poverty and many more to acquire a standard of living so high it would be almost unimaginable fifty years ago. But with this wealth comes responsibility: many are still needlessly destitute and disadvantaged, and our environment is beginning to erode from the effects of excessive demand on limited resources.

It is a source of some relief, even of satisfaction, that governments and central banks realised the need to act quickly and together to divert a global economic meltdown in the face of what could have been an even more catastrophic financial crisis; however, we must now also acknowledge the need for reflection on the deeper issues thrown up by the crisis. We should question ethical boundaries and our collective responsibilities. In so doing, we can better understand what went wrong and what preventative measures we should take to avoid repeating mistakes. This remarkably eclectic collection of essays gathered by Oliver Chittenden for *The Future of Money* is a valuable contribution towards understanding the changing complexities of the global economy.

Vince Cable
London, November 2009

PAST

JAMES ALEXANDER

Was/is the economic cycle inevitable? In a nutshell, yes.

I am not an economist. A few years ago I was lucky enough to become aware of a group of socio-economists, led by Carlota Perez at Cambridge University. Socio-economists, at least as I understand them, look at long-term macroeconomic trends and how these impact the whole of the society in which we live: the way we design and live in our homes; the way we educate; how we govern and legislate; the values and behaviour that become accepted as social norms – a collective common sense.

They believe the only way that capitalist economies develop is through 'waves of creative destruction', a phrase coined by economist Joseph Schumpeter in the 1940s. Their assertion is that each of these waves is based on a technology or set of technologies that over a period of fifty to eighty years transforms the whole of society. These socio-economists trace a path from the first wave, the Industrial Revolution, through the Age of Steam and Railways, via the Age of Steel, Electricity and Heavy Engineering to the Age of Oil, Automobiles and Mass Production and up to our current era, which I believe will be defined by the use of information and computing technology and sustainable living in a resource-constrained world. For example, think of a Lowry print, perfectly encapsulating Victorian industrial Britain: on one side of a large quad a factory with smoke billowing from its chimneys, on the other side the workers' cottages, where women lead gaggles of children towards a school; in the middle of the quad, a number of well-dressed gentlemen plotting the next big project.

In each of the waves a similar trajectory is followed. First a period of *eruption* in which the infrastructure and knowledge are deployed. Then a *frenzy* as an oversupply of capital seeks promises of vast fortune (think the dot.com boom). Then a crash and a *turning point* in which the fundamentals are questioned and a new common sense defined. Then a *golden age*, a period of mass adoption and flourishing of the new technology and common sense across society. Then, finally, a period of *maturity* before the next wave comes.

I believe that what we are witnessing in this current economic crisis is the last hurrah of the previous era – the Age of Oil, Automobiles and Mass Production and the promise of consumerism in a world of abundance. We no longer trust this promise and the common sense that went with it.

For the vast majority of people in developed economies, at least relatively, the last twenty to thirty years has been an era of abundance; frankly, that is all my generation have known. Resources, work and credit have been perceived as a right. We've been brought up to indulge ourselves and taught to value consumption. Marketers have conditioned us to want more, and have made this to seem the norm: for many, success has been defined by accumulation of material wealth; for business, growth was the only game in town; for governments, GDP growth per capita was all that mattered.

We were taught the benefits of growth and the need for leverage, borrowing today to grow more quickly in the future. In business, companies learned how to gear up their balance sheet to optimal levels. Leveraged buy-outs created and financed from private equity and hedge funds, the doyens of the financial industry, became commonplace. Individuals found themselves consuming more and wanting more. They were taught to use 'indulgences' (in a modern-day throwback to Luther), such as the zero per cent balance transfer and credit-card-financed purchases, to absolve themselves, at least until judgement day. We were so indulgent we could even self-certify to obtain the house of our dreams.

But we know that this abundance was not only false but also predicated on false assumptions and beliefs that we no longer trust. Today, we no longer trust the institutions of society. We've lost trust in our companies. We've lost trust in our banks.

And it seems to me that we've been grappling to find a way out of our current problems by using the paradigms and common sense of the last era. We're focused on economic definitions of wealth, on economies of scale and scope, on competitive and comparative advantage in a global market, on supporting mass production, distribution and retail. We're scared, and can't see the future; but people want reassurance and leadership that can guide them through such periods of change. Obama's election campaign is a case in point.

So we find ourselves reverting to type: reducing taxation, lowering interest rates, pumping up public spending, increasing regulation, nationalising failing services and rescuing ailing businesses with state-funded capital to maintain consumption and growth. In some cases we're even witnessing protectionism. And then the best of the lot – this year's silver bullet – quantitative easing. Ah, yes, print more money and then everything will be OK? Let's give it just one more go to get the train over the hill.

Our financial markets are clearly labouring; but somehow I think it's not by accident that our planet is also labouring. As I listen to economists, the news gets gloomier by the day. As I listen to scientists, the time frame shortens and the magnitude of imminent climate change and its environmental impacts grows. There is no going back to normal as we knew it. This is not an option. For those who still do not have a clear picture of the bleak future we must choose to avoid, please read James Lovelock's *The Vanishing Face of Gaia*. And let's be very clear: it is a choice

Today we can see peak oil and climate change as facts and know that the population will grow from 6.8 billion to 9 billion by 2050. We're already witnessing the increased magnitude and frequency of warning tremors that affect our food and water availability and cost, our energy supplies and our global security

My belief is that this economic crisis, like those before it, represents a transition between eras. I believe that this crisis is a warning tremor. I suggest we don't ignore it. I for one don't want to feel the earthquake.

The acute cause of the crisis is the growing difficulty the West has in compensating for its domestic depletion by attracting enough resources from elsewhere. The above-mentioned chain of events is nothing but the visible manifestation of this.

More precisely, the depleted and resource-scarce West instituted the globalisation of markets (especially capital markets) in order to attract resources from the rest of the world, which made it possible for it to maintain its standard of living by creating a worldwide financial bubble. All were interested in this artificial and uncontrollable growth: the nations of the depleted West could maintain their growth and plunder the rest of the world; the governments of the entire world could ensure full employment today with the money paid by taxpayers tomorrow; companies could supply their products without increasing salaries; employees could find jobs and create security for themselves; shareholders would receive significant capital gains; the poorest would have access to housing; banks would make huge profits; the United States would maintain its supremacy without any effort; Southern countries were carried along into global growth by American imports; finally, the global financial system benefited from the world's added value.

Depletion of the West; state debts; lack of rule of law: this spiral, the cause of the crisis, will last much longer.

For ten centuries, Europe, and then America and Japan, have succeeded in mobilising the four elements essential to any material development to their own advantage: population, technology, savings and raw materials. This was done by producing them in their countries, by plundering them or by paying for them. Thus, the major cities in the West would in turn attract all the necessary resources, elites and technologies. This happened in Bruges, Venice, Anvers, Geneva, Amsterdam, London, Boston and New York. Then, the Californian epicentre took over the shift and mobilised a unique part of the world's talents, capital and raw materials; in 2006, foreigners filed a quarter of their patents there; and more than half of the start-ups created in the Silicon Valley between 1995 and 2005 belonged to newcomers.

But this has come to an end because the West is no longer able to contribute itself to that with which it has been entrusted by others; it has lost most of what was essential for survival: self-respect, fear of fading away, the desire to fight, vitality – even demographic vitality. And many of those who had come from other parts of the world and brought their talents and resources started to think that these would be better employed in their own countries. Many Asian investors no longer feel obliged to entrust their money to Western banks. Many students and professionals from Asia and Africa believe they have a better chance of success in their home countries than in the West, which is increasingly reluctant to welcome people from the South. Indeed, while the non-graduate population of the South has always wanted to come to the North, the graduates of American universities coming from the South are more likely to choose to develop their careers back in their hemisphere; young American and European graduates are also more likely to try their luck in Asia, Africa and Latin America; research laboratories are being developed there; discoveries are being made there; the technologies of the future will no longer come exclusively from the West.

To block this trend, the West could try to regain its demographic, intellectual and ideological strength or at least to efficiently attract resources from elsewhere. Instead, it is merely borrowing from the rest of the world without presenting a sustainably convincing project, and waiting for time to bring about a miracle solution.

As always, to compensate for this domestic energy depletion, the stifled epicentre (and this time the entire West), is borrowing from the world's investors to preserve its standard of living. Each time, this leads to a progressive depletion of the epicentre and its replacement by another.

Thus, these private bank debts will be more and more difficult to cover up: in the US, banks will have to transfer household payment failures onto credit cards and home loans (at least half of sub-prime loans will not be refunded). In addition, there are losses on loans for commercial real estate (amounting to $3.5 trillion securitised for a quarter of this amount and already largely unpaid). In Europe, total bank losses will reach at least one trillion dollars. The banks will not have the capital to cover these new losses; on the whole, the weakness of bank capital is a reflection of Western depletion requiring more recapitalisation, which can only come from public funding.

In 2009, OECD governments have borrowed $5.3 trillion, including $2 trillion for the United States, that is 9 per cent of the GDP of all these nations, while the debt is not being contained by any force of recall. Not in the United States, where the dollar is king; nor in Europe, where the euro conceals each nation's individual weakness.

The Asian sovereign funds will continue to provide resources to finance the public deficits of the West, as long as their central banks remain credible: where else could they deposit their savings?

The West therefore maintains an undeserved prominence thanks to the savings of others. But how could it hope to impose self-restraint as long as it finds resources to finance its wanderings?

JOHN BRUTON

The basic problem that led to the global recession was the underlying financial imbalance in the world economy.

This imbalance consisted of excessive imports, spending and borrowing (particularly personal and corporate borrowing) in some countries, and excessive exports, saving, and under-consumption in other countries.

This meant that the under-consuming countries like China, Japan and Germany were releasing large volumes of savings into the world financial system at low interest rates. These savings were then lent on in countries in the overspending category like the United States, the United Kingdom, Spain and Ireland and, when combined with new financial practices, they contributed to a series of bubbles in the stock market and most recently to a bubble in house construction.

The existence of these bubbles was recognised as they approached their maximum extent, but the hope was always entertained by opinion formers that there would be a 'soft landing', i.e. that the bubble would deflate gradually rather than suddenly. The scale of the bubble built up in 2007 proved to be far too big for that, especially because the new forms of financial engineering designed to spread and minimise risks had made much greater leverage possible. Some financial institutions were lending forty times their capital. A small amount of capital or savings provided by the under-consuming countries was thus sufficient to generate ever-increasing amounts of lending in the overspending countries, but the risks were hidden from view by the new forms of financial engineering.

It was not only banks that engaged in this multiplication of credit. Other financial institutions entered the credit market too, but without the regulatory controls normally applied to banks.

Conditions for loans were relaxed. For example, mortgages of 100 per cent of the value of the asset being purchased were offered, with the borrower not having to have any savings and often with a record of earnings that was completely insufficient to support repayment of the loan in the long term. Some lenders offered low-rise mortgages whereby very little interest was charged in the early years. This directly encouraged people to take out loans they could not afford.

Regulators, who might have been expected to rein in such mistaken lending practices, did not do so, partly because different national financial centres were competing with one another for financial business and none of them wanted to be the first to be heavy-handed in regulating 'their' banks in case the banks might simply move their business and the associated jobs to another national financial centre whose regulator applied a lighter touch.

Within the banks themselves, the people who were responsible for assessing and minimising risk by advising against risky loans lost influence to the people on the marketing side of management. Banks and financial institutions were competing for market share and knew that if they were cautious in their lending practices they would lose some part of it.

Rating agencies and media commentators encouraged this by commenting favourably on financial institutions that were seen to be increasing their market share. There was also drive from the institutions and individuals who had invested in bank shares to boost their own short-term returns to increase their share values and their dividends. Bank directors responded to this by supporting aggressive lending practices to win market share, when they would have been much wiser to have reined them in, and they aggravated the situation by designing the remuneration packages of their executives to emphasise the need to increase short-term market share rather than to be prudent.

Consumers do share some of the responsibility for all this in that some of them took loans they should not have taken out. But, in fairness, consumers could not have been expected to have the same knowledge of the precariousness of the overall situation as those lending to them should have had, nor, in many cases, would they have had the financial education necessary to analyse their own capacity to repay realistically. The people who lent them the money must have known this.

The crisis became a global one because the collapse of some financial institutions, and the enforced government rescue of others, led to an immediate contraction of credit globally. This affected normal lending by banks in all parts of the world, because banks everywhere had come to rely on global financial markets to raise funds. It also led to a big reduction in world trade and in trade finance, which reduced economic activity everywhere. This in turn affected the viability of businesses that would normally have been sound.

Warning signs of this collapse were ignored because humans, even at the highest level, have an inbuilt tendency to follow what their peers are doing and to dismiss warnings that are outside the prevailing consensus. Most of the time this attitude is sensible enough, but this time it was disastrous. Public authorities, however independent in theory, will always have an eye to what electorates and governments are thinking. Electorates and governments were not, in many cases, anxious to see artificial elements in the boom brought to an end, because many of them had a vested interest in their continuance.

Rating agencies, who should have probed the unviability of some of the financial arrangements to which they gave favourable ratings, did not do their job well. They often had a conflict of interest because they stood to lose financially themselves if they gave a poor rating to a company with whom they had had a long-term financial relationship.

In the fall of 2008 trust died. About a hundred years earlier, President Teddy Roosevelt proclaimed himself a proud 'trust-buster'. But that was about cartels. Wall Street frauds like Bernie Madoff busted the trust that people had in markets and in government.

Therefore, the collapse of the world economy was not like the Great Depression. It was more like the fall of South Vietnam; or the fall of Rome, with barbarians figuring out how to pick the locks of the gates.

The stock-market crash of 1929 tumbled into the Great Depression when central banks hoarded cash, and the Federal Reserve Board watched as the money supply evaporated like yesterday's rain puddle. Meanwhile, the protectionists of 1930 blamed scurrilous foreigners and then jacked up barriers to trade, led by the US Smoot–Hawley tariff. Politicians compounded the error by strangling American workers with higher tax rates, raising them more than fourfold for lower income earners and threefold for high-income earners.

Today's government economic policy is not so reckless and stupid. Central banks have slashed interest rates, but some protectionist grenades have been lobbed. In September 2009 President Obama slapped a 35 per cent tariff on Chinese tyres. Meanwhile, Russia is placing stumbling blocks in front of imports of cheese and machine tools.

So where does the Vietnam analogy come in? Early in my career, I wrote an academic paper called 'Revolution, Reputation Effects and Time Horizons', arguing that when an invader conquers a country, the economy will collapse, tracking a catastrophic mathematical function. What drives the collapse? Not guns. Not nooses. The catastrophe comes when time horizons shrink. Why? Because merchants must believe that their counterparties will be around next year, or next month. The Latin root for 'credit' means trust. Would you lend to a fly-by-night travelling salesman? The 2008–9 crisis turned nearly every company into a fly-by-nighter, grabbing on to the last chopper out of Saigon.

In late 2008 only a starry-eyed gambler would lend to the Sands Casino company for more than an hour. On the Las Vegas strip you could always find talent who rented by the hour. In the credit crunch of 2008, casino and hotel CFOs had to borrow by the hour.

Even though the Federal Reserve slashed its Fed funds rate and the Bank of England cut its base rate to near zero per cent, commercial credit continued to suffer. A world-class company like AT & T found itself paying 9 per cent to borrow when government debt earned just 3 per cent. No surprise, then, that firms took out meat axes and cut payrolls, driving up jobless rates to levels not seen in twenty-five years.

Was all of the pain and suffering inevitable? Had it been 'baked in the cake' for years? I do not think so. Many 'I told you so' economists are taking credit for forecasting the market meltdown because they 'just knew' that the housing sector had turned into a bubble. I would disagree that housing alone – even combined with rampant speculation and easy credit to homebuyers – would have incited this calamity. First of all, many of the 'I told you so' crowd had been predicting a crash since 1988! The Harvard Joint Center for Housing Studies back in 1990 told homeowners that their home values would soon start cracking and sliding substantially. This was on the eve of a fifteen-year mega-boom!

Here's what really happened: the US, UK, Ireland, Spain et al. enjoyed phenomenal housing booms, fed by easy credit. As the bubble was popping, another equally powerful bubble began inflating to outrageous proportions. That second bubble was commodity prices. Recall tortilla riots in Mexico in 2008, as prices climbed beyond the ability of peasants to buy? Recall rice riots in Vietnam and Thailand? Recall American disgust at gasoline prices hitting $4 per gallon? Every time a consumer went to the supermarket to buy groceries, (s)he paid more for every item (s)he took off the shelf and put into the shopping cart. And so, just as the housing squeeze punished homeowners and wrung out banks, the price of nearly every commodity from oil to gas to cocoa to soybeans exploded higher, ripping from consumers' pockets the final dollar, pound, euro and yen they had available. In the summer of 2008 consumers around the world gave up – they gave up shopping, gave up hope that their houses would maintain their value, and even began to give up confidence that they would keep their jobs. The simultaneous global implosion of housing and the global explosion in commodities wiped out the world economy and devastated the markets.

The commodity bubble did damage beyond wiping out consumer budgets. It also wiped out corporate profits. How could a dishwasher company earn a profit if steel prices climbed sharply? How could a restaurant stay in business if the flour for baking bread busted the budget? Even shampoo makers despaired because the plastic bottles cost them so much more. With almost all input prices rising, neither the household sector nor the business sector could keep up its confidence or its previous spending patterns.

And so, the collapse. Suddenly, banks would not lend to consumers. Banks would not lend to businesses. Banks would not even lend to each other. The LIBOR lending rate used among banks multiplied tenfold! The gates at lending windows slammed shut across the world. It was like a worldwide bomb scare. Without the ability to borrow, firms could not meet their payrolls and had to hoard cash. This was not simply a story of runaway housing prices – this was a story of runaway housing combined with runaway commodities.

Volumes have already been written on the housing collapse and the various causes: The Federal Reserve Board kept interest rates too low for too long; the Chinese government bought too many US bonds, driving down interest rates further; easy lending policies around the world fed speculation; Russian billionaires bought up fancy apartments and tracts of land from Mayfair to Istanbul, etc. In the US, the federal government helped feed the mania. President Clinton's Housing and Urban Development office encouraged sub-prime lending by telling Fannie Mae and Freddie Mac such loans would be an appropriate way to increase so-called 'affordable housing'. With the imprimatur of the government, the private sector took the bait and ran, offering bargain mortgages to even the most dodgy applicants. Finally, we have to allocate some blame to the borrowers themselves, Mr and Mrs 'I Deserve Four Bedrooms and a Jacuzzi', who saved no money, put no money down, lied on their mortgage application and moved into a lovely home they had no business living in.

The housing disaster was not a conspiracy, but it did include too many villains to identify in one essay. The commodity bubble was a less dastardly story, somewhat more subtle, but just as dangerous. Put simply, smart people, who should have known better, became fascinated and blinded by the idea that economic and population growth in China and India would wipe out the world's ability to produce natural resources. Books and articles proclaiming 'peak oil' became best-sellers. So-called experts warned traders and investors that the world was running out of not just fossil fuels but food and metals too. Panic buying began. Pension funds jumped into the game, buying up commodities before the wells went dry and the farming fields went fallow. Of course, it was all exaggerated. World oil demand was rising at a mere 1.5 per cent annual pace, but pundits and environmentalists sent warnings so dire that one would have thought demand was doubling every few hours. While a best-selling book was called *The World is Flat*, investors in commodities were acting as if the world was not flat but *hollow*.

By the winter of 2009, oil, steel, chicken and soybean prices had tumbled, finally giving a little break to the poor beleaguered consumer, who had been clobbered by bad government policy, irresponsible lenders and greedy neighbours, who were now sneaking out the back door of those impossibly expensive homes.

MARTIN FELDSTEIN [1]

I'm pleased to have the opportunity to summarise what I was hearing and reading at the Housing, Housing Finance and Monetary Policy conference in August 2007 and to offer my own thoughts about some of the implications for economic policy.

The housing sector was then at the root of three distinct but related problems: first, a sharp decline in house prices and the related fall in home building that led to an economy-wide recession; second, a sub-prime mortgage problem that triggered a substantial widening of all credit spreads and the freezing of much of the credit markets; and, third, a decline in home equity loans and mortgage refinancing that caused greater declines in consumer spending.

The first two of those are discussed below. I discuss the third on pp. 112–14, and the implications of all three for monetary policy on pp. 245–48.

Falling House Prices

National indexes of real house prices and real rents moved together until 2000 and real house prices then surged to a level 70 per cent higher than equivalent rents, driven in part by a widespread popular belief that houses were an irresistible investment opportunity. How else could an average American family buy an asset appreciating at 9 per cent a year, with 80 per cent of that investment financed by a mortgage with a tax deductible interest rate of 6 per cent, implying an annual rate of return on the initial equity of more than 25 per cent?

But at a certain point home owners recognised that house prices – really the price of land – wouldn't keep rising so rapidly and would decline. That fall began with a 3.4 per cent decline in housing prices over a period of twelve months prior to September 2007 and an estimated 9 per cent annual rate of

[1] These comments are drawn from 'Housing, Credit Markets and the Business Cycle', presented at the August 2007 Kansas City Federal Reserve Conference and published in the conference volume, *Housing Finance and Monetary Policy* (Kansas City Federal Reserve, 2008).

decline as reported by data from June 2007 (a Goldman Sachs estimate) The decline in house prices accelerated offers to sell and slowed home buying, causing a rise in the inventory of unsold homes and a decision by home builders to slow the rate of construction. Home building thus collapsed, down 20 per cent from over a one-year period to 2007, to the lowest level in the decade up to that point. Such declines in housing construction were precursors to eight of the past ten recessions. Moreover, major falls in home building were followed by a recession in every case except when the Korean and Vietnam Wars provided an offsetting stimulus to demand.

Why did home prices surge in the past five years? While a frenzy of irrational house-price expectations may have contributed, there were also fundamental reasons. Credit became both cheap and relatively easy to obtain. When the Fed worried about deflation it cut the Fed funds rate to 1 per cent in 2003 and promised that it would rise only very slowly. That caused medium-term rates to fall, inducing a drop in mortgage rates and a widespread promotion of mortgages with very low temporary 'teaser' rates.

Mortgage money also became more abundant as a result of various institutional changes: sub-prime mortgages were the result of legislative changes (especially the Community Reinvestment Act) and of the widespread use of statistical risk-assessment models by lenders. In addition, securitisation induced a lowering of standards by lenders who did not hold the mortgages they created. Mortgage brokers came to replace banks and thrifts as the primary mortgage originators. All of this had been developing since the 1990s, but these developments contributed to mortgage problems when rates fell after 2000.

As house prices declined enough (by more than 50 per cent) to re-establish the traditional price-rent relation there were serious losses of household wealth and resulting declines in consumer spending. Since housing wealth in 2007 was about $21 trillion, even a 20 per cent nominal decline would cut wealth by some $4 trillion and might cut consumer spending by $200 billion or about 1.5 per cent of GDP. The multiplier consequences of this would easily push the economy into recession.

A 20 per cent national decline would mean smaller declines in some places and larger declines in others. For example, homeowners with a loan-to-value ratios of 80 per cent would find themselves with a loan that exceeded the value of their houses by 20 per cent or more. Since mortgages are nonrecourse loans, borrowers could walk away with no burden on future incomes. While experience shows that most homeowners continue to service their mortgages even when the loan balances slightly exceed the value of the home, in 2007 it was not then clear how they would behave if the difference were substantially greater. It was accepted that the decision to default was more likely when house prices fell further.

Once defaults became widespread, the process snowballed, putting more homes on the market and driving prices down further. Banks and other holders of mortgages saw their highly leveraged portfolios greatly impaired. Problems of illiquidity of financial institutions became problems of insolvency.

Widening Credit Spreads

I turn now to the second way in which the housing sector affected our economy: the impact of sub-prime mortgages on credit spreads and credit availability.

For several years, informed observers had concluded that risk was under-priced in the sense that the differences in interest rates between US Treasury bonds and riskier assets (i.e., the credit spreads) were very much smaller than they had been historically.

Some market participants rationalised these low credit spreads by saying that financial markets had become less risky. Better monetary policies around the world reduced inflation and contributed to smaller real volatility. Securi-tisation and the use of credit derivatives were thought to disperse risk in ways that reduced overall risk levels. Most emerging market governments now avoid overvalued exchange rates and protect themselves with large foreign-exchange reserves. There was also the hope based on experience that the Federal Reserve could respond to any financial market problems by an easing of monetary policy.

Many of us were nevertheless sceptical that risk had really been reduced to the extent implied by existing credit spreads. It looked instead as if the very low interest rates on high-grade bonds were incentivising investors to buy riskier assets in the pursuit of higher yield. Many portfolio managers were enhancing the return on their portfolios by selling credit insurance – i.e., by using credit derivatives to assume more risk – and by using credit to leverage their investment portfolios on the false assumption that the basic portfolio had relatively small risk. Investors took comfort from the apparent risk transfer in structured products. And less sophisticated investors were buying such structured products without actually recognising the extent of the risk.

Most of the institutional investors who thought that risk was mispriced were nevertheless reluctant to invest on that view because of the cost of carrying that trade. Since virtually all such institutional investors are agents and not principals, they could not afford to take a position that involved a series of short-term losses. They would appear to be better investment managers by focusing on the short-term gains that could be achieved by going with the herd to enhance yield by assuming increased credit risk.

But these investors also shared a widespread feeling that the day would come when it would be appropriate to switch sides, selling high-risk bonds and reversing their credit derivative positions to become sellers of risk. No one knew just what would signal the time to change. It was the crisis in the sub-prime mortgage market that provided the shock that started the wider shift in credit spreads and credit availability.

Sub-prime mortgages are mortgage loans to high-risk borrowers with low or uncertain incomes, high ratios of debt to income and poor credit histories. These were generally floating-rate mortgages, frequently with high loan-to-value ratios and very low initial 'teaser' rates. A realistic assessment would imply that the borrowers would have trouble meeting the monthly payments once the initial teaser-rate period ended and the interest rate rose to a significant premium over the rates charged to prime (i.e., low-risk) borrowers.

Borrowers with sub-prime credit ratings nevertheless took these adjustable-rate loans with low teaser rates because they wanted to get in on the house-price boom that was sweeping the country. Many of those who originated the loans were mortgage brokers who sold them almost immediately at a profit to the financial market. The sophisticated buyers of the sub-prime loans could then bundle them into large pools of mortgages and sell participation in that pool. Often the pool was 'tranched' to offer different degrees of risk to different buyers. In a simple case, the highest-risk tranche might represent the first 10 per cent of the mortgages to default and would carry a correspondingly high interest rate. Buyers of the next tranche would incur losses only if more than 10 per cent of the mortgages defaulted. The highest-quality tranche, which would incur losses only after 90 per cent of the mortgages had defaulted, was regarded as so safe that the rating agencies would give it a better than AAA rating.

In retrospect, the riskiness of individual tranches was often underestimated by the rating agencies and by those who bought the participation in the risk pool. These were nevertheless combined with other more traditional bonds and commercial paper in structured notes and even in money-market mutual funds that had high ratings and attractive yields.

This was clearly an accident waiting to happen. The sub-prime problem unfolded quickly with very high default rates on sub-prime loans.

Because sub-prime mortgages are a relatively small fraction of the total mortgage market and therefore an even smaller fraction of the total global credit market, many experts and government officials initially claimed that the sub-prime problem would have only a very limited effect on capital markets and the economy. But the sub-prime defaults and the dramatic widening of credit spreads in that market triggered a widespread flight from risk, widening credit spreads more generally and causing price declines for all risky assets. When those risky assets were held in leveraged accounts or when investors had sold risk insurance through credit derivatives, losses were substantial.

As credit spreads widened, investors and lenders became concerned that they did not know how to value complex risky assets. Credit ratings came under suspicion when failures exceeded levels associated with those official credit ratings. A result was a drying-up of credit for risky investments, including private equity acquisitions.

Loans to support private equity deals that were already in the pipeline could not be syndicated, forcing the commercial banks and investment banks to hold those loans on their own books. Banks are also being forced to honour credit guarantees to previously off-balance-sheet conduits and other back-up credit lines. These developments are reducing the capital available to support credit of all types. One result has been that hedge funds have been forced to sell stocks (or buy back short positions) because they can not obtain credit to maintain their portfolios. It will of course be a good thing to have credit spreads that correctly reflect the actual risks of different assets. But the process of transition has already proved to be very costly to the overall economy.

Someone once said that Karl Marx was dead wrong about communism, but absolutely right about capitalism. As the world struggles to cope with capitalism's near apocalyptical failure in this first decade of the twenty-first century, the observation about Marx is likely to resonate with many. 'How did we get here?' is a question that will dominate debate in the halls of academia, the corridors of power, the boardrooms of commerce and the kitchen tables of suburbia for years to come.

Clearly, the priority of governments all over the world remains targeted on damage limitation and getting their economies back onto a path of growth and stability. If recent predictions are to be believed, the global economy may be out of intensive care but still in the hospital ward, closely monitored and slowly regaining some semblance of health, largely thanks to the sustained IV drip of concerted and coordinated fiscal-stimulus policies by governments the world over.

Much of the discussion of the subject so far has been focused on examining how the crisis erupted in the United States and spread to the rest of the world. But we need to dig deeper into the problem to understand its origins, to know why and how it took root, and also why it was allowed to develop unfettered for so long.

There is a school of thought that argues that, given capitalism's imperfections, the crisis we are experiencing is a systemic failure, a manifestation of the internal and inherent contradictions of capitalism itself, and so long as we choose to make capitalism the organising principle of our economic life, we have to learn to live with its limitations as well as its upsides (echoes of that observation about Marx).

I have a different take on this subject. It is one thing to argue that booms and busts are endemic to our economic system, but quite another to conclude that we the people and our institutions of governance are limited in our ability to manage the gyrations of the economy. This is a simplistic argument and it underestimates the ability of humans and governments to manage the economy better. It also conveniently deflects culpability from those whose duty it is to manage the economy properly and their dereliction of that responsibility. The sub-prime housing saga in America illustrates how economic mismanagement can be attributed to everyone and no one at the same time.

The Making of a Disaster

The timing of economic phenomena can rarely be pinned down to specific dates, but 15 September 2008 is a convenient marker for our purpose. That was the day when Lehman Brothers collapsed (or was allowed to collapse), crystallising a development that had been in the making for a few years.

The basic features of the sub-prime housing phenomenon are well known. Towards the end of the 1990s, demand for houses in the United States began a steady climb, driven by low interest rates, which allowed homebuyers to borrow at low costs to finance their purchases. Mortgage financiers also lowered their credit criteria for homebuyers, thus enabling many to realise their 'American dream'. As demand rose, so did house prices and the numbers queuing up for housing loans. Rising prices also meant homeowners could easily gain access to home-equity loans, furthering their sense of wealth.

This development was accompanied by the growth of a parallel business for investment banks. They bought the home loans from mortgage financiers, sliced and diced them and packaged them as securities, and then traded them in markets all over the world, earning handsome commissions in the process.

It appeared that happy days were not only here, but almost everyone – from the pundits down – was predicting they were here to stay into eternity.

Business boomed, houses sold, inflation was kept relatively in check and everyone made money. A few brave souls ventured to pull aside the curtain and expose the illusion. Houses were being sold at highly inflated prices, loans were being made to people who would never be in a position to repay them and the securities bought and sold by the banks had unreal valuations.

Inevitably, the bubble burst and the gravy train came to a screeching halt. Mortgage financiers, investment banks and the insurance companies that insured their securities tottered. Their over-hyped assets could not be sold and became known as 'toxic' assets. Some, like Lehman Brothers, went bankrupt. Others were acquired by competitors, and some others were bailed out by governments (socialism, anyone?).

Since these banks could not lend – because their balance sheets were full of toxic assets or because they could not attract deposits – credit, the lifeline of economic activities, dried up. Businesses suffered, consumer demand took a dive and jobs became scarce. Within a year, US households were reported to have lost $13 trillion in wealth, more than six million jobs disappeared and unemployment reached its highest level since 1940.

Government intervention became necessary, and a now familiar package of measures was introduced: toxic assets were removed from the balance sheets of banks, their capital bases were strengthened through the injection of more money, credit lines were restored as banks felt able to lend once again, and stimulus packages were launched to encourage spending and get the economy moving again.

The pattern of response in other countries affected by the crisis has been broadly similar, with priority given to rescuing their banking systems, followed by spending programmes to avoid or overcome a recession. In short, Wall Street took priority over Main Street.

Only in America

Time and hindsight have revealed some amazing facts about the way this phenomenon developed. The sub-prime housing and related securities business grew at an amazing pace. In 2000, sub-prime mortgage lending totalled US $130 billion. Of these, some $55 billion were repackaged as mortgage bonds. By 2005, the comparable figures were $625 billion and $507 billion dollars respectively.

Just reflect on that for a minute. It required exceptional talent to grow this business. The bundling of mortgages into tradable securities, and the packaging and repackaging of these securities into various forms of derivatives, were all based on the use of highly sophisticated mathematical models of risk evaluation.

Perhaps the most critical aspect of the sub-prime saga worth noting is that it proceeded largely in a largely unregulated environment. Low interest rates made borrowing inexpensive, and this enabled mortgage financiers to cash in by doing away with their traditional credit-evaluation criteria and give out loans on easy repayment terms. People who had no income or collateral were encouraged to borrow, and repayment instalments were generously deferred. At the end of 2006, eight out of every ten dollars that were lent were provided by unregulated operators.

For investment bankers, the sub-prime market became the source of a lucrative business. Ultimately, it mattered little to them what was the quality of the assets they traded. Risk, the key element of their margin business, became an ephemeral consideration so long as commissions could be earned.

Why was all this allowed to happen?

Ideology or Economics?

The shadow banking business that was integral to the sub-prime crisis developed in full view of the regulatory authorities. At various stages in its development, action could have been taken by regulators to discipline the housing market, curtail the excesses of mortgage financiers and investment bankers and protect individuals from themselves. But the absence of intervention by the authorities is the distinguishing feature of the whole sub-prime saga. How does one account for this?

Nobel Laureate Paul Krugman has observed that 'key policy makers failed to see the obvious'. Former US Federal Reserve chairman Alan Greenspan, he pointed out, had in 2004 dismissed talk of a housing bubble. Krugman also quotes current Fed chairman Ben Bernanke as saying in 2005 that home-price increases 'largely reflect[ed] strong economic fundamentals'.

Krugman and his ilk have posited that the problem is one of ideology, not economics. There is an ingrained philosophical bent in the American psyche that discourages people holding public office from intervening directly in the workings of the economy, preferring instead to allow perceived natural competitive forces to resolve issues of the marketplace. This, of course, is the argument of the invisible hand, the argument of capitalism.

Beginning in the 1970s and gathering steam in the succeeding decades, an extreme – and now obviously virulent – strain of free-market ideology gained dominance in the United States. The market could do no wrong (never mind that there is no such thing as the 'perfect' market or the truly 'rational' calculations of humans), they proclaimed. Hayek reigned, Keynes was dethroned – buoyed by a mood of triumphalism as the Berlin Wall fell. And common sense was banished to the margins.

The makings of a global financial meltdown were in place, with America as its epicentre.

WOLFGANG FRANZ

What fuelled the 2007–8 financial crisis?

The turbulence on the financial markets erupted for the first time in July 2007. It reached a new dimension in September 2008 in due course of the unexpected insolvency of Lehman Brothers. These developments shook the market players' confidence in the stability of banks and insurance companies so massively that credit relationships between financial institutions came to a virtual standstill.

Hence, two obvious questions arise. First, what are the roots of the financial crisis? Second, how could the losses on US sub-prime loans and securities fuel the financial crisis on such a grand scale as observed?

To begin with the first question: the causes of the financial crisis are fairly complex. By dint of an overly expansionary interest policy pursued by the Federal Reserve, a macroeconomic environment was created in the United States in the years 2003 to 2005 that triggered a real-estate boom. In addition, one of the goals of social policy in the United States consisted of granting house ownership to low-income households. As a consequence, even so-called 'ninja households' – 'ninja' stands for 'no income, no job, no assets' – bought houses financed by mortgage loans. Newly developed securitisation techniques then enabled banks in the United States to sell these mortgage loans to investors all over the world. Moreover, securitisation was accompanied by a market lowering of credit standards, not least because it was possible now, through 'product structuring', to magically transform loan portfolios consisting of sub-prime mortgages largely into highly rated financial instruments. As has been emphasised by the German Council of Economic Experts in the 2007 annual report, a key role in this process was played by the rating agencies. These rating agencies were irresponsible enough to stamp the seal of quality on such structured products although they had insufficient experience with them, to say the least.

The biggest threat to the stability of the financial system, however, emanated from the massive maturity transformation by quasi-banks, so called special-purpose vehicles. They served to turn long-term US mortgages into very short-term instruments. Unlike regulated banks, these special-purpose vehicles did not hold a capital cushion as a safeguard against their exposure. Moreover, they irresponsibly neglected the risk that the financing instruments that they issued might be spurned by the potential purchasers one day. As these quasi-banks could operate only via the umbilical cord of credit lines from an established credit institution, the liquidity problems that they encountered in the third quarter of 2007, for example, endangered the stability of the banking system. In many countries the central bank, in its role as the lender of last resort, was consequently obliged to provide lavish liquidity assistance. By contrast, hedge funds – in Germany sometimes discredited as locusts – posed no systemic danger to the financial system in 2007, contrary to widely held fears.

These developments were also supported by the lack of a greater depreciation of the US dollar. Such a depreciation would have dampened household's propensity to borrow by pushing up prices and interest rates. The required depreciation of the US dollar was prevented for a long time by large-scale foreign-exchange-market intervention by central banks from emerging market economies. Another problematic development was carry trades, especially involving the Japanese yen. It offered financial-market players with a high risk appetite a very cheap source of refinancing even after the key interest rates in the United States returned to a neutral level. In addition, it led to a depreciation of the yen against the US dollar, which further amplified the global current-account imbalances.

As has been emphasised at the beginning of these considerations, the causes of the financial crisis are manifold and anything but easy to understand. This holds for the second question, too.

As has been estimated by the International Monetary Fund, the losses on US sub-prime loans and securities as of October 2007 amounted to about US $250 billion. However, the decrease in the value of stock markets – measured as the sum, over all markets, of the decrease in stock-markets capitalisation from September 2007 to November 2008 – amounts to some $26.4 billion, according to Oliver Blanchard from the International Monetary Fund in his November 2008 Munich lecture. This provokes the second question, how that could happen.

The answer consists of two parts that are not mutually exclusive. First, the need of financial institutions for liquidity and the need of financial institutions to maintain an adequate capital ratio.

Investors in many cases want to take their funds out of the institutions if they suspect them to have become insolvent. Sometimes even depositors want to do the same if they are not insured against losses in contrast to the regulations prevailing in most countries. For the sake of simplicity, we can concentrate on investors taking their funds out of the banks. Normally, banks as well as other financial institutions finance themselves to a considerable degree from money markets. But this way was closed in the financial crisis 2008–9. Money markets were drained owing to a lack of confidence between banks. As a consequence, banks had to sell assets, and since many banks over the world have been involved in this necessity, prices of those assets sometimes fell rapidly and deeply to levels such as 'fire sales prices'. The resulting capital losses were, of course, worldwide, since many of the assets have been spread over the entire financial system. This is the first part of the answer of why the sub-prime loan crisis resulted in worldwide losses of values on stock markets.

The second part of the answer is closely related to the first part and the note is 'deleveraging'. More precisely, owing to the decrease in the value of their assets and thus lower capital, financial institutions were then faced with a too-high leverage, i.e. the ratio between outside capital and their own capital resources. They had to re-establish an appropriate leverage, in order to follow institutional regulations or to meet demands by the investors. Many banks decreased the size of their balance sheets by selling assets (again) rather than by acquiring additional funds from outside investors, because there were no investors willing to put in funds. Prices of these assets fell and the crisis spread over the whole world.

STEPHANE GARELLI

The current economic turmoil will have unfolded in three phases: the financial crisis, which peaked in 2008 and led to the destruction of some $50,000
billion in value (share price, credit losses, etc.); the economic crisis in 2009
which translated into a 5 per cent drop in world GDP; and, finally, a social
crisis which will develop in 2010 and threaten the jobs of some fifty million
people worldwide. Each crisis cycle feeds into the next one and despite some
'decoupling' of Asian economies, notably China and India, we are truly
witnessing the first global recession since the Second World War.

Where did it originate? In the US, for sure, but then all significant global
economic news – good or bad – still comes from the US, which represents
23.5 per cent of the world economy. Was it triggered by the collapse of the
sub-prime market? Yes indeed, this sparked the crisis, despite the fact that the
$350 billion default incurred was, in retrospect, quite 'small'. Is the financial
sector the main culprit? Most probably: the reckless behaviour of some financial institutions has shocked not only public opinion and governments but
also the business community at large, at least those involved in the so-called
'real economy'. Altogether, banks were responsible for $3,500 billion of credit
losses, not bad . . .

The truth of the matter is that everybody has been a sinner. Households
have overspent for a decade, piling up debt, with saving rates close to nil.
Maybe the bad example came from above: the US government has not been
very virtuous either. When President Clinton left the White House in 1999,
he was running a surplus of $236 billion. Ten years later; President Obama
inherits a budget deficit of $1,750 billion. This is colossal: if you had put $2
million in a box every day since the year zero, you would still not have reached
such a sum! The US national debt is now in excess of $11 trillion and is
increasing by $3.7 billion per day. And on top of the federal debt, one should
add the debt of US cities and states: California is virtually bankrupt!

In short, the origin of the crisis is that, for years, the US economy has
been over-consuming money. However, the rest of the world is also responsible: we let it happen . . . In general when a country massively increases

deficits and debt, the market quickly reacts: currency is devalued, the IMF and creditor countries step in and impose belt-tightening measures. Latin American has experienced this many times in the past. But for the US it was quite different: nobody really cared. The assumption was that the largest economic and financial power of the world was not a risk. And there were at least two good reasons to think that way:

- The US debt is in its own currency – the dollar – which remains the dominant world currency, managed by the Fed, which is thus *de facto* the world's central bank. Today, more than 60 per cent of the world currency holdings are in dollars, less than 30 per cent are in euros, while the pound and the yen remain negligible. Actually, half of the world economy is pegged to the dollar, mainly in Asia and Latin America, whether countries like it or not. The situation was well summarised by John Connally, the former secretary to the Treasury under President Nixon: 'The dollar is our currency but it is your problem'!

- The second reason is what I call the boomerang effect: in economic terms a trade deficit in a country generates a currency surplus somewhere else around the world. For example, the chronic deficit of the US trade balance has created a currency surplus in China. The boomerang effect theory states that no matter how much money is lost through trade to the rest of the world, it always comes back 'home', i.e., to the US and to a lesser extent Europe. It was mainly invested in government bonds and real estate. For example, China now owns some $800 billion in US treasury bonds, which is more than 20 per cent of the total foreign holding in US treasury bonds. One explanation for this awkward situation is that many countries have earnings in dollars (exports or natural resources). The other is the lack of secured investment opportunities outside the US and Europe.

Thus, the US economy – with the complicity of the rest of the world – has been immunised for years from the risks and consequences linked to the accumulation of debt. The boomerang effect not only induced a careless approach to money but also created the so-called 'saving glut' of the past years, since emerging economies were reinvesting massive amounts of revenues in the US and European banking system. At one stage, there was so much money around that it generated the wildest innovation on financial markets to find new ways to invest it. Money became a commodity used to make . . . money. Financial instruments became so complex that nobody really knew what they contained and/or how to regulate them. On the other hand, as long as the markets increased in value, nobody really cared either. Some scholars even dared to speculate that – finally – we had 'escaped' from economic cycles, or at least, as Alan Greenspan put it one day, that they had become 'quite manageable'.

Well, maybe not ... Recent history has shown that they were not as manageable as expected and that soon or later economic 'gravity' bites back. Today, more and more countries are trying to escape from the 'dollar trap', starting with China. The answer will not be a move towards the euro. 'Emerging currencies' such as the Chinese yuan could become an alternative in the future. It is more likely, however, that several countries – for example, commodities-producing nations – will instead look at the possibility of using 'baskets of currencies' to trade their goods.

Finally the boomerang effect doesn't work any more. Emerging economies are piling up money at an impressive rate, reaching almost $6 trillion at the present. China leads the pack with some $2,000 billion of foreign-currency reserves, followed by Japan, then the Gulf States (together) and Russia, Taiwan, India, Brazil and Korea. Will this money go back 'Home', i.e. to the US? Not to the same extent as before. Much of the cash will now be invested in the rest of the world simply because today huge business opportunities exist outside the traditional advanced economies.

Question: if emerging economies no longer finance the huge budget deficits and the debt incurred by American and European governments during years of careless spending, then who will? Answer: you and me through our taxes! Not good news ...

The most tangible long-term consequence of the crisis is that we are most probably entering an era of higher taxation, not only in terms of rates but also in the scope of what will be taxed, especially in the international sphere. Tracking tax loopholes and tax havens has become a key priority for governments. It is understandable. After the crisis, they need to recover some of the money that they have lent. In the words of President Thomas Jefferson: 'If a government is big enough to give you everything you want, it is also strong enough to take away everything you have!'

FRED HU

The worst global financial crisis in nearly a century has naturally sparked a raging debate about its causes, remedies and how we can prevent similar catastrophes from occurring again in the future.

It is not difficult, at least in hindsight, to identify the multiple factors that might have played a role, individually or collectively, in causing, transmitting, and magnifying the current crisis. The list of responsible factors includes excessive leverage, inadequate capital base of banks, the over-reliance of financial institutions on the whole-sale-funding model, failure to heed against liquidity and counterparty risks, blind faith in external credit ratings, the opacity of markets for credit derivatives, the process of securitisation running amok, lax supervision of sub-prime mortgage lending, the absence of an effective resolution regime capable of the orderly unwinding of large failing financial institutions, and yes, the flaws of the compensation practices that may have contributed to short-term behaviour and excessive risk-taking.

In order to build a more robust financial system far less prone to the kind of crisis of the size, scope and severity we have experienced over the past two years, the financial-service industry must take to heart the painful and deeply humbling lessons from this tragedy, and commit to far-reaching change, from building adequate capital and liquidity cushions, to improving risk management, and to revamping failed and failing business models. Nothing short of genuine and sweeping reform could help repair the battered image of Western finance and restore shattered public confidence.

While fundamental reforms at both the individual-firm level and the industry level are absolutely essential, the single most important lesson we can learn from this crisis is perhaps the close interactions between macroeconomic imbalances, monetary policy and financial instability. There is overwhelming evidence that the root problem triggering the current financial crisis is macroeconomic in nature, that is, a long-running, gigantic housing bubble fuelled an unprecedented credit bubble in the US, UK and other parts of the developed world that ultimately proved unsustainable.

To be sure, the consequences of a bursting housing bubble have been made far more damaging because of the mistakes made by financial institutions, regulators, investors and consumers. But central banks' super-loose monetary policies, as manifested by persistent, extraordinarily low interest rates, rapid credit expansion and the build-up of asset bubbles notably in the housing market have made a crisis almost inevitable.

Therefore, the current calls in the US, UK and other parts of the world to strengthen national and international macro-prudential regulations targeting systemic risks are well justified. In particular, central banks should discard the long-reigning philosophy, as espoused by Alan Greenspan among others, that monetary policy need pursue only narrow inflation-targeting while disregarding asset bubbles. An enduring lesson from this crisis is that to safeguard macroeconomic and financial stability asset bubbles should not be allowed to run their full course.

The second most important lesson I believe we should learn is that complacency would usually blindside people from impending dangers, hence leading to poor risk management. In the quarter-century or so proceeding to the global financial crisis, the world economy experienced a long period of 'great moderation', marked by low or falling inflation, low unemployment and robust growth in corporate profits. The collapse of the Berlin Wall, the rise of China and India as great emerging economic powers, and the apparent, remarkable resilience of the US and other developed economies (except Japan) to a series of shocks including the 1997–98 Asian crisis, the burst of the dot.com bubble in 2000 and the terrorist attack of 2001 have led to a belief that housing prices in countries such as the US and UK could only go up, trees could grow to the sky and financial crises are reserved only for Japan and the most grossly mismanaged emerging markets. A long period of prosperity, macroeconomic stability and buoyant equity, fixed income, commodities and housing markets have lowered guard against risks for lots of players – banks, non-bank financial institutions, regulators and investors. Financial intermediaries, supposedly the institutional experts in risk management, became fat, lax and utterly ineffective when crisis did strike. Investors became fearless and driven only by greed; regulators slept at the wheel, taking comfort from the self-regulating and self-corrective capacity of efficient financial markets. There was an overt display of triumphalism about the invincibility of Western financial capitalism. It was precisely this blind optimism that induced financial titans to keep dancing while the music was still on.

Another very important lesson that we can draw from this crisis, I must add and highlight before the list becomes too long, is that large complex financial firms can pose great risks to the stability of the financial system as a whole, as painfully illustrated by the sagas of Fannie Mae, Freddie Mac, AIG and, especially, the Lehman bankruptcy. The current proposals for financial reform, in my judgement, have failed to address the particularly vexing problem of 'too big to fail' and 'too interconnected to fail'. Rather disturbingly, what we have seen instead since the eruption of the crisis is further concentration of the financial-service industry, as illustrated by the acquisitions of Bear Sterns and Washington Mutual by JP Morgan, the merger of Wachovia and Wells Fargo, and the sale of Merrill Lynch to Bank of America. Instead of slimming down and becoming smaller and simpler, financial firms have astonishingly become even larger and more complex in the aftermath of the crisis.

The proposal for creating a systemic risk regulator is a sensible one in so far as it is intended to strengthen macro-prudential regulation and supervision. But it is a dangerous delusion if people are led to believe that an outside regulatory agency, no matter how professionally competent it may be, can realistically accomplish the task of effectively supervising very large and complex firms to keep them out of harm's way.

It seems strange that this crisis has not resulted in sufficient soul-searching about the consequence of repealing the Glass–Stegall Act in the 1990s, which created financial conglomerates like Citigroup. These large financial holding companies assembled under one roof a wide array of financial activities, often with different business models and warring operating cultures, and become too complex and unwieldy to be managed well. Mixing different businesses, such as those of commercial banking and investment banking, also allowed firms to exploit differences in rules (governing capital, accounting, and profit/loss recognition and so forth) as applied to different parts of the firm. Such intra-firm arbitrage across business activities naturally leads to risk flowing to where it is least monitored and where capital requirements are lowest. Without centralised consolidation of risk management and pricing, toxic asset problems can be left to fester until they suddenly implode to endanger the entire firm and the broader financial system.

If we fail to understand the systemic implications of large complex financial firms, the global financial system will likely continue to be haunted by the 'too big and too interconnected to fail' syndrome for years to come.

WILL HUTTON [1]

This terrifying moment is our one chance for a new world

The past twenty years has seen an unparalleled boom in the money markets. As the free market blossomed, so too did cheap debt, huge bonuses and ostentatious wealth. But when our financial system lay on the brink of collapse, it became time to build a new one, based on fairness instead of naked greed, and with long-term commitment to building businesses and supporting investment.

I never imagined I would live through events such as those during September–October 2008, when the Western banking system faced disintegration. Economists and policy-makers were at loggerheads over how to intervene to stop the panic that swept the world and how to inspire sufficient trust for the key money and credit markets to reopen.

This crisis was thirty years in the making – a Gordian knot of libertarian free-market fundamentalism, unregulated globalisation, the collapse of social and political forces committed to fairness, the explosive impact of financial innovations such as 'securitisation', and sheer greed. Each contributed to the fiasco and all now need to be unravelled if the economy is to have a sustained recovery.

In the seventies, there was a revolution born of a free-market belief that inflation and low growth were the consequence of too much state action – too much public spending, too much taxation, too much union power and too much money being printed. Instead we would rely on what Ronald Reagan once called the 'magic of the market'. Governments should balance their books and let companies, banks and workers make their own decisions liberated by free markets. Thus stagflation would be bested.

Some of this made sense. Nationalised industries were not especially well run, some highly unionised industries such as printing and car manufacturing suffered low productivity, and governments had become too addicted to running budget deficits. Challenging the shibboleths of the seventies was

[1] This entry is based on an article published in the *Observer* on 5 October, 2008.

long overdue, and over the eighties it began to produce some results – lower inflation and more growth.

Then the Berlin Wall fell, the Soviet Union collapsed and the revolution hardened into something more dangerous – an ideological commitment to the view that government regulation had no place whatever in the economy. The left critique of capitalism – that markets delivered instability, booms and busts, monopoly and gross inequity that paradoxically undermined the values of integrity and trust that bind markets together – was proven wrong. There should not even be a mixed economy between private and public sectors. The job was to enlarge the role of markets.

In the United States this would manifest itself in Newt Gingrich's 'Contract with America' that gave free licence to the anti-tax, anti-government, pro-deregulation instincts of an increasingly fervent Republican Party. That wasn't all. The financial markets were exploiting the new freedoms to insist that governments did Republican things. The Bush presidency sealed the market fundamentalists' victory.

This was manna from heaven for the City of London, desperate to recover its place as the fulcrum on which the British economy pivoted. Ditching the gold standard in 1931 had dealt it a harsh blow. Controls directed cheap finance into industry throughout the Depression and into the war. The City hated it, but, by 1951, twenty years of 'proud finance being humbled', as Winston Churchill had put it, had prompted Britain's partial reindustrialisation.

Despite its troubles, the City of London remained the apex of Britain's social structure throughout this period. This is the place to which the privately educated, Oxbridge professionals in law, accounting and banking commuted from their large Home Counties houses to practise 'gentlemanly capitalism' – a capitalism that does not focus on manufacture, science and technology, but on property, international lending, deals and the trading of financial securities. It provided a good living in the fifties, sixties and seventies, but London had ambitions. North Sea oil created the balance-of-payments surpluses that would allow the incoming Tory government to lift controls. The way was open for London to combine with New York to become the centre of world finance.

The regulations that inhibited London's development were progressively eliminated. The 'Big Bang' in 1986 allowed the brokers and jobbers on London's stock market to be bought up by American, European and Japanese investment banks so they could do in London what was outlawed in New York by Roosevelt's Glass–Steagall Act, introduced in the aftermath of the credit crunch that caused the Great Depression. They could manage huge investment funds, trade in any kind of financial security both on their own account and for clients, advise on deals and act as large banks – all under the same roof, despite the conflicts of interest that were prohibited in New York. London began to rise in the league tables of international finance. The foundations of Anglo–American financial capitalism were being laid – and with them planted the seeds of its own demise.

In the early nineties came a breakthrough that would transform the financial landscape. Goldman Sachs took the concept hitherto used by mortgage companies of packaging up mortgage payments and selling them as a financial security and applied it to an Arizona trailer park. The site pledged its income to a new company, specially set up, which then issued securities – backed by Goldman. The market bought them. 'Securitisation' took off: there are now more than $23 trillion of securities backed by a weird and wonderful range of income streams. America, followed rapidly by Britain, did not have to worry that it did not save enough to support its borrowing ambitions; it could sell these securities to all comers from all over the world – especially in Asia and to China's central bank – to finance ambitions to borrow.

And we did. Banks issued bonds allowing huge takeovers. Hedge funds and private-equity companies blossomed. Money flowed into residential housing. In 1999, Bill Clinton abolished Glass–Steagall; it was pointless, given what was happening in London. New York and London were in an unseemly race to regulate less. And if regulators raised an eyebrow, they were told not to worry. The securitised bonds – this packaged income – could always be sold to raise cash; and on top of this banks took out insurance against the risk of default.

Nor should regulators worry if banks directed the investment funds under their management to buying any unsold bonds, which might look like a fraudulent conflict of interest; one day they would rise in value.

So confident did bank directors become that they permitted their managers to run hidden portfolios of securitised assets offshore in secret tax havens; thus would profits be boosted at no risk.

Bonuses grew larger and larger, residential and property prices kept rising, fees from ever bigger deals became juicier and juicier. And when there were setbacks, such as the dot.com bubble bursting, chairman of the Federal Reserve Alan Greenspan was on hand to flood the markets with cheap money. The free-market fundamentalists seemed to be right. Markets never did make mistakes, financial business kept booming, leverage became astronomical. The ever more extravagant school fees were easily paid and Britain's Home Counties – like New York and the Hamptons – became home to parties of astounding luxury and lifestyles of grotesque opulence. Gentlemanly capitalism became super-gentlemanly capitalism. The *Financial Times' How to Spend It* magazine is studded with dresses that cost up to £30,000. Private submarines, jets and yachts became the rage. One hedge-fund manager I knew considered himself underpaid at $200 million for one year's work.

There was no effective opposition. The left and organised labour collapsed as intellectual, social and political forces; there was no conviction that any alternative to this shareholder-value-driven, financial, 'securitised' capitalism existed, or any political muscle to support it even if there were. Mainstream culture moved away from public purpose and fairness; the new priorities were individual self-fulfilment, personal experience and loyalty to self. For example, in the 1990s I fervently opposed the demutualisation of our building societies, built on the values of fairness and collective self-help, arguing that in the interests of pluralism alone we needed a variety of financial institutions to serve the public. They would inevitably try to expand too fast; and inevitably end up being taken over.

So it has proved. Every demutualised building society has been taken over. But nobody wanted to listen. The directors wanted the vast personal gains and the members were only scarcely less greedy. In any case, building societies were collective institutions from another age, rather like trade unions, and no more worth defending.

Investment bankers seemed cut from the same cloth as Russian oligarchs and football stars; their fantastic wealth was part of the new order – one that produced growth every year since 1992 and a never-ending rise in house prices. If the rich were getting very rich, ordinary people were not doing badly either. Britain had stumbled on a new social compact.

Leader writers of right-wing newspapers could dub the high priests of finance 'wealth generators' without demur – and if any regulator tried to limit their operations, the world would fall on their head. When Tony Blair flirted with the stakeholder capitalism that I proposed in *The State We're In* for a few weeks early in 1996, his colleagues, especially Gordon Brown, were appalled. The idea would upset the new gods in the City of London and in any case was wrong, because it challenged the free-market orthodoxies. The only way New Labour could win and govern was to accept the Thatcherite settlement and try to promote social justice within those constraints. And so the madnesses became rocket-propelled.

The suddenness of the early twenty-first-century financial crisis resembles a Kafka parable. One night a couple of years ago, we all went to bed feeling as secure and prosperous as the most solid burgher. But then the next morning we awoke to the real-time nightmare of a contagious bank run which was paralysing the financial system; we were, it seemed, about to be crushed, like cockroaches, by the arbitrary heel of the tottering global capitalist system.

Of course the dramatic 2008 economic contagion – triggered by American banks that had radically over-leveraged their risk on sub-prime mortgages – wasn't quite as shocking as the metamorphosis of Gregor Samsa. Yet the viral speed of the Wall Street banking collapse, its dramatic network effect, its real-time media coverage and the speed of its terrifying electronic contagiousness around the world bring to mind not only the subtle work of Franz Kafka but also more graphically apocalyptic products designed in the dream factories of Hollywood.

Yes, the events in the second half of 2008 had all the hallmarks of a nail-biting disaster movie. EIGHT DAYS: THE BATTLE TO SAVE THE AMERICAN FINANCIAL SYSTEM rang out the headline to a twenty-four-page, 19,000-word piece in the usually understated *New Yorker* magazine. The piece, written by the award-winning business journalist James B. Stewart, covered the week between Friday 12 September and Friday 19 September 2008, seven days that Stewart described as 'the most important week in American financial history since the Great Depression'.

Stewart, of course, wasn't alone is dramatising those dark days in September 2008, when a run on investment banks like Merrill Lynch and Lehman Brothers blindsided the wisest men of Wall Street. Even paragons of circumspection like Ben Bernanke, the chairman of the Federal Reserve system and Hank Paulson, secretary of the Treasury, made dramatic public pronouncements about the fragility of the whole financial system. Things got so serious that even President George W. Bush, the epitome of inarticulate Texan optimism, was worried. 'Someday you guys are going to need to tell me how we ended up with a system like this,' Bush is reported by Stewart to have told Paulson and Bernanke.

In a sense, of course, it was 11 September 2001 all over again – that peculiar early twenty-first-century apocalyptical synthesis of the real and the fictional. Only this time it wasn't hijacked planes that terrorised Wall Street but rather banks like Goldman Sachs and Bank of America, whose illiquidity threatened the very integrity of the global financial system. In 2008, the world's labyrinthine electronic economic system – an enigma of unregulated financial algorithms whose complexity seems to have eluded even their own brilliant architects – appeared to descend from the heights of prosperity to the depths of imminent bankruptcy in the space of a few mouse clicks. One moment we were celebrating the roaring digital noughties, the next we seemed to be hurtling toward the abyss of the Great Depression 2.

So what, exactly, happened in 2008? And what do these surreal events tell us about the inevitability of the economic cycle?

I'll leave the grisly details of the collapse to economists but, yes, I suspect that the economic cycle was, is and always will be inevitable. Every contagious economic upswing is always followed by an equally contagious downswing, every quick boom by an equally speedy bust, all sunny financial optimism by the dark pessimism of quantitative decline. Thus the global 'crisis' – if that's the right word to describe the series of near-death experiences that shook the global economic system in 2008 – is the inevitable consequence of a timeless irrational optimism and an all-too-human greed for economic growth and individual enrichment.

But the most interesting thing about the 2008 crash is not so much its similarities with previous historical crashes but its differences. You see, not all economic crashes are equal, some being more revealing than others, and the latest 'crisis' of the capitalist global system actually offers insight not only into the uniqueness of the early twenty-first-century digital post-industrial economy but also into the contagiously catastrophic nature of global electronic capitalism.

So with which previous economic collapse should we compare today's meltdown? The conventional response, of course, is to juxtapose today's crisis with the Wall Street Crash of 1929 which – with its black-and-white memories of snaking food lines and bankers in bowler hats throwing themselves out of tall buildings – has become the stereotypical media image of a global economic catastrophe.

But a more vivid historical analogy is with the great slump of the last quarter of the nineteenth century – the first global economic bust of the industrial capitalist age, a crisis triggered by the stock-market crash of 1873. Like every great pre- and post-industrial run on money – from the Dutch tulip craze of the seventeenth century to the South Sea Bubble of the early eighteenth century to today's early twenty-first-century electronic miasma –

the 1873 meltdown was caused by a contagion of exuberance, innovation and greed. As a Viennese journalist remembered the entrepreneurial background to the great nineteenth-century crisis of capitalism: 'Those were the days when companies were founded to transport the aurora borealis in pipelines to St Stephen's Square and to win mass sales for our boot polish among the natives of the South Sea islands.'

While human greed and self-deception are a historical constant, what's changed since the late nineteenth century is the speed and virulence with which it reverberates around the world. As the British historian Eric Hobsbawn explains in his incomparable *Age of Capital*, the late nineteenth-century global economic bust was a twenty-year great depression that 'did not seem to end'. For twenty-three long years, from 1873 to 1896, this was a crisis – Hobsbawn cites a German study – which had 'been in everyone's mind'. But the crisis simmered for so long that, according to Hobsbawn, contemporary economists even began to wonder whether the world's economy really was in a severe slump.

So why didn't the late nineteenth-century crisis explode with the speed and drama of today's financial meltdown? The difference lies in one word: communications. In the late nineteenth-century, the inchoate global economic system existed without a global communications network that could electronically compound the exuberance, innovation and greed of financial entrepreneurs. Thus, in 1876 – three years after the great stock-market crash – there were only 380 telephones in the United States and 200 telephones in all of Europe; while, as Hobsbawn reminds us, even the very 'operation of a pump by electricity' caused a huge commotion at the Vienna International Exhibition of 1873.

Today, of course, the electronic network of financial communications is ubiquitous. From the hundreds of millions of electronic nodes in our global financial trading system to the real-time media coverage of its dramas to the ever-increasingly intricate and mostly unregulated technological tools that lubricate this banking system, everyone is connected and everything is speeded up. 'Talk is cheap,' goes the old cliché, incorrectly. Actually it's our increasingly decentralised yet global electronic network – a system that enables traders to instantly talk with other traders – that has dramatically compounded the economic cycle and enriched financial risk-takers.

As the futurist Alvin Toffler put it in his classic 1970 work *Future Shock*, 'The whole world is a fast-breaking story.' And that story is one of dramatically speeded up and more viral economic booms and busts. Toffler talks about something called the 'accelerative thrust', which, he argues, is the driving force of our social and economic life. He's correct. What took twenty-eight years in the late nineteenth-century global economy now takes eight days.

Tomorrow, I fear, it might only take eight hours or even eight minutes to bring down the entire global financial system.

Ironically, it's the owner of the most uninquisitive mind of the early twenty-first century who asked the most searching question. 'Someday you guys are going to need to tell me how we ended up with a system like this,' President George W. Bush asked his treasury secretary and his chairman of the Federal Reserve. For an answer to his question, Bush needs to read Karl Marx, still the most prescient analyst of capitalism. Back in the middle of the nineteenth century, Marx wrote a little book which he entitled *The Communist Manifesto*:

> The bourgeoisie cannot exist without constantly revolutionising the instruments of production, and thereby the relations of production, and with them the whole relations of society . . . Constant revolutionising of production, uninterrupted disturbance of all social conditions, everlasting uncertainty and agitation distinguish the bourgeois epoch from all earlier ones. All fixed, fast-frozen relations, with their train of ancient and venerable prejudices and opinions, are swept away, all new-formed ones become antiquated before they can ossify. All that is solid melts into air . . .

Marx was uncannily right. In an economic system driven by financial greed and by the cult of never-ending innovation, all that is solid does indeed 'melt into air'. The global insurrection in networked communications, the digital revolution in technology, the contagion of unregulated markets have created a financial system that lends itself to more and more transformative booms and busts. In the early twenty-first century, the future has arrived too soon for most of us. We have become victims of a financial system that has no clear moral rhyme or reason. Franz Kafka put this nightmare into words in the early twentieth-century. Today, a century later, those words have crawled off the page and have turned our economic lives into a nightmare of perpetual uncertainty and upheaval.

RICHARD KOO

The financial crisis of the present magnitude inevitably has many causes. For my part, I would point out three failures that stand out in the current crisis: (1) the complete failure of the Greenspan Federal Reserve to issue warnings about the bubble; (2) the failure of rating agencies to rate the risks inherent in the newly securitised mortgage products, and (3) the failure of US monetary authorities to anticipate the consequences of allowing Lehman Brothers to fail.

Firstly, it was remarkable that the US central bank, which should be in the position to warn the economy in general and financial institutions in particular about the danger of a credit bubble, actively refused to do so. In fact, Greenspan refused to use the phrase 'housing bubble' until he retired from the Fed chairmanship. Even though he began to acknowledge the fact that there may be pockets of froth in some isolated housing markets, he refused to accept the fact of the nationwide housing bubble. In many of his congressional testimonies, it was appalling to see the members of Congress pressing him on the dangers of housing bubble and his refusal to admit to there being one. It was a complete reversal of the usual pattern, where the central bank is expected to remove the punch bowl while the politicians insist that the party should go on.

It was true that he was raising interest rates, twenty-five basis points at every FOMC meeting, to tighten monetary policy. Both the magnitude and pace of rate hikes were highly appropriate. But he could have done far more, both through persuasion and via bank regulators under his control. After all, he was referred to as 'the maestro' and enjoyed tremendous credibility with the public. A warning from the maestro would have gone a long way to cool the craze in the housing market. Instead, he worsened the situation by giving his weight to the argument that there was no bubble. In fact, Greenspan was so sure of himself that he even discouraged, if not prohibited, Fed staffers from using the phrase 'housing bubble'.

Since all bubbles have good reasons for starting, it is extremely difficult to stop a bubble from happening. But the eventual size of a bubble and the damage its subsequent collapse causes depends on how soon the central bank removes the punch bowl. During the current episode, the central bank not only failed to remove the bowl, but also kept on replenishing the punch, which made the eventual collapse that much worse.

If the central bank is the public-sector watchdog containing the bubble, rating agencies should have been the private-sector watchdog maintaining the quality of financial transactions. Here too the brakes failed miserably, with rating agencies granting the highest rating (triple A) to some of the worst-securitised products.

The CDOs that are at the heart of the financial crisis are so complicated that it often takes a dozen qualified mathematicians over three weeks to figure out their exact risk characteristics. No investor in his right mind would touch these instruments if it were not for the fact that rating agencies have blessed them with triple-A ratings. In other words, the current financial crisis could not have happened without the collaboration of the rating agencies.

There is also no indication that rating agencies have checked the risk characteristics of each and every paper with a dozen mathematicians working full time for three weeks. If they had done so, the cost of rating would have been prohibitive. Instead, they were swept up by greed to cut corners and maximise short-term profits. In the process, they failed to check the extremely poor quality of origination of those mortgages where people with minimal or no incomes were granted finance. They also failed to fully compensate for the fact there were no reliable statistics on the default rate of mortgages originated by many financial institutions because those institutions had never offered subprime mortgages in the past. The list of overlooked problems goes on.

It is true that securitisation and sub-prime mortgages were both financial innovations, and government bank regulators, who must follow the existing rules, typically fall behind when innovations are introduced. But in the present episode, rating agencies, which should be the private-sector watchdog for quality in financial activities, also failed completely in their tasks.

Lastly, the US decision to let Lehman fail when the US and global banking systems were under such stress exacerbated a bad situation. Even under the best of circumstances, allowing a firm the size and importance of Lehman to fail is a huge policy gamble. Allowing it to fail in September 2008 was nothing short of madness. Treasury secretary Paulson's inability to anticipate the global meltdown was not compensated for by the Fed chairman, Ben Bernanke, who is also responsible for maintaining the stability of the US banking system. For there is no indication that the Fed chairman warned Paulson that he was headed in a wrong and dangerous direction. Only Tim Geithner, the then president of the NY Fed, was working hard to find a solution for Lehman. But he received no help from the above two men in Washington, and the rest is history.

The US leaders again showed their lack of expertise when they both insisted that purchasing bad assets from banks is the best solution when history amply tells us that only capital injection by the government can save the banking system. They subsequently realised their mistake and changed course, but much credibility was lost in the process. It should be noted that Japan's finance minister Nukaga warned Paulson as early as the February 2008 G7 meeting in Tokyo that the US must inject capital into its banks, but Paulson failed to comprehend the importance of Nukaga's advice.

This is in sharp contrast to the clearly focused leadership displayed by the Fed under Paul Volcker during the 1982 Latin America Debt crisis or by the Bank of Japan during the 1997–9 banking crisis in Japan. Both events could have resulted in a catastrophic global outcome, but a prompt and far-sighted approach by the respective central banks managed to contain the crisis. In the 1982 crisis, a large number of US money centre banks were technically bankrupt when all countries south of the Texas–Mexico border defaulted on their loans. In the Japanese crisis, the losses suffered by its commercial banks reached 100 trillion yen or 20 per cent of its GDP. But the average public in both countries hardly felt the pain, unlike the post-Lehman economic collapse we are all experiencing today. In fact, the cost to taxpayers was zero in the Latin American case, and 11 trillion yen or 2 per cent of GDP in Japan's case.

The latest IMF estimate on the amount of losses US financial institutions might suffer from the current crisis is 2.7 trillion dollars or 20 per cent of US GDP. This loss is *smaller* than the one Japan suffered because the Japanese 20 per cent is just commercial banks, whereas the US 20 per cent includes hedge funds, insurance companies and other financial institutions in addition to banks. The poor handling of the current crisis in the US, however, has ended up making everybody suffer so much more.

A lengthy recession was entirely possible even without the Lehman fiasco, but the sharp contraction in economic activity and the huge bill for rescuing both the economy and the banking system could have been avoided if the policy makers had handled the Lehman incident along the lines of Bear Sterns or Merrill Lynch. As a former NY Fed economist who was directly involved in the rescue of the global banking system following the 1982 Latin American Debt crisis, I regard the post-Lehman meltdown as the most unfortunate and unnecessary suffering brought about by the incompetence, if not arrogance, of US policy makers.

NORMAN LAMONT

This recession has really been two recessions. Firstly there has been a general economic, cyclical downturn and then there has also been, specifically, a banking crisis. The two are related and it is debatable which was the prior crisis. I, personally, believe there would have been a slowdown even without the banking crisis, though it has greatly exacerbated it.

It is frequently said that we have not experienced a 1930s-style recession, although the falls in output in some countries like the UK have been broadly comparable to those of the 1930s. The great difference between the policy response of the thirties and now is that banks have been saved by the intervention of governments. That does not mean, however, that the crisis is over or that the outlook is bright. It isn't.

It was right that, in the UK, the government took stakes in major banks like the Royal Bank of Scotland (RBS) and Lloyds. I support the general principles of the Banking Act with its special-resolution regime leaving temporary nationalisation as a last resort.

A big mistake was made by the UK government in suspending the competition rules, with the connivance of the EC, to facilitate the merger of Lloyds and HBOS. The disastrous consequences were that the government, in effect, created two banks with problems when before there had been one.

The big problem facing the banking sector has been that of how to deal with so-called toxic assets. I say 'so-called' because some of these assets in time will recover part of their value. The UK government opted for an asset-insurance scheme instead of the classic way of tackling the problem, which is to separate the impaired assets into a bad bank alongside a good bank. Germany and Ireland are two countries that have followed the classic 'bad bank, good bank' route.

It took the new administration of President Obama and Treasury Secretary Geithner several attempts before they came up with policies that commanded any confidence from the markets. The US administration also stress-tested American banks, though there have been doubts whether these tests were tough enough and included the worst possible scenarios.

What of the future? What will the supervisory regime be for banks?

Undoubtedly they will face greater, more detailed supervision. In the UK we will have to face increased supervision at domestic, European and global levels. Although coordination and cooperation between international regulators is important, the most effective regulation, the one that might actually work is at a national level, and it would be a big mistake to concentrate too much authority at an international level, which will inevitably be the lowest common denominator of what people will accept.

In the UK we have to be careful European proposals on regulation are not such as will harm the City. Other countries might have an interest in seeing the flexibility and ability to innovate of the City of London diminished. More attention will be paid to remuneration packages. Quite rightly, governments and regulators have been critical of incentives that do not align risk and reward but encourage excessive, short-term risk taking.

I am sceptical of the case for separating investment and commercial banks, as is fashionably advocated. The banks that failed tended to be on either side of the divide – either investment banks or commercial banks. Furthermore, the distinction between investment and commercial banks is not so easy to make today.

This banking crisis was, above all, caused by too much leverage of banks' balance sheets, together with irresponsible lending. Colossal amounts of impaired debt will have to be written off. The fear is that banks have still not yet adequately faced up to the losses that are embedded in their balance sheets and that will inevitably have to be declared at some point in the future.

In July 2007, the Federal Reserve chairman, Mr Bernacke, estimated sub-prime losses at $50–100 billion. Institutions like the IMF were reporting world-wide losses on securities of something like $3–4 trillion. The EU Commission suggested that impaired assets might amount to 44 per cent of European banks' balance sheets. It will take several years to work these losses out of the system.

The above losses are only the first crisis. They reflect the excesses of the boom. We have yet to experience the full effect of second wave of bad debts and defaults from the recession. The more bad debts there are, the more difficult it is for banks to lend to other customers: A loss of $1 billion from a bank's capital may mean that it can lend $10 billion less.

The most important need is for the banks to recognise losses and to declare them realistically as quickly as possible. Mr Strauss Kahn, managing director of the IMF, has said that the lesson of 122 past crises is: 'You never recover before the cleaning-up of the banking sector has been done.' Mario Draghi, the governor of the Bank of Italy, has said, 'The main thing we need now is a sense of transparency, where we can put a credible floor to the banking losses.'

One cannot rule out more capital injections being required. The weakness of the banks is such that it seems unlikely they will be able to finance anything other than an insipid recovery and that sluggish lending will persist for years. The need for banks to repay governments will be an added burden and inevitably their first priority.

Everywhere banks are being told by governments they must keep lending at previous levels to justify the support from the taxpayer. It is doubtful if this is achievable. There has been a sharp drop in transnational lending and in many countries a large financing gap has been left by the departure of foreign banks.

Another huge gap is that left by securitisation. It was the packaging of loans from banks and selling them on in securitised form that helped to fuel the boom. Packaged loans were removed from balance sheets, providing banks with scope to lend even more, and this got hopelessly out of control. In the United States in 2007, there was around $2,500 billion of securitised debt lent. In 2008, there was hardly any. There is an even larger sum of nearly $9,000 billion of assets in the US still held in securitised form. Some of this debt has to be refinanced, and if there is no replacement, global economies will be forced to contract.

All in all, I remain pessimistic about the ability of the banking system to service economies. With a few exceptions like Canada and Australia, the industry has been severely impaired and compromised. Lending is becoming profitable again but the priority will be to rebuild balance sheets. Even with all the government aid that has been poured into it for some time yet, it is unlikely the sector will be able to finance a robust recovery.

MAURICE LEVY

Given that there were plenty of data offering stark evidence of a dangerous credit boom, why were these warning signs ignored by economic institutions and public authorities?

First, let's admit that data existed for all governments and regulators to see, yet central banks and government let the bubbles happen. Were they blind? Were they incompetent?

I do not believe there is one simple explanation. It is probably a complex mix of several reasons:

- The exhilaration that comes with growth, and with the bubble; everyone wants to believe that they have found the solution for future growth. For politicians, it is nirvana, a return ticket for re-election. For heads of companies, it is the solution to the short-term pressures of the market to deliver today – no matter what happens tomorrow.
- The belief that the market is always right; with this kind of blinkered (and also short-term) ideology, as long as the market is heading north, it is hard to focus people on any underlying problems (or even wrongdoing), especially over a medium or long term.
- Some brilliant minds saw the potential risks and decided to remain silent and not to act simply because they did not want to be responsible for putting an end to a feisty growth era.
- In a globalised economy, no single state could take one isolated action. And G7, G8 were too busy generating growth instead of acting on some of the negative consequences of current policies.
- The USA had to fund the war against terror, as well as the war in Iraq and so growth was essential.
- The CEOs of the financial sector had to show comparable or better results than their competitors, no matter how.

And everyone else had their own reasons to perpetuate the system: banks with their huge fake profits, bondholders who did not want to see the value of their investments diminish, poor people getting access to their dream of their own house and, of course, traders and brokers making a lot of money (and their shareholders).

They fell back on the ultimate excuse – or perhaps the ultimate hypocrisy, because they knew it was wrong – the famous expression of Bert Lance, President Jimmy Carter's budget director. He said: 'If it ain't broke, don't fix it.' And so they pretended it wasn't broken.

'Those who can't remember the past are condemned to repeat it.' This quote from Spanish novelist George Santayana gives us some more insight into what happened. The fact is, we *did* go through something like this before, although on different scales, and not too long ago. Over the past two decades, we had the real-estate bubble and then the Internet bubble.

Yet, this time – and even as it grew to enormous proportions – some people just didn't want to hear about the looming largest financial crisis ever: '*Il n'est pire sourd que celui qui ne veut pas entendre.*' (There are none so deaf as those that will not hear.) Indeed, there were too many people benefiting from the expanding bubble, who really did not want to hear the warnings that others did express. Call it 'bubble denial'. And those who did raise concerns either did not want to take responsibility for possibly stopping the party that everybody seemed to be enjoying or they simply had no power to do much.

So what lessons can be learned?

Let's go to another quote: 'First, let's kill all the lawyers' – a famous line from Shakespeare's *Henry VI*. I'm referring here to the witch-hunt that governments have launched, with unbridled hypocrisy. This time, they are going after bankers. Yet where were *they* – the regulators – when the bubble was clearly building?

Will we learn these lessons?

If we manage to get the right balance of private-sector self-governance and public policies that encourage recovery based on prudent policies plus careful oversight that is truly independent of national political policies, we have a chance to learn from the past and thus not repeat it.

AUGUSTO
LOPEZ-CLAROS

The 2007–8 financial crisis reflected a combination of various factors which ended up reinforcing each other. Among them one can point to the low-interest-rate environment following the bursting of the dot.com bubble in 2000 and the events of 11 September 2001 in the United States. The easy monetary policies that followed from these were, without a doubt, a contributing factor behind the emergence of real-estate bubbles in the United States and in other markets. A 'light' regulatory environment based on a theory that financial markets were self-correcting and that deviations tended to be the result of some external shock, lying outside the system, led to a prudential and regulatory regime that was highly Balkanised with very dispersed responsibilities. This, in turn, was associated with financial innovations in the 'shadow' banking system (investment banks, hedge funds, various investment vehicles) which resulted in the emergence and rapid growth of all sorts of financial instruments, such as collateralised debt obligations and credit-default swaps, whose systemic implications for the risk profile of the financial system were difficult to assess. The low-interest-rate environment prevailing in mature markets also created in investors a desire for higher yields and the consequent search for more sophisticated instruments.

Yet another feature characteristic of this period and which intensified the effects of the crisis was the existence of high and rapidly growing levels of leverage within the financial system, which reinforces the boom during an upswing in asset-prices but has deeply destabilising implications during periods of asset-price weakness, as investors have to liquidate positions in the middle of falling markets. Indeed, low interest rates turned investors, homeowners and broad segments of the population into highly leveraged speculators.

Finally, although it is seldom noted, I believe, like Amartya Sen, that lack of transparency in the workings of the global financial system has been very much at the heart of the present crisis. Had the authorities been more effective in monitoring the explosive growth of increasingly sophisticated and opaque financial instruments (the so-called 'weapons of financial mass destruction', to use the term coined by Warren Buffett), it is quite conceivable that the current crisis might not have been so severe in its intensity. Sen notes that societies operate better under some presumption of trust and that, therefore, they will benefit from greater openness. In a recent *Financial Times* piece he observes: 'The far-reaching consequences of mistrust and lack of confidence in others, which have contributed to generating this crisis and are making a recovery so very difficult, would not have puzzled Adam Smith.'

On the global ramifications of the crisis, it is useful to note that the idea was put forward in late 2007 that some countries could 'decouple' from the crisis then emerging in the US. Needless to say, this notion has been proven to be premature, or fanciful, or both. Indeed, the spillovers from the global crisis have been intense and have hit Asia with particularly impressive force. Asia has been affected because of its integration with the global economy. The trade exposure of the region to advanced economies has increased in the past quarter-century. The region is specialised in sectors that have been hit especially hard by the credit crunch. I am referring in particular to medium- and high-technology exports like cars, electronic goods and machinery, items that rely on financing. A fairly dramatic example, for instance, is Japanese auto exports, which, according to the IMF; fell by close to 70 per cent between September 2008 and March 2009. More generally, manufactured exports in Asia fell at an annualised rate of close to 70 per cent, three times the drop seen during the 1997–8 crisis. Exports to China from the rest of Asia have likewise fallen at rates in excess of 80 per cent, given China's role as a hub for final products in the Asian supply chain. This impact has been especially severe for Hong Kong and Taiwan.

On the financing side, because Asia's financial ties with the rest of the world have strengthened, it has exposed the region to the impact of global deleveraging. (There has been a huge increase in recent years in the volume of shares of foreign equities held by Asians and Asian securities held by foreigners). Obviously, access to bond financing has become much more difficult.

Recoveries after financial crisis are slower than other recoveries, particularly now, given the synchronised nature of the global downturn. In particular, unlike 1997–8, it is more difficult to 'export your way out of the crisis'. The crisis has hit other markets as well. Huge repatriations of capital from Russia, for instance, and the associated collapse of energy prices will result in a close to 10 per cent contraction of the Russian economy in 2009. Countries that financed high growth through large inflows of capital – particularly foreign direct investment in the case of countries in Central and Eastern Europe and the Baltic, as well as Iceland – have also been hit hard. Other countries for which international trade has been an important engine of growth have also been strongly affected. Nevertheless, the path to recovery in Asia and elsewhere could be similar to that of past recessions: a recovery of global demand coupled with currency depreciation allowing for a rapid rebound of exports.

I would like to suggest – as I did in the pages of the *Financial Times* in December 2008 – that, in fact, we do not know whether 2009 will not witness the definite beginnings of a recovery, in response to an unprecedented combination of looser monetary policies, fiscal stimuli and the whole battery of government-sponsored interventions that have taken place over the recent past and are still likely in the pipeline.

While the present crisis is of a totally different scale when compared with previous episodes of financial-market turmoil, it is the case – as argued by the IMF – that during the US stock-market crash of 1987, the Russian crisis of 1998 and the associated collapse of Long Term Capital Management, the technology crash of 2000, and the aftermath of 9/11, the near-term outlook was also grim. All of them involved a sudden increase in uncertainty and created conditions where policy makers and markets found it difficult to assess risks. All of these episodes were characterised by increased market volatility and a flight to safer assets. But, with some lags, it soon became evident that the world was not coming to an end. Output growth in the US picked up after 1987 and 1998 and was largely unaffected by the events of 9/11. The bursting of the technology bubble in 2000 was followed by a short recession.

The main danger we face is not that the continued flow of macro-economic and earnings news will be much worse than expected but rather that by late 2009 the global economy will be perking up again (because the housing sectors will have bottomed and the unwinding of commodity prices will boost consumption among oil importers) and governments will go back to business as usual, missing a once-in-a-life-time opportunity to address the serious vulnerabilities in the world's financial system that the current crisis has revealed. In that scenario, the next crisis would find us with little ammunition left. That is the real danger.

GERARD LYONS

This was a financial crisis made in the West. Its impact, however, was global, highlighting the interconnectedness of the world economy and financial system. Just as the implications from this crisis were global, so too are the lessons.

The crisis was triggered by a combination of factors. Three in particular stand out: a systemic failure in the financial system; a failure to heed the many warning signs; and an imbalanced global economy that saw savings flow 'uphill' from Asia and the Middle East to economies in the West whose growth was fuelled by debt.

While this crisis took everyone by surprise, it was also the most predictable in history. How can that be? An analogy is that if you drive a car at 200 miles per hour on a winding road in the dark, and you do not know what is ahead, I will tell you with certainty that you will crash. However, I cannot tell you when you will crash, how bad the accident will be and who will be injured. So it was with this crisis. There were many warnings, but it was impossible to say when problems would materialise.

Although the seizing-up of the money market was not expected, there had been many warnings about the build-up of debt and excessive leverage. I know of no one who did not think, for instance, that UK property prices had risen too far. Also in the middle of this decade, lest anyone forgets, there was also a heated debate over the size of the derivatives market, and the problems this might cause.

There were countless concerns that markets were not pricing for risk. Pride of place should go to the Bank for International Settlements (BIS), the central bankers' bank, who gave many warnings. The Bank of England's Financial Stability wing, also for instance, highlighted the dangers of crowded trades.

Despite all this, behaviour did not change. 'People heard but did not listen.' This is a critical lesson, explaining much of what went wrong.

Even with the warnings, it was the systemic failure within the financial system that was of most concern. There were many, sometimes complex, factors, but the crisis highlighted a failure of risk management; a lack of liquidity management, particularly under stressed conditions; and pro-cyclicality.

Other features added fuel to the fire, such as capital reserves that were based on artificially low default levels; the incentive structure within the financial industry; the influence of rating agencies and the use of mark-to-market accounting, which created a vicious cycle, particularly as prices fell and expectations deteriorated during the downturn, triggering asset write-downs and panic selling.

Asset-price inflation and rapidly rising house prices were a central feature of those economies that suffered most. Within parts of the financial sector there was a willingness to use too much leverage.

The procyclicality problem can be best summarised by the three Gs: Glass–Steagall, Greenspan and Greed. The abolition of the last vestiges of the 1999 US Glass–Steagall Act removed remaining barriers between retail and investment banks. The Greenspan effect was that policy rates were too low. As we moved through the last decade, the world witnessed one of many consequences of China opening up, as it exported low inflation to such an extent that CPI figures around the world – or consumer price indices – could have been renamed China Price Indices. In turn, central banks in the West kept interest rates lower than they should have been. That, in turn, contributed to the greed. It was a collective greed: investors wanted higher returns, so too did savers. The financial industry became incentivised to sell higher-yielding – and, thus more complex, or more risky – products.

Some of the post-crisis debate has centred on a view of the world where the choice is outlined as between narrow, domestically focused banks versus global banks that are seen as big, complex, interconnected and too big to fail. Some of the discussion has focused on avoiding the latter, and concentrating on the former. Breaking up banks seen as too big to fail is one outcome. Certainly we need to avoid the problem, identified by Governor Mervyn King, of where banks are 'international in life and national in death', and thus taxpayers pick up the bill.

Although abolishing Glass–Steagall was a culprit, it might be wrong to reinstate it.

The world has moved on. One challenge is that there are many banks that do not fit into a single category. Such banks can include large domestic banks, regional banks and international banks that help facilitate trade, and who service the increasingly global needs of their clients.

The crisis demonstrated many things, one of which was that banks are the lifeblood of an economy, playing a central role in its workings. Money, in its most basic uses, is a store of value and a medium of exchange. Banks are vital for the operations of the payments system and for safe custody. Banks help raise money from those who have it and transfer it to those who need it. They help look after people's savings and, via their lending, allocate it to people and companies to invest, creating employment and wealth in the process. Banks are central to the credit system. As we saw during the crisis, cross-border finance and promoting trade is vital to many economies and for jobs.

All of these sound basic. It is because we accept them and take them for granted. Yet some of these basics can be potentially risky. Maturity transformation is a central feature as banks raise short-term funds and thus accumulate liabilities in the form of short-term deposits and translate these into assets of longer tenor. But it is risky, leaving the banking sector heavily exposed both to liquidity challenges and to the term structure of interest rates. This risk was compounded as some banks did not have sufficient deposits to fund their lending, leaving them, in addition, exposed to the need to fund in the wholesale market.

It is vital that banks are good at the basics. Risk is at the centre of banking and should not be a destabilising influence that threatens a bank; it should not be excessive and needs to be measurable and monitored. Ideally, the management and governance structure within banks should ensure this. In addition, the regulatory and financial-stability environments need to ensure sufficient checks and balances exist.

A banking sector needs to be well capitalised, liquid and resilient to shocks. Despite the crisis, the banking sectors in some countries survived better than others: Canada and Australia, where leverage and liquidity problems were avoided; Hong Kong, where low loan-to-value ratios limited the amount that could be borrowed in relation to house prices; and India and China, where central banks had sufficiently tight monetary policies, including higher reserve-requirement ratios. Are some of the more direct methods used in China, in addition to reserve ratios – such as loan quotas – of greater potential use elsewhere in controlling credit booms?

Even in the UK, badly impacted by the crisis, not everything broke. Those banks that stuck to the basics of banking and managed risk fared well, and parts of the wider financial system in the City of London – such as insurance and financial services – were largely unscathed, although they have since been hit by the recession.

In many businesses if a competitor fails this may be seen as good. But in banking if a competitor has problems it can have an asymmetric impact if it undermines overall confidence and trust. This contributed to the freezing of the interbank market during the crisis, causing severe disruption in the wider economy and forcing central banks to add liquidity. The motto of the London Stock Exchange was, 'My word is my bond,' and until the middle of the 1980s it was the phrase used across the City of London. Trust is central. And it needs to be won back and re-established as quickly as possible.

Some sort of economic cycle seems embedded in human behaviour, but the 2008–9 downturn was more serious than it need have been, had policies been different.

It would be wonderful if we were able to explain why economic cycles should exist because then the policy makers might be able to make a better fist of curbing them, or at least damping down their amplitude. We can't. What we can do is describe some of their features and hence give some possible explanations.

We know, for example, that investment tends to rise during a boom. Companies are profitable and find they are running hard to meet demand. Because they are profitable they have both access to finance and their own resources to deploy. Because they have strong demand they have the expectation of a continuing increase in demand. So they invest: they build factories, they put in new computer systems, they move into new headquarters – and they probably take on staff.

A parallel movement happens in financial markets. Companies are profitable, shares are doing well and in the quest to find new sources for capital, money flows into more and more exotic causes. The dot.com boom of the late 1990s was a classic example of that; the complicated financial instruments of the most recent boom, another.

In addition, ordinary consumers find themselves caught up in the mood, particularly if they find their principal asset, their homes, rising in value. So they spend more, thereby driving growth yet further.

We also know a bit about why such a process comes to an end. In several post-war cycles it was rising inflation, which had to be checked by rising interest rates. The most extreme example of that was during the 1970s, when inflation reached double digits in most developed countries. That was tackled by raising interest rates but at a cost of severe recessions in the 1970s and 1980s. It was also to some extent the reason for the end of the 1980s boom, though that was also associated with a surge in property prices. The 1990s boom, by contrast, saw very little inflation, but was associated with a surge in investment, most notably in the new communications technologies. When it became clear that the investment had been excessive, a slowdown duly followed.

And the most recent boom–bust cycle? Well, it is too early to produce an definitive comment, but when the economic historians get to work I expect that they will see that excessive asset prices played a key role and I expect the principal blame will go to the central banks around the world that permitted that to occur. The central banks, I suggest, were lulled into complacency by the very low inflation in current items – the prices of goods and services. As a result they failed to see that they had a wider responsibility for general financial stability, which meant paying attention to inflation to asset prices, particularly property. The financial regulators may have been weak – indeed in many countries they were – but the principal cause of all inflation, including asset inflation, is an excessively loose monetary policy.

That judgement is controversial and many would place emphasis more on the banking system. As I say, we will just have to wait and see how history judges the performance of the principal players. What is not in dispute is that there does seem to be a natural economic cycle, maybe somehow embedded in human nature, from which we seem unable to escape.

Two further points are worth making. One is that looking back over the past generation, there had been an apparent trend for the amplitude of successive cycles to diminish. The numbers vary a bit from country to country, but in general the 1980s downturn was less serious than the 1970s one, the 1990s than the 1980s, and the early 2000s was less serious still. Policy was perceived to be successful, or at least progressing. This complacency was shattered by recent experience.

The other is that for many of the emerging economies and in particular the two most populous ones, China and India, the economic cycle has been much less marked. Growth slowed in both countries (and some of the other emerging economies have indeed experienced recession) but the 'new' world has as a whole done much better than the 'old' world. So from the perspective of China and India, is it not so much a question of the economic cycle being inevitable. Rather it is one of how to be best prepared for a downturn in the rest of the world and how to make sure that instability elsewhere does not undermine their development progress.

When the history of the latest downturn is written I suspect it will be seen in similar vein to the upheavals of the 1970s. It will be seen as a failure of policy, just as the 1970s inflation was a failure of policy. In terms of crisis management, the various central banks, government agencies and governments themselves, will probably receive a reasonably favourable report card. Once the crisis struck they did what was needed. The criticism will be directed to their policies in the run-up to the crash. But the costs of their action, particularly in terms of the debts encountered, will persist for at least a decade, maybe longer. The legacy of the 1970s was two decades of monetary restriction as inflation was forced out of the economic system. Expect two decades of fiscal restriction to follow.

Historically, it is common in the aftermath of financial crises to look for villains. The celebrated economist, author and public servant J. K. Galbraith, reflecting on periods of financial euphoria through history, stated that it is always the case that we look for individuals to blame, and preferably for those whom we can incarcerate as well. In the wake of the financial meltdown in 2008 we did this with gusto.

Bankers were the obvious villains, because of their actions: irresponsible lending and failure to manage risk properly. Supervisors and regulators were also pilloried for having allowed financial excesses to develop in the first place, when it was their duty to rein in imprudent institutions and behaviour. Credit-rating agencies, such as Moodys and Standard and Poors, were blamed for having lent their authority to the high credit ratings assigned to complex financial products that were poorly understood, and for having benefited financially in the process. Central banks were deemed to have ignored the warning signs of rising asset prices between 1997 and 2007, especially soaring house prices, and to have sustained for too long a regime of low interest rates adopted after the dot.com bust in 2001. Households, especially in countries, such as the US, UK, Spain and Ireland, that have experienced housing busts, have also come in for criticism for having taken on excessive amounts of mortgage and credit-card debt in the naïve belief that house prices could only ever rise. Readers can take their pick, for all were agents of the financial crisis. Businesses are the only group not to have been singled out for blame, and that is because, for the most part, they did not repeat the debt accumulation that found them out at the end of the 1990s.

However, behind every crisis there are systemic causes, and these are much harder but more important to identify. The 2007–8 crisis was one of excessive debt accumulation, used to support asset-market bubbles, notably in housing. Once US house prices began to plummet from late 2006, the fragile structure and weight of debt became exposed, many lenders and borrowers were revealed as insolvent or bankrupt, and a deep recession ensued. The outcome was not helped by the incompetence of the previous

US administration's handling of the fate of the investment bank Lehman Brothers.

The financial crisis and the recession did not remain confined to advanced nations. Emerging and developing countries also buckled, in some cases even more than their richer peers. For Asia, Latin America and Africa, however, the problem was not financial failure, as it had been a decade earlier. The slump in demand in the West led to a collapse in their exports. Trade finance dried up for a while, commodity prices tumbled, and they experienced a sharp decline in growth, or stagnation. Eastern European countries were the most badly affected, not just because of their reliance on Western European markets, but also because many had borrowed substantial sums in euros or US dollars to finance economic development and housing. As their currencies weakened, their financial position grew increasingly precarious as their access to new borrowing shut down. For major emerging markets, however, the economic downturn was much more traditional and lacked the distorting effects of a financial crisis. Their recovery has been faster and more assured.

During the 1990s and 2000s, household debt in the US soared over the decade to 2007 from less than 70 per cent to 120 per cent of disposable income, while in the UK, the ratio rose to 160 per cent. Banks, which typically maintained loan assets that were ten to fifteen times as large as their capital, grew them to the point where they represented 30–40 times their capital. As well as having inadequate capital, while they had to fund these larger assets with increasing levels of short-term borrowing. In the US, financial-sector debt rose from 60 per cent to 120 per cent of GDP between 1997 and 2007, whereas it had taken almost forty years to increase from 20 to 60 per cent.

The crisis began in the esoteric world of US sub-prime mortgage financing, where irresponsible lending and borrowing had fuelled an unprecedented boom in house prices. When these started to decline, the entire debt-financing structure in this sector was undermined, and the rot spread quickly to conventional mortgage markets, a host of other financial products and instruments, and the rest of the world economy. Sub-prime debt was merely the large tip of a massive debt iceberg. So the question about what fuelled the financial crisis is really about what allowed the debt mountain in our economies to build up to levels that were imprudent and then destructive. There were four contributory causes.

First, global imbalances provided the essential backdrop for the debt mountain in many Western economies to evolve. After 2001, the US balance-of-payments deficit doubled to about 6 per cent of GDP, or some $800 billion. This was matched on the other side by the increase in the surpluses of China and commodity-exporting countries. External balances reflect the difference between how much countries save and invest. In a nutshell, the US did not save enough, and had to borrow the excess savings of the surplus countries. Other countries, such as the UK, Iceland, Spain and Hungary, also borrowed substantial sums abroad. The surplus funds coming to the US and Europe helped to fund the significant expansion of what we know as wholesale money markets, the failure of which contributed directly to some well-known bank failures and critical problems for many others.

Second, deregulation allowed financial entities and households to conduct their financial business with increasingly fewer obstacles, and draw on a rising tide of global liquidity. The process of deregulation began with the ideological shift of the 1980s, in which the primacy of markets was underscored and in which increasingly large financial entities were able to innovate, expand and make substantial profits. By the time the crisis hit, the financial and housing sectors were generating roughly 60 per cent of the growth in the UK's GDP, and a little more than 50 per cent in the US. Bank profits rose from about 12–14 per cent of total profits in the late 1990s to about 25–33 per cent. The laissez-faire approach to financial entities, structures and products was unquestionably a major driver of the credit boom.

Third, poor regulation and oversight, by definition, allowed dangerous financial structures and myopic practices to continue unchecked. There probably isn't too much to add. The regulatory apparatus failed, and the reasons will be addressed, more or less, in the tide of regulatory reform that has already begun.

Fourth, central banks and governments committed bad policy errors that helped fuel or sustain the debt boom. After the dot.com bust in 2001, interest rates were cut aggressively, but central banks kept them low for too long. Moreover, they were preoccupied with low consumer-price inflation, paying scant attention to the warning signs of asset-price inflation. Even in 1996, when former Federal Reserve chairman Alan Greenspan first posed the question about 'irrational exuberance' in equity markets, there were opportunities and instruments to quell speculation, but these were never used. Nor were they elsewhere. Governments were busy taking credit for the apparent strength of public finances and the economy, but embarked on spending programmes (including war) without prudent attention to the durability of the tax revenues needed to finance them.

These systemic issues and failures were really what fuelled the financial crisis. While it is popular, maybe even necessary, to point the finger at individuals, adequate resolution of the crisis and its legacy effects over time will not occur if the systemic cases are not addressed effectively and boldly.

THIERRY MALLERET

Numerous and varied causes lay behind the crisis that erupted in 2007. Most have now become accepted wisdom: the over-stimulatory monetary policy; over-reliance on mechanistic risk-management models; excessive leverage (i.e. debt); corporate-governance-agency problems (the misalignment of interest); conflicts of interest that afflicted rating agencies; perverse incentive structures, and so on. Going back further, it is also important to remember that the crisis is rooted in the long-standing macro imbalances that fuelled an unprecedented liquidity bubble – the so-called 'malign interaction' between some countries' propensity towards chronic excess supply (mainly China, Japan and Germany) and other countries' opposite propensity towards excess demand (mainly the US and the UK). But when trying to reduce the complexity of what triggered the global crisis, it all boils down to (1) high leverage coupled with (2) opacity and (3) domino effects.

Today's predicaments began in 1998 with the emergence of a consensus that real estate was a bargain. Sensing a great opportunity, the financial markets conspired to make it easier for buyers to obtain loans by transforming the traditional mortgage industry – centred around banks, which kept the risks on their balance sheet – into a global market in which investors from all over the world could pool money to lend. By spurring competition and innovation, this globalisation of the mortgage business brought down mortgage fees, which in turn compelled global investors to demand better returns. All this took place against the background of the reduction in interest rates that followed the tech bubble of 2000. In the middle years of this decade, the US had negative real short-term interest rates, which meant free money and all the distortions that it entails in terms of (in)efficient allocation of capital. In addition, low interest rates effectively allowed investors to further increase their returns by leveraging their investment.[1]

---

[1] To understand how leverage magnifies both gains and losses, consider the following example: an investor makes a $50 million bet with $1 million of his own money and $49 million in debt. If the value of his investment rises to $5 million, he makes a return on his capital of 100 per cent. If the same investment were to lose just $1 million of its value, the investor would lose 100 per cent of his capital.

In such an environment awash with liquidity (courtesy of rising commodity prices and the Asian economic boom), Wall Street offered sub-prime mortgages as a response to global investors demanding better returns. By charging higher interest rates to people who couldn't really afford a mortgage, the lenders did in effect obtain better returns on their investments, which were sliced into different pieces subsequently bundled into CDOs (collateralised debt obligations[2]) and sold to different investors.

The conventional wisdom which says that 'nobody saw it coming' is wrong. Numerous articles started to appear in the press as early as the end of 2006, warning about the impending crisis. Economists and a few market participants expressed then their concern about the markets being over-stretched, observing that in the credit markets, 'deals [were] being made with almost no due diligence'. The complexity of the new instruments (CDOs and others) created a 'pass the parcel' game, where nobody really knew where the risks were. Derivatives offered the possibility to slice and re-bundle risks in new, complex structured products that ended up on many different balance sheets, including those of institutions not equipped to understand the risks they were dealing in. The sophistication and complexity of most new financial instruments clearly outpaced the comprehension of regulators, central bankers and most market participants in a world where many investment banks were behaving like hedge funds. In the words of one very senior banker at the end of 2007:

> The best arbitrage play on Wall Street may simply be working on Wall Street: banks and hedge-fund investors are willing to pay upfront money without seeing back-end results. It is a free-rider's paradise, where individuals can stack up the short-term benefits for themselves, while letting the institution bear the brunt of their actions. The result is a banker getting handsomely rewarded in January for making a loan that blows up in August. The hedge-fund manager, meanwhile, is able to buy up billions in suspect sub-prime real-estate loans and derivatives, clipping a 2 per cent management fee along the way.

New instruments that were supposed to contain the risks by dispersing them in reality simply ended up amplifying them.

---

[2] CDOs have the particularity of being quite illiquid. It is indeed a distinct irony of the twenty-first-century financial world that, while many bankers hail them as the epitome of modern capitalism, many of these newfangled instruments have never been priced through market trading. Unless circumstances arise that force a market trade, valuations often remain at the investment manager's discretion – so a large gap can suddenly emerge between the market price and its book value.

Proof of the extent of this phenomenon of amplification emerged when portions of the sub-prime risk were found in the most improbable places (municipalities in Norway, state-owned banks in Germany), triggering in turn an atmosphere of profound distrust and uncertainty. Similarly, the Icelandic risk turned up on some most unlikely balance sheets (among, in particular, many high-net-worth individuals in different corners of the world). In such situations, when nobody knows exactly where the assets and bad loans lurk, financial institutions hoard cash and counterparty risk increases dramatically.

When bubbles burst, asset prices decline, net worth of non-financial borrowers shrinks and both illiquidity and insolvency emerge in the financial system. Credit growth slows, or even goes negative, and spending, particularly on investment, weakens. Because of the acute nature of the credit crunch, the financial world found itself for some months in 2008 in the midst of a multi-layered systemic crisis in which most institutions had to reduce all kinds of positions (from 'tainted assets' to all those further up the quality curve), triggering a wave of falling prices. This simple contagion mechanism explains how a disruption in an arcane and small segment of the financial markets (sub-prime) eventually affected all asset classes and pushed the global economy into recession, as consumers started to face negative wealth effects and much more stringent credit conditions.

In mid-October 2008, the markets ended up in the 'revulsion stage' of the crisis – the indiscriminate and contagious selling of distressed assets that eventually forced banks to stop lending on the collateral of such assets. The global economy's circulatory system – the flow of credit from savers to investors, from lenders to borrowers, from one bank to another – completely clogged up. In such circumstances, all previous solutions of central banks trying to inject liquidity by cutting rates, expanding access to discount windows and creating new funding programmes, proved ineffective. The flow of credit was interrupted because the intermediation system was broken. To restore confidence (and to ensure the solvency of the financial system in order to reignite credit markets), governments pledged to inject equity. The US Treasury eventually decided it would invest US $125 billion in nine of the biggest US banks in the form of preferred shares, and another US $125 billion would be used to recapitalise other financial institutions; while Europe committed on 12 October 2008 to a 1900-billion-euro bail-out.

Both announcements prevented Armageddon at the cost of a massive expansion of global debt and deficits.

The debacle was fuelled by 'deleveraging' – the process of purging the financial system of too much debt, the shift from excessive debt towards more capital. Everyone had borrowed too much money (from the homeowner buying a house he could not afford in the hope of realising capital gains to the investor buying complex debt products with high yields because of the extra 'carry') and was directly or indirectly beholden to the banks (even when money was borrowed from the market, lenders – hedge funds, conduits or structured-investment vehicles – had themselves borrowed money from banks in the first place). Towards the end of 2008 and the beginning of 2009, the process of deleveraging took place in a situation where confidence and trust had completely evaporated because no one knew which institutions held suspect securities, how much the losses were and who was ultimately safe. CDS (Credit Default Swaps – unregulated financial derivatives) in particular exacerbated uncertainty.[3]

It appeared that large parts of the financial system were much too thinly capitalised and too dependent on unreliable short-term debt, with leverage ratios often reaching 30 to 1 (US $30 of debt for every US $1 of capital) for investment banks and hedge funds. In such conditions, the dynamic of unwinding the leverage entailed a domino effect, as deleveraging generates negative feedback loops: the plunge in stocks, for example, was driven in part by hedge-fund selling (hedge funds often buy stocks by borrowing from their prime dealers – such as Goldman Sachs or Morgan Stanley – which in turn borrow from commercial banks. If banks deleverage by reducing loans to prime dealers, then prime dealers tighten up on hedge funds, which react by selling stocks, putting the negative feedback loop into motion). The last resort remedy practised by the US, the UK and the eurozone of a taxpayer-funded transfusion to the banking system was the only way out, and was seen as an 'emergency battlefield medicine to keep the guy from bleeding to death' (Paul Krugman). It indeed dramatically reduced the odds of a catastrophic outcome, but did not prevent the world economy from experiencing a deep and prolonged recession.

[3] At the time of writing (mid-September 2009), the CDS market is estimated at about US $43 trillion, for which there is no central clearing house, meaning that nobody really knows who owes what to whom. Contrary to normal insurance, financial institutions that sell CDS are not required to have funds in reserves should the loans default. CDS trading has expanded 100 times since 2001. Creating a central clearing house for credit derivatives is now perceived as essential to restore confidence. Should it not happen, 'it will take years rather than months for confidence to return to the credit markets', in the words of one banker.

MIKE MOORE [1]

No one in retrospect is surprised at the latest global economic crisis. Indeed many central banks, credit agencies and think tanks did sound warnings. Alas, these warnings were ignored. Politicians like to do things, to be seen to be helping people. That's how people who could never repay loans were sent, by irresponsible companies, credit cards in the post. Home loans were offered to people who didn't even have jobs. I saw, in the UK, advertisements for 120 per cent loans, and a trip to Spain thrown in.

When governments guarantee loans and businesses, something bad is always going to happen. In this particular economic crisis the family banker, who for generations had a similar reputation to the family doctor or lawyer, became more similar to the local bookie, who always had a winner – without any prudent oversight. It was unfashionable to talk of thrift, or for governments to talk of regulation and oversight. This financial hubris was a little like the hubris in the first days of the Iraq War. To question the policies was close to being unpatriotic. As a practical politician, I can recall the Treasury advice about listening to the markets, about confidence as all-important to economic management and in running for office. Economic spin became a part of political spin. Keep the good news on the front page – that was the message. Woe betide anyone who questioned convention.

It's true that there are those who oppose capitalism and globalisation and they, too, are wrong. Unfortunately, when militant moderates like myself raised questions, we were labelled as old-fashioned, leftists or worse: provincial nationalists. It's sickening to witness those who think the last fifty years have been a mistake and to now say that the crisis is the fault of democratic capitalism, free trade and possibly even democracy, but these naysayers have no contrasting success stories or examples they can point to. No one flees South Africa to go to Zimbabwe, South Korea to North Korea, West to East Berlin . . .

[1] This entry previously appeared in *Saving Globalization: Why Globalization and Democracy Offer the Best Hope for Progress, Peace and Development* (Singapore: John Wiley and Sons (Asia), 2009).

The last fifty years have been the most economically successful in our history: hundreds of millions have been lifted out of extreme poverty and life expectancy and literacy have skyrocketed. This is most apparent in societies that are open to trade, to the ideas and the participation of their people. China has rejoined the global economy, with stunning results. Now, the world's prosperity and safety are based on the prosperity and safety of our neighbours: we are all each others' customers. Of course there are still other problems: more people now die of obesity-related diseases than through famine and starvation, notably in the least-globalised economies; however, the votes are always with the protectionists at election time. It's easier for politicians to raise money from those who fear for their future than from those who may benefit from change, the most feared word in any language. Regardless, we must accelerate, widen and share the virtues and opportunities of globalisation. We all want, and need, investment; gone are the days when a common refrain was: 'Yankee, go home.'

JIM O'NEILL

Perhaps one of the reasons why the current global crisis has been so severe is partly that so many, including lots of sane people, started to believe that the economic cycle had been beaten. This was due to the longevity of the previous up cycle in many developed economies that had largely withstood a number of shocks since the mid-1990s, including the Asian crisis, the Russian crisis, the LTCM debacle in 1998, Y2K, the bursting of the tech bubble and, of course, 9/11 and related terrorist events. In some ways, they all contributed to this creeping feeling. Maybe globalisation, low inflation, inflation targeting and quick, adaptive policy-making all combined to create what was now, perhaps, to some degree, an illusion. Together with the ability to manage inventories in a smoother manner given the advance of technology, much evidence appeared to suggest that the boom–bust cycle of the 1950s through 1980s had finally been beaten. Many economies showed symptoms of such sustainable growth, including the likes of Australia, the UK, Spain, some of the Scandinavian economies, and of course the US.

Add on the growing emergence of China, some of the other large emerging-market nations such as India, Russia, Brazil – the BRICs – as well as the Middle East, and at times, during the 2003–7 era, it often seemed as though the world might have entered a new, sustainable nirvana, where GDP growth of close to 5 per cent could be sustained, allowing even many of the world's poorest to emerge into prosperity.

While the challenges of resource availability and climate change became apparent consequences, to some extent these were seen as 'quality' problems compared to those that we appeared to have left behind.

Of course, we now know that in fact what was really happening was that the size of the shock that would test this new nirvana hadn't been strong enough, and when one with the severity of the banking crisis hit, in brutal reality, the economic cycle clearly still existed. And given how long and sustained the up cycle was, the down cycle has been brutal and painful.

Many of us worried about lots of warning signals along the way but would often be regarded as Pollyannas, and indeed, given the smoothness of the expansion, many of us also started to forget about these warning signs. Amongst these, the persistence of a very low domestic-household savings rate in the US, the related seemingly never-ending rise of the US current-account deficit, and the associated large inflow to US capital markets, were both amongst the clearest and the most long-lasting reminders. In addition, the strong rise in housing prices, to levels well above those justified by domestic-income levels in the US, UK, Ireland, Spain and many other countries were perhaps the strongest warning signs. Indeed for us at Goldman Sachs, the rise in US house prices had become so concerning by early 2005, we started to increasingly believe that a reversal, and the first ever nationwide modern house-price decline was inevitable. Many people, including policy makers thought we were too pessimistic. In some quarters it became fashionable to argue that the combination of US demographics, a stronger long-term growth trend and the life-cycle-type hypothesis of consumption, were offered by many as to why our gloom might not pan out. We were early, but in this instance, as is often the case, it really is better to be early than late.

The reversal of US house prices, the emergence of problems in the sub-prime mortgage area, and the onslaught of the banking crisis brought reality to us all, and ideas of the end of the cycle vanished. The collapse of Lehman Brothers meant that even those areas of the world that had escaped the first twelve months of the crisis got dragged into the abyss, as literally the complete seizure of world credit markets last September and October caused world trade to collapse. Suddenly many industries dependent on credit were forced to slash inventories and an exaggerated version of the typical destocking process that causes recessions took hold, again. The world fell into deep recession.

Could the crisis have been prevented and are cycles inevitable? Looking back through the period to the build up to the crisis, and two years on from its onset, I think we now know that inflation targeting, while admirable for the price stability it appeared to provide, while a necessity for lasting growth, unfortunately is not sufficient. A significant amount of theoretical and practical evidence suggested that inflation often lay at the heart of many historical boom–bust cycles. What we now suspect is that if goods and services prices are suppressed, life for many seems better, but uncontrollable increases in the value of financial assets can be even more devastating. We need to find a policy prescription that allows inflation to be controlled and financial bubbles to not materialise – no easy task!

In terms of the proxy cause of the bubble, and today's crisis, are the forces briefly mentioned above primarily responsible? An unsustainable rise in US and other nations' house prices was bound to correct. Other countries around the developed world – the UK, Australia and Switzerland would be three good examples – all have experience of such collapses. While many regions in the US also share some of these experiences, for the country as a whole, this house-price decline is a first in modern history, and it is this that has almost definitely lain at the heart of the collapse of the financial system.

While many find it fashionable to bemoan the poor standards upheld by financial institutions, it is not clear that such poor standards would have prompted the catastrophic fall-out if house prices had not dropped. As many others frequently suggest in their writing there are many things that banks shouldn't have done, and hopefully with guidance from smarter and sharper, effective regulatory policy (not necessarily more), these mistakes will be not repeated. However, it seems as though the bank problems themselves were probably more of a symptom, and not an underlying cause.

What caused the housing excess is probably the key to understanding the US crisis, and related to this, almost definitely, what forces allowed clearly unsustainable current-account imbalances around the world to persist? Could US housing prices have been stopped from rising so much if the Federal Reserve had tightened monetary policy more quickly after the technology crash? Is the perceived asymmetric bias to Fed policy that has seemed to often exist when the Fed has eased quickly and aggressively in response to many shocks, responsible for a build-up in events to the crisis? Many like to think so, and there are some grounds for it. However, it also seems to be true that the dependency of the US on foreign capital and the ease with which it arrived greatly complicated monetary policy for the central bank of the world's reserve currency. Linked to this, the excessive size of current-account surpluses elsewhere, especially that of China, might indirectly have had a big role to play. In this regard and, as I will argue later, perhaps as with many crises, so long as we learn, this crisis might lead to a better world, and certainly one with fewer global imbalances.

MICHAEL O'SULLIVAN

Given that we have had some twenty-seven recessions (in the US economy alone) over the past 150 or so years, the contraction in the economic cycle was inevitable, though the shock that brought on the recession is of course much less typical of the kinds of slowdown we have become used to. Indeed, the banking crisis and general panic of 2008 in particular are probably more like the crashes seen in the late nineteenth and early twentieth centuries than those of the 1990s.

At the same time the economic cycle of the past fifteen years has been unusual, in length and rate of growth – it has been a period of great prosperity, not just in the developed world but especially across a range of emerging economies, with the recession of 2001 marking only a brief interlude in an otherwise remarkably healthy period of growth. This period has been termed the 'Great Moderation' – strong and steady economic growth against a backdrop of generally low inflation and burgeoning globalisation. For a while this almost perfect state of affairs was referred to as the 'Goldilocks' scenario, where like the porridge in the fable, developed economies like the US were neither too hot nor too cold.

We are now largely disabused of the illusions and 'miracles' behind the Great Moderation – it produced its own enormous excesses and imbalances, and to a very large extent its success led to a dangerous complacency on the part of many bankers, policy makers and politicians, and to a fatal lowering of expectations of volatility and risk.

In my view the elongated nature of the expansion caused many financial-market practitioners and economists to embed very optimistic views of return and risk into models, and consequently their behaviour. In this sense, markets and many economies were unprepared for the shock when it came.

There is a much broader and very interesting psychological or behavioural issue here that relates to how humans create and allow themselves to be prone to asset-price bubbles. One book, which has been rediscovered by many recently, is Charles MacKay's *Extraordinary Popular Delusions and the Madness of Crowds*. The book is an examination of asset-price bubbles going back to the Crusades. When he wrote the book in 1841, MacKay may very well have imagined that it would alert people to the dangers of bubbles and that as a result they would not recur. But from the Railway Bubble of 1847 to the dot.com bubble of 2000 bubbles have regularly reappeared in financial markets.

What is interesting about these bubbles is that we very often see the same template repeated over and over again. Usually a shift in expectations or new technology (the Internet, for example) sparks an upward move in prices. This boom then becomes a bubble, where cheap money and easy credit are made available. Then investors discard fundamental forms of analysis for somewhat less rational ones, and their general zeal and appetite for risk are more than a match for the aptitude of regulators.

When the bubble is in full flow it produces many side effects – such as the revision of economic logic ('This time it is different') as well as plenty of spurious wealth effects. One of the great bubbles was created in France in 1720 by John Law, a Scot. While at the same time the Mississippi Scheme bubble was taking hold in England, Law's initially successful plan to swap government debt for corporate equity led to a thriving derivatives market, exaggerated money supply, inflation (especially in luxury goods) and, finally, a brutal economic crash. Though Law can be credited with developing a range of economic theories and innovations, he was essentially an alchemist.

His tradition has been proudly continued by bankers, mortgage brokers, financiers and some policy makers over the past ten years, reaching its climax with the credit crisis. So-called innovation dulled the transparency of many financial products and sharply increased the complexity of interconnected financial markets, while at the same time failing to innovate away liquidity and tail risk. Poor regulation and skewed incentive structures meant that bankers and mortgage-sales people had an interest in building up large mountains of low-quality debt, while having little downside in that debt's default.

In the Anglo-Saxon countries of the UK, US and Australia as well as Ireland and Spain, these trends were pronounced. In Ireland and Spain, matters were made worse by the fact of their entry to the eurozone. As a result, interest rates were inappropriately low, setting off a flood of credit into these economies. Indeed, levels of household debt (relative to GDP) and house prices (relative to income) in these countries have hit extremes in recent years.

Against this backdrop the financial engineers and alchemists were bound to be found out, and to use Goethe's phrase, they have been shown up for 'sorcerers' apprentices'. If the lessons of the credit crisis are learned, then financial sorcery will need to be curbed. So far the regulatory backlash after the credit crisis is not as severe as some financiers had feared and not as far-reaching as others would hope.

It will take some time before the many imbalances that caused and result from the credit crisis have settled. Then we can think again about 'normal' economic cycles. Ensuring that these business cycles are not 'abnormal' requires a number of important changes in policy making. They are the creation of new institutions to help adjust national fiscal policy and regulation to imbalances arising from regional/multinational monetary policy, more explicit consideration of asset-prices and the potential for asset price bubbles by central banks, more clever and in-depth regulation of important financial institutions and an end to the widespread and indiscriminate separation of risk taking and risk bearing.

My great-grandfather died when he was 106. Needless to say, I hope I have those genes in me. But I will have to live that long (I am in my early forties now) to see another boom and bust of this magnitude happen again. That is the good news. The bad news is that most of us will be dead by the time something like this happens again.

Last time we had something similar was back between 1924 and 1928, and that period carries incredible similarities with 2003–7. During that period (which was great for business results and we all enjoyed it) we witnessed a major surge of easy money, easy liquidity, too much leverage, financial innovation that spilled over into outright fraud, as well as ignorance about multiple warning signs such as sky-high house prices, globally imbalanced economy, speculative trading (that no one bothered to observe, let alone try to understand or regulate) and insanely high levels of private and corporate debt (particularly in the Anglo-Saxon world, but not exclusively). Mix corruption, fraud, bad regulations, easy money, greed and stupidity and you destroy two of the basic pillars on which capitalism stands: confidence and trust.

I often wondered how it was possible that at the beginning of the new century we could see a crisis of this kind. Then I thought some more and realised that most economic theory we learn at universities tells us that human beings are rational and that therefore most things in economics can be measured by endless and often complicated mathematic formulae. Maths indeed took over economics during the last few decades. In fact, economic science should finally admit that a large chunk of it is more often about irrational human behaviour and that more professional psychologists should be employed with central banks, governments and even regulators.

I like to divide the build-up to the crisis into four points.

First, it is true that the last fifty to sixty years have brought steady economic growth to large parts of the planet. The progress was not a straight line, but as usual had its ups and downs; but the basic line was going up. However, the normal peak was replaced by a super-cycle peak lasting several years prior to 2008. The peak was fuelled by unprecedented amounts of cheap or even free money, and the subsequent build-up of mountains of debt (which fuelled demand for all kinds of businesses). But by any historical measure it was not sustainable and it could not last. Many commentators had been pointing to it, but which politician or central banker would have wanted to spoil the greatest economic party in living memory? If this super peak was going to be the only thing that caused the crisis, the ensuing deleveraging sequence would hurt everyone and we would have a relatively mild and manageable recession. But we would not have lived through the largest crisis since the 1930s. For the real meltdown, the three other factors were needed in the mix.

Second, during the boom build-up to the crisis, the global economy was like a drunken man, leaning to one side, desperately unable to stand straight and always on the verge of falling. The United States of America was building its largest deficits in absolute and percentage terms since 1776, while on the other hand many other markets were running large surpluses. Asian (particularly Chinese and Japanese) and other export-oriented economies were happy to buy any number of debt instruments sold by George W Bush. They bought almost $3 trillion with one single aim, which was to keep their own currencies cheap so that they could export in a competitive fashion to the USA. But what they also accomplished with this exercise was a clear subsidisation of US consumption that further fuelled the imbalances, pushing the drunken man further to the verge of a fall; and in the end he fell. Now we have started the process of painful rebalancing of the global economy – a process which will be neither easy nor fast, causing false starts and disruptions in the years to come. If this second factor had been the only cause of the crisis, it would have been very disruptive, probably causing a slowdown and a few national recessions, but we would not have seen a real meltdown. Two other factors were needed for that.

Third, quasi-financial institutions which did not have any retail deposits loved the game of borrowing in liquid wholesale markets for short-term money and then investing it in a longer-term, often illiquid way – setting the scene for potential panic once something triggers it. Normal banks often played a similar game. If the amounts are large in such games (and they were), major disruptions will follow once lenders stop paying their debts. That is precisely what happened. But the bigger question is this: how was it possible that these institutions were able to borrow so much when their capital base was so tiny? It turns out now that many were hiding their liabilities in off-balance-sheet vehicles and special-investment vehicles, thus convincing the world their balance sheets were always somehow healthy. In addition to hiding, they also mass produced and packaged debt into instruments with fancy names. The idea was to sell liabilities to someone else, rather than keep them on their own books. A lot of garbage that we now commonly refer to as toxic waste was packaged into sexy-sounding names, credit-rating agencies happily rated them triple A and unsuspecting buyers were told they were buying great stuff that could never fail, was secure and gave a good return. If any buyer had been so stupid as to ask: 'What if it fails?' he would have got the answer: 'You can insure it and we will sell you the insurance contract. If you do not trust us, go to the little unit within AIG. They will sell you insurance for your purchase. No need to worry. Nothing can go wrong.' If this is the financial innovation that the financial lobbies now refer to when they say it is needed in the future too, draw your own conclusions how useful it is. The industry has been telling us that packaging debt and reselling it is good because it diversifies and spreads the risk around the world. Sadly, this became conventional wisdom no one dared to question. But the practice spread the risk around the world indeed and we all felt the devastating earthquake it caused. The lawsuits against credit-rating agencies now allege they received $6 million every time they rated a packaged instrument triple A, plus they apparently earned extra fees every time the underlying value went up. In the end almost 70,000 instruments were rated triple A, all at the time when only twelve companies worldwide had a triple A rating.

Fourth, unsuspecting buyers accumulated mountains of toxic waste, thinking it was a solid investment. If these buyers were other financial institutions, they put those things on their balance sheet as assets, used then as a collateral to go to the wholesale market for money themselves and lent more than their basic capital base would allow. Many of course also engaged in the same game of hiding and reselling debt, as well as selling insurance policies to each other (so called credit-default swaps).

Needless to say, there came a time when banks came to the conclusion: 'I do not want to lend to other banks because I know what I did and I suspect my counterparties did the same.' Perfect start for the credit crunch and subsequent perfect storm!

EDMUND PHELPS [1]

Some forty years ago, in a series of models, I argued that monetary policy cannot keep the unemployment rate for ever below (by a non-vanishing amount) its structural tendency. In the medium run, in which firms have fully adjusted their workforce for the time being, unemployment tends to its medium-term structural equilibrium level; a similar statement applies to the long run. [2] It was a huge error, then, to view monetary policy as a static problem of achieving a 'balance' between unemployment and inflation. *Optimum* policy solves a *dynamic* problem: it forgoes the temptation of short-term benefits in order to contain the expected inflation rate; if the latter is already too high, it invests in a temporary cutback of jobs to lower inflation in order to reduce expectations. Now everyone understands that monetary policy manages inflation expectations. But how much more do we understand?

One of the towering lessons of the present crisis is that it has made vivid to us what has long been obvious to all but the most doctrinaire academicians. Radical uncertainty, known as 'Knightian uncertainty', is always present in some respects and is always a significant consideration – at least, in a modern economy or even a traditional economy operating in a modern global economy. When a novel shock or a concatenation of novel or infrequent shocks occurs, the level of Knightian uncertainty spikes. The economy's participants feel at sea – lost.

An important consequence of this flare-up of uncertainty is that the central bank does not know the level to which to set the 'policy rate of interest' and thus the direction in which to start moving the policy rate. The bank may mistake where the rate of structural unemployment is headed relative to the

---

[1] Director, Center on Capitalism and Society, Columbia University, and the winner of the 2006 Nobel Prize in Economic Science. This paper expands upon a dinner speech at the 7th Annual BIS Conference on Monetary Policy, Luzern, 26 June 2008, and a lecture at the Borsa Italiana, Milan, 11 June 2008.
[2] The main publications were my paper 'Expectations of Inflation and Optimal Unemployment Over Time', *Economica*, 1967, and my book *Inflation Policy and Unemployment Theory*, (New York, Norton, 1972).

present unemployment level. If these points are accepted, the Taylor Rule in the usual interpretation is not operational in the context of the US economy or any economy experiencing gradual or abrupt structural shift: the policy interest rate – think of this as the short-term expected real interest rate – is to be raised in response to an increase of unemployment rate in relation to its medium-term structural tendency. But the change in the latter is not known. Similarly, the policy rate is to be raised, other things equal, in response to an increase in the natural level of the real short-term interest rate. (In other words, if expectations of inflation are on target and likewise the unemployment is already at its medium-term natural level, the real policy interest rate is to adjust point-for-point with each change in the natural real rate at the short-end or medium-term maturities.) But the latter change is likewise not known. The natural real rate could go up or down after a contractionary shock.[3]

That must apply to market participants too! We economists commonly assume that a market economy will have a tendency to reach some medium-term rest point – the point at which things have settled down, relatively speaking – if the bank does not wreak too much havoc in the markets.[4] But prevailing uncertainties may be such that employment overshoots or falls short of the 'medium-term structural equilibrium', since market participants likewise do not 'know' a whole lot, so employment may be driven for a time by too much optimism or pessimism; and employment may come to 'rest' for a while at a point that is not very close to the economy's medium-term structural equilibrium level, where average opinion will turn out to be correct, upon averaging over the prevailing opinions.

In sharp contrast to these possibilities, the Keynesian economists of this world, of whom there are still quite a few, and even the textbook writers, who know better, regard nearly every market force that contracts employment as operating only through the channel of 'aggregate demand' while creating no change at all in the structure of the economy. But, in general,

[3] It might be thought it would do no harm to interpret the Taylor Rule as taking both the structural-equilibrium unemployment rate and the natural real interest rate as *constants*. But that would not escape problems. The rule, so modified, would not be forward-looking at all. It would, for example, call for a zero response of the policy real rate – the nominal policy rate *minus* the expected inflation rate – as long as the actual unemployment rate has not changed yet following a shock. Furthermore, if the supposed natural real interest rate is a constant that is always too low – lower than what the actual real rate will tend to be once the unemployment regards its long-run natural level – there will have to be an increase in long-run inflation in order to induce the central bank to bring its policy real rate, which would otherwise be too low, up to the level of the true natural real rate.

[4] So I will try to refer to a medium-term structural 'tendency' or 'destiny' rather than to 'equilibrium' in any general-equilibrium, perfect-knowledge sense.

and in particular in the situation of the US economy for more than a year, now, it can hardly be doubted – with the benefit of hindsight – that the economy's structure *has* changed.

To support that contention I am going to argue that recent shocks in the US have almost certainly caused a serious increase in the structural-equilibrium unemployment rate on the medium-term horizon – the 'natural' unemployment rate. In fact, I will suggest that the medium-term structural rate has risen *more* than the actual unemployment rate to date. One line of explanation is to say that it takes time for the actual unemployment rate to reach the vicinity of its medium-term structural level; and since the unemployment rate still shows no sign of slowing down – as it would tend to do if it were getting ready to dock at the medium-term level (or to loop around it) – it is plausible to infer that the unemployment rate still lies below its medium-term destination. Another line of explanation is to say that we have good theoretical reasons for thinking that the two or three or four structural forces occurring have, on balance, driven the medium-term unemployment to a very much higher level than it had been in the benchmark years of 1995 and 1996.

I also argue that once the US economy has come into the vicinity of the 'medium run', the medium-term level of what we call the 'natural real rate of interest' (at the short end but also further out on the natural yield curve) will be markedly higher than it was in, say, the pre-boom times, such as the benchmark years of 1995 and 1996.

In my informal analysis several lessons from the recent experience are clear.

- First, as already noted, because of the structural shifts that have taken place there is the strong possibility that in the US and some other countries, the 'structural tendency' of the unemployment rate is well above recent levels: 5.7 per cent in August 2008. In that case, the policy rate – which was set low because the economy was weak – is unsustainably low.

- Each month (or open-market committee meeting) that a central bank persists with a very low policy rate costs the bank some of its credibility, so that even if inflation expectations do not utterly break loose from their moorings, the next time the bank needs to count on expectations to hold firm it will start with a smaller fund of credence.

- Similarly, it would have been argued by the Austrians that the longer the policy rate is held down the further it defers the healing of the financial sector. (Vincent Reinhard, a former student of mine, suggests that the low interest rates in the US induce the banking industry to delay their needed transformation.)

- The housing boom, which got started as early as 1997 and peaked only after ten long years, expressed a neurotic obsession with home ownership, as I argued to Amity Shlaes in a recent column. This must have crowded out some business investment, even though the US economy is highly open.
- Another lesson: the increases in the uncertainty premium both before Bear Stearns and in the past month or two constitute a global shock. It would be a shock to any economy outside the US even if no outward capital flow resulted, since it is somewhat like a universal tax on investing in projects, innovative or otherwise, that present considerable Knightian uncertainty.
- Still another lesson: although some brilliant economists spotted flaws in the Austrian contention that ill-founded booms are inevitably counterbalanced by a compensatory slump, the flaw seems specific to a build-up of capital that enters production functions and thus raises the marginal productivity of labour; a housing boom and a financial boom that leaves toxic assets on the books of financial institutions *do* tend to produce overshooting.
- We should expect employment to overshoot on its downward phase before recovering to its new medium-term natural level – of course it will not have any tendency to recover to its overextended levels during the crazy part of the boom.
- Finally, the recent experience is a dramatic refutation of the neo-neoclassical doctrine of Rational Expectations. It is unimaginable that anyone could believe that the recent boom made optimal use of all information in a world in which the workings of the national economies are *perfectly understood*! Yet it is that kind of position that the Rational Expectations Lobby have been arguing for decades!

JONATHON PORRITT

What fuelled the 2007–8 financial crisis?

The simple answer to this question is that there are still too many greedy and gullible people in the world today, and far too many of them in positions of influence in every area of our economy. The greedy were not constrained by adequate regulatory systems, and our ever-compliant financial media (who are now all too wise after the event) did little to rescue the gullible from their all-but-inevitable fate. But these regulatory and media failures were all part of a much deeper, systemic failure that lies at the heart of contemporary capitalism.

It would be easier by far to pin it on a few individuals. Bernard Madoff has been seamlessly transformed into our scapegoat of choice as we continue to stare in disbelief at the way in which seemingly endless billions of dollars flowed into a scheme that was (like all such Ponzi schemes) literally too good to be true. The kind of returns that investors achieved during the 'good years' with Madoff were not untypical for that time; but the fact that they continued rolling in through thick and thin alerted a few sceptics. Their words of warning, however, were promptly ignored by those who needed this particular emperor to be as regally clad as possible in the interests of the financial-services sector's ever greedier aristocracy.

Others might look to Alan Greenspan (chairman of the US Federal Reserve of nineteen years) as their favourite fall guy. Throughout his time in office, Greenspan refused to acknowledge that he might be contributing to a wholly unsustainable 'bubble' in the US housing market. His favourite euphemism under attack was to make light of the institutionalised mis-selling of credit as 'irrational exuberance'. He seemed to believe that house prices in the US would never fall, but would continue to rise indefinitely. Unbelievable that the world should have been in awe, for so long, of a man capable of such crass nonsense.

And certainly we have to ask how it was that a whole army of regulators in both the US and the UK failed so egregiously to do what was expected of them. In October 2002, the Financial Services Authority (FSA) in the UK published a fascinating discussion paper entitled 'An Ethical Framework for Financial Services'. In its foreword, Howard Davies (then the chair of the FSA) expressed deep concern that the kind of rules-based compliance introduced since 1997 through both the FSA and the Bank of England seemed to have done little to prevent serious ethical breaches in the financial-services sector.

> The principles of the FSA – our high-level standards – are based on ethical values. But it is not clear that this ethos is fully understood or applied consistently by everyone working in the industry. This paper considers why that might be, and how we might move beyond rhetoric and aspirational goals to have a tangible impact on firms' and individuals' motivation to do 'the right thing'.

The paper went on to suggest that the industry needed an ethical training programme alongside compliance training if it was to move beyond 'tick-box compliance' to achieve genuinely ethical integrity. But Howard Davies himself promptly moved on, no such programme was introduced, and his words now resonate in a highly disturbing way. Ethics, it seems, means nothing more than what the rule of law demands, and deliberations about what 'the right thing' might be, from a moral point of view, are of no apparent value within the financial-services sector.

For such a moral person, it is strange to have to attribute at least some small part of this debasing of the moral sphere to Gordon Brown. He was the architect of this regulatory system. And it is no accident that Gordon Brown thought so highly of Alan Greenspan. History is, of course, already being rewritten by those anxious to protect the reputation of the Labour Party's two most recent prime ministers, but it is worth reminding ourselves that both Tony Blair and Gordon Brown advocated and defended the policies that go right to the heart of the 2007–8 financial crisis. The idea that it was all down to the inadequate regulation of the sub-prime mortgage market in the US is frankly laughable.

Ministers really did believe that the marketplace could miraculously transform private greed into public good. They felt quite comfortable in the company of a generation of irresponsible speculators as they plunged us all into this vortex of artifice. They endorsed a financial system that encouraged mainstream mortgage providers to act as loan sharks, that eulogised the innovation involved in off-balance-sheet funding and inadequately regulated hedge funds, and embraced corporate privilege with born-again zeal. They were prepared to slash capital gains tax, promote off-shore tax havens, placate 'non-doms' at any price, and exercise the lightest of touches in terms of pursuing tax avoidance or even fraud.

In all of that, Blair and Brown were merely continuing with the inheritance they had received from Margaret Thatcher. They remain convinced to this day that economic success for any single nation depends entirely on the speed with which the global economy as a whole can be opened up to the full rigour of deregulated neo-liberalism. Just as Thatcher was the handmaiden to Ronald Reagan in seeking to build global institutions (as in the World Bank and WTO) and global processes (as with the Doha Trade Round), so Blair and Brown became compliant stooges in George Bush's ideological crusade – even to the point of committing the UK to a transparently illegal and massively costly war in Iraq.

And in which higher cause were these actions (so many of them so painful to the Labour Party itself) being taken? The answer is obvious: increased economic growth. There is not much that governments do these days that is not done in the interests of securing higher economic growth. 'Increased growth at all costs' may be a bit of a rhetorical flourish (as there are still some costs that even today's growth-obsessed politicians will not entertain), but it still characterises the degree to which growth has become *the* all-important macroeconomic objective to which governments now commit themselves.

Space does not allow for any detailed reprise of that increasingly critical growth debate. I would strongly urge readers to download the recent report from the Sustainable Development Commission, 'Prosperity Without Growth?', which lays out in a calm and evidence-based way why it is that consumption-driven economic growth, indefinitely into the future, is an inevitable disaster in the making. Its author, Professor Tim Jackson, even suggests that it was in fact the obsessive pursuit of growth (through the mindless expansion of credit in both the housing market and in personal debt) that lies at the heart of today's economic recession. This may sound counter-intuitive, but I've yet to unearth a stronger underlying reason.

ANDREW SENTANCE

There have been important lessons for economic policy from the recent financial crisis and the recession that has followed from it. One key lesson is the potential for the financial system to be a powerful destabilising force across the world economy. That is something we had not experienced in such a dramatic way in previous post-war recessions, which were driven mainly by the build-up of inflationary pressures and subsequent monetary tightening.

Another key lesson has been the way in which the development of the global economy contributed to the build-up of imbalances and transmitted the effects of the financial crisis around the world. The economic turbulence of the late 2000s and the global credit boom that preceded it have been heavily shaped by the key characteristics of the 'new global economy', which has developed over the last two decades.

The 'New Global Economy'

Economists have been talking about the process of globalisation for many years. Flows of international trade and investment have been increasing in economic importance since the 1950s and 1960s. In the UK, the total value of trade – exports plus imports – has risen from about a third of GDP in the mid-1960s to over 60 per cent last year and similar trends have been seen in other major economies. At the same time, the growth of multinational businesses has led to increasing investment flows across borders.

But, in recent decades, this process of globalisation has deepened and intensified in two critical respects. First, the 1990s and 2000s saw the integration into the global economy of many emerging market economies, including China, India, Russia and much of Eastern Europe. Many of these countries have successfully exploited their access to world markets and low labour costs, coupled with high rates of saving and investment, to develop their economies based on export-led growth. Second, the deregulation and liberalisation of financial markets in many countries from the 1980s onwards has created much more globally integrated capital and financial markets, with financial institutions – especially banks – developing as international businesses as a result.

These two elements, combined, have extended the effects of globalisation beyond the traditional spheres of trade and investment by multinational corporations and into the markets for capital and labour. As financial markets and institutions have become more integrated internationally, capital has flowed more freely across borders. And problems of financial instability, which originated from bad lending in the US mortgage market, have been transmitted around the world through a highly complex and integrated global financial system.

The operation of labour markets has also been affected by globalisation. This has happened partly because of the increasing potential for migration of labour from low-income countries – such as Eastern Europe – to boost labour supply in higher-income countries – such as the UK. But, more significantly, companies have been increasingly willing and able to outsource manufacturing production and back-office service activities to low-cost locations around the world, including China and India. As a result, workers in high-income countries, such as the United States and the UK, are increasingly exposed to competitive pressures from a massive global labour force in the emerging markets and developing economies. (Asia alone is home to over half the world's population.)

Globalisation and the Financial Crisis

The evolution of the global credit boom between the mid-1990s and mid-2000s, and the financial crisis and recession that have followed, have shown this 'new global economy' in action. Globalisation has contributed to the build-up of financial imbalances and the transmission of shocks around the world economy in a number of ways.

First, starting in the mid-1990s, the globalisation and liberalisation of financial markets provided a plentiful supply of global capital to support the inflation of a global credit bubble, centred on the United States. These developments also provided an environment in which financial institutions, and in particular banks, pursued aggressive strategies to develop as global businesses – not necessarily recognising the risks attached to these strategies. While there were other factors that contributed to the development of the global credit boom which has imploded so spectacularly since the summer of 2007, increasingly globalised capital markets and institutions certainly provided a fertile environment in which financial risks could be underestimated. The growth-orientation of banks and other financial institutions, coupled with the excessive sophistication and complexity of the financial instruments they were developing, masked the increasing risks attached to their balance sheets.

Second, the extension of globalisation to many countries with low labour costs helped to contain inflationary pressures that might otherwise have arisen from a long period of economic growth. Many factors contributed to this muted response of inflation in the late 1990s and early 2000s, including the establishment of more credible monetary frameworks in many economies and the stability of inflation expectations. But the 'China effect' – which drove down the costs of manufacturing goods across the global economy – was a very significant factor. The impact of competition from China and other low-labour-cost economies drove down manufacturing prices directly, holding down the imported component of inflation for the economies of the West. In addition, the potential for outsourcing processes to the Far East and other emerging market economies acted as a disciplining force against wage inflation.

That meant that a significant monetary tightening – which might have stopped the credit boom in its tracks earlier – was not applied until the mid-2000s. One point at which a monetary tightening might have been applied was after the strong growth of the late 1990s, which was supported by the inflation of the dot.com bubble in the United States and rising equity prices. But the muted response of inflation to this period of strong economic growth meant that, in the early 2000s, monetary authorities around the world were relaxing rather than tightening policy. This provided added momentum to the growth of credit and the financial exuberance in the mid-2000s, inadvertently further stoking up the global credit boom. And the resulting combination of a long period of growth accompanied by low inflation – stretching back to the early 1990s – fuelled the belief in a new era of 'Great Stability' or 'Great Moderation'. That, in turn, encouraged financial investors to underestimate the macroeconomic risks attached to their asset portfolios, adding to the vulnerabilities in the financial system.

A third aspect of the 'new global economy', which has become apparent as the financial crisis has unfolded and the recession taken hold, is the ability of trade and investment linkages to transmit shocks very rapidly across the world economy. In autumn 2008 and in early 2009 the negative shock to business and consumer confidence surrounding the failure of Lehman Brothers rippled around the world, driven by financial markets and reinforced by highly integrated global supply chains, stretching from the US and Europe across Asia and back again. The initial downturn in demand was amplified by a global stock cycle affecting many key sectors of manufacturing and distribution, including high-tech goods and motor vehicles.

These linkages highlight the vulnerability of national economies to global shocks. However, as business and consumer confidence improves and the period of heavy destocking comes to an end, they have the potential to reinforce the momentum of the recovery too.

GUY VERHOFSTADT

The many effects of the actual crisis cannot be underestimated. Though it was introduced as an American real-estate credit crisis in August 2007, we now face a major financial and economic crisis on a global scale. Unleashed in September 2008, one of the most devastating months in world economic history, the crisis is everywhere. All over the world banks and assurance companies are faltering, or must be saved by public authorities. Within a few months, global stock markets have lost half of their value. Economic growth has been reversed, to be replaced by a worldwide recession. Deficit spending is back, as well as economic nationalism and even collectivism. Trillions of dollars or euros have vanished, many times more than the billions mobilised by national authorities to save their banks and their assurance companies. Millions of jobs have been lost, hitting the poor even more than the rich. And even more jobs are being threatened by the first global economic recession since 1945. Can it be worse? Or do we take the necessary steps to overcome this crisis, and to save globalisation as the most creative movement of our times?

Our first task, I guess, is to understand what happened. Who is to blame for this crisis? What went wrong? Is there anything we could do better? And what should be done to overcome this crisis? – questions I cannot answer in this short introduction. But these questions should guide us for the coming months and years. As long as we do not see what happened, we are condemned to repeat the same mistakes.

In a nutshell, I guess the current financial and economic crisis to be the result of eight elementary failures:

- A failure of financial markets, inventing or reinventing financial instruments (hedge funds, derivates, enhanced yields, dynamic asset-backed funds, diversified mortgage-backed securities . . .) out of any control and transparency, paving their own way of destruction, not hindered by rational control, accepting no other master than faltering confidence.
- A failure of risk, transferring risk from age-old banks and assurance companies, knowing their clients by name and credibility, to those new

'financial products' out of acceptable standards of risk. Traditional standards of risk should have prevented the American credit crunch on the housing markets, the harbinger of the present crisis. Unacceptable standards of risks did not.

- A failure of responsibility. Who is to blame for the present crisis? No one. In a certain sense we all are. Up to the birth of the present crisis we all accepted 'the invisible hand' to lead world economics in the right practices. Doing so, we all expected responsibility to be global or collective. We were wrong: responsibility should be personal; otherwise, it is unidentifiable, particularly in financial and economic matters.

- A failure of control and transparency. Particularly new or renewed financial products proved to be out of control and opaque. But control and transparency can only be guaranteed by national governments, who failed to manage financial markets when confronted with globalisation. This failure is obvious, as national governments are not entitled to do so. But international or supranational agencies could not fill the gap. That's why international control faltered.

- A failure of confidence. Public trust in our financial institutions may be the first and most lasting victim of this crisis. But at the same time a failure of confidence preceded or activated the actual turmoil. As we all know, confidence-building is a long process, while losing confidence can happen in an astonishingly short term.

- A failure of regulation. Markets need to be regulated and guaranteed – they are no gift of nature. They need to follow international rules. I am a liberal, not a libertarian. Libertarianism does not accept any rule. Liberalism wants the rule of the many, not the few. The many should make the rules for anyone to follow. Regulation is not the opposite but the complement of liberalism.

- A failure of globalisation. This failure is the most important for me. Up to now globalisation only concerned economies, financial institutions, markets and technologies. It did not involve politics. Globalising markets and industries need political authorities to intervene with rules – rules that must be followed. These rules can only be set by political assemblies, which, at the national or international levels, did not move. Industrial and commercial globalisation was not followed by political globalisation. In my opinion, this was the major failure leading us to this global crisis.

- A failure of policies. The contrast between globalising economies and national policies can not be greater than it is today. While financial and economic decisions are taken at global levels, political decision making in these matters does not transcend national boundaries. Even within the EU this unbearable contrast prevents politicians from taking tough decisions.

Fortunately we have a European Central Bank, safeguarding monetary stability in these dark times. But even a central bank does not make a unified financial and economic policy. Even within the EU, implementation of economic policy is still decided at national levels. We cannot afford this failure to be ignored.

Given these pivotal failures, the ongoing world financial and economic crisis will not be solved unless we face these failures and unless we take the most elementary decisions to change what went wrong. Knowing there are no simple solutions, tough decisions will take time to implement and bear fruit. It will take time to restore confidence, to rebuild our ailing institutions and to create new ones, and to encourage growth and welfare on a global scale. But we should start now if we want to survive, and combine both a global and a regional approach.

When considering what went wrong, and trying to understand the current financial and economic crisis, I would like to refer to the Japanese recession in the 1990s, which in my opinion was the clearest harbinger in the industrialised world of what happened in 2008 on a world scale. In many aspects, indeed, this Japanese recession already included nearly every characteristic of the current world crisis. It began with a tremendous growth of Japanese GNP in the years 1954–71, an average 10 per cent growth per year, a fivefold increase of Japan's production per capita over the years. During the 1970s and the 1980s, Japanese growth lost its double-digit figures, but in 1989 Japan's economy reached its highest peak in percentage of world production, 14 per cent, twice the economy of the reunited Germany in 1991. Around the year 1990, however, the Japanese economic miracle collapsed. An enormous real-estate bubble, preceding the American housing bubble by ten years, introduced a stock-market crisis and a lasting economic standstill. Japanese economic growth fell from 8 per cent in 1990 to zero per cent in 1994. Japanese stock markets lost half their value in three years. Japan never fully recovered from a lasting 'Japanese winter', condemning economic growth to a meagre 1 per cent per year since then. Having tried any classical recipe for recovery – deficit spending, reducing expenditures, enhancing public debt, twelve recovery plans in twelve years – Japan's economy has only gradually recovered since 2003, after having saved its bank sector for about $500 billion. Therefore, the Japanese experience may help show the rest of the world what should be done, and what should be avoided to survive a crisis of this magnitude.

NORBERT WALTER

Financial markets contribute to the growth and dynamism of an economy in a variety of ways: first, they contribute directly to growth – the banks, insurance companies and other providers of financial services such as stock exchanges create around 4 per cent of annual gross value added in Germany. This is higher than the contribution from Germany's fêted flagship sectors such as the electrical and chemical industries – a fact still unknown to most people. In terms of employment, the financial sector is a major player, with no fewer than 650,000 people (1.6 per cent of the total workforce) working for banks and 1.2 million (2.5 per cent) in the combined credit and insurance businesses. This direct growth contribution is not a reflection – though some may suppose it is – of an irrational ballooning of the financial sector that accompanied the formation of the global financial-market bubble which burst in 2007/08; in fact, the contribution in Germany is still relatively low by international standards. By comparison, in the US the contribution of the financial sector to gross value added is around 8 per cent in the UK it is no less than 7.5 per cent and in Switzerland it is as much as 13 per cent.

Second, and more significant, is the indirect contribution of the financial markets: financing economic activity and allocating scarce resources for alternative purposes; the inherently associated assumption and spreading of risk and the mirroring of their financing function by investing savings in order to smooth and moderate consumption over the life cycle. The decentralised mechanism of the financial markets ensures the most efficient allocation of available savings. The more efficient the financial system, the more effective the performance of the allocation function. Notably, empirical evidence demonstrates that economies with a more efficient and developed financial system grow faster than those without. This efficiency is measured on the one hand by the depth of the financial system (i.e. the ratio of loans and other financial assets such as stocks and bonds to GDP) and on the other by the completeness of the financial market (i.e. the breadth of the range of financial instruments offered). The latter is extremely important, as the total capital supply can be employed more effectively if the available funding instruments correspond with the individual risk appetite of the providers of capital. The capital market therefore needs a diversity of financial products to satisfy the demands of its customers.

The relevance of the completeness (or breadth) of financial markets relative to their depth is often underestimated – mistakenly; however, it should be obvious that different funding projects require different instruments. For illustrative purposes we shall compare an investment to expand capacity in an established-sector company with the investment financing of a start-up-sector company. In the first case, the body of available historical data allows us to make a relatively reliable forecast of the stream and profile of the return on investment; in addition, the company presumably has access to collateral owing to its many years in business. In such a situation the investment can largely be financed using a fixed-interest loan, since on the one hand the funding burden (relative to the revenue flows) can be reliably projected by the investor, while on the other hand the potential risk for providers of capital is low, thanks to the company history and availability of collateral. By contrast, in the case of the start-up, a funding structure is required that takes into account the uncertain future of the revenue stream, which cannot be projected and which rules out a fixed, regular interest claim for the capital provider. This uncertainty may also warrant guaranteeing rights to the providers of capital to exercise influence that would safeguard their investment. In this case the appropriate solution would be quasi-equity financing instruments that grant the investors a say in decision making and a risk-adjusted high return on their capital if the venture is successful.

It is precisely those so often harshly criticised investment-banking products that offer the variety of financing instruments that can meet the requirements of the diverse financing projects and help to satisfy the respective preferences of both the providers and recipients of capital. This underlines how misguided it would be to phase out this segment of the financial markets in favour of simple types of financing (like traditional bank loans) that are presumed to better serve the interests of the real economy.

Note also that the correlation between the heterogeneity of the financial system and the contribution to growth applies not only to corporate finance but also to household financing. For example, a report prepared by Mercer Oliver Wyman for the European Commission showed that economies with a broader range of instruments for private real-estate financing grow faster than those with only a limited number of financial instruments. It would be counterproductive to whittle down the range of available funding investments by imposing onerous regulation. Incidentally, this applies not only with regard to the potential growth contribution, but also with respect to the social policy dimension: more flexible funding models – for example, with variable repayments or longer repayment periods – also allow demographic groups with initially low incomes and few assets to acquire real estate. The important function of the financial markets of dispersing risk also applies beyond the realm of the straightforward financing of investments by companies and households and is illustrated by the example of the hedging of currency risk. As a rule, companies that export their products to, or acquire goods from, other currency areas want to avoid exchange-rate-fluctuation risks. These risks can be hedged by using currency derivatives and forward transactions. Here, too, the availability of such financing instruments makes a significant contribution to growth: it is well known that open economies grow faster than ones that are closed. If and to the extent to which the availability of instruments for hedging exchange-rate risks boosts the willingness of companies to become integrated into the international division of labour, this makes a direct contribution to growth. What is less well known is that using other derivatives allows other categories of risk to be managed, including commodities derivatives, which protect companies from the risks of fluctuations in commodity prices, and the recently introduced weather derivatives, which utility companies and other weather-sensitive sectors may use to hedge against weather-induced fluctuations in their output and corresponding payment streams.

Households and individuals also use financial instruments to hedge risk, to protect against sickness, accident and property risks by using insurance products. What is less obvious is that the ability of a financial sector to provide cover for such risks results in increasingly close ties with the insurance sector in the traditional sense and the capital markets: the ability of insurance companies to assume risks is determined – as we know – by the probability and potential size of loss or damage. While these parameters for traditional risks like mortality are easily calculable, there are several areas of the property-insurance segment where there is growing uncertainty about the probabilities and sizes of losses. This is obviously the case with disaster risks that are dependent on extreme weather events or terrorism.

There is a danger of an incalculability of such risks that results in either unaffordable insurance premiums or, in the worst case, non-insurability, which in turn threatens to hamper economic activity. A wider public became aware of this following the 11 September terrorist attacks, when the continuation of civil aviation was threatened by the prospect of airlines being unable to insure their aircraft. Less dramatic, but of increasing importance on account of global climate change, are the concerns of insurance companies that they will face excessive burdens from climate-induced losses.

The complement to the financing function is the investment of savings. From a saver's point of view it represents delayed consumption. A particularly important aspect of this – given that the demographic shift is flagging up the limitations of the state-financed, pay-as-you-go pension system – is safe-guarding one's standard of living during old age. From the saver's point of view the key is striking the right balance between the conflicting objectives of a return on investment regarded as satisfactory (the higher this is, the more likely one is to refrain from consumption) and the security of the investment (so that they have reliable access to the desired amount of funds in their old age). In this connection the international nature of capital markets is partic-ularly important: the demographic contraction of rich nations like Japan or Germany will be accompanied by a decline in the potential growth rate of these economies. A reasonable return on savings can therefore only be attained via an international diversification of invested assets – with this diversifica-tion having to be hedged suitably to mitigate exchange-rate and other risks in order to ensure the security of the investment. This shows once again that the more developed, the deeper and more diverse financial markets are, the more likely they are to succeed in fulfilling the desired objectives of old-age provision.

To prevent any misunderstanding, note that financial markets per se do not generate growth (apart from their direct contribution to growth); effi-cient financial markets are, however, essential for the efficient utilisation of scarce resources in an economy and boost its growth impact. Growth is not only the basis and expression of a country's increasing prosperity, it is also the best means of ensuring that broad swathes of the population can play their part in the economy and benefit from prosperity or – should they be unable to do so for whatever reason – that they can obtain some form of financial support, via transfer payments, for example. These payments should not, however, destroy incentives for the jobless to search for re-employment.

Admittedly it may appear inappropriate to point this out in the current environment, but even following the outbreak of the financial crisis the funda-mental truth remains that open financial markets have an important indicator function with regard to the quality of the economic policy of a country. Financial markets punish, for example, monetary policy that is inflationary compared with that of other countries, as well as countries whose debt policy is too lax, by demanding higher interest rates and/or by withdrawing (or reducing the flow of) capital.

Likewise deep and wide stock markets can be an indicator of the attrac-tiveness of a country as a business location. Of course too much cannot be, nor should be, read into every swing in the stock market as an assessment of a location's appeal for investors; however, if a country's stock-market valu-ation and capitalisation systematically lag behind those of other nations, this must and should certainly be interpreted as a vote of no confidence in the country's economic fundamentals and performance. Note that this does not mean the financial markets determine the choice of a specific economic model – each country is free to choose its economic policy in accordance with the political preferences of its population; in this sense the financial markets perform merely an indicator function, illustrating more clearly the economic consequences of the selection of a specific policy. Unlike in elections, this assessment is not only made at the extended periodic intervals of polling day, but is more of an ongoing process – which is certainly positive in the decision-making process, but may not always be welcome as far as the (political) players involved are concerned.

In turn, those that derive the most from this indicator and control function are the socially disadvantaged: those on low incomes, pensioners and people with few assets, for example, benefit from monetary stability. The rich should be able to diversify their assets more easily or shift them abroad if necessary to protect themselves from the negative consequences of currency devaluation.

So, efficient financial markets not only make a contribution to financing investments, hedging risk, smoothing consumption and boosting the potential growth rate of an economy. They also perform an important social-policy function. Both political leaders and financial institutions should therefore attach high priority to communicating this importance and intensifying the promotion of viable financial markets. Currently, this task is even more pressing, with uncertainties in the markets and growing doubts about the effectiveness of the market economy as a whole. The private sector banks are working to solve the problems and discrepancies that have been revealed as the financial crisis has unfolded. However, the private sector must remain able to act after the implementation of regulatory policy measures.

Financial structures and individual institutions that have been the bedrock of the financial system for decades have in some cases disappeared literally overnight; therefore central banks and governments must respond with corrective measures to complement private-sector initiatives and encourage inter-sectoral cooperation.

Although it is certainly true that excessive risk taking by financiers and inadequate regulatory supervision are to blame for the global financial crisis, global macroeconomic forces should not be overlooked as a contributing factor. As a major player in the new global economic structure of the 2000s, China along with other emerging economies had a part in shaping the macroeconomic context that framed the disastrous financial crisis.

The economic crisis of 2008 has its roots in the last recession. Ever since the US Central Bank used loose monetary policy to stave off a technical recession in 2001 after the dot.com bubble burst, low interest rates were the norm for the next several years in developed economies, even as economic growth was strong. That is the usual use of monetary policy, but the fundamentally altered structure of the global economy of the 2000s made the outcome unpredictable.

The mis-priced risk at the heart of the US sub-prime mortgage crisis is a result of low interest rates and excess liquidity. Credit was cheap and plentiful, which is peculiar in a country with a low rate of saving and a high level of consumer debt as well as highly leveraged firms. Normally, a savings deficit requiring borrowing to consume would increase the cost of borrowing on account of the low supply of funds. Moreover, the liquidity did not cause inflation. This is due to globalisation and the global appetite for US debt, which kept down prices and the cost of borrowing. The US Federal Reserve then missed the signal that money was too cheap, and lenders continued to seek borrowers, even if they were sub-prime ones.

This strong demand for US treasuries stemmed from the trade surpluses in the Middle East (due to oil exports) and China and elsewhere in Asia (due to cheap manufactured goods). The rapid increases in current-account surpluses of these countries are largely matched by the gaping current-account deficit of the United States since the late 1990s. When combined with a high savings rate, particularly in Asia, large foreign-exchange-reserve holdings accumulated in their coffers. As a result of the fixed exchange rates operated by these countries, purchases of US treasuries were necessary even if the American interest rate, and therefore returns, were low.

European primary and external positions did not experience the same deterioration as the United States. However, measures undertaken in the 2000s in Europe facilitated the financial sector raising funds from US wholesale money markets instead of funding their lending through deposits, spreading the liquidity across the developed world and contributing to housing bubbles in Britain, Ireland and Spain, among others. Financial derivatives and securitised assets moved easily in globalised markets, which led to the prospect of systemic banking-sector failure in Western Europe as well as the United States for the first time since the Great Depression of the 1930s.

With such global imbalances, one question must be why there was not a rebalancing when global savings/borrowing and trade were misaligned. The fixed-exchange-rate regimes of these emerging economies also forestalled a rebalancing of the global economy. When China, for instance, recorded trade surpluses since 2005 which reached some 12 per cent of GDP, the RMB was bound to experience irresistible pressure to appreciate. If this had happened, goods purchased from China would have been more expensive for American consumers, who would then have bought less, thereby reducing the US trade deficit and concurrently causing the Chinese trade surplus to fall. This, however, did not happen, as the Chinese intervened to keep its currency in a managed band and instead used measures to raise reserve requirements in its banking sector, among other measures, to manage the large increases in liquidity in its economy. This has not been entirely successful, as sterilisation of the inflows was incomplete and China experienced the prospect of overheating when investment, particularly in fixed assets and construction, grew rapidly and led to the prospect of an asset bubble.

Fixed exchange rates are not the only reason. The US dollar further has the status of being a reserve currency – demand for which does not fall purely on the basis of demand and supply following from trade balances and capital movements. If that were the case, then the US's 'twin deficits' (budget and trade) should have been unsustainable long before. Indeed, the US external deficit reflecting consumption based on borrowing from abroad was a phenomenon even before China's significant opening to the world economy. Thus, it is not unusual for China or other developing countries to want currency stability and maintain competitiveness while growing. Nevertheless, the so-called global imbalances meant that the West, with low savings, was importing savings from the (Far and Middle) East, and the appetite for the US dollar kept liquidity high and cheap (as well as interest rates low) in America. As European banks drew on US wholesale money markets, the effects spread widely. The financial crisis followed, as financiers created ever more sophisticated instruments and sold them around the world.

The global economy will need to be rebalanced. However, the process should proceed gradually, as liquidity from China and emerging economies is needed to help the West in its credit crunch. It would alleviate some of the necessary belt-tightening of Western consumers and also help deflate the asset bubbles building up in emerging economies with liquidity coming through inadequate sterilisation. It would help to stabilise the rich countries, which provide a great many of the world's consumers upon whom most emerging economies depend for export growth.

Also, Western governments will have to borrow fairly heavily to fund the rescue packages that are necessary to prevent systemic banking failure. These government bonds are likely to be bought by emerging economies with high savings and external surpluses, such as China. Therefore, rather counter-intuitively, although global imbalances led to this crisis, they should be maintained whilst the battle ensues to rescue the financial sector and real economies of the West. Cutting off liquidity at a time when the West is drawing upon it to fund its rescue efforts would likely lead to a long and painful period of austerity. The recovery of the West and its markets is in the global interest, particularly China's as the world's second-largest trader.

Therefore, emerging economies played a notable, albeit indirect role, in the global financial crisis. They can also help in ameliorating the impact. The challenge, however, is the type of global leadership role that China, along with other emerging economies, is willing to take on. Providing liquidity has been argued for, and otherwise easing of capital flows would help finance the recovery in a way that continues to preserve the Chinese exchange rate. Allowing greater convertibility and flexibility of exchange rates, however, would also be helpful, particularly as it enables these countries to absorb the balance-of-payments shocks nominally through exchange-rate movements instead of painful real adjustments such as a rise in unemployment as exports contract. This does not necessarily mean floating currencies, but ones which are more easily traded and moved within a band that allows them to navigate a middle path between stability and flexibility. Doing so is not just geared at aiding a Western-led crisis, but at restoring global economic and financial stability that has brought real prosperity to China and much of the developing world over the past decade.

PRESENT

JAMES ALEXANDER

As explained on pp. 3–5 I believe we are experiencing a societal shift from an era defined by consumption in an age of abundance to an era defined by sustainable living in a resource-constrained world. This transition will change how individually and collectively we see the world and how we behave in it; however, it is important to remember that this societal shift has not been caused by the financial crisis but that the financial crisis is merely a sympton of it.

In my view, the single biggest implication of the financial crisis on social behaviour has been the further erosion of trust in society. And to a naïve Sagittarian optimist this is a sad thing, as it has further undermined the very fabric of a collective and thriving society. Now, please don't misunderstand me here. The financial crisis has quite rightly shone a blinding light on those individuals and institutions that represented and defined all that was success and excess in the last era. From Lehman's and Northern Rock to Madoff and Fred Goodwin, our former idols and heroes have been as exposed as the emperor in his new clothes. And this is a very good thing, as it has caused us to pause and question our current economic and societal models.

This exposure was ultimately caused by readier access to relevant information, which has opened our eyes, taught us to question more and to trust less; and this is exactly what we might expect, given the wider transition that society is going through.

In the last era, the Age of Oil, Automobiles and Mass Consumption – the promise of consumerism in an era of abundance – we became conditioned to a certain common sense and way of operating. In commerce, the economics of scale and scope dominated as businesses sought to mass-produce, mass-distribute and mass-retail homogenous products at low cost. And boy, was it successful! With fridges, washing machines and vacuum cleaners we were increasingly liberated from time-consuming household chores; with cars and planes we liberated ourselves from our immediate locale. These benefits reinforced our faith in the advantages of high-growth, energy-intensive mass production, distribution and exchange ordered and orchestrated by overseeing global institutions such as the World Bank and the UN.

But the new era, of sustainable living in a resource-constrained world, is defined by information and communication technologies that put the individual users in control, thereby allowing them to be defined by self-reliance, without the need for the institutions of society, which they no longer trust; thus, they're more able to choose to lead more enriched and diverse lives, with multiple-income streams that they've made possible by leaving conventional corporate employment. In this new world people value authenticity – for example, they pay more attention to the food they eat and where it comes from – and are more at ease defining themselves by their individuality rather than by their material possessions. Above all, they value control, transparency, community and ethicality.

I have witnessed this transition first-hand in financial services. As strategy director at Egg, the Internet bank, and in co-creating Zopa, the peer-to-peer social-lending marketplace, I spent much time trying to get under the skin of the concept of trust in the financial-services industry. Trust is not absolute. It typically takes a long time to earn and can be lost rapidly. It is also context-specific; for example, if a few years ago, I had asked: 'Do you trust your bank to keep your money safe?' I suspect the answer would have been yes; if I asked the same question today, and you'd been a customer of Northern Rock or an Icelandic bank, it is likely you'd give a very different or qualified answer. Similarly, if I asked: 'Do you trust your bank to make payments from A to B?' I suspect that most would answer yes. But if I asked: 'Do you trust your bank to help you with your money?' I suspect that, sadly, most would answer no. If I ask Robin, our six-year-old son, to draw a picture of a bank, he inevitably draws a building with bars on the window and a safe in the corner – not exactly a welcoming image. So when we created Zopa in 2005, it was with the vision that people could trust one another with money. This may seem a somewhat ludicrous notion as well as a fabulous aspiration post-Madoff, Northern Rock and the demise of Lehman, but with the growth of community banks and cooperatives the world over, this notion seems significantly less fanciful.

This wider transition in society has taught us to question everything and everyone – as our received wisdom and common sense have unravelled and because we have not settled on the new rules by which we play. This includes people and institutions that previously many trusted implicitly: doctors, teachers, religious leaders, politicians – even parents. In the 2007 conference 'Politics and the Media in the Internet Age', the UK shadow chancellor George Osborne stated:

> With all these profound changes – the Google-isation of the world's information, the creation of on-line social networks bigger than whole populations, the ability of new technology to harness the wisdom of crowds and the rise

of user-generated content – we are seeing the democratisation of the means of production, distribution and exchange.

This new democracy is a good thing.

It is challenging our existing sources of authority, in the media and in politics, and so it should . . . People are no longer prepared to sit and be spoon-fed. They are taking matters into their own hands . . . They are the masters now.

So within this context it is critical that political, religious and indeed all leaders examine their roles. They can no longer rely, as perhaps many have done in the recent past, on the erstwhile status quo of their place in the hierarchical authority. Instead, their role today must be about demonstrating true ethical and moral leadership – about defining the values, morals and ethos of our society in the new era.

JACQUES ATTALI

Are we seeing a 'global' response to the first 'global' financial crisis?

In order to regain equilibrium without bankrupting the affected states, it is necessary for certain outside forces to be able to ensure that the states balance their budgets. There are no such forces domestically and the role of international financial regulation would be to create constraints limiting these imbalances: politically, as the euro experience demonstrated, it is easier to accept restraint from outside forces than to resolve these issues from within.

While strict banking regulations were introduced back in 1934 separating the activities of commercial banks and investment banks, this time nothing has been done despite announcements made by various summits, from the G8 to the G20, because everyone knows that these constraints will ultimately lead to extremely unpopular and strict regulations.

In the United States, whilst a silent battle is being fought between Chicago and Wall Street in order to gain control of the derivative markets (the main derivative markets for raw materials are located in Chicago), the ABA (American Bankers Association) is doing its best to ensure that the improvement of bank capital does not lead to nationalisations and the Fed does not become the main regulator, as nevertheless has been decided by President Obama, and it is also against the creation of a government agency responsible for consumer protection. On the whole, the Obama administration has failed to pass any reform in Congress and has capitulated before Wall Street.

In Europe, the twenty-seven member states of the European Union, divided over the nature of controls that should be enforced against the banks, are leaving them under the responsibility of each national authority, thus paving the way for regulatory chaos.

Globally, the initiatives proposed by the G20 for monitoring rating agencies, hedge funds and LBOs, and for preventing speculation in raw materials, uncovered positions in credit-default swaps, non-recourse debts and speculative transactions are not being adopted because of opposition by banks and governments, who fear the depression that might ensue.

DAVID BLANCHFLOWER [1]

The UK economy is in dire straits. In the final quarter of 2008 GDP growth contracted by 1.5 per cent, the sharpest rate of decline since 1980, and output continued to contract through the first half of 2009 with a range of macro-economic forecasters now expecting 2009 to be the sharpest contraction of the UK economy in the post-war period.

In the three months to December 2008 ILO unemployment was close to 2 million people – its highest level for ten years. And since the beginning of 2009 there has been a stream of redundancies across a wide range of firms. At the same time the graduation of the high-school and university classes of 2009 grows closer, threatening further increases in the pool of unemployed labour.

In past recessions rising long-term unemployment had a persistently adverse effect on the supply potential of the economy. Fiscal measures to sustain employment may also be an important part of the overall macro-economic-policy response to the credit crisis. In this section I shall discuss the overall macroeconomic context of rising unemployment.

Where Are We Now? And Where Are We Going?

How long is the downturn likely to last? Economists typically tend to under-predict the length and depth of recessions.[2] Recent recessions have typically been associated with five quarters of negative output growth and financial crises tend to have particularly severe consequences.

Consensus forecasts around the time of the last recession of 1991 projected that GDP growth would be over 2 per cent but the final out-turn ended up being around minus 2 per cent; however, even when economists had been consistently surprised by the depth of the recession in 1991, they failed to realise that growth would continue to contract in 1992 but then became so

[1] This entry was taken from an open lecture given at the University of Stirling, 25 February 2009.
[2] David Blanchflower, 'Macroeconomic Policy Responses in the UK', Nottingham University, Thursday, 29 January 2009.

pessimistic that they failed to appreciate the strength of the upturn in 1993 and 1994.

This financial crisis is certainly the worst in my lifetime. We must consider the plausible possibility that the recession may be more protracted than those recessions that occurred in recent decades[3]. Some commentators have characterised the surprising severity of the recession as reflecting a stream of unexpected events in the financial sector; for example, amongst many other events, the collapse of Northern Rock and Bear Stearns, government interventions in Fannie and Freddie Mac and the AIG insurance group, and the bankruptcy of the Lehman Brothers investment bank.

I find these arguments tenuous at best. The collapse of Lehman Brothers was clearly a symptom, not the cause of the credit crisis. It is hard to imagine a counterfactual in which the Lehman Brothers investment bank might have been propped up at the last minute by public funds, and global confidence in the financial sector would have been markedly better. Rather, a realisation of the magnitude of the underlying problems in the financial sector, leading to adverse effects on confidence, spending and investment intentions was always likely, and sooner rather than later. Clearly policy makers did not come to a realisation of the problems in the financial sector quickly enough.

Concentrating on these events abstracts from a proper appreciation of the underlying causes of the recession. Perhaps it is this habit that leads so many macroeconomic forecasters during recessions to assume that the adverse shocks to economic activity have largely passed and will dissipate going forward. Hence, using some macroeconomic model, they extrapolate that growth will return to its trend or average rate more quickly than it actually does. Few forecasters expect the underlying shocks to activity, and our responses to them, to intensify. Every bad data release is treated as the trough and the next quarter is forecast to be better, but it isn't. Initial projections for a 'V-shaped' recovery are then revised to a 'U-shaped' and as optimism turns to pessimism, eventually to an 'L-shaped' just as the recovery arrives.

This experience suggests we must not be overly optimistic. Hence, the Bank of England's February 2009 *Inflation Report* central projections are for growth to begin recovering by 2010 but also include the possibility that annual GDP growth will remain negative through 2010. The risks to the central projection are clearly weighted to the downside.

Commensurate with the problems in the financial sector there have been significant macroeconomic policy responses, both fiscal and monetary. In the UK the bank rate has been cut by 400 basis points. But the size of this response must be set against overall conditions in financial markets and credit availability.

[3] Sir John Gieve, 'Seven Lessons from the Last Three Years', London School of Economics, Thursday, 19 February 2009.

That is, the transmission of monetary policy has been impaired. Cuts in bank rate have not been fully passed through to the rates faced by households and firms in servicing their debts. Overall credit conditions have tightened.

Ultimately, the medium-term prospects for the economy are dependent on a healthy financial system to channel our savings into the most productive investments. To this end a range of public-policy initiatives have been announced to restore more normal conditions to financial markets, and ensure that lending to households and firms improves. For example, these measures include steps to reduce uncertainty about banks' capital adequacy by providing insurance against future losses from holdings of risky assets.

I certainly hope these measures will work and allow the UK economy to gradually recover. However, the risks of a protracted recession are clearly evident. It may take longer than expected for policy initiatives to restore more normal lending conditions in financial markets. Additional policy initiatives may be required if conditions continue to deteriorate within the financial sector. The possibility of further unexpected events cannot be ruled out. Alternatively, the more general downturn in the British economy might have a more negative impact on the financial sector than we expect.

Hence, a second risk relates to the rising level of unemployment in the economy.[4] As redundancies rise and house prices fall, more British households will face the grim prospect of experiencing both unemployment *and* negative equity in their homes. Forced selling in the housing market could lead to further downward pressure on house prices, pushing more households into negative equity and reducing the amount of collateral they have to secure their mortgages against. In this case mortgage arrears and defaults will rise, putting further pressure on the financial sector. Such a scenario would lend a new dynamic to the existing vicious circle of falling house and asset prices and reduced credit availability. These are plausible possibilities we must consider.

How bad will the downturn in the labour market be? In past recessions the rise in unemployment has been persistent and lagging the contraction in output. Survey measures of current economic activity, confidence and investment and employment intentions remain close to historic lows. In a recent survey by the Bank of England's regional agents, many contacts suggested that their next stage of adjustment to weaker demand could involve more substantial job cuts.

---

[4] Even two years ago I noted that the labour market was loosening: 'In my view, the labour market for the UK, as a whole, has continued to loosen over the past twelve months or so. Labour demand has remained firm or picked up in many sectors, but on the whole has not kept pace with the additional supply. Consequently, while employment has risen, so too has the degree of slack in the labour market.' David Blanchflower, 'Recent Developments in the UK Labour Market', speech given at the University of Stirling, 26 February 2007.

The deterioration in employment prospects is being felt in muted wage growth. At the same time, sharp reductions in bonus payments will push down on overall wage and salary growth in 2009. As nominal wage growth retreats in 2009 this will add to the broader degree of disinflationary pressure within the economy. Annual CPI inflation has already fallen sharply from its peak of 5.2 per cent in September 2008 to 3 per cent in the release as of February 2009. Falling oil, commodity and input prices will push down on firms' costs; and as the degree of spare capacity within the economy widens, firms will be more likely to cut their consumer prices to maintain market share. In the February 2009 *Inflation Report* CPI inflation was expected to fall back to well below the 2 per cent target with the possibility that CPI inflation would fall below zero.

So the MPC must consider the risk that the UK may experience deflation. Of course, some measures of retail-price inflation which include house prices or mortgage-interest payments are very likely to move into negative territory. This raises serious questions regarding whether the CPI inflation target is the correct measure of inflation for the MPC to consider.

I echo the comments by my colleague Sir John Gieve that setting a target for a measure of consumer-price inflation that excludes the costs of home ownership has done us no favours.[5] How might monetary policy have been set differently had house prices been included in the index? Interest rates might have been increased more quickly as the house-price boom began, and have been cut more quickly as house prices began to fall.

Measures of inflation that include the costs of home ownership have the advantage of including a larger basket of goods than in the CPI. House prices are also the most important asset price for many households, as it is the price of their home that households secure their mortgages against. The large boom in house prices meant households were able to obtain ever more favourable mortgages relative to the bank rate as their loan-to-value (LTV) ratios fell. And the rise in house prices also reflected financial institutions lending ever greater multiples of the incomes of first-time buyers.

The MPC considered these effects in their policy decisions when targeting CPI, but not sufficiently. Because house prices are so intimately linked to developments in credit markets there are advantages in explicitly including house prices in the target the MPC considers in setting monetary policy.

[5] Sir John Gieve, 'Seven Lessons from the Last Three Years', London School of Economics, Thursday, 19 February 2009.

JOHN BRUTON

I believe that the financial crisis gives people an opportunity to get their values back into perspective. Values are the criteria we use to decide what is more, and what is less, important in our lives. It is arguable that these criteria have become disconnected from what actually brings us contentment on a day-to-day basis.

For example, social theorists such as Professor Barry Schwartz of Swarthmore College have pointed to what he calls the paradox of choice. He suggests that increased spending power and the increased mobility that has come with wealth have immensely increased the number of choices we can make as individuals, but that this widening of choice has not, of itself, brought us greater happiness or contentment. In fact, too much choice often becomes a source of anxiety and disorientation.

Economic growth as experienced in the last twenty years in the West has led to an explosion of choice that has affected every aspect of life – multiple choices of television programmes to watch, of goods to buy, of holiday destinations to visit, of options to invest one's money and even of which home to be in, as more and more people have two homes. But apparently all this freedom and choice has not made people more contented.

For example, while the American gross domestic product more than doubled in the past thirty years, the proportion of people describing themselves as 'very happy' declined by 5 per cent. By some estimates, clinical depression in 2000 was ten times as likely as it was in 1900. This may be due to expectations rising too fast, and to increased anxiety when one does not keep up with peers, even though one may be living well by objective standards and by comparison with how one was living a few years back.

Professor Thomas Naylor of Duke University has written that modern families 'work themselves to exhaustion to pay for stuff that sits around not being used'. The amount of food we buy that goes to waste is enormous.

Much spending is dictated by a need to be seen to keep up with neighbours, with in-laws or with work associates. If one of them has a higher-range car or takes a more distant holiday, one feels pressure to maintain one's status by doing the same. A whole category of status goods has developed. As general income levels rise, the whole process becomes self-defeating because yesterday's status good has become today's out-of-date trash.

While there is now great anxiety about this fall in income being experience by most economies in 2009, it is also worth noting that, in the West, people's average income per head will still, even at the end of 2009, be five times what it was *before* the crash of 1929. So, if we do have to economise as societies or as families, we still have a far greater margin of downward flexibility to do so, without threatening the essentials of civilised life.

The evidence of social surveys suggest that the experiences that bring us contentment have more to do with our relationships with family and friends and with our sense of belonging, than with the amount we consume or the amount we own. It is necessary for us to put greater emphasis now on the first category of experience than on the second. As they say, 'freedom is the recognition of necessity'.

Indeed, some of the adjustments we may make now are ones we were going to have to make now anyway, as the baby-boomer generation retires and the size of the active workforce declines relative to the retired population.

Political and religious leaders can play a big role in helping people to understand these trends, to be less anxious about them, and to recognise that they can in fact cope with change. They can help people to take the time to reorder their priorities, to de-emphasise status goods and to emphasise the things that make one genuinely content – such as time with family and friends, and voluntary service.

In the short term, governments also have a role to play in preventing a sudden destructive collapse in economic confidence and in creating conditions in which necessary adjustments can take place gradually without destroying the structure of our economies, as happened in the 1930s. That is why government financial-stimulus packages and credit relaxation by central banks are sensible now, even if a price will have to be paid for them in higher government debt and higher interest rates later. All policy choices have a price.

I have no sympathy for Mr and Mrs 'I Deserve Four Bedrooms and a Jacuzzi', the couple who saved no money, put no money down and worked with a crooked mortgage broker to move into a McMansion – from which they are now sneaking out. And yet I have grown weary of all the scolds who are treating consumers like naughty dogs, rolling up newspapers and smacking them on the snouts, shouting: 'Bad American! Bad Brit! Bad consumer! Stop spending! Get yourself a small car, a small house, or – even better – a pup tent in a national park!'

Maybe amid the financial wreckage we feel a natural yearning to go back to simpler times. But some of our commentators have taken this urge a little far. In April 2009, the *Chronicle of Higher Education* carried an article subtitled 'The Gift of Financial Insecurity', noting that, as a result of the crisis, 'perhaps Americans can now begin to temper their ingrained optimism with a more elegiac sensibility'. A sweeping *Time* cover story told readers: 'It's time to ratchet back our wild and crazy grasshopper side and get in touch with our inner ant'. Baron Layard, a British economist and the author of *Happiness Lessons From a New Science*, seems to think that we would be better off psychologically if we erased a few more zeroes from our bank accounts. 'After all,' he says, 'extra income has done so little to produce a happier society, there must be something quite wasteful about much of it.' And if you type the word 'affluenza' into Amazon's search engine, you'll come up with four books and a PBS special bemoaning our rise from poverty.

None of this is new, of course. *Small Is Beautiful* by E. F. Schumacher was a book that millions of undergraduates had to read in the 1970s, until roughly the time Jimmy Carter gave his fireside 'malaise' speech in a cardigan sweater and looked so sad that the fire went out. Mr Schumacher, the world's first German-born, Buddhist-British economist, and the chief economist for the British Coal Board, argued for 'enoughness', a Buddhist view that we should get by with far less. For Mr Schumacher, modern society 'requires so much and accomplishes so little'. True, until you consider that in 1900 life expectancy was just forty-seven years.

In fact, small is not necessarily better, and there is a difference between a simpler life and the life of a simpleton. At what point in time should we declare: 'Stop. Enough progress. Let's keep things simple'? Would 1 BC have been a good time to hit 'pause'? Or 3 July 1776? Or on the eve of the 1964 Civil Rights vote? It's a good thing Teddy Roosevelt did not lock us into the standard of living of 1904 or we would never fly on airplanes, get a polio vaccination or expect to live past the age of fifty. With all due respect to medicine men, who did sometimes come across valuable herbal tonics, it was daring science, not the jungle, that produced Jonas Salk. Grants from the Mellon Foundation helped, too.

Without the progress of the twentieth century, Milton Berle said, we'd all be watching television by candlelight. (Of course, postal delivery might be roughly the same.) The point is that we cannot know what we might be missing by halting our climb toward affluence and greater possibility, any more than Emperor Joseph II could help Mozart by declaring that his opera had 'too many notes'.

And there is something unfair about decrying consumption at this stage in the game. Even if we simplify our lives and forswear 'extra income', we will still benefit from centuries of innovation and wealth-creation that others have yet to enjoy. Make no mistake: to embrace the 'small is beautiful' ethos is to crank up the drawbridge and leave a crocodile-infested moat between elites who already own Viking ranges and the world's unwashed masses yearning to gain access to indoor plumbing. Never mind that in the past twenty years, thanks to the explosion of American consumption, millions of people around the world, now with jobs to meet US import demands, have eaten three meals in one day – for the very first time in their lives. This is a war on poverty that we are winning! Snobs would rather downsize and turn victory into defeat.

As for the simple life, its charms wear off fast. Many tourists have tramped around Walden Pond snapping photos, but few would take seriously what Thoreau would probably advise today: to throw away our BlackBerrys and start growing real berries.

Yet there are plenty of books on happiness urging us to do something like that: to surrender our raw capitalistic drives and leave the rat race before the entire world turns into a Habitrail. I would argue that it is the excitement of competition – sloppy, risky and tense – that brings us happiness. It is the pursuit of knowledge, money and status that releases dopamine and ignites our passion. Neuroscientists report that when a person begins to take a risk, whether gambling on roulette or ginning up the nerve to ask a pretty girl to the prom, his left prefrontal cortex lights up, signalling a natural 'high'. Alpha waves and oxygenated blood rush to the brain. Sitting alone in a pup tent does not yield the same effects.

Humans have competed ever since Cain picked up a rock and knocked Abel on the head. And, from a historical point of view, the idea of competition has not imprisoned us but liberated us, psychologically and materially. In 2009 I served as a visiting fellow at St John's College, Cambridge, in a charming old office just a few blocks from the pub where Watson and Crick interrupted lunch to announce they had found 'the secret of life' (the DNA double helix). They were driven by beer, moxie, ego and competitiveness.

As Albert O. Hirschman noted in his book *The Passion and the Interests*, traditional societies believed that the noble classes living in the castles were composed of fundamentally different kinds of humans from the rest of us. Kings and queens, it was thought, should pursue their passions, whereas the rest of us should just tend our sheep, drink ale and forget about the mannered and manored life. But all that changed with the rise of democracy and industrial society – and the arrival of a broad 'affluence'. Now is no time to condemn ourselves to a new life of simple serfdom.

MARTIN FELDSTEIN [1]

Declining Mortgage Credit for Consumer Spending

The housing sector now contributes to the adverse outlook of the American economy and the substantial decline in consumption in response to lower home-equity withdrawals through home-equity loans and mortgage refinancing.

An important feature of the US mortgage system is that most borrowers can repay at any time without penalty. When interest rates fall, the borrower can replace the existing mortgage with a new one at a lower interest rate. If the value of the property has increased since the existing mortgage was obtained, refinancing also provides an opportunity to withdraw cash – the so-called mortgage-equity withdrawal (or MEW). Starting in 2001, the combination of lower mortgage rates and the rapid rise in house prices led to widespread refinancing with equity withdrawals, a practice heavily promoted by banks and mortgage brokers. Someone who obtained a mortgage at 7.7 per cent in 1997 could refinance at 5.8 per cent rate in 2003 and extract substantial cash at the same time.

A massive amount of such refinancing and equity withdrawal occurred. In 2005, 40 per cent of existing mortgages were refinanced. The 'flow of funds' data imply that mortgage equity withdrawals between 1997 and 2006 totalled more than $9 trillion, an amount equal to more than 90 per cent of disposable personal income in 2006.

This new borrowing was used to pay down other non-mortgage debts, to invest in financial assets, and importantly to finance additional consumer spending.

There is a vigorous professional debate about the extent to which MEWs led to additional consumer spending.

Alan Greenspan and James Kennedy, in Federal Reserve Bank research,

[1] These comments are drawn from 'Housing, Credit Markets and the Business Cycle', presented at the August 2007 Kansas City Federal Reserve Conference and published in the conference volume, *Housing Finance and Monetary Policy* (Kansas City Federal Reserve, 2008).

concluded from an analysis of survey data that substantial fractions of the MEW funds were used to finance home improvements or general consumption. It is significant in this context that home improvements would generally be treated in the national-income accounts as a form of consumer spending rather than investment.

Some economists are sceptical about the effect of mortgage-equity withdrawals on consumer expenditures, pointing out that individuals may choose to undertake mortgage refinancing simply because they want to increase their spending or undertake home improvements. While that may be true in some cases, I believe that the combination of rapidly rising home prices that more than doubled the value of owner-occupied housing between 1999 and 2006 – an increase of more than $10 trillion – and the substantial fall in interest rates were the primary drivers of the large rise in mortgage-equity withdrawals. I believe that it was the availability and low cost of mortgage-equity withdrawals that caused the increased consumer outlays.

The economist John Muellbauer notes that the relatively long time series evidence on the relation between mortgage-equity withdrawals and consumer spending is inconclusive, with some studies pointing to substantial effects of mortgage-equity withdrawal and others the opposite. I am quite sceptical about the relevace of this evidence because variations in national home values only became substantial after the year 2000.

Others argue on theoretical grounds that MEW should not change consumer spending, since consumption should be a function only of income (including expected future income), wealth and the rate of interest. If so, the transformation of housing wealth into cash should not affect consumption but should be used only to reduce debt or invest in financial assets.

I'm not convinced for two reasons First, as Muellbauer notes, individuals who are liquidity-constrained will consume more in response to an increased opportunity to borrow. Second, consumers can regard the increased spending on home improvements and major consumer durables as a form of investment that will provide services for years to come, even though the national-income accounts classify these outlays as consumer spending.

The national-income accounts, recently revised as of 2007, show that personal saving fell sharply from 2.1 per cent of disposable income in 2003 and 2004 to less than 0.5 per cent in 2005 and 2006, a decline equal to about a $160 billion annual rate. I believe that a substantial part of that decline and the relative increase in consumer spending was due to the concurrent rise in MEW that resulted from low mortgage-interest rates and increasing home prices.

The potential implication of this for the future is clear. A decline in house prices and a rise in mortgage-interest rates should shrink MEW and cause the household saving rate to rise to a more normal level. This is clearly good in the long term, permitting increased investment in plant and equipment and reducing our dependence on capital from abroad.

But in the short run a rapid rise in the saving rate and a decline in consumer spending would mean less aggregate demand and contribute to pushing the economy into recession as an effect of the magnitude and speed of the adjustment in mortgage-equity withdrawals, on the impact of the MEWs on consumer spending and on the state of aggregate demand as this occurs.

The volume of mortgage refinancing began to decline in late 2007 and the level of revolving home-equity loans has declined since the beginning of the that year, which also saw a rise in household savings rates. We know now what the impact has been of the sharp reduction in available mortgage credit that began in those few weeks.

An American Contagion in Europe

In the summer of 2009, at the Paris Air Show in June, I was being interviewed by the media. One of the questions was about whether the rapid spread of the A(H1N1) virus, or 'swine flu', posed a serious threat to air travel, and whether it had affected AirAsia.

I responded that AirAsia's passenger loads continued to be strong, and that forward bookings were holding steady (even rising, on some routes). I went on to add that the bigger threat to AirAsia and other reputable companies was the difficulty in gaining access to credit. 'The only swine now are bankers,' I said.

It was a comment made in jest. But it got published all over the world, and I received hundreds of text messages and emails from people whom I didn't even know (including from people in Nigeria, of all places!). Unanimously, they congratulated me for my remarks and expressed support for my views about banks and bankers.

For me, as an entrepreneur whose company's future depends greatly on access to credit, the virtual shutting down of the credit flows by banks created massive concerns. That a reputable, successful and much-honoured company like AirAsia faced such hurdles was indicative of the general tenor of the times in the financial industry. The choking-off of credit lines by banks clearly indicated that the pendulum had swung from one extreme to the other – from the days of easy credit to a situation where even reputable corporations were shut off by bankers.

Bankers claimed they were merely being prudent in the wake of the excesses that nearly brought the world financial system crashing down. In reality, however, this 180-degree turn in their attitudes and practices threatened to push into bankruptcy – with all the attendant concerns – viable, well-managed and thriving corporations.

How did we get to be here? Well, when America's housing bubble burst in mid-2006, it triggered a financial crisis and recession that swept across the globe. Countries that had embraced American-style capitalism in particular were badly hit. In Europe, banks that had invested heavily in mortgage-backed securities offered by American financial institutions found their balance sheets peppered with toxic assets. Confidence in these banks took a dive, and some were forced into bankruptcy; others had to be rescued by governments.

As banks struggled to survive, they reduced their lending activities and short-term liquidity became scarce. The domino effect came into play. With liquidity running scarce, the rest of the economy took a hit. Businesses suffered, consumer demand fell and jobs were lost. Many countries slid into a recession.

Governments have had to intervene and damage limitation began with trying to restore confidence in the banking system. This usually meant removing toxic assets from the banks and injecting funds to strengthen their capital bases. There have been instances, too, where governments have had to guarantee the private savings of bank customers. Governments were going by the assumption that injecting public funds into banks would eventually lead them to lending out this money, beginning the virtuous circle once again. Those hopes initially failed to materialise, although there are signs now (in the fall of 2009) that tight-fisted bankers – concerned about the survival of their own institutions – are now slowly beginning to provide credit again.

Asia: Same, but Different

Asia did not escape this contagion but has been affected in a different way. Many countries, including Indonesia, Thailand and Malaysia, had been victims of the financial crisis of 1997–8 and have since taken steps to clean up and reorganise their banking systems. Defence mechanisms were erected. Strict supervision had helped rein in the wild excesses, and poorly capitalised banks had been required to look for additional funds or merge with stronger banks to strengthen their bases.

In a sense, therefore, it can be said that Asia was more prepared for the contagion that came from the West, and it is to the credit of many Asian governments that this time round the headlines in the East have not been dominated by news of bank runs or bank failures. But Asia could not escape unscathed, especially from the secondary effects of the crisis. The slowdown in economic activity in the United States and in the industrialised countries of Europe has resulted in reduced demand for goods manufactured on its side of the globe. Factories have had to close down and workers retrenched in many countries. Economies that are heavily dependent on trade with the West are experiencing negative growth. It has been estimated that primarily as a result of a fall in exports, nearly 200 million additional people will be thrown into poverty. China, for one, will have difficulty maintaining the 11 to 12 per cent growth rate it has achieved in recent years.

The contagion from the West has also affected Asia in another way: the reduction of foreign direct investment. Overseas investments have been a major contributor to growth and development in Asia. The slumping levels of FDI will affect the recovery and development plans of several Asian nations.

If there is one lesson this crisis has emphasised, it is that the international economy has never been more integrated. What happens at one end of a supply chain will have an immediate and real impact along the rest of the links in that chain. Any notion that the economies of Asia can be 'decoupled' from those of the industrialised West is but a fallacy.

The 'Stimulus IV Infusion'

The purpose of stimulus packages is to use government funds to compensate for the reduction in spending by the private sector. It is worth noting that there was hardly any ideological opposition to the huge stimulus packages approved by the US government sitting in the capital of the nation that provided the neo-liberal framework for polices under the rubric of the 'Washington Consensus'.

No ideological hang-ups have curtailed government intervention in Asian countries, where the credo remains that the job of governments is to govern, and to do what is necessary in the public interest. Stimulus packages of various hues have been introduced by several governments, the biggest being the one launched in China.

But there are stimulus packages – and stimulus packages. Two basic issues come to the fore. The first is making sure the money is spent on the right project. Stimulus packages work best if money is spent on projects that have a flow-on effect on the rest of the economy. China's stimulus package is reported to have been successfully targeted on infrastructure spending and has helped to compensate the reduction in exports to the United States.

The second issue is to ensure that the money spent is properly accounted for. Transparency and accountability are crucial. If not properly monitored, the money can end up being spent on some politician's pet project or leaked into pockets in which it does not belong. Some governments are clearly in no hurry to provide a detailed accounting of where the money has gone.

Coordinated Action: Local vs Global

Since most countries are experiencing a simultaneous downturn in economic activity, it makes sense to take coordinated action to prevent the slowdown from worsening. The most high-profile of these attempts has been the G20 summits.

But there is an inherent contradiction in what these industrialised nations are trying to do. EU countries, for example, are committed to a single-market philosophy and there are rules to promote competition and govern state aid to domestic institutions. But in the wake of the crisis, governments have adopted measures to protect jobs and businesses in their own backyards. By any definition, these are protectionist measures and are inconsistent with a commitment to open competition and the free movement of capital and labour.

We have also witnessed attempts by the industrialised countries to coordinate the launching of their respective stimulus packages, the theory being that this will maximise the impact the measures will have across borders. Again, in practice, this has rarely been achieved.

There is a simple explanation for all this. Although the crisis is global, its impact on countries has been unequal, and each country has had to scramble to find a response suited to its own needs. At the end of the day, the nation state still trumps any notion of a global, one-world order.

WOLFGANG FRANZ

What are the implications of the financial crisis on social behaviour?

The global financial crisis has, at least in Germany, reanimated a public debate about the functional viability of a free-market economy, namely the German model of a social market-based economy, the so-called *soziale Marktwirtschaft*. The major reproach culminated in calling this model 'cowboy capitalism'. More specifically, it was lamented that this system is conceptually wrong because profits are supposedly privatised while losses are nationalised. In particular, bank managers were accused of an unscrupulous greed for money, highlighted by exorbitant bonus payments despite the losses of their employers being at remarkable orders of magnitude. In its place the critics are calling for a much more active or even dominant role for the state, and at the very least much heavier regulation and the protection of domestic enterprises, such as 'national champions'.

By and large, this view is mistaken, although it contains a grain of truth. This holds especially for those bonus payments of bank managers that focus only on short-term success but neglect losses in subsequent years. Hence, the summit of the G20 states in September 2009 was right to demand appropriate bonus-payment systems that are based on a mid-term performance of bank managers. From an economic viewpoint, bonus payments constitute a suitable incentive system for providing greater efforts. These efforts, however, should result in a performance of the bank that lasts for more than simply one year. On the other hand, claims by prominent politicians to restrict these payments by introducing a nominal upper limit overshoot the mark. Given the globalisation of financial markets, banks have to meet international competition for excellent managers. Moreover, there is no justification other than a vague belief in social fairness, for fixing bonuses at a certain amount of money, such as €500,000, as was then proposed by the German ministry of finance.

Similar considerations hold for bank managers who claim their bonus payments although their bank only survives by virtue of taxpayers' money. These bonuses were based on the provisions of the employment contract and a common legal principle says that *pacta sunt servanda* (agreements are to be honoured) as long as the legal ground of that contract still holds. The latter prerequisite may, of course, be questioned seriously and should be subject to a court's decision rather than to public excitement. To demand that those bank managers should voluntarily do without their bonus payments may be popular, especially for those who will never earn so much money. Although extremely speculative, it would be interesting to elaborate on the behaviour of the same critics if they would be entitled to such payments. *Honi soit qui mal y pense* (Evil be to him who evil thinks).

Turning from these aspects of social behaviour to more fundamental problems, the criticism of social market-based economies overlooks that regulatory interventions in financial markets constitute an integral characteristic of each economic system and have nothing to do with the specific model of a market-based economy. In fact, financial markets in nearly every industrial country are subject to a far higher level of regulation than many product markets. As has been emphasised by the German Council of Economic Experts in its annual report for 2008, there are good reasons for government interventions in financial markets. As a general principle, government intervention is warranted whenever markets fail to function properly and if the government can resolve the associated problems better than the private sector. To put it differently, the threat of market failure must always be weighed up against the threat of government failure. Market failure may be caused by several different factors. In the case of financial markets one of the principal causes of a malfunction is problems concerning the asymmetric distribution of information between lenders and borrowers. The example of second-hand car markets may illustrate. The buyer of a used car frequently has incomplete information about the quality of the car by contrast with the previous owner or the seller. In financial markets this holds, for instance, for securitised and structural financial products. The major difference between the two types of markets concerns the possibility of a systemic risk.

While the consequences of asymmetric information in the second-hand car market are restricted to this market, the collapse of just one financial institution might trigger the implosion of the entire financial system and would also drag down the real economy. Therefore, in the case of the second-hand car market it suffices for a regulation to protect the buyer if he or she is betrayed by the seller. Usual legal terms of business will do this job. In contrast, financial markets must be subject to a much higher level of regulation.

Therefore, the criticism of allegedly unbridled financial markets completely misses the point. This criticism fails to recognise that financial markets are already heavily regulated. In other words, the key issue is not the undisputed need for regulation but rather the need for a more efficient system of regulation. Such an improved system of regulation is now under consideration and the G20 states have paved the way at their summit in Pittsburgh. Such an improvement should lessen the systemic risk to financial markets by ensuring more transparency and better risk buffers. More specifically, a stronger global orientation of financial-market oversight is in order, such as, first, an international early-warning system that must have access not only to macroeconomic information but also to micro-prudential data on individual large financial institutions. Secondly, the system's risk buffers should be perceptibly strengthened, so that they unleash smaller pro-cyclical effects.

It goes without saying, however, that the issue at stake is not a question of eliminating each and every individual risk. Earning higher returns inevitably entails incurring higher risks. While this seems to be a commonplace, many bankers have not been fully aware of this basic principle of their business. The same holds for savers. They want interest payments as high as possible and make savings deposits in banks that pay higher interest, indeed, but are not subject to national systems of deposit securisation, such as Iceland's Kaupthing bank in Germany. Despite the bad experience of losses due to the financial crisis it is perhaps necessary to inform people better on that basic principle: higher returns mean higher risks. People know that from other activities: better opportunities of achieving success entail a higher risk of failure. Such is life.

An excess of spending, debt and liquidity led to the financial crisis, which in turn stalled the world economy in 2009. However, financial exuberance alone cannot explain the formidable economic expansion that took place between 2001 and 2008. During that period of time, exports from Germany and the Netherlands almost tripled, and those of China were multiplied by six! Only the US had a weaker performance, with exports not quite doubling. As a consequence, most industrialised nations saw their GDP double while emerging economies saw a record explosion of their wealth. One could have expected that this formidable expansion would not last for ever. In reality, the world economy is suffering from a massive hangover after a great party!

Most of the economic expansion of recent decades was the result of a huge 'catch-up' competition engaged in by the emerging economies. Thirty years ago the world market economy was for the most part serving US, European and Japanese consumers: some 700 million people. Half of the world was still living in state-planned economies. Today, the world is open and only a few isolated countries remain on the margins of economic progress. The world economy now serves some 6 billion people. Nations that had been excluded from prosperity and wealth for decades embarked on high economic growth policies in order to catch up as quickly as possible with industrialised nations. In 1950, China had a GDP per capita of $439, about the same as 2000 years ago . . . In the past twenty years only, it has been multiplied by ten!

The industrial revolution in emerging economies has had exactly the same consequences as in the West during the nineteenth century: the birth of a middle class. During the past fifteen years, the world middle class (defined by the IMF as people living on between $2 and $13 a day) has surged from 1,428 million to 2,644 million. Most of this growth obviously took place in the BRIC countries and Central Europe. According to McKinsey, the middle class in India will increase from 50 million in 2006 to 580 million in 2025. As Ayn Rand, the American writer, put it: 'The upper class is the past of a nation; the middle class is its future.'

The traditional view is that emerging economies are low-cost-producing countries that live from exports to advanced economies. This is only partly true: the globalisation of companies in the early 2000s was certainly triggered by the cost attractiveness of many countries. Outsourcing, or off-shoring, activities has significantly lowered the cost of operations for most global companies. As a consequence, inflation had disappeared from our vocabulary. In addition, many emerging nations moved from cheap labour costs to cheap brain power (for example, India) providing the world economy with highly qualified young professionals for the service industry. However, this 'supplier' strategy is being battered by the economic crisis, forcing emerging nations to reorientate their economic policies towards the development of their domestic markets. The desynchronised development of emerging economies that eradicated inflation for more than a decade is now being reversed: it will feed inflation. Why?

One of the simplest explanations of an economic crisis is when production exceeds consumption. An early-warning sign that this is occurring is when inventories surge in companies. A high level of inventories in the system is always a bad omen for future growth. However, something is different in this crisis: for the first time – and especially in Europe and the US – we see excess inventories not only in companies but also in households. The world is now split into two: a 'replacement economy' (Europe and the US) and a 'first buy' economy (emerging economies).

How many items of furniture and other goods can be found in an average European household? Statistics are woefully lacking there. However, as an indication, when I made an inventory of my home for the fire-insurance company, I reached the astounding number (to me) of 654 items – and I do not live in a castle. Second question: how many more items can I bring in? Actually none . . . unless I throw out an older product first! And this is the point: every new product that we buy is to replace an older one – a new car, a new cellphone, a new sofa replaces an older one. We live in a replacement economy. After seven years of exuberant growth, spending and debt, households are now saturated with products. With the crisis, most of us discover that we can last a full year without spending anything on non-essential goods without experiencing a drop in our standard of living. This is bad news for stimulus plans ($ 3,200 billion of them worldwide), because in such a situation people will save, and not spend, the money that they get from governments.

In emerging economies, the situation is different. The birth of a middle class is putting enormous pressure on domestic consumption: one of the definitions of middle-class status is having the ability to use one-third of income on discretionary spending, such as a car, travel, consumer electronics, home appliances, branded goods, etc. In short, the new middle class want to 'buy happiness'. And there is no desire to wait. A few years ago a Gallup opinion poll asked Chinese people which were the words that would best represent their value system: 62 per cent answered 'work hard and get rich'. In this environment, traditional Keynesian policies do work. If people get money from the government, they will spend it. As they do so, they put massive pressure on world commodities, which are a major source of inflation.

The consequences for global financial and industrial companies are dramatic. A decoupling of the world economies is occurring again. Emerging nations are now – whenever they can – concentrating on developing their domestic consumer markets. Their stimulus plans assume that exports to 'saturated' households in the West will not resume former levels in the near future and that sustaining domestic consumption is the strategy for the future. These plans work better than in the West precisely because the emerging middle class is eager to consume. This should be good news for companies in advanced economies. They are moving from a supply strategy to a market-serving one. The assumption is that Western companies have all the products and financial services that a middle class want to buy. If we look at luxury goods, this analysis would appear to be correct so far.

The problem is that, in the longer term, it may not be sustainable. The other characteristic of a middle class is that it creates companies. Very often, at the beginning, they are family owned, small and with a niche technology. This is what happened in Britain and Germany during the industrial revolution in the nineteenth and twentieth centuries. Today, the *Mittlestand*, which is the layer of medium-sized enterprises in the German economy, is probably the most competitive part of the country. The same is happening in the emerging nations. New local brands in China, India, the Gulf region, Russia, Turkey, Brazil, Mexico, etc. are quickly becoming fierce competitors not only on domestic markets but also globally. Ten years ago very few people had ever heard of Haier, ZTE, Mittal, Infosys, Wipro, MTN, Koç, Severstal, Cemex, etc.

Many of these new companies are now enjoying not only a strong domestic market but also the financing or back-up of their government, mainly through sovereign-funds funding. They are definitely part of a new world business community which is much more diverse than before. And the new world which is emerging from the crisis – a new middle class and new brands – is more multi-polar and competitive than it has ever been. The economic, and soon the political, power is shifting to new regions. It is not a cosy world any more. This will require a change in companies' strategies, in business models, but especially a change in mindset. In the words of Winston Churchill: 'We change the world faster that we can change ourselves; we apply to the present the habits of the past!' Reinventing the world may also mean first reinventing the management competencies and the personal skills to succeed.

The unprecedented interventions by governments and central banks around the world following the 'great panic' sparked by the Lehman bankruptcy in September 2008 have succeeded in averting a devastating collapse of the global financial system. The world economy is extraordinarily fortunate to have, just narrowly, escaped from a 1930s-style Great Depression.

In the face of the rapidly deteriorating and spreading crisis in the fall of 2008, Hank Paulson, the US secretary of Treasury, and Ben Bernanke, the chairman of the Federal Reserve, demonstrated pragmatism and decisiveness. They clearly understood the gravity of the crisis and showed determination to keep the US and the world from sliding into the abyss of another Great Depression. Though their actions and decisions at the time seemed unconvincing in their efficacy, and were extremely controversial, there is no doubt that they have eventually started to work.

Initially the government authorities took a case-by-case approach in dealing with the financial crisis, as shown in the cases of Bear Sterns, Northern Rock, Fannie Mae and Freddie Mac. However, governments and central-bank authorities in the US, UK, Europe and elsewhere have all adopted a comprehensive crisis-management approach in the aftermath of the Lehman bankruptcy, by deploying sweeping and drastic intervention strategies, including capital injection, asset and/or liability guarantees, and liquidity support. In a number of cases, governments engineered emergency takeovers or outright nationalisation of extremely troubled financial institutions.

The blanket interventions by governments around the world have effectively drawn a line in the sand, avoiding the chaotic collapse of any additional ailing large financial firms. Direct capital injection and liquidity support through bank-debt guarantee programmes have played a crucial role in shoring up banks' capital and liquidity positions, thereby slowly stopping the panic about a generalised financial-sector meltdown.

Since the end of the first quarter of 2009, especially after the 'stress tests' conducted by the US authorities on the systemically important financial institutions, there has been growing evidence that the Western financial system has been largely stabilised, if not yet fully rehabilitated. The much vilified TARP programme, first introduced by the Bush administration in the fall of 2008, and other programmes notably TALF, together with a massive injection of liquidity by the Federal Reserve and other central banks around the world, have helped contain the spreading panic, unfrozen the credit market and gradually restored the functioning of the broader financial markets. It is worth noting that this fact has been largely overlooked in the raucous debate and investigations on the US Capitol Hill into the role of the US Treasury and of the Federal Reserve in managing the financial crisis. Equity markets in particular have made a stunning recovery since March 2009, underpinning the return of investor confidence that the recovery of the world economy is slowly under way.

The global financial sector, after suffering from a staggering loss of US $1.6 trillion, has broadly made progress in repairing the battered balance sheets, with reduced leverage, increased liquidity cushion, and an enlarged tier-one capital base. Not all are yet out of the woods, however. Small- and middle-sized lenders continue to fail at a high rate, and several large complex financial firms, currently on government life support, are still fighting for survival on their own. Disturbingly, disposal of toxic assets has been snail-paced, despite government efforts, via the Public Private Investment Program (PPIP) and the like, to jump-start the market for illiquid toxic assets. With the stabilisation of housing prices, especially in the US, and resumption of the broader financial markets, however, one might hope that investors may be more willing to bid and banks burdened by legacy assets may have greater incentive to sell than so far has been the case. If non-performing assets were not disposed of quickly, the banking system would remain too burdened to resume normal credit provision to support the economic recovery. As shown by Japan's experience in the 1990s, the crisis won't be truly over until the bad-asset problems are fully dealt with.

The rather swift recovery of the financial stock prices and improvement in bank revenue and earnings have caused fresh concerns that banks might return to the old ways. Such concerns are indeed justified. As a Chinese saying puts it, 'the pain is forgotten once the wound is healed'. Therefore, governments, regulators and the general public should maintain the pressure for genuine financial reforms, and refuse to tolerate 'business as usual'.

Worldwide, attention has now clearly shifted from crisis containment to post-crisis reforms. The fully loaded reform agenda includes tightening capital, leverage, liquidity and accounting rules, overhauling over-the-counter credit derivatives and rating agencies, strengthening regulatory standards and practices, improving cross-border banking supervision, revamping macro-prudential policies and institutions, setting up resolution regimes for large financial institutions and changing compensation practices. Only strong and comprehensive reforms can successfully reshape the global financial system and make it more efficient, more stable and resilient to future shocks.

But it should also be warned against the danger that populist politicians might overdo it by imposing draconian regulations and interfere excessively with the normal working of financial markets and operations of financial institutions. Tragic as the crisis has been, it does not refute the fact that the Western financial capitalist model has, over the long term, functioned well in capital allocations and contributed to increases in productivity and economic growth. The goal of post-crisis reform is to curb the system's excesses, fix its weaknesses, but not to stifle it altogether. Prudent risk taking, and socially beneficial innovation should be preserved as the essence of financial capitalism. Going back to the old ways of greed without fear is clearly unacceptable; nor is throwing out the baby with the bath water.

Every crisis brings about a new opportunity, as suggested by the ancient Chinese wisdom. This financial crisis is no exception. One extremely encouraging development in its aftermath has been the general acceptance of the need for close international cooperation and coordination. In that regard, the G20, first created in the wake of the Asian crisis but always in the shadow of the G7, has for the first time gained political prominence for global policy making. The two G20 summits, held in Washington in November 2008 and in London in April 2009 provided impetus to joint actions to combat the financial crisis and stimulate the global economy. Emerging market economies, especially the BRIC countries, and China in particular, have gained a voice in the G20, IMF and the enlarged FSB. This is an extremely positive trend coming out of the current crisis, boding well for future peace and prosperity of mankind.

What's particularly comforting is the shared global consensus against protectionism. While the fiscal-stimulus package passed by the US Congress included a controversial 'Buy American' clause, and many other countries also had slippage in free trade, on the whole the leading economies such as the US, Europe and China have avoided repeating the fatal mistake of the infamous Smoot-Hawley Tariff Act introduced by the US in the 1930s, which deepened the Great Depression. This time around countries have refrained from the destructive 'beggar thy neighbour' protectionist policies prevalent in the 1930s. If the global financial crisis caused a collapse in world trade, there are hopeful signs that a pick-up in trade could help lead or reinforce the global economic recovery.

WILL HUTTON [1]

Now the roof has fallen in, setting up potentially the most dangerous vicious circle since the Great Depression. The belief that securitised loans could always be sold or insured has proved illusory. Worse, too many have junk assets as security: commercial property, buy-to-let property, junk American loans and overstretched buyers in the residential property market. The debt will stay toxic until the economy recovers again. But worse, the margins on any new loans the banks could offer are tiny or non-existent. They have dried up. The communal property market is in existential crisis. The debt is becoming even more toxic. Because everybody knows this, and nobody trusts anybody else, the banks are in a trap.

Should the taxpayer shore up the banks' core capital to give them capacity to lend? Or should the taxpayer buy toxic debt, as the American Paulson plan proposes, and release the banks from their crippling, if self-inflicted, burden? And if so, would toxic debt from every international bank registered in London be included? In addition, should there be some form of government-sponsored insurance to support new lending? So far the British government is committed to a case-by-case, go-it-alone approach in which risking taxpayers' money is seen as an instrument of the last resort. In Japan that approach left the country saddled with zombie banks that devastated its economy for a decade. Britain's refusal to drop the laissez-faire ideology risks both that fate and a complete financial seizure in the interim.

Yet despite the government's instincts, we have nationalised £150 billion of bank assets in Northern Rock and Bradford & Bingley – and last week effectively nationalised the money markets. The Bank of England has been forced to step in as a sort of ringmaster, now lending more than £100 billion to banks under its special liquidity scheme, and another £100 billion-plus because banks will not lend to one another. But despite this £350 billion of public support, the money markets remain frozen while ordinary savers move their cash to safe havens such as National Savings, Premium Bonds, Northern Rock and

[1] This entry is based on an article published in the *Observer* on 5 October 2008.

Irish banks. Credit flows are dwindling to nothing. Unless there is a reversal, there will be a major economic recession – even a slump.

The problem is that panics occur because of the primeval desire to protect oneself and one's own. The fear feeds on itself, and unless some major event brings everyone to their senses it will grow. This panic is international. What transfixed London on Tuesday 30 September 2008 was less what had happened in Britain – the necessary and inevitable action on Bradford & Bingley – but the failure of the US House of Representatives to pass the Paulson plan. Meanwhile, bank collapses required public bail-outs in France, Holland, Iceland, Belgium and Germany. Then came the Irish guarantee of every deposit in its banks.

The Irish 'beggar thy neighbour' policy shocked Europe; such an extreme response could only have been prompted by the potential collapse of a bank. Ireland had jumped straight to the last-resort policy of a blanket deposit guarantee, potentially forcing the whole of Europe to follow in fear of losing deposits to Dublin's secure accounts. The need for better European collaboration could not be better dramatised, and [the 4 October 2008] Paris summit called by President Sarkozy, expected to limit such a Dutch auction in deposit guarantees, is a start. Eurosceptics in Number 10 and the Tory Party may wish otherwise, but Britain alone does not have the muscle to support the vast international financial centre that is the City of London – British bank assets are five times British GDP – let alone the assets of international banks domiciled here.

We are as vulnerable as Iceland, Switzerland and Ireland, as one top financial regulator told me. We need Europe. If the scale of the threat is obvious, so is the opportunity. A political fortune awaits the government that seizes the opportunity to rebuild the delinquent casino that is the British financial system, and around different principles – a long-term commitment to building businesses, support for investment and innovation, and fairness. Anglo-Saxon capitalism may have delivered a ten-year boom, but the price has been savagely high. Now there is a once-in-fifty-years opportunity to create new institutions, new practices and new incentives. If Gordon Brown and his government eschew it they will deserve to be trounced at the general election and then have to live with having passed up the golden opportunity of their lives.

Talking of making bankers pay for the mess they have created, as they do in America over the Paulson plan, is pointless. The task now is to survive without a slump, and create a new financial system that moves decisively away from the mores of super-gentlemanly capitalism.

We have to mimic the Paulson plan and set up a so-called 'bad' bank, with up to £100 billion of purchasing power. We must buy toxic loans from all British-based banks, with the object of selling them in better market conditions. Most such operations, as in Sweden in the nineties or Britain in the seventies, end up losing no money whatever. This will stop the banks becoming zombie institutions.

Second, we have to reopen the markets in securitised assets. This requires two initiatives. The taxpayer will have to find £50 billion-plus to invest in the shares of our leading banks so there is no doubt that they are solvent and can support both the existing level of debt and the new issue of more. The taxpayer should also give an additional stimulus by running a temporary insurance scheme so that overseas and domestic buyers of securitised loans know there is no risk of losing any money – in other words, a form of targeted and temporary deposit insurance.

The government will become the biggest single shareholder in the financial system. It can require the banks to behave differently – to move from financing casino capitalism to productive enterprise. There can be a new emphasis on relationship building and offering cheap long-term loans to business. We should create a long-term investment bank. Casino banking, trading in derivatives on the bank's own account, and commercial banking should be split, reinforced by a British Glass–Steagall Act. The British vogue for takeover can be constrained.

The regulatory regime must be overhauled; never again should regulators turn a blind eye to offshore banking and wild ratios in which lending can reach thirty or forty times a bank's capital. EU and American regulators need to work much more closely – and Britain needs to be part of the process. The UK taxpayer does not have the firepower to support a bust international system – one of the reasons that Brown's reluctance to consider a joint European initiative is shortsighted. We may even have to consider joining the euro to get the necessary financial power behind London.

A thirty-year experiment has come to an end. The world of go-getting investment banks has gone for ever. The danger is that we go from feast to famine; debt remains a vital element in any economy, and if we too suddenly try to live without it, we will crush ourselves economically. What we are witnessing is a system failure that requires a systemic response – the creation of a new system that sponsors a fairer, more productive capitalism in its place, while maintaining high flows of credit and debt.

This is a terrifying moment; but it is also our generation's once-in-a-lifetime chance to change British capitalism. Brown has an awesome responsibility to his party and his country. I hope he rises to the challenge.

ANDREW KEEN

Explaining the implications of the financial crisis on social behaviour is tricky. That's because today's crisis isn't independent of society – errant social behaviour being as much a cause as a consequence of today's economic meltdown.

So what kind of social behaviour contributed to the financial crisis in the first place?

You can blame it on the 'L-word'. No, not liberals. The guilty party here is the libertarians, those radical ideologues of individual liberty and the free market. Today's economic crisis can't be detached from a late twentieth-century libertarian rebellion against traditional authority, particularly that of the state. And it's the ethic of financial libertarianism both on Wall Street and in society – what *Time* magazine economics columnist Justin Fox called 'the myth of the free market' – that primarily caused the 2008 financial crisis.

Libertarian economics is a secular religion with its own catechism of appropriate social behaviour. The worship of free-market theorists like Milton Friedman and Friedrich Hayek over the last quarter-century has created a cult around the ideal of individual liberty and free economic choice. It has resulted in the withdrawal of the state from economic life, the absence of real centralised regulation over financial speculation and the failure of both domestic and international organisations to control the flow of capital.

This fetishisation of the free market is only a part of the general libertarian revolt against all forms of traditional external authority. From public cynicism about politicians to a popular rebellion against the authority of mainstream media to an infatuation with highly individualised evangelical movements, libertarianism has emerged as the most corrosive ideological force in the early twenty-first century.

Populist libertarianism does away with the traditional left–right distinctions of the nineteenth and twentieth centuries. Conservative libertarianism is built around both the rational market, hostility to taxation and a general antipathy towards the right of external authority to interfere in social or cultural life; while progressive libertarianism inherited much of its hostility towards authority from the sixties and thus tends to focus more on the supposed liberating impact of technology, particularly the Internet in freeing individuals from the external control of big business or mainstream media.

As the work of critics like Thomas Frank has revealed, the ideology of libertarianism has become a powerful engine of cultural change, fuelling not only the global entertainment business but also Madison Avenue. Selling the ideal of rebellion against authority has emerged as an effective way of branding companies and products. Thus companies like Apple, Nike and Virgin have all built their identities around challenging the status quo and questioning the credibility of traditional cultural orthodoxies. And so today's youth increasingly idealises start-up culture and the most iconic figures in popular culture – from Richard Branson to Steve Jobs to Facebook's youthful founder Mark Zuckerberg – tend to be disruptive entrepreneurs rather than moral philosophers or even creative artists.

Given the libertarian ethos permeating much of American social behaviour, today's typical popular response to the economic crisis is to demand more autonomy from traditional institutions or organisations. Conservative libertarians are opposed to any kind of state intervention in the economy, arguing that politicians are, by definition, ill equipped to deal with the challenges of economic innovation; while progressive libertarians see the current crisis as an opportunity to challenge the legitimacy of traditional business elites and politicians and replace them with younger, supposedly more transparent and democratic elites.

The problem with both these strains of libertarianism is that they give us the excuse to blame everybody but ourselves for the economic crisis. The one thing that libertarians aren't well equipped to do is take any moral responsibility for their own actions. And so the global financial meltdown doesn't seem to have triggered much popular soul-searching. Property owners who are no longer able to pay their mortgages, for example, blame the banking industry for their own failure to read the small print in their mortgage agreements. Politicians get blamed when public investments don't magically materialise in a revitalised economy. Meanwhile, everybody blames those 'greedy' financiers on Wall Street – even though there was never any resentment against highly compensated financial entrepreneurs when Wall Street was riding high and the American 'people' was benefiting from the stock-market boom.

So what to do? As the Slovenian cultural critic Slavoj Žižek observed in a 2006 essay entitled 'The Liberal Communists of Porto Davos', the contemporary popularity of libertarianism has redrawn the ideological landscape. Today, it's the free-market elite of Davos and the counter-elite of the anti-globalisation Porto Allegre community that represent the 'twin cities of globalisation'; while it's the old left with its 'big struggle against capitalism' and the old right with its 'ridiculous belief in authority, order and parochial patriotism' who, Žižek tells us, are now the real outsiders in our brave new libertarian world.

Žižek is absolutely right. The implications of the financial crisis on social behaviour can only become meaningful if we accept the existence of undeniable truths outside ourselves. And both the old left and the old right – with their big moral certainties about capitalism, tradition and God – do have the opportunity to leverage the current crisis to vindicate their own worldview. Thus the issue that the old left and the old right could agree to address is the value both of the state and of rebuilding the authority of traditional intermediary institutions as public forces in controlling and managing the excesses of the free-market economy.

There's no doubt that social behaviour and values have to change in the wake of the crisis. We need politicians and public figures to critically evaluate the impact of endless innovation not only on the economy but also on society. Schumpeterian economic innovation isn't necessarily always destructive, but in league with a free-market economy, a popular culture of libertarianism and an unregulated financial system, it will inevitably lead to both moral decay and economic breakdown.

Above all, however, today's economic crisis should provide authoritative politicians, churchmen and business leaders in the United States with the opportunity to have a serious conversation about the moral and cultural value of the supposedly rational market. Given the almost religious veneration of the free market over the last twenty-five years and its self-evidently central role in the crash, this is a long-overdue conversation that, had it taken place before 2007, might even have averted the current economic crisis.

RICHARD KOO

The global recession that began in 2008 is characterised by many unusual features. They include massive budget deficit, need for fiscal stimulus, inability of monetary easing to turn the economy or asset prices around, government guarantees and injection of capital to banks, and rating agencies threatening to downgrade governments running large deficits. Indeed the seeming inability of zero interest rates and massive quantitative easing to turn the US and UK economies around fly in the face of conventional economics, which suggests that monetary easing of such magnitude should produce a strong response from both the economy and asset markets. These difficulties, in turn, made people more cautious, as they realised that something was awfully different in this recession compared with past recessions.

All of these unusual features, however, were observed in Japan during its Great Recession from 1990 to 2005. In fact, what is happening abroad seems like a replay of the Japanese drama, especially for those of us in Japan, with the same confusion and sense of uncertainty reflected in the policy debate.

The shocking similarities between the two recessions are no coincidence. Both recessions were triggered by the bursting of asset-price bubbles. The collapse in asset prices, in turn, left millions of private-sector balance sheets in tatters as the liabilities incurred in purchasing those assets remained at their original values. With their balance sheets in a shambles, people had no choice but to reorient their economic priorities from their usual profit maximisation to debt minimisation in order to put their financial houses in order.

This shift, in turn, nullified the effectiveness of those economic theories and policies that were based on the assumption that private sector was maximising profits, and the biggest casualty here has been monetary policy. This is because those with debt overhang are not interested in increasing their borrowings at any interest rate, and there would be few banks interested in lending money to those with impaired balance sheets. Moreover, those with balance sheets underwater will try to pay down debt as quickly as possible to regain their credit ratings, regardless of the level of interest rates. By 1995, the Japanese interest rates were almost zero, but instead of increasing their borrowings, the corporate sector in Japan became a net repayer of debt for fully ten years until 2005. In some of the bigger years, the net debt repayment reached 30 trillion yen or 6 per cent of Japan's GDP.

No economic or business textbooks have suggested that the private sector should pay down debt when interest rates are zero, but that was what was happening in Japan for a full ten years. The textbooks never mentioned such a possibility because they assumed that private-sector balance sheets were clean and sound. But that assumption is broken when a nationwide debt-financed bubble goes bust. And that is exactly what happened to Japan after 1990, and the world after 2008.

It is also no coincidence that one hears so much about 'deleveraging' in those countries, such as the US and the UK, where the effectiveness of monetary easing has fallen most dramatically. The private sectors in these countries are now minimising debt instead of maximising profits, and that shift has thrown the affected economies into balance-sheet recession, a very rare type of recession that happens only after the bursting of a nationwide asset-price bubble.

In a national economy, when someone saves money or pays down debt, there had better be someone else out there borrowing and spending those saved or repaid funds in order to keep the GDP from shrinking. In the usual economy, the task of equating savings and borrowings is performed by the adjustment of interest rates. But in a balance-sheet recession, demand for funds may remain far less than supply, even with zero interest rates. This is due to lack of borrowers; as a result, unborrowed funds will remain stuck in the financial system and will constitute a leakage from the income stream and a deflationary gap in the economy. If left unattended, this gap will throw the economy into a deflationary spiral as the economy loses demand equivalent to the saved but unborrowed funds each year. And that is exactly what happened during the Great Depression, the last great balance-sheet recession, where the US lost half of its GDP in just four years.

Since the private sector has no choice but to repair its damaged balance sheets, the only thing the government can do to keep the GDP from falling is to borrow and spend the excess savings in the private sector and put them back into the economy's income stream. This explains why fiscal policy centred on government spending becomes so essential in this rare type of recession. With the private sector deleveraging, there is no danger of government spending crowding out the private sector or misallocating resources. After all, without government actions, those resources will go unused, which is the worst form of resource allocation.

Japan suffered a staggering 87 per cent fall in the value of its commercial real estate nationwide when its bubble burst, but was able to keep its GDP at above the peak of its bubble level for the entire period because the government borrowed and spent the excess savings generated by the deleveraging of its private sector. In the process, the government debt increased by over 460 trillion yen or 90 per cent of its GDP. But that action helped maintain over 2000 trillion yen of GDP over the fifteen-year period. Without government action, Japan's GDP could have easily fallen to the pre-bubble level of 1985. With 460 trillion supporting 2000 trillion, it was a huge success by any standard.

Policy makers around the world are beginning to realise the importance of the Japanese experience, and are now implementing fiscal stimulus following the strong plea by Prime Minister Taro Aso of Japan during the emergency G20 meeting in Washington in November 2008. The IMF has also argued for global fiscal stimulus since early 2008. Some of these actions are already producing positive results.

The challenge going forward is to make sure this fiscal support is maintained for the entire duration of private-sector deleveraging. This is an extremely difficult task in peacetime, because when the economy begins to recover, the temptation to cut government deficit will become tremendous. Opposition politicians as well as well-meaning citizens who find reliance on government distasteful will argue that with fiscal pump-priming already working, the time should be right to reduce (wasteful) government spending. But if the recovery is actually due to government spending and the private sector is still in a balance-sheet-repair mode, a premature fiscal reform would invariably result in renewed meltdown, as the Japanese in 1997 and the Americans in 1937 found out.

The Japanese mistake in 1997 not only resulted in five quarters of negative growth, but also a massive increase in budget deficit which took nearly eight years to bring back to pre-mistake levels. This mistake also increased government debt by nearly 100 trillion yen and lengthened the Great Recession by at least five years. The US mistake in 1937 was so devastating that it took the massive military spending of the Second World War to pull the country out of recession. With corporate deleveraging continuing and the household-savings rate rising in so many countries, even with record low interest rates, this is no time to contemplate an exit strategy for the fiscal stimulus. On the contrary, policy makers should be prepared to implement seamless fiscal policy centreed on government spending as long as deleveraging by the businesses (including financial institutions) and households continues.

Those rating agencies that do not understand the concept of balance-sheet recession will also stand in the way of needed fiscal-policy response by threatening downgrades for those governments running large deficits. Some countries have already been downgraded, and more are likely to follow.

Japan saw its ratings cut to the level below that of Botswana in 2002 because the agencies were so certain that its skyrocketing government debt would eventually result in higher interest rates and the total collapse of the economy. Although participants in the Japanese government bond market were badly disturbed by successive downgrades at first, they soon realised that the amount of funds the government must borrow and spend to keep GDP from falling was exactly equal to the excess savings generated by the deleveraging private sector. In other words, there was no financing problem because the excess private-sector savings had no place to go except to government bonds. With this realisation, bond-market participants ignored the rating agencies, kept the bond yields at the lowest level in human history, and helped the government play the role of 'the borrower of last resort' to pull Japan out of balance-sheet recession.

The fact that businesses are deleveraging and households are increasing their savings rate in so many formerly 'low-savings countries' such as the US and UK means that these countries can also finance their deficit domestically. Policy makers and market participants in these countries are therefore advised to ignore downgrades from those agencies that have not grasped the concept of balance-sheet recession. Fiscal retrenchment should be implemented only after it becomes absolutely certain that those funds left unborrowed by the government will be borrowed and spent by the private sector.

NORMAN LAMONT

The economic success of Britain and America has been terribly exposed as a debt-fuelled illusion. We face the grave risk of losing international authority as well as our prosperity.

Shortly after I became chancellor of the exchequer in 1990, I had a meeting with my Japanese opposite number, a charming, able man, who insisted on speaking English without an interpreter. His English was better than my non-existent Japanese, but I could hardly make out a word he said. Eventually, leaning forward, I was able to discern one phrase endlessly repeated: 'the bursting of the bubble'. Over the years, I met many Japanese ministers. The speech was always the same because the pain lasted a long time.

What we have been seeing is the bursting of the Brown bubble. This is not the import of some problem from the US to Britain. America has had its own bubble, but so have we in the form of the highest personal debt per capita in the G7 combined with an unsustainable rise in house prices, which we conveniently chose to confuse with prosperity.

The Government has talked for years about the need to 'maintain stability', but what we have had in the past few years is anything but stability. It is not stable, nor sustainable, to have a rise in house prices of more than 140 per cent in ten years.

It is extraordinary how a Government that produced endless heavy government publications on so-called stability, could not see that soaring personal debt and ever-increasing house prices would eventually hit the rocks. The longer the illusion lasted, the greater the boasting became. At first it was 'the longest period of expansion in the twentieth century'. That was always untrue, as the period 1950–64 was longer. Then it became the longest period of expansion 'on a quarterly basis' for 100 years, and then even '250 years'. These claims were ridiculous because records were not kept on the same basis for these periods.

Just how great an illusion it was can be seen by comparing the growth in real, personal disposable income (after tax) under the present government and under the Conservatives. During the governments of Margaret Thatcher and John Major, post-tax disposable income grew steadily. Since 1997, take-home pay has only grown very slowly because of increased taxes. The illusion of rising prosperity has been maintained by borrowing to spend, often in the form of equity withdrawal from increasingly expensive houses. The impression is given that this is entirely some self-generated crisis from within the financial system. There has certainly been irresponsible lending. But the primary responsibility for where we are today belongs to governments and central banks.

In the United States, the boom was fuelled by too-low interest rates and the Fed continually pumping large amounts of money into the system to avoid 'deflation'. Far from working, injections of money only delayed the problem and, indeed, exacerbated it. Here, the Bank of England's remit, set by Gordon Brown in 1997, was too restrictive, as it targeted a narrow definition of inflation that excluded house prices and did not give any weight to the growth of money. As the boom took off, financial institutions rushed to satisfy the insatiable demand for credit, creating ever more esoteric financial instruments, hard to understand and apparently not understood by those who created and sold them. In the US, profits of financial companies increased to no less than a staggering 41 per cent of total company profits in 2007. There were lots of warning signs – and many did warn at the time.

What we have been through was potentially the most serious financial crisis since the 1920s. But there can be no certainty that even now in the financial sector the problems are now completely over. The actions of the American government have been awesome in their scale, but also involve risk. The $300 billion to take over Fannie Mae and Freddie Mac, the US housing-finance corporations, doubled at a stroke the government's liabilities. The securities the Fed has taken on to its balance sheet from the private sector could fall in value, or be subject to defaults. It was a sobering moment when one of the rating agencies felt it necessary to announce that it was not proposing to downgrade the rating of the US government.

The problems of the banks have been intertwined with those of the residential property markets. At present in the UK, house prices have hit a bottom and even risen somewhat. But this is on low turnover and is a fragile situation.

Even when the financial sector settles, the effects will be felt over the next few years in the wider economy. Banks will be more cautious and will have less capital to lend. As credit shrinks, so will private-sector demand. There are plans for more regulation. Ironically banks are already heavily regulated because of their privileged access to the lender of last resort, the Bank of England. But if banks are wise, they will take a long look at their own remuneration practices. Too many people have been allowed to make massive sums of money and then walk away, leaving nothing but wreckage behind them.

The government was right to support key parts of the financial system, but we must be careful that in solving this crisis we do not again sow the seeds of the next. It was never the view of Walter Bagehot, the great nineteenth-century financial writer, that central banks should bail out unwise lenders, but rather that they should make finance freely available to bona fide institutions at a penal rate.

The consequences of this crisis will be with us for a long time. They will be political as well as economic. So our standing in the world, and that of the US, has been diminished. Other countries will be less inclined to listen to lectures from us as to how they should run their affairs. And perhaps they have a point.

MAURICE LEVY

When it comes to public opinion it is difficult to separate the overall international financial crisis from the unfortunate coincidence of the Madoff scandal. This is particularly true of public opinion in the industrialised, developed world. In developing countries, wealth creation is more recent and the consequences of the crisis did not have the same impact.

The first measurable consequence is loss of confidence in the system, in market economy and in the financial system. There is a profound doubt about the elites who are patronising, lecturing on TV and explaining the situation. People ask: 'Where were they? Why didn't they speak up?'

Yet the public has a terrible sense of déjà vu, which exacerbates this loss of confidence. That is, they know that, just as the latest and biggest-ever bubble is not the first one we have ever seen, the Madoff scandal is one whose ancestor is the Ponzi scheme created in 1920.

So they are asking: 'How could this have happened again?' – a question that makes confidence-building even more difficult for governments who missed calling the bubble before it burst, with terrible consequences for the general public as well as the financial sector, and which, itself, already had a tough time inspiring confidence.

And confidence has been seeping out of the system for a longer time than we might want to admit. Remember a song called 'Money for Nothing'? It was in 1985 – almost a quarter of a century ago – when the rock group Dire Straits had that hit. It was about a furniture-moving man making fun of the rich (rock stars in this case) who were earning 'money for nothing', as it appeared to him.

Two years later, Oliver Stone's film *Wall Street* put that same question to the financial sector. In the film, an unprincipled financial manipulator, Gordon Gekko, led audiences worldwide to conclude that the Wall Street financial establishment was also making obscene amounts of 'money for nothing', while the average worker was sweating on the end of month to make ends meet.

What is needed to restore public confidence? Perhaps the recipe is for some honesty and transparency about the past from the people who were responsible for oversight – financial regulators – and more honesty from government leaders who are tempted to place the blame elsewhere.

One could argue that political leaders were incapable of avoiding the financial crisis, which overwhelmed them like a tsunami from a financial sector that was out of control. One could also defend the idea that they stepped in very courageously and boosted spending to reboot the economic machine, even though there was not much they could do because most countries live above their means and are hugely indebted.

Yet, to restore confidence that, in itself, is a key to economic recovery, shouldn't all governments now address their own mea culpa? Only very recently did the SEC admit that it was asleep at the switch on the Madoff scandal. And one can justifiably ask whether that kind of negligent oversight also encouraged the financial sector to take imprudent risks.

I am not talking about the partisan blame-game. For the fact is that this problem spanned all political-party lines. It wasn't just the Bush administration's lack of effective oversight; it was also the direct result of government intervention in the US, when the Clinton administration began pushing banks to lend to people who wanted to have their own home, but who simply couldn't justify loans on any reasonable basis. So the sub-prime financial disaster, the root case of the international financial crisis, was, at least in part, the direct result of 'sub-prime' government decisions and policies.

More generally, the recent news on big profits of the banks and multi-million-dollar bonuses is provocative for people. Why did we help all these banks avoid failure with taxpayer's money if it is to see them go back to their same old bad habits? Are there really no lessons learned? The G20's inability to act on these questions made countries look like they have different agendas and led people to think that very little can be achieved to 'moralise' financial-sector behaviour.

People are facing a crisis of values. What are the values of the free world? What is the role of money? Why did people lose homes – why are they now losing jobs – and governments did not punish those who created the crisis and benefited from the situation? What are the values governing the free-market economy? And what is the value of the things I'm buying?

People are questioning the values they have lived with and are 'resetting' their minds. That is because fear has set in: people live in fear of losing the value of what they own as well as losing the source of their future wealth – their jobs. Research shows that, indeed, we have reached a real turning point as the general public no longer believes and no longer trusts the institutions in which they used to believe. They certainly do not trust the financial system any longer; they believe it is simply too cynical, and too selfish.

Religious leaders have not shown much leadership here; indeed, some are selfishly surfing on the wave of doubt, of questioning in order to explain that the answer is their faith. So people are left alone with their problems, which leads to anger. And anger is never a good thing.

Consumers are trying to find ways to consume differently, more rationally, getting more value for money. Brands continue to be trusted; some are loved. But they have to demonstrate that they are useful to people and that they deliver value.

In a way, that is also what governments and all institutions in the public and private sectors need to do: demonstrate once again that they are useful to people and that they deliver value. Then they will have a chance to restore the public confidence that they have lost through this global financial crisis.

AUGUSTO
LOPEZ-CLAROS

I am not confident at all that we have moved to the type of regulatory environment that is necessary to prevent the next crisis. I tend to agree with the IMF assessment that our model of financial regulation was deeply flawed. Loan brokers and mortgage originators had few incentives to more realistically assess risk which, in any case, they sold on to others – this was part of the 'financial innovations' so warmly welcomed by market participants. Investors relied too unthinkingly, in assessing asset quality, on unrealistic or overly optimistic analyses done by credit-rating agencies, which, again, proved a time-tested ability to be *lagging* indicators of crisis (remember the 1997 Asian financial crisis?). Regulation and supervision were too concentrated on firms and not sufficiently focused on issues of systemic risk. None of these weaknesses is being addressed in a credible way yet.

The shadow banking system – investment banks, mortgage brokers, hedge funds, among others – were lightly regulated by a multitude of agencies. The assumption was that only deposit-taking institutions needed to be regulated and supervised, thereby encouraging financial innovation in the rest of the system, which, the thinking went, would act under a regime of self-imposed market discipline, spurred by the self-correcting nature of financial markets. Obviously the system had a huge amount of moral hazard built in, which, regrettably, the financial crisis has not eliminated. Excellent results in some financial institutions in recent quarters – and levels of compensation that in many cases are no worse than those last seen in 2007 – are partly the result of risk profiles fuelled by public funds.

We need to move to a system where, as noted by the IMF in its latest World Economic Outlook, 'all activities that pose economy-wide risks are covered and known to a systemic stability regulator with wide powers'. This would include banks, institutions issuing CDOs attached to mortgages or insurance companies selling credit-default swaps. Disclosure obligations within this 'extended perimeter' should then allow the supervisory authorities to determine relative contributions to systemic risk and to calibrate the scope of the prudential oversight needed. For instance, one would discourage the emergence of mega-banks. The financial system has become too concentrated. Over the past twenty years, the share of US financial assets held by the ten largest US financial institutions has risen from 10 per cent to 50 per cent. This is not desirable and, not surprisingly, has led to calls for change – Chancellor Angela Merkel recently stated that 'no bank should be allowed to become so big that it can blackmail governments' – a thoroughly sensible proposition. One way to achieve this is to simply force very large financial conglomerates to spin off assets, although there is also merit in proposals to do this via capital ratios that rise with the contribution to systemic risk. Indeed, many of the recommendations put forth by the IMF in the aftermath of the crisis are quite sensible, but we are not moving anywhere near fast enough to implement them. In particular, there seems to be a reluctance to address the issue of institutions that are 'too big to fail' and the moral hazard that they imply. As expected, vested interests are working full-time to prevent the implementation of such reform proposals. Paul Krugman is certainly correct in lamenting the extent to which vested interest (or, as he puts it, 'corporate cash') has 'degraded our political system's ability to deal with real problems'.

The IMF also thinks that it would be desirable to mitigate pro-cyclical behaviour, for instance by raising minimum capital requirements during upswings (when, in the US, the Federal Reserve has tended historically to take a hands-off approach) and allowing these to come down in a downturn, when, again, the Federal Reserve in the US has tended to be aggressive in loosening monetary policy. Many think that one could do the same for leverage – introduce a supplementary leverage ratio for banks. There is also a need to reform the system of incentives for compensation, which remain perverse and, at the moment, are rewarding many players in the financial system, as noted above, for assuming risk with public funds. It would also be desirable to sever or, in any case, weaken the connection between compensation and annual results and link it more to medium-term return on assets. An interesting question is whether it was a terrible mistake to have repealed in the United States the Glass–Steagall Act, which separated commercial from investment banking. I am very sympathetic to the idea that in the financial system household deposits (which are insured) should only be invested in low-risk assets, which is not what we had at the outset of this crisis, when deposits were being used in high-risk activities.

Central banks need to broaden their definition of 'financial stability' from an often exclusive concern with stabilising inflation to looking at asset-price increases, credit booms, leverage and ways in which financial innovations might be complicating the task of the authorities in setting monetary policy – you know you are in trouble when some instruments are so complicated that you can no longer tell whether they should be included in the definition of some appropriately broad monetary aggregate. The IMF is right when it says that it matters a great deal whether or not the boom is associated with high leverage. For instance, the dot.com bubble of the late 1990s was associated with limited leverage and thus its bursting had limited impact on economic growth. In the current crisis, asset-price collapses have greatly affected the balance sheets of financial institutions.

However, there are several other issues, beyond purely aspects of the new regulatory regime that need to be brought into being, which are a source of concern. I would like to highlight several. First, there is the question of fiscal sustainability.

There are several reasons why we should worry about the remarkable increases in public debt under way. One has to do with the constraints on government policy that high levels of debt normally imply. With debt levels in excess of 100 per cent of GDP, governments are less able to invest in education, infrastructure and other productivity-enhancing areas, to say nothing of moving to a lower-tax environment. This undermines growth. High debt service becomes an important constraint on the ability of governments to respond to pressing social and other needs, including possibly responding to other unforeseen crises in the future.

Second, in a large number of the bigger economies there are unfavourable demographic trends that are resulting in the ageing of populations. Increases in life expectancy combined with declining fertility will have systemic implications for the sustainability of pension systems and the ability of governments to remain faithful to the key elements of the social contract.

In fact, governments are having a tough time in getting the thrust of policies right. On the one hand, there has been and there may well continue to be a need for fiscal stimulus, to mitigate the effects of the recession. On the other hand, too much fiscal stimulus risks undermining government credibility, as debt levels are perceived by markets to be unsustainable; by 2014 many rich industrial countries will have debt levels on a par with Italy's, an inevitable consequence of the bountiful flow of red ink everywhere. Particularly worrying is a scenario where foreigners become concerned that higher government financing will push up long-term US bond yields, leading them to want to reduce their exposure, which would then put strong pressures on the dollar. One way to deal with this tension is to be judicious in the choice of stimulus measures. For instance, governments should target measures that bring long-term benefits to the economy's productive potential – infrastructure spending is very helpful, but I think that the crisis has also given us a great opportunity to spend more money for environmental protection and conservation. This might be an ideal time to introduce carbon taxes, to move a little closer to a world of full-cost pricing, which we are not doing by largely ignoring some of the more deleterious effects of global warming.

Third, we need to address fiscal challenges posed by ageing populations. What does this mean? Let's take the case of Europe. Solidarity and social cohesion are very much at the centre of European policy debates. One element of the solution will be to work longer and retire later. We must, therefore, boost training of the workforce, to extend the useful productive life of workers, perhaps in increasingly flexible settings. This, in turn, will force governments to reconsider expenditure priorities with a view to making resources available for retraining. This is a key element of better management of the globalisation process.

We must also deal more effectively with global imbalances. This is a reference to large current-account deficits and surpluses in countries such as the US, Japan, Germany and China, which, under some scenarios, could cause a reversal of capital inflows into the US and a massive drop of the dollar. Massive capital inflows have been associated with excessive risk taking, exchange-rate risk and other sources of systemic risk. I have done some quick calculations which show that the current-account deficits of the US, the UK and Spain (a combined $909 billion in 2008) are just offset by the current-account surpluses of Germany, Japan, China, Switzerland, Norway and the Netherlands ($903 billion).

But this is largely a US, China, Japan and Germany phenomenon, as the surpluses of these last three countries account for about 112 per cent of the US deficit. These imbalances have been a huge source of risk to the global economy. Among the causes: structural high savings in China linked to the fact that in this country there are no effective mechanisms of social protection, no pensions, no unemployment protection. The large Chinese population saves for old age because of lack of mechanisms of social protection; in the presence of such a system surely they would have a higher demand for American and European consumer goods, which would bring their 9.5 per cent of GDP trade surplus down.

In any event, it is evident that we need to have more effective mechanisms of international coordination to deal with the global nature of the crisis and ensure that we do not go back to a world of destructive protectionism.

The outcome of this financial crisis depends on three key factors: the policy response, the economic fundamentals and confidence.

The policy response has been impressive. Over a year ago, when the US unveiled tax cuts, the talk was of the need for policy to satisfy the three Ts: timely, temporary and targeted. Following the crisis, the global policy response can be thought of as achieving the three Ss: synchronised, sizeable and successful. Although the stimulus measures have varied to suit domestic needs, there has been a remarkable degree of consistency, with injections of liquidity, lower policy rates and relaxed fiscal stances, involving tax cuts and increased spending.

To emerge from the crisis, the world economy needed demand now followed by balance in the future. Policy stimulus pulled us back from the brink, preventing depression and ensuring some stabilisation of output. The challenge, though, is: when the policy stimulus is withdrawn, will the world economy be able to cope? This is not clear. Thus there has been much talk of exit strategies, particularly in terms of monetary policy and the liquidity provided to the financial sector.

Already signs are that policy makers have heeded some of the lessons from Japan's lost decade. Then, premature fiscal tightening in 1997 hit a fragile economy. Thus, when Japan embarked upon quantitative easing in 2001, even they announced the preconditions for their exit strategy many years before implementing it in spring 2006. Whilst it is important to signal to the markets that an exit strategy is in place, it is also vital that it is not implemented prematurely, before the economy is able to cope. Thus the West may witness a prolonged period of low policy rates.

Across the emerging world, many countries relaxed policy from a position of strength, as they headed into the downturn with fiscal positions in much healthier shape than economies in the West, interest rates generally higher and, in many instances, high levels of currency reserves. China's huge fiscal boost was particularly impressive, although more recently it has triggered worries about asset-price inflation.

Fears that policy easing around the world will trigger inflation need to be taken seriously, but in my view are misplaced. Yes, there will be asset price inflation in some countries. And there is a concern that, in coming years, recovery led by emerging economies will trigger higher commodity-price inflation. Economies where domestic demand is more resilient are thus likely to tighten policy sooner, whilst many export-dependent countries are likely to wait, possibly some time, before reversing their stimulus.

Even though the focus is on recovery, levels are important. The world economy has taken a big hit. The slump in demand and the amount of spare capacity in the world economy suggests little near-term pricing power. In addition, it is hard to imagine a surge in wage inflation. There has already been evidence of labour flexibility in Western economies, and this may persist, with unemployment yet to peak and set to rise in 2010.

Furthermore, the recovery may see many companies opting to invest in emerging, high-growth markets in the East, suggesting a recovery without a lessening of unemployment in the West. This may trigger protectionist measures. Moreover, if Eastern economies receive the investment they need, we are likely to see a surge of new, low-cost, possibly high-skilled workers coming on to the global labour market in years ahead.

The most controversy has been over the use of fiscal policy, particularly in the West, but if firms and companies are not spending, then it makes sense for a government to do so. In the wake of the financial crisis the imperative for the world economy was to see increased demand to limit the downside risks from both the bursting of the asset bubble and the deleveraging that was already taking place. So demand now and, in the future, a more balanced global economy. Boosting demand, even if it delays the move to a more balanced world economy, may be better than the alternative, which could be an ever-deepening downward spiral.

Equally, within the financial sector, it is vital to fix the parts that were broken; but not everything needs fixing. Many parts of the financial system worked well and, even in the parts that broke, there were well-run institutions that did not get into trouble. All of this suggests the need to differentiate, from both an economic and a financial-markets perspective.

Equally the economic outlook may also be different, as it is emerging economies that are likely to rebound sooner and more strongly from this recession. But even they cannot avoid a downturn. Yet whereas the West faces recession followed by stagnation, Asia's downturn this year will be followed by a stronger rebound in 2010.

One of the many remarkable features of this crisis was the extent to which many countries who were the least to blame for the financial crisis were hit the hardest. Emerging economies proved to be the victims and not the culprits.

World trade collapsed in the autumn of 2009. The slump in demand was the key factor, but this was compounded by the difficulty of obtaining trade finance and insurance and by the need to cut excess inventories that had been built up as commodity prices had soared earlier in the year. Generally it takes two years for world trade to return to pre-recession levels, but in the early eighties it took four, and early signs are that this time the hit could be just as hard.

No one should underestimate the immediate downside risks. Even ahead of the financial crisis of autumn 2008 the US was already two years into its downturn and was in recession, the advanced economies were slowing and this had already started to filter across the emerging world, with equity markets hit hard and exports slowing. Autumn's financial crisis moved us into a different space, leading to a loss of trust within the financial sector, a collapse in confidence across the globe and a deterioration in expectations about economic and financial prospects.

The problems are more acute for the advanced economies, either as they come to terms with the crisis or as they try to reposition themselves to compete in a world where the balance of power appears to be shifting to emerging economies. The shift from G8 to G20 is a reflection of this.

Yet even across the emerging world there is a need to differentiate. Regions like Central and Eastern Europe are vulnerable, as are economies that saw housing booms, such as Dubai, or that have large trade deficits. In contrast those economies with large savings, healthy surpluses, or with plenty of room for policy manoeuvre, look in good shape. A number of these economies are in Asia, and the biggest is China. But even China, like the rest of Asia, has been hit hard this year, highlighting that the world economy is not decoupled.

Finally, there is confidence. This is the hardest aspect to call. Policy measures have worked by pulling the financial sector back from the brink. There is the need to see how this feeds through into the wider economy. The earlier stages of recovery could be strong, particularly as policy feeds through. The likelihood, though, is that confidence is likely to recover sooner, and prove more resilient, across many emerging economies, particularly those where domestic demand is more resilient.

There is no doubt that we need to move to a more balanced global economy, and this adjustment eventually requires deficit economies in the West to spend less and save more, surplus countries in the Middle East, Asia and elsewhere to move more of their savings into spending. Currency adjustment will have to be part of this future process, with a ticking time bomb under sterling and the dollar.

What are the implications of the financial crisis on social behaviour?

Financial crises have their greatest social impact when they reinforce changes that were taking place or about to take place, and as a result speed the pace at which those changes were happening.

Within the developed world there were several huge social changes starting to occur. These include the consequences of ageing populations, the greater mobility of labour in terms of both geography and occupation, the move out of manufacturing to services and the loss of trust in many forms of authority. While it is hard to be confident about the impact of this downturn on social issues – we won't be able to make much of a tally until growth is secure and we have gone through the whole economic cycle – it is worth making some educated guesses.

The first point concerns ageing and its consequences for the workforce. There was some evidence that as the baby-boomers throughout the developed world reached retirement age there would be a new conservatism in social attitudes. This is most evident in Japan, which is ageing most rapidly, but also in Germany, which has the oldest population among the large European countries. In both cases savings have been high and consumption depressed. The workforce in both countries is now shrinking and there has been relatively slow growth in both countries, indeed hardly any in Japan. In the rest of Europe there are similar trends, though these are not yet so advanced.

This shift in the average age of populations has affected different people in different ways. For those in secure jobs or on generous pensions, the prevailing desire has been to hold on to what has been achieved. For the elderly who are less secure it has been a disturbing period. But for the young there has been a sense of frustration: 'bed blockers' have prevented them from getting ahead.

Now add to this the recession. For the secure elderly it has reinforced their desire to have no surprises and to hang on to what they have. For the insecure elderly it has been more disturbing. Many have seen their savings eroded or their pensions slashed. For some the response has been to carry on working beyond the age at which they had planned to retire. In the UK the willingness of people of retirement age to carry on working has been, along with immigration, the main reason for the increased supply of labour. Paradoxically this insecurity of older workers has put more pressure on the young. Youth unemployment has been rising throughout the developed world, in most cases faster than unemployment in general. Quite why this should be happening remains a puzzle. In theory young workers, given their relative scarcity, should be in great demand. Many of the skills needed in the new industries require high levels of computer literacy, which one might reasonably think are more likely to be qualities of the young. Presumably, too, young people are more mobile than older ones. So why are youth-unemployment levels so high and why have they risen particularly during the current recession?

It may be partly that when employers are looking to shrink their workforce they are not going to take on many new young workers, however skilled. That would be common sense. But that would not explain the phenomenon during the boom years, so we have to look further. I suspect that part of the problem is the levels of education and 'soft' skills of the young: that they are less well prepared for job opportunities than earlier generations. If that is right, one of the lasting social effects of this recession will be for there to be more pressure on the education system, naturally from employers but also from students, to prepare young people better. In the UK, where university students are having to contribute more to their education fees, there has been a noted shift in student attitudes: they demand more from their professors.

This leads to a further huge social shift that is just becoming evident. It is for young people to be aware that they are competing not only against their peers in their own country but against people from all over the world. Thus an American computer programmer is competing against someone in India, who is probably just as well qualified and is on a significantly lower salary. As companies have sought to cut costs during the recession, there has been great pressure to use the most cost-effective talent, wherever it is located.

This trend is particularly evident in service industries, and as the weight of global employment shifts from manufacturing to services the trend can only increase. That is a further shift that has speeded up during the recession, particularly in the advanced economies. For example, we may not know how much of the global car industry will shift from Europe and North America to Asia, but we do know that, for the first time ever, China is in 2009 producing more cars that the United States. Manufacturing in Europe and North America will not disappear. But it will decrease as a proportion of the total economy and it will move upmarket. As a result the workforce will be smaller but higher skills will be required of it. So one lasting consequence of the recession will be even greater pressures on our society to up-skill our people.

Finally, a word about authority. The recession has shattered many illusions. Self-evidently the financial-service industry has suffered grave damage to its reputation but the damage surely goes beyond that. Many leaders, be they financial, commercial or political, have been proved wrong. The inevitable result is a questioning of the market-driven economic model. It is irrelevant whether this scepticism is fair or justified. It is irrelevant whether greater state intervention is desirable or effective. The market system will be more closely scrutinised and more strongly challenged for a decade, maybe a generation. The business community has to accept that and deal with it. That will require patience and understanding.

GEORGE MAGNUS

We had many telltale signs that a serious banking crisis was in the making during 2007 and the first half of 2008. The banking system meltdown later that year necessitated government and central-bank intervention on a massive scale. By the summer of 2009, announced financial assistance measures in the form of capital injections, asset purchases and lending, liquidity support, and debt and loan guarantees amounted to about 30 per cent of the GDP of advanced economies. In the US, the figure was nearer 45 per cent, in the UK about 48 per cent, and in Germany, the Netherlands, Austria and Belgium it was between 20 and 40 per cent. In Ireland, it was 2.5 times the country's GDP.

According to the US Federal Deposit Insurance Corporation's website, 106 banks had failed in the period from the start of 2007 to October 2009, compared with twenty-seven banks in the prior five years. Most of these banks were small, local and inconsequential on a national scale, but not all. In Ireland, Iceland and the UK, large or locally important banks have been nationalised. In the US and many European countries, several large banks have received government capital in exchange for so-called preferred shares, giving the government significant ownership stakes.

In 2009 there was both great relief and gnashing of teeth about the strong recovery in the earnings of several large banks. Both reactions were wrong. The earnings rebound said little about sustainable economic recovery, let alone the health of the banking system. The bounce in profits came from the normalisation in financial markets brought about by public authorities, virtually zero financing costs to banks, and from sharply reduced competition. The 'noise' on bank profits and bonuses jarred with what is probably an inevitable trend towards a smaller and more regulated financial sector. It is imperative to underline that the repair of the banking system is a work-in-progress, which is both politically fractious, and likely to take years, not months. The continuing weaknesses in the banking system fall into two main categories. First, the repair of balance sheets, and second, the repair of the structure of banking organisations.

According to the IMF's Global Financial Stability Report, produced in October 2009, the estimated write-downs of loans and securities in the US, Europe and Japan between 2007 and 2010 amount to about $3,500 billion, of which a little more than $2,800 billion were accounted for by banks. By the middle of 2009, about $1,000 billion of write-downs had been recognised by banks. Precise numbers are complicated by the combination of as yet unknown bad debts as the default cycle continues through 2010, the illiquidity of some assets and loans, the suspension of fair value accounting for some types of assets, and the vulnerability of banks to macroeconomic risk.

The most urgent priority was and remains the rebuilding of adequate capital to strengthen the ability of banks to withstand losses. Some progress has been made, particularly in the US and the UK. By mid-2009, about $900 billion of capital had been raised by banks in advanced economies, of which about a half was in the US. This extra capital, raised both privately and via public-sector injections, roughly balanced the estimate of write-downs taken to date. In the period to the end of 2010, the recovery of bank earnings and low funding costs can be expected to help banks build up their capital even further. However, it is unclear how far the banks will have to go, not least because it is widely expected that regulatory change will demand that banks hold levels of capital that are higher than in the past, adequate for current business-cycle purposes, and possibly greater when the cycle turns up again so that they are better prepared for future economic downturns.

The IMF estimated, in April 2009, that banks might have to raise another $560 billion of capital so that they could meet a widely noted 4 per cent ratio of tangible common equity (ordinary share capital) to total assets. The bulk would have to be raised in European countries, especially as US banks raised nearly $100 billion of new capital in the second quarter of 2009, following the announcement by the US government that it would conduct stress tests for major banks to determine how much each bank was required to raise.

On the other side of the balance, bad assets still clog the balance sheets of major banks. The UK authorities introduced an asset-insurance scheme. The US created a Public – Private Investment Programme designed to get banks to sell bad assets to pools of private investors, with the state subsidising the transactions. Early enthusiasm quickly dissipated as it became clear that the plan suffered from numerous weaknesses, and would probably not address more than a small proportion of total bad assets. In the next two years, the problem of bad assets on the balance sheet needs to be revisited. If not, the experience of Japan in the 1990s suggests that many banks might remain 'zombies' – that is, they would survive but without really being able to intermediate credit properly, and would sour the operating environment for their healthier peers.

The repair of banking organisations and the disappointment about the pace of regulatory change really speak to the aftermath of the systemic crisis between September and December 2009. While the initial response to the crisis stabilised the banking system and contributed to a partial normalisation of many market functions in 2009, the follow-up policy effort has been flawed. One policy option, viscerally opposed by most governments, was to nationalise formally insolvent financial entities, apply the process of triage to the banks themselves and to their operations, restructure them, and sell them back as soon as possible. Instead, some banks have been all but nationalised, but we pretend they are still private-sector agents, while others have been encouraged to remain or become 'too big to fail' as an alternative to proper nationalisation. As many, including the governor of the Bank of England, Mervyn King, have noted, if a bank is too big to fail, it is simply too big – from the standpoint of systemic risk at least.

Everyone acknowledges that greater regulation is needed, but the exact template for regulatory reform is unclear and often disputed between banks and national public authorities, and between the latter themselves. However, 'too big to fail' represents a major escalation in moral hazard. In the US, for example, banks have returned to profit, and many have paid off loans they borrowed from the US government. If in the next one to two years' profits were to decline again or, worse, if the economy went into a second or double-dip recession, 'too big to fail' means that the government would again have to come to the rescue. It was hard enough the first time, and evoked an understandable but incoherent public rage. Next time, who knows?

The critical weaknesses in the banking system that need to be tackled are the size of our largest banks, and the political courage needed to take on strong vested political and financial interests that represent a major hurdle to the kind of regulatory reform and restructuring that are needed. The endgame has to provide for tightly regulated and fully protected banks that engage in low-risk lending and borrowing, and even better capitalised providers that undertake higher-risk operations but that know they may not be eligible for any bail-out in the future. The status-quo structure of banking organisations is compatible with this objective.

THIERRY MALLERET

When historians look at the mid-2009 recovery, they will observe that it was only the systematic socialisation of market risk combined with the sheer scale of policy intervention that prevented the global economy from slipping into depression. The worst had indeed been avoided, but the expansion that took place around the third quarter of 2009 was primarily driven by the various national fiscal and monetary stimuli put in place the year before combined with a massive inventory adjustment (the industrial restocking). If, therefore, the recovery was driven by temporary factors, the key question then becomes: what happens when governments step back and the positive effect of their aggregate US $3.2 trillion in (fiscal only) commitments wanes? What happens, in other words, when conditions cease to be accommodative? The rebound is indeed fraught with uncertainties that will span several years.

At present (September 2009), it is much too early to tell what shape the recovery will take (a 'V' for a strong rebound, a 'U' for a sluggish recovery, or possibly a 'W' for a double-dip recession) and how the global economy will evolve over the years to come (so much depends on policy decisions that nobody can predict). The global landscape, however, has changed irrevocably. We review below just some of the few 'lessons' drawn from the crisis that are the most likely to affect the way in which decision and opinion makers think about the 'big picture' and how they make decisions.

It is often tempting to think that, once the crisis has passed, we will soon return to the situation as it was before. Not this time! We are entering a new era, which Pimco (one of the largest fixed-income fund managers in the world) has called the 'new normal'. It is characterised by heightened government regulation, higher unemployment and lower consumption, which will lead to slower growth in economies, which in the meantime will have become overly dependent on sectors driven by public spending. Some economists such as Olivier Blanchard (the chief economist, of the IMF), go as far as venturing that economic growth may be 'permanently' impaired by the recession, with a potential output much lower than before, primarily because to the need to rebalance global aggregate demand. This entails a necessary shift from domestic to external demand in deficit countries – primarily the US – and a reverse shift from external to domestic demand in surplus countries – primarily China. It represents a long-term adjustment that also constitutes a US strategic imperative, as there is an inherent tension between superpower status and net foreign indebtedness (the two do not go hand in hand).

The crisis has made it blatantly clear that a growing disconnect exists between the long-term nature of the global problems we face and the short-term solutions proposed by policy makers and the markets to address them. The failure of leadership is obvious, but furthermore the now inadequate global governance itself – inherited from Bretton Woods – has reached its limits. 'Short-termism, and the endless quest for growth and higher returns associated with it, is killing us.' Unless some externalities are internalised to become properly priced, we face a very bleak future. This is particularly true for climate change.

One of the greatest casualties of 2008 is simply economics itself, while one of the greatest winners is neuro-economics! Almost all long-held ideas at the core of the economic discipline (such as the resilience of the markets, the power of monetary policy and the stability of the business cycle) have been shattered. Conversely, the phenomenal progress made in neuroscience over the past years is changing the way we see ourselves and make decisions (as it sheds light on the role that emotions play in this process). In the face of ever-growing complexity, we are all victims of what neuro-economists call 'bounded rationality'. The disturbing consequence in terms of policy making is greater uncertainty: how can a minister in charge of devising economic or financial policy make up his mind when he is being offered contradictory advice by two equally competent advisers?

Beyond economics itself, the long-held belief in finance that the market's forces guarantee efficiency and stability has also been shattered. We now all know that markets are not efficient, because they are beset by problems of asymmetric information. As a result, the efficient-market theory taught in all MBA classes has taken a battering, and yet business schools and fund managers continue to behave as if nothing has changed. New research puts a further nail in the coffin of the theory by showing that one key driver that guides professional investors' decisions is the fear of losing one's job (the so-called 'career risk'). In such conditions, a fund manager may well be tempted 'to fail conventionally rather than to succeed unconventionally', as Keynes used to say. This could again lead to a 'melt-up' in asset prices, as fund managers follow the herd (buying into the market, not wanting to miss an upturn).

In our increasingly interdependent world, our capability to mitigate the global risks we face (pandemics, terrorism, financial shocks, extreme weather events – in a nutshell, all the risks that don't stop at the borders) seems to be rising in conjunction with the increase in their occurrence. A fundamental disconnect exists between the global nature of these risks and the way in which they are being addressed by national governments (or institutions): in relative isolation one from the other. In reality, these risks can only be mitigated by cooperative responses. We live in an era in which catastrophes are bound to occur at an accelerated rhythm, with a hyper-concentration of the value at risk. In our 'just in time' society, preparedness and celerity are key, but again, governments and regulators are bound to be outpaced.

The idea that the financial elite has hijacked the political establishment and that 'the underlying cause of this crisis is the economic supersizing of finance, as manifest particularly in the rise of big banks to positions of extraordinarily political and cultural power' (Simon Johnson, professor at MIT and former chief economist of the IMF) is gaining traction. Many consider the Obama plan for regulation as too timid and unable to 'stop bankers from making huge, risky bets with other people's money' (Robert Reich). No effective regulation of the financial sector will be achieved unless national governments sing from the same hymn sheet – a very tall order!

The long-term fiscal costs of the current crisis and the associated bail-out programmes are becoming apparent. So far, systemically important countries have massively increased their debt; but none has yet committed in a credible manner to a primary surplus that might subsequently reverse the debt dynamics. In a nutshell, short-term policy imperatives conflict with long-term ones (the short-term/long-term disconnect highlighted above).

The crisis has made obvious the disconnect that exists between the real economy (which produces value) and the financial economy (which too often gambles with taxpayers' money). More and more people realise that the connection between effort and reward must be proportionate and the playing field needs to be level if we are to secure a fully functioning market economy underpinned by political stability. To a certain extent, the consensus on the virtues of individualism, liberalism and consumer capitalism is now unravelling with potentially profound consequences. The 'outrage factor' caused by sentiments of unfairness and inequality is erupting and manifesting itself in various ways – from the uproar about bonuses to various protests in different parts of the world and even physical attacks on some bankers' properties. The social contract between the markets and the state, the value systems and social hierarchies are being turned upside down as more and more people come to the realisation that finance does not create value (production does, while finance just supports it). The world of finance is in the midst of a tectonic shift. In a nutshell, the financial system will operate with far less debt and far more supervision.

The country that has emerged as the most significant winner from the financial and economic crisis is China, where – like the rest of Asia – the reputation of the West for financial and economic competence is in tatters.

To understand today's predicament, one must grasp that there is/are simply too much debt and too few assets around (implying that the deleveraging process is far from complete). In the words of economist Paul Krugman, 'The surge in asset values has been an illusion, but the surge in debt has been all too real.'

MIKE MOORE [1]

The Doha Development Round, which aims to lower trade barriers around the world, therefore allowing countries to increase trade globally, was launched when I was director general of the WTO, in 2001; however, it has yet to be finalised and moves painfully slowly ahead, particularly with regard to agriculture and its related subsidies. If the deal were done, it would return up to five times more to Africa than all the aid and debt relief put together. The obscenity of the rich OECD nations' agricultural policies, which spend a billion dollars a day to make food dearer with their subsidies and protection, is still in place. This is a tax on poor people in rich countries that robs the poor in poor countries. To right this, politicians need to stand up to powerful, vested interests. Concluding the Doha Round would represent the greatest redistribution of wealth and opportunity in history. It should be the top priority for our leaders.

The grim reality is that while our economies have globalised and integrated, our international institutions and their processes have not changed and therefore cannot cope. Environmental issues, as well as global economic issues, are locked together in a deadly embrace. No country can be safe from disease or terrorism, or fight the war against drugs, manage airlines or even run tax systems without the cooperation of others. We borrow from each other as well as trade with each other, our national economic activities now have a wider financial impact: a series of housing-loan defaults in the US may cause a city council in Sweden to go bust; a crazy investment decision in Iceland may cause a UK bank to close down as a result; when the Eastern European banks look shaky, then Italy and Spain tremble; when there is a health scare in China, farmers in New Zealand and Brazil need to worry. A world without walls cannot be a world without rules or values. A definition of civilisation is that societies live by the rule of law; thus, we need firm, predictable and transparent global rules of conduct, which, along with our global institutions, should reflect the world as it is, not as it was.

[1] This entry previously appeared in *Saving Globalization: Why Globalization and Democracy Offer the Best Hope for Progress, Peace and Development* (Singapore: John Wiley and Sons (Asia), 2009).

We should be optimistic: there will be no new Great Depression, despite such dire, even gleeful, predictions of a year ago. We have learned our lessons, but only just. The Great Depression was prolonged and deepened because of anti-trade protectionism and competitive devaluations. From this grew the twin tyrannies of the last century: fascism and Marxism. And after the war, smart people established the UN, World Bank, IMF and the GATT (later to become the WTO). Imperfect as these institutions are, they have fostered the best fifty years in our economic history, with the erstwhile poor benefiting most especially from this upward trend.

At the moment, world leaders are saying the right things about protectionism, although, alas, eighteen of the twenty have put in place some form of protectionism, albeit modest. Most nations have pumped money into the system to keep purchasing power up. We can argue about the quality of this expenditure and the fairness of tax reforms, but only the barking mad are calling for balanced budgets at this time. The countries that are best able to cope are those that have built up surpluses in the good times. Indeed, the last ten years of the fifty have been the strongest in terms of growth, with more wealth created than ever before. Most accept that this is not the time to call for a better past. Challenges remain: inequality, poverty, the dangerous denial of climate change, and the threat of war and terrorism still looming. The questions remain: What to do? And how? What have we learned? And why?

I believe it is extremely important to think carefully when assuming this crisis was truly global. Perhaps because it was such a huge crisis in the United States and spilled over into many other countries, developed and developing alike, this is the presumption, but as with many other aspects of this crisis, it is complex. Has there really been a real 'financial' crisis in Australia or Canada? Has there been a real 'financial' crisis in China, India or Indonesia? Yes, all of these countries have seen their economies weaken, but it is not clear that they have been part of the true financial crisis.

Of course, on one level this is perhaps even an irrelevant issue, as everyone did get hit after the Lehman failure when the Western financial system effectively froze for a few weeks and, as discussed earlier, world trade collapsed. However, in terms of thinking about any recovery, and where we are now, this is not just a finer technicality, as it might be able to tell us something about the nature of the recovery.

Another angle to this, which has grown in my mind linked to the way I have tried to answer this question, is perhaps that this is the first 'Facebook' crisis, in which so many people all over the world have such a strong opinion about it partly as a result of access to some sort of information, which results in almost definitely distorted albeit powerful opinions. Indeed, the popularity of the view that there was a strong likelihood that the grim days of the 1920s–30s were going to be repeated last winter and in the spring made me very confident that it was, on the contrary, highly unlikely. The fact that so many policy makers were born to parents who had probably been alive in the 1930s, and many of them had read of how inappropriate policy probably caused the Great Depression to be such a depression, made it unlikely that they would sit idly by and do nothing in the face of the shock the world experienced post-Lehman. Indeed, while it is now popular to criticise governments for their excessive fiscal deficits and debt, back around the turn of the year, many were rightly desperate for them to undertake the fiscal stimulus most have done.

It was clear that a lot of people feared we were heading towards a repeat of the Great Depression and it was even clearer that policy makers feared that prospect and were going to do something about it.

So, has that risk receded, and what is the state of play today?

We simply can't be that confident of the answer, not least because, if we didn't know before, this crisis should have demonstrated that economics is merely a social science, not an exact one. Many of us are well trained in it, quite experienced, but we need to remember that always. We don't ever know with confidence whether our models will work. With that in mind, here is what many of our objective proprietary indicators are showing.

Post-Lehman, when suddenly everything seemed problematic, we developed an index to measure the system financial risk. We call it the GS-FSI, Goldman Sachs Financial Stress Index. We calculate it in a very simple manner, in an attempt to capture the essence of financial stress. It includes four equally weighted variables. They are the spread between official US policy rates and short-term market rates, the so-called OIS–LIBOR spread. When it is wide, it shows that there is no confidence in the banking system, as it increasingly did throughout mid to late 2008, especially post-Lehman. Banks simply didn't trust each other, so wouldn't lend to each other. Fortunately it has improved a lot. We include the amount of commercial paper issuance, as a guide to how much short-term paper borrowers can raise. We also use a measure of the health of mortgage borrowing, using the US Government to Mortgage 'repo' spread. Lastly, to measure risk aversion we monitor the spread between the amount held in money-market funds and the equity-market capitalisation of the markets.

A picture of this index shows the weighted average of all four back to where it would have been in May 2007, i.e. just as the crisis was blowing up. While this can not tell us anything about the health of individual banks, it strongly suggests that the systematic risk of the banking system has been reduced.

We also use a number of other indicators that give us some colour.

For the past fifteen years, we have used a financial-conditions indicator, an FCI, as a leading indicator for the US, as a measure of the effectiveness of US monetary policy. It too, includes four variables, this time weighted according to econometric testing. Ninety per cent of the weight is three-month LIBOR, and an index related to the performance of triple-B-rated corporate credits. Five per cent weight goes to the trade-weighted dollar, and the remaining 5 per cent to an index linked to the Wilshire stock market, the market which has most stocks owned by the public. Historically speaking, when the FCI eased 100 basis points, within a year, all else being equal, the US economy would improve by 1 per cent. Moreover we find that US financial conditions are very important for the world economy. Also pre crisis, a 100 basis points' worth of easing would result, all else being equal, within a year, in the world economy being 0.6 per cent better than otherwise.

Obviously, when financial conditions tighten, the opposite is true, and the US and world economies weaken.

If you look at a chart of US financial conditions, you will find that in 2008 they tightened by a degree more, especially post-Lehman, than we can ever find having happened before. Not surprisingly, therefore, soon afterwards the US and world economies began to weaken dramatically.

Now, fortunately, since the US authorities have come up with their really aggressive policy response, which really got going last November, our FCI shows around 90 per cent of that tightening has been recovered, albeit at times tough to maintain, and not in a straight line. But this suggests that, all else being equal, the US and the world will recover 90 per cent of what it might have otherwise lost.

Is all else equal?

We also have financial-conditions indices for elsewhere, in fact for nearly thirty countries. Perhaps the other one which is critical to consider currently is China. Like my earlier example, our FCI for China is also constructed with four variables, again weighted econometrically based on past sensitivities. The main difference is that, as China doesn't have a developed bond market, we use M2 money supply instead. That and short-term interest rates make up around 85 per cent of the index, the rest being the trade weighted yuan, and the Shanghai stock market. Now take a look at a chart of our Chinese FCI: it has exploded by 630 basic points in the seven months since November 2008, a massive easing – unprecedented for China or anywhere else we monitor. Why? Linked to what I said at the start of this section, the Chinese financial system has not been 'broken' and, in circumstances of a massive policy stimulus, Chinese financial conditions eased dramatically. On the back of this, it would be likely that economic activities sensitive to such conditions – real estate and auto sales, consumer spending in general – would all show really positive signs, as indeed is now in evidence.

To complete the picture, now let's finish with our Global Leading Indicator – the GLI, as we call it. This is an index designed to predict industrial production in the developed world three to six months ahead. We use about fourteen time sensitive yet regular indicators from around the world, such as Korean exports (Korea being the first country to report each month) and weekly US jobless claims, for example. It fell dramatically in late 2008 and early 2009, foreshadowing the steep drop in activity. Highly interestingly, it appeared to bottom out in March, about the same time as world stock markets, and suggests at the moment more 'green shoots' ahead.

All in all, our best indicators, with all the caveats mentioned earlier, suggest that the world is, at a minimum, stabilising from the credit crunch, and perhaps before the year is over some modest positive GDP growth might reappear.

MICHAEL O'SULLIVAN

This is most definitely a global financial crisis, occurring against a backdrop of nearly twenty years of globalisation. At the same time, I feel that we are not quite there in terms of a credible, coherent global policy response, though at the very least there is so far a lack of sharply divergent or protectionist actions.

In broad terms, globalisation refers to the increasing interdependence and integration of economies, markets, nations and cultures. Though many of the artefacts of globalisation such as technological advances make it look and sound new, it does have a precedent. There are two generally recognised waves of globalisation, the first taking place from 1870 to 1913, and the current one, which effectively began in the late 1980s.

As the now well-worn quote below from Keynes shows, the first period of globalisation placed an array of goods and services at the disposal of (wealthy) people that they could acquire with new-found speed. The confidence and optimism reflected here are emblematic of the outlook of many in developed and emerging markets over the past fifteen years:

> The inhabitant of London could order by telephone, sipping his morning tea in bed, the various products of the whole earth, in such quantity as he might see fit, and reasonably expect their early delivery upon his doorstep; he could at the same moment and by the same means adventure his wealth in the natural resources and the new enterprises of any quarter of the world, and share, without exertion or trouble, in their prospective fruits and advantages, or he could decide to couple the security of his fortunes with the good faith of the townspeople of any substantial municipality in any continent that fancy or information might recommend . . . Most important of all, he regarded this state of affairs as normal, certain and permanent except in the direction of further improvement, and any deviation from it as aberrant, scandalous and avoidable.[1]

[1] Keynes J M, *The Economic Consequences of the Peace 1919* (New York, Dover Publications, 2004), p. 4.

The 1870–1913 period of globalisation was also remarkable for the levels of emigration that were witnessed. Over sixty million people migrated to the New World between 1820 and 1913. It is estimated that from the 1880s to the early 1900s 6 per cent of the population of several European countries migrated overseas.

However vibrant globalisation was at the turn of the century, burgeoning levels of trade, finance and technological advances (in transport and communications) soon led to imbalances in the European, Latin American and American economies, which were dealt fatal blows by poor policy making. Openness quickly gave way to protectionism and the application of tariffs. The rise in poverty and unemployment that was brought about by inflation in the price of goods and deflation in asset prices forced an eventual response from governments who had come to fear the greater say that the poor had in politics because of the expanding franchise. Where small government had previously been in vogue (in 1912 government expenditure in developed countries was about 13 per cent of GDP) governments were now expected to spend and protect their way back to prosperity. Thus protectionism, economic decline, nationalism and finally war brought down the curtain on the first period of globalisation. In many ways, save for some cross-Atlantic discussions on central banking, there was very little attempt at coordinating a 'global' response to the end of globalisation and to the various banking crises that punctuated its end.

Parallels and Differences

There are many parallels between the first wave of globalisation and the current one. The main ones are the rise in trade, the growth of financial systems and the rapid diminution in the cost of doing business as transportation and communication costs fell. It is also interesting to note that stock-market bubbles arose during both periods of globalisation, driven by the advent of new technologies. In the early twentieth century it was primarily the railway, telephone and radio stocks that led the rise in share prices, while in 1999–2009 information technology and finance were the chief culprits.

Still, there are crucial differences. Chief amongst them is that today more countries and more people are touched by globalisation, and in most cases are better off as a result. Globalisation today has a much greater reach. This is partly due to the fact that, compared to the twentieth century, more people than ever before enjoy electoral franchise and the freedom of democracy, and today popular opinion has a greater say in politics, at least in developed countries. Within the majority of developed countries the role of government is greater than it was one hundred years ago and the notion of welfare insurance is now well accepted in the developed world.

Advances in technology are now more rapid and in fields like communications have speeded up the transfer of ideas and information and made globalised forms of production more feasible. Corporations have grown in size and influence over the last one hundred years to the extent the corporation is the dominant force behind globalisation today. As a result there are now far many more 'global' products or brand names than there were in the period 1870 to 1913.

A final difference between globalisation now and that of the nineteenth century is the growth of institutions and trans-national governance. While the nation state is still very much a viable entity, power is increasingly placed in the hands of unelected policy makers. This is reflected in a number of quarters, such as the standardisation of accounting and financial measures. Institutionalisation increasingly seems to be replacing the role played by the gold standard, Pax Britannia and the ideological consensus that prevailed in the nineteenth century. It is manifest in bodies like the EU or IMF, and has broadly speaking been beneficial in preventing and resolving crises, in particular in placing a premium on negotiating skills rather than military power.

Given this backdrop, the ingredients exist, in the form of multinational corporations, international institutions, interwoven trade patterns and public opinion for more coordinated responses. This time around is also different in that so far there has largely been an absence of broad-based, ugly and persistent economic nationalism and protectionism.[2]

Overall, while the response, or rather responses, to the credit crisis so far have often been more miss than hit, they have been enormous in size, particularly with the introduction of quantitative easing by central banks and some very aggressive fiscal spending plans announced by the likes of China. Also, it could be argued that authorities have moved at a fast pace compared to previous crises – for instance, central-bank discount rates have fallen faster and further than at the same stage of the Great Depression and growth in money supply has been much more aggressive in the past year than in the early years of the Depression. Similarly, governments today seem to be much more willing to undertake fiscal stimulus, or rather to run large deficits, than they were in previous crises.

[2] There are nonetheless some signs of protectionism. India has raised tariffs on steel and iron imports and has stated it would impose safeguard or anti-dumping duties on products from any countries selling below costs. Indonesia is thinking about introducing special licences or tariffs in textiles, footwear, toys, food and beverages. Russia hiked duties on pork imports, cut poultry quotas and introduced temporary customs on imports of agricultural equipment. Brazil and Argentina have imposed tariffs on automobile and meat imports.

Central banking is perhaps the one area where coordination or at least communication has been evident on a global scale. Exchange of expertise, policy views, coordinated capital infusions into banks and large swap agreements are some of the ways large central banks have cooperated. Much of this was made necessary by the interconnectedness of banking systems and the global nature of derivative markets and the shadow financial system. Where divergences occurred (such as the ECB's unswerving and public focus on inflation (up to the peak in eurozone inflation in August 2008)) this resulted largely from differences in mandates, culture and structural economic issues (such as the relatively low sensitivity of European households to short-term debt and house prices), rather than a refusal to 'cooperate'.

Governments have been less conspicuous in their efforts to coordinate. In the darkest moments of the crisis, policy moves (such as Ireland's blanket guarantee to its banks) appeared selfish and took on a 'beggar thy neighbour' tone. In general, though, outright examples of economic nationalism and protectionism have been relatively few, given such trying economic conditions.

Where the fiscal response to the crisis has diverged it has been because of differences in cultural and political attitudes (such as the reluctance of German politicians to use debt or budget deficits to counter the crisis), priorities (some countries like Saudi Arabia are using the crisis as an opportunity to push ahead spending in areas like education), strategy (China is arguably using this weak point in the global economy to strengthen its strategic position economically) and of course government finances (countries like the UK have very limited scope to borrow). At the same time, international institutions like the IMF have provided the conduits for targeted financial action for certain emerging markets (notably in Eastern Europe), while technologies like the internet (witness blogs like www.voxeu.org, or www.irisheconomy.ie) and groups like the G20 have provided centralised forums for policy debate.

At the time of writing, moves are afoot to construct a global regulatory framework, though structural and policy differences between regions (notably the US and EU/Switzerland/UK) are likely to impede a credible global framework, and may in time lead to regulatory arbitrage by banks and investment funds. In particular international standards like Basel II need to be intelligently reformed, and wide-ranging measures are required to limit global systemic risk.

As a final point, the very nature of globalisation means that countries that have symbiotic links in trade and finance (such as China and the US – China owns a third of US government debt) have a strong mutual interest in coordinated policy moves. This of course does not mean that there will not be disagreements, but there are at least two key near-term risks. One is that emerging economies diversify their currency reserves away from the dollar and increasingly trade with each other in their own currencies or other non-dollar currencies. This could potentially weaken the dollar, with a risk that this becomes disorderly, which in turn provokes selfish policy responses.

The second risk is that dollar-pegged or dollar-related emerging economies suffer asset-price bubbles and/or consumer inflation because of low US interest rates. This is also a threat for some of the smaller eurozone countries and potential new eurozone members in Eastern Europe. One lesson from the Asian crisis of the 1990s and the property bubbles in Spain and Ireland in recent years is that there needs to be much, much better coordination of monetary and fiscal policy within currency regions.

Overall, though, this crisis has been global in cause and effect. The policy countermeasures could have been better coordinated globally, but they have also been much less selfish than in other crisis. As a result, we will likely suffer a great recession, but not a Great Depression II.

This is not a normal recession. This event is cyclical, financial and more global than any other in history. Its complexity is mind-boggling, only more visible now that the earthquake dust has almost settled. In terms of its size this is the largest crisis in peacetime in human history. It is four times larger as a percentage of global gross domestic product than the Great Depression and yet the Depression was avoided. This is due to a very different response than during the Great Depression.

Back in the late twenties and early thirties, the mantra was that the markets were self-correcting, that nothing should be done and that the good dose of suffering was needed to get back to normal. And nothing was done for three years. As a consequence of inaction, US GDP collapsed by a staggering 33 per cent and more than 9,000 banks were allowed to fail. The idea of a stimulus and action was seen as all wrong.

Today we know better and yet we still ended up in great recession. The reason is that the policy response was overall good and unprecedented by historical standards, but sadly it was always running a bit behind the curve. The response included monetary and fiscal easing, bank rescues and recapitalisation, guarantees to bank liabilities and deposits, purchases of toxic waste, bypassing the banking system, providing unlimited liquidity and in the end in some markets even printing money (popularly called these days 'quantitative easing'). All fine, good and appropriate, with one problem: it was always coming a little late, as authorities waited for numbers to be published (this indicates the continued lack of sophistication of economic science), then debated what needed to be done (political reality); and only then the reaction came. To be fair, any other speed of reaction was probably not possible anyway, considering different opinions in political circles. Also, the complexity of the crisis and the speed were unprecedented, catching everyone by surprise, and by the time numbers were published they were very old indeed.

The delayed reaction, despite its overall soundness, caused fears and ended up being a crisis of confidence – on top of the crisis of trust caused by financial problems (see pp. 72–4). At this point there was no way, historically, to avoid a recession and that is where we ended. Crises are very psychological once confidence and trust are shattered and it always takes time to rebuild them. It will be like that this time.

The risks to recovery are many and it will require a serious change in the architecture of the entire financial system to get it right. One of the main pillars of that future stability is to improve supervision, based on new and tighter regulations. While regulations should not prevent *all* kinds of innovation, they should be targeted at useless ones. If the new regulatory environment is not in place with proper implementation and punishment (and punishment for breaches should be severe), then we have a chance of getting into more problems again fairly soon.

Global response and consensus on what needs to be done will again be debated at the upcoming G20 meeting and it remains to be seen what exactly will be done. The financial industry has become influential and in reality some kind of compromise will be made. But if that compromise includes higher capital requirements for banks, the squeeze of quasi-financial institutions, tracking of the derivatives markets (including credit-default swaps), instruments to prevent speculative trading of commodities (whereby you have to physically buy and take them rather than just trading a piece of paper), then we are already on the right track. After all meetings, national authorities will probably have different regulations, but hopefully at least some of those will be common to all.

We also need more capital controls in emerging markets and a different involvement of the IMF. Emerging markets were asked to liberalise their capital accounts too early, allowing everyone to speculate with their currencies and debt instruments. This caused massive and sudden inflows and outflows of hot money. We should use the model Western Europe used for decades after the Second World War, which was to allow currency trading of their own currency only if it was used for productive purposes. Ever since premature liberalisation happened, we have had more financial crises in emerging markets in the last three decades than in some three centuries before that. The IMF should be helping economies during the crisis with fiscal stimulus (even if they are heavily indebted) and then restructuring debts when the crisis is over, rather than asking for deep spending cuts when we know this makes recessions worse in the short-term.

EDMUND PHELPS [1]

My thesis in recent years is that the just society requires the good economy; the good economy requires high dynamism and wide inclusion; and these qualities require a well-chosen mix of economic policies: some aimed at dynamism, some at inclusion. If further goals of economic policy are valuable, as productivity might be, either they derive value from what their achievement would add to dynamism or inclusion, or their pursuit does not get in the way of dynamism or inclusion.

What Is Economic Dynamism?

I began working with the concept of economic dynamism when doing research on the Italian economy in the late 1990s. By the dynamism of an economy I mean its innovativeness in commercially viable directions.[2] It is important to note that episodes of rapid growth in a country or in the whole global economy can come purely from market opportunities of a transitory or exhaustible kind, such as Europe's fast growth from the mid-1950s to the mid-1970s, when it had opportunities to pluck for its own use the low-hanging fruit of overseas technologies and business practices; so dynamism and growth are not the same thing and the growth rate is not a measure of dynamism. What, then, *are* the indications of dynamism?

Dynamism – or the lack of it – tends to manifest itself in a variety of ways. Higher dynamism in an economy delivers faster productivity growth most, if not all, of the time, so with time it leads to a consistently higher level of productivity. Dynamism creates a distinctive sector of economic activity:

[1] This paper expands upon a dinner speech at the 7th Annual BIS Conference on Monetary Policy, Luzern, 26 June 2008, and a lecture at the Borsa Italiana, Milan, 11 June 2008.
[2] My use of 'dynamism' began in my reports for Italy's science foundation in the late 1990s, later published in Phelps, *Dynamism and Inclusion in the Italian Economy*, (Springer Verlag, Berlin 2002). The same concept and term are at the centre of the fine book by Virginia Postrel, *The Future and its Enemies* (Pocket Books, New York, 2003).

employment in the financing, development and marketing of new commercial products for launch into the marketplace; and a cadre of managers deciding what to produce and how to produce it. These added avenues for employment, it may be argued, generate higher levels of total labour force and total employment. There is also evidence that higher dynamism results in workers reporting higher job satisfaction and employee engagement. Finally, higher dynamism also tends to produce a relatively high rate of turnover in the members belonging to the economy's largest firms, as some new firms grow large and displace old members.

In recent years I have been testing the hypothesis that dynamism is so important and the disparities in dynamism across countries are so pronounced that where a country ranks in the 'league standings' with respect to productivity level, employment, job satisfaction and turnover among the big firms is largely determined by the relative dynamism possessed by its economy – its economic institutions and economic attitudes. This hypothesis can be found in the writings of Friedrich Hayek, Alfred Chandler, Richard Nelson, Roman Frydman and Andrzej Rapaczynsky, and Amar Bhide, to name some seminal contributors.

Many of the general public, though – in the United States and elsewhere – are under the belief that high productivity and job satisfaction (there is some debate about job creation) are driven by the great technological advances of scientists and explorers. Productivity growth and many jobs would gradually vanish were it not for the occasional *deus ex machina* from outside the economy – a Christopher Columbus, an Alessandro Volta or a Michael Faraday. That view underlies the model of innovation in the 1911 book by Joseph Schumpeter, *Theory of Economic Development*. In this model, the Schumpeterian entrepreneur considers the many unexploited opportunities for new commercial developments made possible by the previous discoveries of scientists and explorers and then the entrepreneur identifies the project that will best fit his or her abilities; the Schumpeterian banker inspects the entrepreneurial projects brought to him and ably selects the ones with the highest prospective profitability. No player in the economy conceives of anything that the other players have not conceived. The agents of change are all outside the economy. This view started with the German school led by August Spiethoff, who taught that innovation comes in great waves, each one linked to some new fundamental scientific breakthrough.

The historical record since the mid-nineteenth century supports the dynamism theory more than the Spiethoff–Schumpeter theory. If they were right, we would see productivity growth arriving mainly in great waves; and, looking across countries with satisfactory property rights and rule of law, we would see only insignificant differences in productivity, job satisfaction and turnover among the big firms. But we do not see such homogeneity. In Canada and the United States there is an almost unbroken record of relatively high employment, high productivity and rapid turnover.

Productivity in these countries is particularly remarkable for the *sustained* nature of its growth: it did not slow even during the Great Depression of the 1930s, though it was awfully slow between 1975 and 1990. Looking at other countries in the G10, we see in France, Italy and Sweden a strong rise of relative productivity, employment and turnover among the largest firms from the late nineteenth century until the First World War followed by a decline during the 1930s that, in most respects, is still evident to this day. Both turnover among the largest firms and reported job satisfaction have been strikingly low in France and Italy; and in Sweden there have been no newcomers to the twenty largest firms since 1921.

Many who believe in the feasibility of dynamism in the economy maintain that dynamism can best be produced by a top-down system in which the state fosters technological advances that will in turn give inspiration and a competitive advantage to national firms. This was the strategy of Italy when in the 1930s it instituted the Consiglio Nazionale delle Ricerche and the strategy of France (and to a lesser extent Germany) where nationalisations established some giant state-owned enterprises that were allowed, even encouraged, to produce technological advances in their laboratories.[3] But the impression of many experts is that little dynamism tends to result from society's investments in this 'techno-fetishism', since so little business expertise and commercial calculation – and so much self-dealing – go into the proposals and selections of scientific projects. Even if scientific projects in one country or more did boost productivity by enough to cover the investment cost, the increase in productivity would be minuscule next to the potential contribution that improving business practice could make. Productivity in Italy, France and Germany during the 1920s and 1930s lagged far behind productivity in the US in spite of an abundance of scientists. Productivity in the Soviet Union lost ground to rival economies in the 1970s and 1980s in spite of a heavy expenditures on scientific research. These economies could have *pockets* of creativity – researching rockets, Sputnik, bullet trains and later the Concorde – but the creativity did not pervade the commercial sector, so there was no financial and managerial discipline that could bring cost management and, above all, strategic vision: seeking the highest returns without fear of failure. If it would take a supernatural leadership by the state to generate much dynamism, how

---

[3] In the US as well, a report just last year by the National Academy of Sciences and another this spring by David Baltimore urged the federal government to expand state-sponsored scientific research on the stated grounds that it would quicken productivity growth in the American economy.

is it that some countries do generate it? What is their secret?

The existing theory, beginning with work by Friedrich Hayek in the 1930s, argues that appreciable dynamism in the creation and adoption of new commercial ideas can be generated by an intricate system with six bodies of actors: a diversity of conceivers, or dreamers, of new commercial ideas each drawing on his or her unique experience and private knowledge; a diversity of enterprising figures each well matched to his or her developmental project by virtue of his or her unique background and talent; a diversity of financiers each with a contrasting experience and education for use in selecting which projects to back and nurture; and a diversity of managers and consumers some of whom will have the preparation and specialised background to pioneer the adoption and mastery of a new method or products. (Even if the system is in place, it can be blocked.)

In some of the countries having economic institutions of the capitalist type just this system for dynamism is found in relatively unfettered operation. With the key freedoms protected by the rule of law, participants will sort themselves out among the six bodies: some participants will step forward with new commercial ideas; some others will each take up an entrepreneurial project to develop a new idea into a marketable product or method; still others will make the decisions to finance some of these projects and refuse others; finally, many will act as end-users, as managers and consumers evaluating new products and methods and sometimes pioneering their adoption. It may be that the system for dynamism is also found in some other type of economy – perhaps some more 'cooperative' type of economy. But before we come to economic policies for dynamism we first have to consider whether dynamism is something that is really required for a good economy, whatever its full description.

The Good Economy: Dynamism with Inclusion

A great many people are very unsettled by such a system: they feel pulled along by a headless horseman. It is true that an economy of considerable dynamism is on an indeterminate course: it is indeterminate because there is no way to determine in advance what the new ideas yet to emerge and be developed in the economy will be. Hence the participants themselves cannot fully know what will be the results of their own innovations and, even more, the unforeseen innovations undertaken by others. More precisely, even the *probabilities* of the known influences on the outcome are not known and not all the influences are known – the situation called 'Knightian uncertainty' (see p. 75). A lot of people have no appetite for being entrepreneurs once they understand that entrepreneurs need 'animal spirits' – that to commit to a really innovative project is to leap into the void.

Numerous observers, including me, have described how uncertainty manifests itself and the kinds of challenges it presents in setting monetary policy, managing a business and so forth. There are hazards in acting, which most businesses must often do, with limited understanding. In the past dozen years we have seen blunders in monetary policy, regulatory mistakes, astonishing financial losses and worldwide financial crises that are a result of imperfect understanding. This sort of uncertainty and the resulting instability are widely seen as an objection to economies possessing appreciable dynamism. Capitalism was widely seen as receiving a black eye when the US financial system contracted in 2007. The other objection to dynamism is that it causes inequalities in wealth that have no immediate or obvious defence. They seem morally arbitrary. There is also in some countries noticeable hostility to anyone's succeeding in becoming rich – much more than to anyone's *being* rich. If a person inherits great wealth it is not his fault – perhaps it was hard to avoid it without causing offence. It is seen as part of the *downside* of an economy of dynamism that it is a system in which people dream – dream of wealth, fame, whatever – and while some succeed, many fail, for no fault on their part.

What kind of reply can be made to these two objections? Is the choice between an economy of dynamism with its attendant uncertainties and inequities and an economy of tradition with its attendant routine and familiarity simply a matter of taste? Or are there some fundamental principles involved? I saw that there is a very basic consideration that must not be ignored. Dynamism opens the door for participants to engage in novel activity – the conception, financing, developing, marketing and adoption of products and methods not known before. This is an economy in which entrepreneurial types are free to seek opportunities to exercise their creativity by venturing something innovative, and financial types can exercise their judgement.

Is this so crucial as to trump concerns over uncertainties and inequalities? Humanist philosophy, as I read it at any rate, suggests that, whatever the other dictates of justice may be, an economy cannot be a just economy, or a good economy, if it does not permit and facilitate the good life; so the answer may lie in what we take the good life to be. There is a classical conception of the good life that originated in ancient Greece and has continued to evolve even in the twentieth century.

In humanist thought, the classical conception of the good life originated with Aristotle and has continued to evolve right through the twentieth century. Aristotle saw the good life as one devoted to the acquisition of knowledge –

not that everyone could afford such a life. Aristotle was followed by a school of humanists who might be called pragmatists. Virgil, a poet of ancient Rome, celebrated the human capital acquired by the Roman farmer. Later there was Voltaire, and in the twentieth century John Dewey and John Rawls and Amartya Sen.

The vitalists are a parallel school of humanists: starting with Benvenuto Cellini in Renaissance times and Cervantes in the baroque era and continuing on to William James and Henri Bergson early in the twentieth century. This humanist tradition clearly implies that dynamism, even though it is a cause of some irremediable fluctuations and some irremediable inequalities, is necessary for the good life. An economy of dynamism meets some of our very basic needs: to exercise our imagination, to enjoy the mental stimulus of change, to have an endless series of new problems to solve, to expand our capabilities, to feel the thrill of discovery and to sense our personal growth. The primary importance of this self-realisation and self-discovery surely trumps the point that such a life poses uncertainties and the risk of failure.

Well-accepted notions of economic justice imply that *economic inclusion* is also necessary for a good economy. When, in the early 1990s, I began urging government measures to increase inclusion, my first argument was Adam Smith's point that you will be more effective in raising a person's income if you enlist his self-help alongside your own contribution rather than simply throw money at him unconditionally, which will probably diminish his motivation to earn additional income. I also argued in my 1997 book *Rewarding Work* that people of sound mind and body who are unable to gain employment or are in and out of employment for any of a variety of reasons suffer a loss of dignity, of economic independence and of the sense of belonging to the central project of society. And they need the money.

Yet in that book I also saw that inclusion is of primary importance in part because, for most people, jobs are virtually the only source of mental stimulation, problems to solve, expansion of talents and self-discovery that they are likely to find. Because the more fortunate of the advanced economy are full of dynamism, it is particularly important in those economies that people be able to participate in the economy. Justice, John Rawls would have said in this context, requires that society help people into jobs lest they be deprived of any prospect of self-realisation.

So the moral necessity of dynamism and the further moral necessity of inclusion, if the economy is one of dynamism, spring from a common consideration. It is a kind of death not to be able to have a career of challenge, change and personal growth – which only a career can provide. The evidence does not bear out the claim that family can deliver the same rewards. Data show that reported happiness does not increase with the number of children!

I go on to argue that dynamism and inclusion are largely non-competing. Dynamism boosts inclusion. The reason is that dynamism creates jobs and raises wages in the process, which benefits everyone – including the marginalised and the disadvantaged. I have also come to see that inclusion can boost dynamism. The entry of the marginalised and the disadvantaged into the economy increases the diversity of the participants, thus opening up added sources of new commercial ideas. That may be why a society's outsiders look surprisingly more creative to us.

Economic Policy

The biggest threats to the good economy – to dynamism and to inclusion – seem to me to be the same three dangers throughout the Western world. A classical kind of rhetoric in defence of the welfare state holds that welfare payments bolster people against market forces so that we can have a market economy. The successful pressure to legislate additional welfare entitlements to cushion the middle class and the elderly from everything, even death, drives out economic policies (actual or potential) to preserve or foster dynamism and inclusion. These entitlements are not a left-wing conspiracy to soak the rich – the rich hardly care about the modest increase in tax rates on payrolls. They are more nearly a right-wing conspiracy to buy the solidarity of the middle class at the expense of government efforts to build an infrastructure and a regulatory system aimed at raising dynamism and government efforts to build an education system and a wage-subsidy system aimed at raising inclusion. Some economists think that this welfare state is not a burden on society's capacity to do other things as long as the middle class sees the entitlements as worth the taxes paid; but this is terrible economics: the receipt of the new entitlement is itself made a burden by weakening employee loyalty and zeal, thus aggravating unemployment and reducing incentives to stay in the labour force. In the struggle between Hillary Clinton, who campaigns for welfare, and Barack Obama, who campaigns for work and development, I know perfectly well which side I am on!

Another threat to dynamism and to inclusion is the pressure from 'stakeholders' and the 'social partners' to limit the property rights or incentives of entrepreneurs, financiers and managers to make innovations – innovations that would involve downsizing an existing business facility, or require new ownership of a company, or require CEOs to exert discipline over featherbedding and nepotism, or require shareowners to discipline the CEOs, etc. The post-war and inter-war economic history of Western continental Europe (and some other nations) provides powerful evidence for the thesis that private ownership with only vestiges of scope and control on the part of the owners, owing to social pressures, is disastrous for dynamism, and thus for high employment and job satisfaction. This is an old story: the struggle between *Gesellschaft* and *Gemeinschaft* – business and community. The pressure on politicians to refrain from opening the economy and even to take steps in the direction of less openness is not just bad policy from a neoclassical standpoint – from the viewpoint of free-trade advocates. This pressure also operates to reduce dynamism, which is much worse than lowering real incomes by a few percentage points. Taxes that restrict imports and taxes that restrict exports, such as Argentina's notorious *retensiones*, both operate ultimately to narrow *both* exports and imports. In doing that, these policies have the effect of narrowing the size of the market for entrepreneurs, actual or potential, when they are deciding whether to innovate or not. So policies in a country structured to constrict the scale of its foreign trade operate in this way to reduce dynamism.

I would also argue that economic policies in a country that are profligate or hostile to competition or to foreign capital, so that the country's currency is weakened, also reduce dynamism. A real exchange-rate depreciation increases the shield that domestic producers have from foreign competitors. That, in turn, induces all or most of these producers to raise their mark-ups – in short, to act more like monopolists and less like competitors. This is just like a contraction of supply and one effect is a cutback of employment, which I think is confirmed by some statistical studies. Another effect is to induce domestic firms to cut back their innovative activities, since, at least for a time (until the increase in customers makes up for the reduced supply to all), the size of the market has shrunk.

I am not a 'neo-liberal'. An optimal set of economic policies is not orthodox in every respect. Programmes to nurture dynamism and subsidise inclusion are required. Yet a wholesale failure to prize work and enterprise over welfare benefits, to favour real owners over stakeholders and social partners, to encourage innovators by allowing them to keep the money, and to support openness over protection, will prevent any country from achieving high economic performance and doing well in the international competition for influence and prestige.

JONATHON PORRITT

We seem to have become a very quiescent citizenry here in the UK. It's difficult to believe that we have just gone through eighteen months of deep economic disruption, with still worsening impacts on the lives of millions of people, and only a handful of heads have as yet rolled for their share of the responsibility for what has happened.

Most of them got off pretty lightly. Even Sir Fred Goodwin of the RBS eventually kept his critics at bay by 'voluntarily' taking a small reduction in his gargantuan pension settlement. Four out of five of his senior banking colleagues faced their moment of ritual humiliation in front of the Treasury Select Committee in the House of Commons, pleaded personal innocence ('It's the system, guv'), and promptly faded away into what can only be described as extremely well-heeled obscurity.

It's still too early to predict the full fall-out in terms of 'social behaviour'. But one thing already seems crystal-clear. The levels of debt that have now accumulated in order to bail out the banks and to put in place 'recovery programmes' all around the world will take decades to pay back. In the UK, it looks as if the impact will be particularly serious; all that is now in dispute between the major political parties is the *scale* of the necessary cutbacks in public expenditure and where those cutbacks should come.

That may not necessarily be such a disastrous thing. Vast amounts of public money are indeed wasted here in the UK, and will continue to be wasted until such time as a radical overhaul becomes completely unavoidable. There are many in the NHS, for instance, who both welcome the huge increase in funding that the Labour government has so successfully maintained and despair of the continuing wastage on administration and endless structural re-engineering.

This is not just about operational efficiencies. In his 2002 Review for the Treasury, Sir Derek Wanless warned that if people were not encouraged to lead healthier lives, NHS costs would continue to spiral out of control. He outlined three scenarios: 'fully engaged' (with a focus on preventing illness and making better use of health resources), 'solid progress' and 'slow uptake'.

Taken over a twenty-year period, he found, the 'fully engaged' scenario would not only be the least expensive but would also deliver the best health outcomes – and the gap between this and the worst scenario would have grown to around £30 billion – half of what the NHS spent in total in the year he was writing.

This makes a compelling case for all the different sectors and services, including education, employment, planning, housing, benefits, transport, sport, leisure and environment, to share responsibility – and work together – to address the underlying causes of illness and health inequalities.

But it is still going to be painful. Paying back debt will impact not just on the government but on millions of individuals who somehow took it for granted that their own little credit bubble (as a mini-microcosm of the nation's massive credit bubble) could just grow and grow. The information here is confusing. On the one hand, our newspapers and magazines are full of stories about the 'New Age of Austerity' as more and more people pay off outstanding debts and cut back on discretionary expenditure. On the other hand, levels of consumer spending have *not* collapsed (as some predicted), and would appear to be startlingly resilient. Politicians are hoping that that remains the case and that the problem described by John Maynard-Keynes as the 'paradox of thrift' (where anxious citizens go into risk-averse savings mode at exactly the same time as governments would like them to be out there consuming away to keep the wheels of the economy turning) is somehow going to be avoided.

It seems inevitable therefore that debt will dominate our lives in one way or another over the next few years. Astonishingly, however, I see little indication that this unprecedented focus on debt has as yet spilled over into increased awareness about the most serious debt of all: the debt that we collectively owe the natural world.

Some time ago, the Global Footprint Network and the New Economics Foundation launched a new initiative (under the name 'Ecological Debt Day') to mark the point in the calendar year at which society exceeded the total volume of resources available to us every year – if we were intent on maintaining intact our stocks of natural capital. In 2009, their report demonstrated that we went into 'overshoot' on 25 September. In 2005 it was 2 October. In 1995 it was 21 November. In 1986 it was 22 December. The direction of travel is crystal-clear, as are the moral consequences: this kind of deficit consumption is, in effect, drawing down on the capital entitlements of future generations.

Given that I've never heard a single politician indicate the slightest awareness of this phenomenon (let alone any declared intention of planning to redeem these ecological debts), we should recognise this for what it is: inter-generational larceny on a staggering scale. Those politicians that *are* concerned about the environment are principally focused on the threat of accelerating climate change. However, they still see it not so much as just the worst of many symptoms of our failure 'to live within environmental limits' over the last few decades, but rather as a stand-alone problem that we can somehow sort out through technology and a bit of behaviour change.

So I suppose I shouldn't be too surprised that by far the wisest voices on the deeper implications of the recession are those of our religious, rather than our political, leaders. Though I am no great admirer of the current Pope (whose views on family planning I find deeply repugnant), the latest encyclical issued by the Vatican has more to tell us about the deep systemic flaws (*moral* flaws) in the global economy than anything offered up at a seemingly endless sequence of G8 summits.

But even these insights are trumped, for me, by the profound reflections of Rowan Williams, the Archbishop of Canterbury, both on the causes and the consequences of the recession, and on our new responsibilities in such a trouble world:

> Renewing the face of the Earth is not an enterprise of imposing some private human vision upon a passive nature, but of living in such a way as to bring more clearly to light the interconnectedness of all things and their dependence on what we cannot finally master or understand. This certainly involves a *creative* engagement with nature, seeking to work with those natural powers whose working gives us joy, as Saint Augustine says, in order to enhance human liberty and well-being.

This is perhaps the most positive way of seeing it. Turn the concept of imposed austerity into joyful frugality; turn the banalities of 'respect for the environment' into reverence for the created world; and turn all the whingeing about heedless materialism into the deepest compassion for others and for all those who come after us. That way we might just find a viable alternative to the cruelties of today's neo-liberal economic orthodoxy, with or without a belief in God.

JEREMY RIFKIN

We are at a precarious point in history. The decision to rescue banks by infusing hundreds of billions of dollars of government funds directly, in the form of purchasing bank shares, will not be enough to restore market confidence and fully avert a global economic situation. The sad truth is that the global credit crisis is eighteen years in the making and not amenable to quick fixes.

What is even more troubling is that this global credit crisis is compounded by the global energy crisis and the global climate-change crisis, creating what amounts to a potential cataclysm for human civilisation, unlike anything we've ever witnessed before. These crises are interwoven and feed off each other.

The credit crisis is visceral, painful and immediate therefore, it gets the attention of government, industry and the general public – to the detriment of the far more insidious global energy and climate-change crises, which creep up on us, slowly and inexorably strangling the global economy with far more profound long-term consequences to our economic way of life. While governments are pouring hundreds of billions of dollars into bailing out the banking and financial community, they are far less willing to entertain the idea of spending comparable funds to address the two more dangerous global crises that threaten the very extinction of civilisation.

The credit crisis that has spread throughout Europe and the wider world began in the early 1990s. Wages had been stagnant and falling in the US for nearly a decade. America emerged out of the 1989 to 1991 recession – brought on, in part, by a contraction in the housing market – by extending a massive amount of consumer credit to millions of Americans. Readily available credit cards allowed US consumers to purchase goods and services beyond their means.

In turn, this boosted purchasing power, putting American companies and employees back to work to meet the demand for these goods and services and propping up the global economy. The price, however, for maintaining a global economy on the shoulders of increasing US consumer debt has been the depletion of American family savings. The average family savings in 1991 were approximately 8 per cent, but by 2006 the average American family began to spend more than it earned. The term for this is 'negative income', an oxymoron that represents a failed approach to economic development.

As savings turned into debt, the mortgage and banking industry created a second line of artificial credit, which allowed the purchase of homes with little or no money down, at low or non-existent short-term interest rates (sub-prime mortgages). Millions of Americans took the bait and bought homes beyond their eventual ability to make the increased payments, which were affected by the rise in interest rates once the initial 'teaser' rates had run their course. This created a housing bubble. Strapped for cash, home-owners used their homes as if they were ATM cash machines, refinancing mortgages – sometimes two or three times – to secure more cash. Now that the housing bubble has burst, millions of such debt-ridden consumers have suffered foreclosures; likewise, many banks have teetered on the verge of collapse, or indeed fallen over the edge.

The upshot of so many years of living off extended credit is that the United States is now a failed economy. The gross liabilities of the US financial sector, which were 21 per cent of GDP in 1980, have risen steadily over the past twenty-seven years and were an incredible 116 per cent of GDP by 2007. And because the US, European and Asian banking and financial communities are intimately intertwined, the credit crisis has swept out of America and engulfed the entire global economy.

To make matters worse, the global credit crisis began to escalate further as oil prices soared, reaching US $147 per barrel on world markets in July 2008. This increased price stoked inflation, dampened consumer purchasing power, slowed production and increased unemployment, wreaking further havoc on an already debt-ridden economy.

We now face a new phenomenon. It's called 'peak globalisation' and it occurred at around US $150 per barrel. Beyond this point, inflation creates a firewall to continued economic growth, pushing the global economy back down towards zero growth. It is only with the contraction of the global economy that the price of energy falls as a result of less energy use.

The importance of 'peak globalisation' can't be overemphasised. The essential assumption of globalisation has been that plentiful and cheap oil would allow companies to move capital to cheap labour markets, where food and manufactured goods could be produced at minimum expense and at high profit margins then shipped around the world. The rise of oil prices, thus the cost of fuel, has disintegrated this bedrock assumption with ominous consequences for the globalisation process.

To understand how we got to this point, we need to go back in time to 1979. That is the year that global oil per capita peaked, according to a study done by BP, the British oil company. The public is far more familiar with the term 'global peak oil production', which refers to the point in time when half of the world's oil is used up. Geologists say that global peak oil production is likely to occur sometimes between 2010 and 2035. Peak oil per capita, however, is why peak globalisation has occurred well before peak oil production.

After 1979, the amount of oil available per capita began to decline; however, when China and India began their dramatic economic growth in the 1990s, their demand for oil skyrocketed. Demand began to outstrip supply and the price of oil began to climb. And while more oil reserves have been found it is still barely enough to distribute amongst the growing human population.

With the likely possibility of there being less oil available it has made it more difficult to bring one third of the human race – the combined population of China and India – into an oil-based second industrial revolution. And with this increased demand on finite oil reserves, prices are pushed up. When oils hits $150 per barrel, inflation becomes so powerful that it acts as a drag, contracting global economic growth.

The rising price of energy is connected to every product we make: our food is grown with petrochemical fertilisers and pesticides; our plastics and building materials and most of our pharmaceutical products and clothes are also fossil-fuel-based, as well as our transport and electricity. The increased price of energy impacts every aspect of production and makes long-haul transport by air and tanker so costly that it becomes increasingly prohibitive. Whatever marginal value companies previously enjoyed by moving production to cheap labour markets is cancelled by the increasing cost of energy across the entire supply chain. This represents the real endgame for the second industrial revolution and occurs well before the point of peak global oil production.

At the same time, the effects of 'real-time' climate change are further eroding the economy in regions around the world. The cost in damage to the US economy just from Hurricanes Katrina, Rita, Ike and Gustav is estimated in excess of $240 billion. Floods, draughts, wildfires, tornados and other extreme weather events have decimated ecosystems on every continent, crippling not only agricultural output but also infrastructures, slowing the global economy and displacing millions of human beings in the process.

What the world needs now is a powerful new economic narrative that will push the discussion and the agenda around the global credit crisis, peak oil and climate change from fear to hope and from economic constraints to commercial possibilities. The great pivotal economic changes in world history have occurred when new energy regimes converge with new communication regimes. When that convergence happens, society may be restructured in wholly new ways. Today, the same design principles and smart technologies that made the Internet possible, along with vast 'distributed' global communication networks, are just beginning to be used to reconfigure the world's power grids so that people can produce renewable energy and share it peer-to-peer, just as they now produce and share information, creating a new, decentralised form of energy use. We need to envision a future in which millions of individuals can collect and produce locally generated renewable energy in their homes, offices, shops, factories and technology parks, store that energy in the form of hydrogen, and share their power generation with each other across a Europe-wide intelligent intergrid.

This new economic narrative is just now emerging as industries begin to hurriedly introduce renewable energies, zero-emission and positive-power buildings, hydrogen and other storage technologies, intelligent utility networks, and electric and fuel-cell plug-in vehicles, laying the groundwork for a distributed post-carbon third industrial revolution, which should have as powerful an economic impact in the twenty-first century as the convergence of print technology with coal and steam-power technology had on the nineteenth century, as well as the coming together of electrical forms of communication with oil and the internal combustion engine on the twentieth century.

European and US leaders will not resolve the current economic crisis until they recognise that their main problem is not financial but legal. The primary cause of the current global economic crisis is the trillions of dollars of 'toxic paper' on the balance sheets of financial institutions, scaring off potential creditors and investors who lack the legal means to understand what this paper signifies, how much there is, who has it and who might be a bad risk. To get credit flowing again, policy makers must target their real enemy: the debasement of the legal financial documents that represent value, allow it to be transferred and signal risk.

Look around: everything of economic value that you own – house and car titles, mortgages, checking accounts, stocks, contracts, patents, other people's debts (including derivatives) – is documented on paper. You are able to hold, transfer, assess and certify the value of such assets only through documents that have been legally authenticated by a global system of rules, procedures and standards. Ensuring that the relationship between those documents and each of the assets they represent is never debased requires a formidable system of legal property rights that produces the trust allowing credit and capital to flow and markets to work.

It is through paper that we connect and know the global economy. It is impossible to do business on a national level – never mind in a globalised marketplace – without reliable legal documentation. Yet this worldwide web of trust is now crashing down. In recent years, governments have debased paper by carelessly allowing into the market a biblical flood of financial instruments derived from bad mortgages nominally valued at some $600 trillion or more – twice as much as all the rest of the world's legal paper, whether it represents cash, traditional financial assets, or property, tangible or intangible.

The astonishing quantity of these documents, and the fact that they're so tangled up and poorly recorded, is making it difficult to determine how much there is, what it's worth or who holds it. Given that the volume of these derivatives dwarfs all other paper, the mess is also undermining one of the greatest achievements of property law: the power to identify and isolate with precision every asset and every particular interest on that asset. Thus a meagre 7 per cent default on sub-prime mortgages that were funded or insured by derivatives – maybe only a few hundred billion dollars' worth of toxic paper – is debasing the rest of the economic paper and contaminating the entire economy. There is no other vehicle available for representing and ensuring value; by debasing paper you demolish the trust that holds the global economy together. Because this toxic paper refers to credit and capital, it affects all economic activity; the loss of trust spares no one, spreading out in all directions and beyond local bubbles, whether sub-prime housing or dot.com. And then staring you in the face may be the worst recession in modern history.

The solution could not be clearer: we must restore trust in paper. That requires finding this toxin and purging it. I have identified at least five obstacles that authorities must overcome to come up with a complete and convincing plan and move on it without hesitation.

Obstacle 1: Governments know more about controlling the money they issue and preventing it from being debased than they do about protecting credit. Though money can become credit, the overwhelming amount of available credit is made up of proprietary paper, such as mortgages, bonds and derivatives, all of which is not money per se but has some of the financial attributes of money – what economists used to call 'moneyness'. To prevent the debasement of paper and adequately infer its value, the Obama administration must turn to the well-tested rules ensuring paper's credibility:

- *All documents and the assets and transactions they represent or are derived from must be recorded in publicly accessible registries.* It is only by recording, arranging and formatting such factual knowledge – and updating it constantly – that we can detect overly creative financial and contractual instruments whose growth could lead to recession.
- *The law has to take into account the 'externalities' or side effects of all financial transactions – according to the age-old legal principle of* erga omnes *('in relation to all'), historically developed under property law to protect third parties from the negative consequences of secret deals carried out by aristocracies unaccountable to no one but themselves.* Applying this rule to financial paper would help ensure that derivatives always move in step with the general interest and allow government to protect those not directly involved in the deal but suffer from its effects.
- *Every financial deal must be firmly tethered to the real performance of the asset from which it originated.* This ensures that the amount of debt secured or created on the basis of assets does not become dangerously 'out of scale' with those assets that underlie or guarantee the debt – a discrepancy that

is the most prominent cause of a recession, according to the economist John Kenneth Galbraith. By aligning debts to assets, we can create simple and understandable benchmarks for detecting quickly whether a financial transaction has been created to help production or to build a casino for making bets on the performance of distant 'underlying assets'.

- *Government should never forget that production always takes priority over finance.* Finance supports wealth creation but in itself creates no value (as both Adam Smith and Karl Marx stated). It should be treated as a kind of infrastructure, like roads and bridges. We should not support solutions to the crisis that sacrifice the property and the wealth of producers to subsidise the mess created by unruly financing – unless it benefits the commonweal.

- *Government can encourage assets to be leveraged, transformed, combined, recombined, sliced and diced, and repackaged into any number of tranches – provided the process intends to improve the value of the original asset.* The principal justification for bestowing the legal privilege to manufacture a new financial instrument should be to create additional real wealth and not just another opportunity for gambling.

- *Government can no longer tolerate the use of opaque and confusing language in drafting financial instruments; clarity and precision are indispensable for the creation of credit and capital through paper.* Much derivative paper lacks transparency and is not standardised, scattered helter-skelter all over the market in thousands of idiosyncratic types of documents so complex and unreadable that even to put a value on them or gauge their risk is a stretch. A satisfactory estimate of the value of derivatives will be difficult, until authorities categorise them and clear up the existing confusion.

Obstacle 2: US and European authorities find it difficult to believe that the fundamental cause of a recession could be a poorly paperised legal system. But in emerging markets, like the one I come from, the importance of paper is obvious. Most of our people are poor and live in the anarchy of the shadow economy, where their assets and contracts are covered by paper that is endemically toxic: not recorded, not standardised, difficult to identify, hard to locate and with a real value so opaque that ordinary people cannot build trust in each other or be trusted in global markets. Credit paralysis is a chronic condition. So when I look at this recession – triggered by toxic paper – I feel really at home. Western politicians must not forget what their own greatest thinkers have been saying for the last three centuries, from Kant to Charles Sanders Pierce and Wittgenstein – namely, that all our obligations and commitments are derived from words recorded on paper with great precision.

Obstacle 3: Some authorities still cling to the hope that the existing market will eventually sort things out – that all that is required is recapitalising banks, stricter oversight and injecting money into the economy. That won't be enough. Modern legal markets only work if paper is reliable and people have access to credit and explicit information. 'Let the market do its work' now means, in effect, 'let the shadow economy do its work' – where the main beneficiaries are vulture capitalists and loan sharks, who devour producers with good credit scores but no credit.

Obstacle 4: Many now claim that it is virtually impossible to identify and value all the toxic paper now on the financial institutions' books. Yet in the past US and European lawyers and bureaucrats have proved brilliant at sorting out toxic paper, whether it referred to bad debt, confusing claims or opaque legislation. They thus have untangled claims after the California gold rush, picked up the pieces of Europe's crumbling pre-capitalist order, converted Japan's feudal enclaves into a market economy after the Second World War and reunified Germany after the fall of the Berlin Wall. That's the process of capitalism: continuous detoxification. And we're hard at it today, too, in developing countries, searching for toxic paper – informal titles, licences, contracts, laundered money and identity documents – in an effort to bring people into the mainstream.

Obstacle 5: Governments can no longer delegate the solution exclusively to financial specialists who operate within the narrow context of the derivatives market. The law that governs derivatives lacks the standards required to keep paper tethered to reality, the indicators to size up the damage and the tools to sort out the growing conflicts of interest between the holders of derivative paper and the rest of society. Nor does the financial community have the inclination, the incentives or the economic interest for such a down-and-dirty job.

The Real Economy is the Law

There is a myth that 'the real economy' is about natural resources, production and hard work. Yet in Latin America, we export gold, copper, soybeans, airplanes, cars, natural gas and oil. But a real economy where everyone can get connected to the rest of the world is a goal that we are still striving for. What has bestowed prosperity on the West is the ability to trust and cooperate on an expanded scale, form credit and capital, and combine ingredients from a variety of sources into products of increasing complexity. That requires legal property paper, and therein stands the real economy.

Escaping this recession requires restoring order, precision and trust to financial paper. That will be a daunting legal and political challenge – legal, because government has allowed the paper that represents assets to cross the line from the rule of law into the incomplete legal space of derivatives; political, because only fixing the law can eventually stop the recession, and those responsible for making laws are politicians. The hard decisions about locating, valuing, and isolating the toxic paper, and figuring out who will foot the bill for the losses – taxpayers, banks or vulture capitalists – will be easier to make the sooner politicians realise that the alternative could be the collapse of the very system that has generated the most prosperity in history – and all hell breaking loose.

GUY VERHOFSTADT

Recalling what has happened to solve the current world economic and financial crisis since its outbreak in 2008, facts and figures prove my theory that the brunt of anti-crisis measures was borne by national public authorities, not by international bodies who could have fought the situation in a more effective way. Every nation first of all was trying to save its own banks, insurance and other companies, its own institutions and its own workforce for a combined amount of an estimated $5,000 billion. As a result, little money was left for a regional or global approach. While these national efforts did not match the estimated $20,000 billion that evaporated in the worldwide crisis (not just virtual money, to be deleted by one fingertip, but also the savings of millions of our co-citizens and the financial resources of our investment funds), the effects of these efforts cannot yet be estimated; however, they did not dampen my scepticism, based on empirical evidence, that national efforts cannot prevent or solve a truly international crisis.

Of course, the world crisis was met by a growing awareness of the need for international cooperation. Since the outbreak no week passed without an international meeting in America, Asia or Europe. G4, G7, G8, G20, the International Monetary Fund, the OECD, the World Bank, ordinary and extraordinary meetings, including the European institutions, APEC, ASEAN and ASEM. All contributed to a new sense of urgency; nevertheless, the staggering number of meetings was not matched by impressive results, with few conclusions going further than freewheeling recommendations, with financial resources to be invested in a regional or global approach too meagre to divert the crisis.

For 2008 and 2009, the changing emphasis of G8 to G20 was the most promising step taken. Indeed the G20 includes not only the most industrialised nations (represented by the G8 and the European G4) but also the emerging economies (Argentina, Australia, Brazil, China, India, Indonesia, Mexico, South Africa, South Korea . . .), representing a massive 90 per cent of world production and 80 per cent of world trade. Particularly important was the April 2009 G20 summit, where it was agreed that $1,000 billion was to be injected into global economics. This was paramount for rising expect-ations of a global response. But I did not see any prospect of President Obama's 'historical turning point' or of 'the most drastic reform of the world's financial system since 1945', echoed by the French President Sarkozy. Strength-ening existing institutions is no reform. National not global interests still prevail within the realm of many institutions, including the IMF and the World Bank and unless these institutions can be reformed effectively in the interests of the many, not the few, additional means will not change their course of action. On the contrary, such means prevent change.

But things are now even worse. Even the European institutions within the union did not take up the challenge of the times in 2008 and 2009. Throughout the worst economic or financial crisis since the 1930s we did not hear one single European solution. We have yet to see one European economic and financial policy that would save our banks and companies. We did not even find, nor did we follow, one European economic recovery plan. What we saw in Europe and within the Union was twenty-seven member states trying to save themselves.

First of all an economic and monetary union, the EU, even in its core business, failed to develop a common approach to recovery to save its financial infrastructure. Europeans still stick to twenty-seven separate plans, which are often the most protective. Even when combined, these twenty-seven plans represent only €200 billion, or roughly 1.5 per cent of EU GDP, for €170 billion to be financed and to be devoted by the single EU member states, not by the union. Even if we take into account the dubious 'automatic stabilisers' (such as unemployment compensation and corporate and indi-vidual income-tax adjustments), European recovery plans still only amount to €400 billion, or about 3 per cent of EU GDP, half the American figure. Compare this meanwhile to the USA, where President Obama introduced a recovery plan worth about $787 billion (€600 billion), 6 per cent of American GDP, and to China, which went even further, devoting a staggering 14 per cent of Chinese GDP (about €450 billion) to its recovery plan.

One recovery plan for the USA, one for China; twenty-seven for the Euro-pean Union – twenty-seven 'national' recovery plans, allowing any member state first of all to save its own banks, its own enterprises, its own 'crown jewels', its own employment figures. Introducing 'sovereign funds' to save 'vital' national sectors; a catalogue of different priorities, nationalising banks in the UK, recapitalising them in Germany, lowering taxes here, investing in education and infrastructure there. However you look at them, they are still protective measures and as such the absolute opposite of European princi-ples. 'British jobs for British workers', we heard from the United Kingdom, the European counterpart of the 'buy-American clause' in the first Obama recovery plan. European states joined nationalistic protective ranks, as if the European Union did not exist.

One reason for the fragmented and scattered European approach to the crisis is the standstill of European integration these last five years. Five years after the greatest enlargement of the union, going from fifteen to twenty-five member states in 2004, the long-awaited reform treaty of Lisbon, signed in 2007 but not yet ratified by the twenty-seven member states, involves crucial proposals to deepen the union: adaptation of its major institutions to an ever-enlarging union; the presidency; the high representative for a European foreign and defence policy; changes to the Commission and the European Parliament. We should also see a review of the union's constitutional framework, enhancing the efficiency and democratic legitimacy of the union, improving the coherence of its actions to provide more decision making by qualified majorities, while giving a new impetus to the union's Charter of Fundamental Rights and Liberties. After about five years of virtual standstill, Europe, I hope, is moving again. And it's up to the new European Parliament to take the lead and use its enlarged competences to foster a more united Europe.

But this virtual standstill of European integration – since popular referendums in France and the Netherlands in 2005 turned down the European constitution we signed in 2003 – is not the only reason for European impotence to formulate and to implement a truly European recovery plan. Even within the reform treaty of Lisbon, the union does not have the means nor the competences to adopt a federal approach for the twenty-seven member states combined. That's why I wrote *The United States of Europe* in 2005, now translated into eighteen languages, inviting the member states to accomplish and to complete the most powerful economic, financial and commercial union in the world by installing a federal European authority, under European parliamentary control and regulation, at least for those willing to move further on their way to European unity, beginning with the sixteen member states of the eurozone – member states with a single currency and already gifted with a European Central Bank. I am convinced this eurozone and the ECB in 2008 and 2009 played a pivotal role in preventing a worst-case scenario for the most threatened European economies within the eurozone. But the eurozone countries could have done better with a unified economic and financial policy, yet to be introduced.

NORBERT WALTER

It is highly questionable to call on banks to maintain or even expand lending volumes as a quid pro quo for state support in the financial crisis. It is well understood that the rationale of state support is to maintain the intermediation function of the financial system. At the same time, asking banks to expand lending volumes in the face of an imminent crisis is likely to be counterproductive. What should be called for is prudent lending and, if need be, government guarantees for lending using traditional forms of governmental support scheme for lending to corporations. Moreover, expanding lending would be tantamount to making the same mistake twice: after all, the crisis was caused not least by excessive lending.

A major dilemma in the current situation is how to prevent a severe contraction of viable credit to households and to non-financial firms, while at the same time facilitating an orderly reduction of excessive leverage in the financial system. This dilemma is, however, even more serious for economic policy makers than for individual banks.

Are political institutions working to develop a clear view about the level and rate of growth of bank credit that is desirable to cushion macroeconomic activity and asset prices in the current downturn? Such a view could help to clarify the time span and the rate at which the banking system as a whole should deleverage as well as what this means in the short and medium term for private- and public-sector actions to strengthen banks' capital adequacy.

So far, deleveraging is primarily affecting trading-book assets, not the loan book. Instead, traditional lending to non-banks in Europe has hardly suffered at all. In fact, loan volumes to both non-financial corporations and private households continued to rise in many European countries throughout 2008, defying the often-cited 'credit crunch' even though growth rates have been receding steadily since the beginning of 2008. Most banking groups report that they are willing to lend, but that there is a lack of loan demand.

The official line therefore requires consistency: if banks are to be criticised for being reckless and careless in their lending decisions prior to the outbreak of the crisis, they should not be criticised for now applying the lessons they have learned. Similarly, if regulators discuss measures that will drastically reduce leverage (e.g. leverage ratios) or make equity more expensive (e.g. retention on securitisations) then it should come as no surprise if banks reduce their balance sheets in anticipation.

We should also be aware that the modern banking model of active risk and balance-sheet management will survive, though in a modified form – but there will be no return to the outdated model of pure on-balance-sheet intermediation.

Many people surmise that it was the ever-growing sophistication of financial markets that led to the financial crisis. Indeed, many commentators have suggested that bankers were like the sorcerer's apprentice, conjuring up the spirits but unable to control them. Specifically, these critics point to securitisation and other forms of credit-risk transfer as possibly the main culprits in the crisis. Against this background, some in the industry predict that we will return to the 'good old days' of traditional banking, when banks took deposits, assumed risk in the form of loans and held it on their balance sheet until maturity. Correspondingly, many politicians, regulators and academics want to make securitisations and other forms of credit-risk transfer more difficult, if not impossible to attain.

As indicated, many commentators have seized on the death of the archetypal Wall Street investment banks and have declared the end of the era of modern finance based on capital markets. Again, this seems premature. What is true is that the model of the highly leveraged investment bank conducting short-term refinancing in wholesale markets is defunct. This, however, does not mean that investment-banking services are also defunct. These services include issuance business and underwriting, commission business, trading and market making as well as advisory; henceforth, these will be provided by the respective business divisions of large, diversified financial institutions with a strong capital base, a reliable funding structure and a global reach.

The crisis has shown the value of a diversified business model. Pure investment-banking models may survive in the form of smaller institutions that are likely to be partnership-based. These institutions will, however, be niche players, who may lack two features demanded by bigger clients: global coverage and the balance-sheet clout needed to handle large transactions.

To be fair, large and diverse financial institutions have their own problems: they can be difficult to manage and, crucially, investors now tend to be sceptical of opaque, unwieldy conglomerates. Large, diversified financial institutions therefore present special management challenges that require strong leadership: firstly, to impose discipline on business divisions (e.g. internal pricing of funding); secondly, to realise synergies (one face to the customer; joint product development); and thirdly, to impose transparency on corporate structure and on performance of individual business divisions.

To paraphrase Bill Gates: investment banking is important, investment banks are – probably – not.

It is fitting that a new Bretton Woods is being discussed now. It is, in many ways, a welcome 'global' response to this 'global' financial crisis, by reconsidering and reforming the out-dated international governance structure of the world economic system.

The original Bretton Woods institutions were created after the Second World War in recognition of the fact that even developed countries can experience liquidity crises and that global efforts are required for economic development. In the throes of this formidable economic crisis, it is appropriate to consider the ways in which the international economic system can be reformed to govern globalised financial markets and interlinked economies.

Although there have been calls for some time for the current international financial institutions to be more representative of emerging economies, it took this financial crisis to underscore the extent to which the global economic structure has changed. Namely, this pertains to the global imbalances which permitted the West to access cheap credit despite their low saving rates, particularly the US and the UK. The worst banking crisis since the Great Depression strongly suggests that a global rules-based system is necessary to oversee financial markets and coordinate economic management. The issues are rather different from those of the Bretton Woods era, and would require further development of international economic institutions and laws to govern an increasingly multipolar world economy.

A new Bretton Woods has to be accommodative of the shifting global economic weight towards emerging economies, but also able to act quickly to stabilise financial markets. This would require promulgating international economic law and regulations as well as reforming the current international financial institutions, such as the IMF. The financial crisis has revealed the extent of the interlinkages between markets, making it apparent that cross-border dealings require regulation. For instance, there should be an international clearing house for financial transactions and also a body to monitor cross-border capital flows. The latter of these could be under the auspices of an institution like the Bank for International Settlements (or BIS, which is the central banks' bank) with power to demand greater transparency in financial dealings in all major markets. This need not be more burdensome than what national regulations already require, though clearly reform is needed there as well. The resultant multilevel system of governance could be modelled after federal regulatory systems such as in the US. However, regulation cannot be the entire answer, as active engagement by regulators will always be needed, since written rules are unlikely to keep up with innovative markets. In a new Bretton Woods system, there should then exist regulators operating under the auspices of an international regulatory framework to monitor world markets. Second, banks are indeed global or at least regional, such as in Europe, so there should be a coordinated and efficient deposit-insurance scheme up to a widely accepted limit so that confidence is assured and bank runs are not a possibility even if there are bank failures, as is the system in America. Third, the existing international institutions continue to have important roles, but need reform, including expanding their membership to reflect the shift of global economic power to the East. Even before this crisis, there was much talk about increasing transparency and accountability in the IMF in particular. As a provider of liquidity when countries are in trouble, it is telling us that Iceland and Pakistan were reluctant to seek their assistance and turned instead to the emerging powers of Russia and China, respectively. Similar reforms to strengthen the mandate of the World Bank would also be warranted. Fourth, a likely response to looming national recession is an increase in protectionist sentiment, evidenced in the Smoot–Hawley Act passed in the US in the Great Depression, which had the effect of slowing global trade and worsening the economic downturn. Any new Bretton Woods system should encompass reforms to the World Trade Organization (WTO). The WTO helps to establish a rules-based system for trade and should work to ensure that trade is not disrupted by protectionist tendencies that can arise in times of crisis. Its operation in the past decade suggests that it is a fairly efficient forum for resolving disputes, though the Doha Round extending its coverage to more traded goods and services has stalled. Enhancing the WTO should be part of any new system so that rules rather than power (and politics) are the premise of international trade; in other words, the development of international economic law.

Finally, an international body or forum cannot force its mandate on sovereign nations, but must appeal to the mutual self-interest of countries in maintaining stability by, for instance, monitoring the development of the so-called global imbalances that led to excess liquidity and mispriced risk. The onus cannot entirely be on one country, as macroeconomic forces are intertwined – e.g., if America didn't consume so much, then China would not be such a significant lender. A new set of Bretton Woods institutions that identified these economic flows and assessed their consequences would help policy makers coordinate responses to try to lean against future asset bubbles. Indeed, the next one could be in emerging economies, as cheap currencies and high levels of domestic savings fuel real-estate bubbles even as interest-rate cuts to stimulate the West promote global liquidity searching for the next investment opportunity, which will be in Asia in the next couple of years. It is therefore in the interest of all countries to have a system of international economic law and associated institutions, and a new Bretton Woods could be a positive legacy of this financial crisis.

FUTURE

JAMES ALEXANDER

As the world makes the transition into the age of sustainable living in a resource-constrained world we will see sweeping societal changes, not only for the individual but also for business and government.

Historically, Schumpeter's 'waves of creative destruction' have transformed society around the dominating set of technologies and context for a given era. In each era a new 'common sense' has emerged – and it is the innovative application of this common sense that drives success.

So what might this new common sense look like? Well, this is what I see in my crystal ball:

- A move towards being defined by our values, our ethos and our social networks, with a shift from conspicuous consumption to conscious consumerism.
- A move towards the leading of more fulfilled lives today, rather than seeking the promise of happiness in the future, with a rejection of borrowing to fund our purchases and an acceptance of individual and collective responsibility.
- A move from growth as defined purely by economic production (e.g. GDP) to growth as defined by sustainable wealth in its broadest sense, and which would include well-being as one of its measures. It is interesting to note that in his *Wealth of Nations*, Adam Smith did not define wealth solely in financial terms; instead, that interpretation was one we chose to adopt in our capitalist and consumer-driven era.
- A move from an era in which there has been a global tragedy of the commons to one in which communalism reins (e.g. look at the flourishing network in the UK of transition towns such as Totnes, Devon – see www.transitiontowns.org). We will look back on the previous era as the Age of Stupid, when we doubted the veracity of scientific studies into climate change and as a result fished our oceans dry and polluted our skies to such an extent that we warmed the planet.
- A move towards smaller and more nimble network-based systems and away from big and inefficient command-and-control structures; e.g. note the

rapid emergence of smart grids, which will use digital technology to gather and distribute electricity from scattered sources, thereby saving energy, reducing costs and increasing reliability and transparency. Of course there will continue to be 'big' companies, but these will increasingly become networked amalgamations; e.g. look at the ecosystem that Amazon has created.

- Successful brands will no longer be just marques, they will reflect their customers' values and represent new outlooks and lifestyle choices; Timberland, Patagonia and Howies are examples of these new brands.
- A move from trust in global institutions to trust in individuals; from empirical analysis and evidence-based policy making to policy making that looks to a new morality based on community, transparency, ethicality.
- The need for intervention and strong leadership from government to see us through a period when the required market mechanisms establish themselves, not yet working quickly enough to adjust to living in a resource-constrained world; e.g. look at the shambles of European carbon markets and their tiny impact on the power generation market as an example of this.
- We will see innovation in the financial world and a flourishing of business models that harness new technology, put the user in control and adhere to strong community ethos. For example, witness the growth of community banks around the world and the development of – and I declare an interest here – Zopa and social-finance models such as Muhammad Yunus's Grameen Bank.

The transition from one era to another is often a time of turbulence and fear, but it is also a wonderfully exciting time – one that will bring in a new wave of technologial development and societal evolution, to forge the new common sense and create a better way of leading our individual and collective lives. It is our opportunity to create a better future.

JACQUES ATTALI

The most certain and perhaps the most unsettling development of the next decade will be an increase in the world's population of a billion people, which will exceed 8 billion, equalling the increase in world population between the beginning of AD and the middle of the Second World War. The majority of this new population will be made up of Africans, India's population will outnumber China's population, the population of Europe will stagnate, the population of the US will continue to rise, reaching nearly 330 million compared to 300 million today, with immigration accounting for two-thirds of it and reducing the average age of the population in the future.

Furthermore, over a billion of the rural population will migrate into cities, where almost two-thirds of human beings will be living, and the number of people who will move to live in a country different from the one in which they were born will double, from 200 to 400 million. Most of the new migrants to the United States will be of Mexican, Chinese, Filipino, Indian and Vietnamese in origin. In 2020, nearly one in five Americans will be an immigrant and one in three Americans will be of Hispanic origin.

Longer life expectancy and the decrease in the number of children being born per woman will lead to an increase in the average age of man, which is presently twenty-eight, while family support networks will disappear along with rural migration. People aged over sixty-five, who are becoming more numerous throughout the world, will have additional needs and will become even greater in number. By 2020, there will be more than 300 million people aged over sixty in China; more than a quarter of Chinese people will have passed the age of retirement, while there will still probably be no widespread retirement scheme in the country.

By 2020, particularly because of continued economic growth in Asian countries, the global middle class will grow by nearly 2 billion people, representing nearly half of the world population compared to one-third today. Six hundred million of them will be in China and India. This new middle class will want the same kind of life as in the West: freedom, care, housing, cars and education. They will buy a car when their annual income reaches the equivalent of $5,000 today, which could then lead to an increase of one-third in the number of vehicles by 2020, unless a global economic depression occurs. They will travel and increase the number of foreign tourists from 900 million to 1.2 billion.

The scientific and technological breakthroughs of the next ten years will follow largely predictable work patterns.

As has been the case for millennia, these breakthroughs will primarily aim to allow people to accomplish the same tasks with reduced effort. And to achieve this, they will improve energy efficiency and the way data are transmitted. These will be implemented when they can overcome an obstacle to productivity growth. For instance, the crisis that began in 1873 (which led to the seizure of power by the United States from Great Britain) brought about the emergence of the oil industry and the development of the modern banking industry, which finances the former. Similarly, the 1929 crisis was accompanied by a wave of technological advances revolving around the use of electricity (elevators, radios, television, and household appliances). Finally, in the seventies, the rising cost of white-collar work in large American and Japanese companies led to the emergence of the microprocessor and to the widespread use of computers.

In the next decade, population growth will lead to further scarcity of all natural resources, which will increase their prices, slow down growth and lead to the emergence of a new wave of technological advances forming an apparently disparate group but in actuality an extremely coherent one, for which we can retain the English acronym NBIC (nanotechnology, biotechnology, information technology and cognitive sciences).

Nanotechnology will open new opportunities for the miniaturisation of microprocessors, with countless applications in logistics, energy saving, and medicine; carbon nanotubes, which will make up the first application, will be particularly suitable for hydrogen storage and will transform, for example, the textile industry by virtue of their exceptional physical properties.

Biotechnology will raise the odds in cattle breeding, agriculture and health; we will soon know how to produce drugs tailored to specific genetic defects and how to genetically study the impact of combinations of known drugs. We will also know how to produce plastic within plants or specific tissues. It will then become possible to reprogramme tissues, to use bacteria to produce chemicals, medicines and textiles, or to store data. In more general terms, we will have a better knowledge of how to take biological complexity into account when finding complex yet more realistic solutions, such as 'pleotherapy'. Given the major reduction in the cost of genome decoding, more accurate diagnoses will be much more likely, and it will be possible to create artificial cells and organs from stem cells or to return specialised cells to the state of stem cells.

Information technology has not completed the transformation of industrial and service-related processes. The Internet will revolutionise communication between objects and people. Three-D, cloud computing and parallel processing will transform industrial processes; the semantic Web will change all teaching, medicine and consulting professions. These technologies will rapidly develop the foundations of the hypersurveillance of objects and people, also called 'traceability'. New robots, mainly Japanese, Korean and American, will be present throughout production, daily life and games; they will be able to transport heavy loads across challenging terrains, to help in the most sophisticated surgical procedures and assist people in household tasks.

Cognitive sciences and neurosciences will revolutionise behaviour analysis, brain medicine and learning processes at a time when knowledge and health will account for an increasing share of spending, where ageing will require devoting many more efforts to treating degenerative brain diseases and where the increasingly rapid accumulation of knowledge will require a radical change in the learning process. In the long term, these new sciences will have staggering effects on what we know about self-consciousness, self-esteem, and the idea that we have of freedom and happiness.

The development of each of these technologies depends on the development of the others: no genetics without information technology; no biotechnology without nanotechnology; no traceability without nanotechnology, biotechnology and information technology; no robotics without biotechnology and nanotechnology, which will build robots the size of flies and controllable by the brain; no neuroscience without all the others. This combination will allow exponential breakthroughs. Moreover, unexpected technologies will appear by the mere combination of existing technologies, as was the case of the Wii, the unlikely combination of two well-known and very simple technologies.

These technologies will revolutionise the practices of many industries and services, particularly those of health, education, media, banking and consulting.

Each of them however, will pose considerable ethical problems because of the uncertainty of their impact on human nature and democracy. For instance, carbon nanotubes could have a destructive impact on human cells; genetically modified organisms may have an irreversible impact on the structure of DNA; traceability instruments could become instruments of political control capable of destroying democracy. Finally, we might wonder what will remain of freedom once we are able to decipher the chemical processes governing the tangle of neurons and synapses in making a particular decision. These concerns could slow down the development of such practices, as long as their threats are not eliminated.

The cumulative effect of demographic and cultural vitality, the evolution of saving sources, the emergence of technologies, and new debts caused by the current crisis and by all other crises to come will cause a major geopolitical change marked by an accelerating decline of the United States – at least a relative decline and sometimes even an absolute one: much of the American population is already worse off than twenty years ago.

After 2012, the Asian financial capital will exceed that of the United States. After 2013, China's GDP will be half of the US GDP, compared to a fifth in 2006. Thus, the United States could lose its economic supremacy in the next ten years, but no other nation looks powerful enough to replace it politically. If it is not able to become an industrial nation again and to have a positive balance of payments, it will be politically dependent on its creditors and go into decline. However, as nobody is interested in chaos and many are interested in having a very powerful American army, its creditors will therefore help it to maintain its supremacy, at least for a time, even on credit.

Europe seems set to stagnate in the coming decade, unless there is an unlikely political surge.

Africa's emergence will accelerate, owing to the ongoing changes in governance, demography and technology. The GDP of the continent, gone from $130 billion in 1980 to $300 billion in 2008 and with an annual average growth rate of 7 per cent for ten years should continue to grow at a rate of 3 per cent over the rate of world growth in the next decade. Corruption will be reduced, governance will be improved and democracy will progress. Capital markets will open in all these countries: there are already sixteen African countries that deal in the shares of 500 companies. Foreign investment will increase.

Only the Middle East (stuck between a high-powered, declining West and the booming Africa and Asia) will stay away. In particular, the Arab world will accrue all inequalities and a high level of poverty, despite its considerable natural resources; its population will reach 400 million people, of which 60 per cent will be urban, with an area comprising over 69 per cent desert and an average age of twenty-two compared to the world average of twenty-eight.

This already existing trend will accelerate towards a polycentric and fragmented world, looking a lot like the one in the late Middle Ages, and with the same proportions: as in the fourteenth century, cities and corporations will have more power than nations; forty city regions are already producing two-thirds of the world's wealth and are home to 90 per cent of its innovations. They will be increasingly run in a relatively authoritarian manner in general, in a kind of a state capitalism; we will be witness to the proliferation of epidemics, the denial of the future, the return of religious intolerance, a disregard for the natural world, while the number of lawless zones will increase. We will see how new dictatorships, criminal authorities, warlords, pirates and privateers, enclaves of the rich and timeless ashrams will settle.

The few existing elements of global governance will be threatened. Indeed, this is already the case: no significant new international agreement has been signed in any field since those creating the World Trade Organization in 1994 and the Nuclear Nonproliferation Treaty in 1995. Many other initiatives aiming at putting global rules in place (concerning climate or poverty) have failed or unravelled. Thus, the world is heading for chaos. All alone, corporate models of coordination persist and increase as in the Middle Ages. We will witness the advent of corporate coordination mechanisms in many areas, especially technological, financial and those related to raw materials, just as in football, on the Internet, in aviation security and in banks and insurance companies.

JAGDISH BHAGWATI [1]

When the twin crises erupted on Wall Street and Main Street, each one of them fierce in itself but far more frightening when they interacted, populists rushed forward to celebrate the demise of capitalism and, for added gratification, plunge their pitchforks into its dead corpse. Since then, they have had their champagne parties. By now, however, the fizz is gone and the rush to judgement by capitalism's obituarists has left us with tattered myths and egregious fallacies that invite scrutiny and refutation.

I can do no better than begin by citing a prominent populist, an icon to the madding crowd who would like to drive a stake through capitalism and globalisation (which is viewed, not without some justification, as an international extension of capitalism). I am speaking of my Columbia University colleague Joseph E. Stiglitz. In 2001 he shared the Nobel Prize in Economics with the remarkable George Akerlof of Berkeley, who pioneered the study of asymmetric information with his brilliant paper on 'the market for lemons', the first to draw on the insight that the sellers of used cars (i.e., lemons) had more information than the buyers, a situation that would generally lead to 'market failure'. In the long sweep of market failures, with virtually every generation since Adam Smith's focusing on a different one appropriate to its time, asymmetric information is just one more, of course, and not even among the most important, it could be argued.

But Stiglitz made a much-cited claim that the current crisis was for capitalism (and markets) the equivalent of the collapse of the Berlin Wall. Now, we know that all analogies are imperfect, but this one is particularly dicey. When the Berlin Wall collapsed, we saw the bankruptcy of both authoritarian politics and an economics of extensive, almost universal, ownership of the means of production and central planning. We saw a wasteland. When Wall Street and Main Street were shaken by crisis, however, we witnessed merely a pause in prosperity, not a devastation of it.

[1] This entry is based on a longer article printed in *World Affairs Journal*, vol. 172, issue 2, October 2009.

We had enjoyed almost two decades in which the liberal reforms under-taken by China and India, with nearly half the world's population between them, had produced an unprecedented prosperity that (and this must be emphasised) had finally made a significant impact on poverty, just as we reformers had asserted that it would. The rich countries, with a steady expansion of liberal policies during the 1950s and 1960s, had also registered substantial prosperity. (This was episodically interrupted by exogenous circum-stances like the success of OPEC in 1971 and the Volcker-led purging of the 1980s, but generally always resumed with robust growth.) Meanwhile, an increasing number of the poor countries had turned to democracy, altering the status quo ante in which India had been the one 'exceptional nation' to have embraced and retained democracy after independence.

Some will object that economies have at times registered high growth rates for long periods despite bad economic policies. But we must ask: are such growth rates sustainable? I tell the story about how my radical Cambridge teacher, Joan Robinson, was once observed many years ago agreeing with the mainstream Yale developmental economist Gus Ranis on the subject of Korea's phenomenal growth. The paradox was resolved when it turned out that she was talking about North Korea and he about South Korea. Now, more than three decades later, we know who was right. In a similar vein, Soviet growth rates were high for a long period, thanks to exceptionally high investment rates and despite the horrendous absence of incentives and the embracing of autarky. But then the Soviet Union descended into a steady decline until a mismanaged transition with perestroika plunged the country into negative growth rates.

The effort to make the anomalous into the universal is a polemical exercise. Some economists, such as Dani Rodrik, like to cite occasional high growth rates in countries without liberal – or, as some critics prefer because it sounds more sinister, 'neoliberal' – policies as a refutation of liberal policies. This, however, misses both the point of the issue and the sweep of history.

Other critics then shift ground, claiming that higher growth is beside the point and that we need to judge capitalism by whether or not it works for the poor. But slowly growing or stagnant economies cannot rescue the poor from their poverty on a sustained basis. In countries with massive poverty, such as India and China, economic success has had to come principally through rapid growth of incomes and jobs. This is, of course, common sense. Just as firms that make losses cannot finance corporate social-responsibility policies, countries with stagnant economic performance cannot rescue the poor from their poverty.

It was bad policy that kept China and India from growing in the first place. Only after liberal economic reforms did these countries register accelerated growth rates that, during the last twenty years, finally pulled nearly 500 million people above the poverty line. However grim the current crisis has been, it cannot be used to deny this elemental truth.

Arguing the other side of the coin, the AFL-CIO and other labour unions in the United States claim that trade with poor countries has produced paupers in the richer countries by depressing real wages. But this dire conclusion is not supported by empirical findings. My own analysis, dating back at least a decade (and extended in my 2004 book *In Defense of Globalization*), argued that, if anything, the fall in wages which labour-saving technical change and other domestic institutional factors would inevitably have brought about was actually moderated by trade with poor countries. This benign conclusion has since been reasserted by Robert Lawrence of Harvard's Kennedy School (despite an unsuccessful attempt by Paul Krugman in a recent Brookings paper, commissioned by Lawrence Summers, to prove otherwise). Indeed, the same goes for the effect of unskilled immigration on the wages of our unskilled workers. Giovanni Peri of UC Davis has shown for unskilled immigration what I showed for trade with poor countries: that the effect is benign.

Thus, we need not apologise for liberal policy in terms of its effects on overall prosperity, on poverty in poor countries, or on the wages of the poor in rich countries. To compare an interruption of this remarkable progress to the collapse of the Berlin Wall is like drawing a parallel between a tsunami and a summer storm that brings rain and a rich harvest to parched plains.

These critics, including Stiglitz and, ironically, George Soros (who has done rather well by working the markets), also argue that the current crisis spells the end of 'market fundamentalism'. My Swedish friend Leif Pagrotsky, who was a cabinet member in Prime Minister Goran Persson's government and is on the left in his country's Social Democratic Party, told me with amused astonishment that at a panel meeting at Columbia University in New York, Soros had accused him of exactly this sin. 'Market fundamentalism' has now become a phrase of scorn in these fringe populist circles, much like 'liberal' is in the fringe right-wing circles.

The presumption from which these critics start is that our markets were based in a pragmatic centre but then moved to the fundamental right, letting markets rip – and rip us apart. But this is totally wrong for much of the world, and certainly for many developing countries that had been mired in quite the opposite problem, an anti-market fundamentalism that was reflexively and irrationally hostile towards markets and reliant on knee-jerk interventionism that went so far that Adam Smith's invisible hand was not only not seen but never felt. When these countries finally realised the costs of their anti-market fundamentalism, they moved to the pragmatic centre. So, yes, there has been a shift in recent years, but it has not been from pragmatism to market fundamentalism, as critics such as Stiglitz and Soros would have us believe, but from anti-market fundamentalism to the centre.

A myth related to those above is the notion that somehow there was a consensus in Washington among the Bretton Woods institutions that drove the world into liberal reforms, which evolved into a malignant market fundamentalism. But anyone familiar with the measures undertaken with gusto in the Soviet Union (and then Russia), India and China, which together claim a gigantic share of the world population, has to know that these measures were endogenous, not imposed from without. The reformers in all of these countries were not bullied into submission, but driven by their increased awareness that without these liberal reforms their societies would continue to stagnate.

The precise mix of politics, institutions and history did matter in the specific trajectory of reforms chosen. In my Radhakrishnan Lectures at Oxford in 1993, I discussed the factors driving Indian reforms, which began in earnest in 1991 with the current prime minister, who was then the finance minister, leading the way. These included the fact that the reforms became inevitable as the dissonance grew between India's superiority complex about its 'ancient culture' and the 'inferior status' that its sorry economic performance had wrought. And as for the former USSR, the Russia expert Padma Desai has written that Mikhail Gorbachev and Eduard Shevardnadze finally decided that, without reforms, Soviet decline would continue to get worse and their superpower would be reduced to the size and influence of a super-beggar in world politics.

None of these reformers cared about what Bretton Woods institutions, or Washington more generally, thought. The idea of a 'Washington consensus' is little more than a Washington conceit developed by witless Western media and spread by anti-globalisationists and critics of capitalism, who find that the anti-Americanism this phrase invokes gets their critique greater mileage than its content actually merits.

Inevitably, the crisis on Wall Street has revived the never-ending notion that markets undermine morality. Oliver Stone, ever restless to recapture the days of former glory, has begun production on a sequel to the 1987 movie *Wall Street*, which immortalised Gordon Gekko as the symbol of markets and greed. But the debate on how markets affect morality has not always been a slam dunk for capitalism's naysayers. Matthew Arnold, especially in his influential 1868 book *Culture and Anarchy*, might have been spectacularly critical, but Voltaire's passionate defence of markets, most eloquently stated in his 1734 *Philosophical Letters*, made him the most influential hero of the new bourgeois age. He proposed quite reasonably that peace and social harmony, as opposed to the religious strife common until then, would flow from the secular religion of the marketplace.

After two and a half centuries of this fascinating debate, I have to say that my own sympathies lie with those who have found markets, on balance, to be on the side of the angels. But I should also add that I find the specific notion that markets corrupt our morals, and determine our ethical destiny, to be a vulgar quasi-Marxist notion about as convincing as that other vulgar notion that ownership of the means of production is critical to our economic destiny. The idea that working with and within markets fuels our pursuit of self-interest, greed, avarice and self-love, in ascending orders of moral turpitude, is surely at variance with what we know about ourselves.

Yes, markets will influence values. But, far more important, the values we develop will affect in several ways how we behave in the marketplace. Consider just the fact that different cultures exhibit different forms of capitalism. The Dutch burghers Simon Schama wrote about in *The Embarrassment of Riches* used their wealth to address the embarrassment of poverty. They, the Jains of Gujerat (from whom Mahatma Gandhi surely drew inspiration), and the followers of John Calvin were all taking values from religion and culture to bring morality to the market. Many economists, perhaps most noticeably André Sapir of Brussels, have used their study of the diverse forms of capitalism that flourish in the world to deny the claim that markets determine what we value. The Scandinavians, for example, have an egalitarian approach to their capitalism, which differs from what we find in the United States, where equality of access, rather than of success, is the norm.

So, where do we get our values? They come from our families, communities, schools, churches, and indeed from our religion and literature. My own exposure to the conflicts of absolute values came initially from reading Dostoevsky's *Crime and Punishment*, wherein Sofya Semyonovna Marmeladov turns to prostitution to support her family. My love of the environment came from reading Yasunari Kawabata's famous novel *The Old Capital*, which proposes a harmony between man and nature, rather than the traditional Christian belief that nature must serve man.

How does one react then to a phenomenon like Bernie Madoff? Does it not represent the corrosion of moral values in the marketplace? Not quite. The pay-offs from corner-cutting, indeed outright theft, have been so huge in the financial sector that those who are crooked are naturally drawn to such scheming. The financial markets did not produce Madoff's crookedness; Madoff was almost certainly depraved to begin with. The financial sector corrupts morality in the same sense that the existence of an escort service corrupted Eliot Spitzer. Should we blame the governor's transgressions on the call girls rather than on his own flaws?

Something more needs to be said about the notion that, at least in the financial sector where the collapse began, it was the ideology of markets and deregulation rather than factors such as lobbying by Wall Street to make profits that drove the crisis. That proposition is simplistic and therefore wrong.

Of course, the notion that freer financial markets and increased reliance on self-regulation would help the greater good played a role in what happened. The post-war period had shown, as noted above, the powerful effect of liberal economic policies on trade and direct foreign investment. But to carry over the legitimate approbation of freer trade in particular to the altogether more volatile financial sector, which represents the soft underbelly of capitalism, was surely unwarranted.

Pressure from the IMF and the US Treasury on developing countries to embrace capital-account convertibility (i.e., free capital flows, so one could walk into a bank and convert limitless domestic currency into whatever foreign currencies one chose) had been palpable, and was indeed a principal cause of the East Asian financial crisis in the late 1990s.

We must ask why some of the world's best economists, such as Larry Summers, went along with the assumption that the indisputable advantages of freer global trade would extend into the financial sector, when in fact they had to be aware of the asymmetry. Their blind spot was caused by what I called the Wall Street–Treasury Complex. The constant movement of people like Robert Rubin and lesser but still influential figures between Wall Street and the Treasury Department created a euphoria – shared by a large group of influential people who sport Brooks Brothers suits, belong to the same clubs and travel on the same circuits – about how markets that would serve the interests of Wall Street would function just as well in the financial sector as in trade. This euphoria led these gifted economists at the Treasury and the IMF to drop their guard and join in the chorus for freeing up capital flows.

Furthermore, we should not underestimate the role that good old-fashioned lobbying played in the crisis. One of the seminal moments occurred when the heads of the big five investment banks, among them future Treasury secretary Hank Paulson (then CEO of Goldman Sachs) 'persuaded' the SEC to impose no reserve requirements on their lending. The result was reckless over-leveraging that accentuated the crisis when the housing bubble burst and securitised mortgages became toxic assets. But this had to do more with lobbying for profit than with ideology. An ardent environmentalist and graduate of liberal-leaning Dartmouth College, Paulson was surely no ideologue on markets, the way Alan Greenspan, outspoken fan of Ayn Rand, had been during his time as Fed chair.

But why did the SEC agree to this demand? Answering this question takes

us right into the role played by governmental failure, not 'market fundamentalism', in creating the crisis. Senator Chuck Schumer, whose Wall Street
PAC contributors come with his political territory, is known for having indulged
in Japan-bashing, then India-bashing and now China-bashing. This time around,
though, he bought into the argument that Wall Street would lose out to
London if the demands of the investment banks were not met. So, he played
a crucial role in the 'race to the bottom' that was central to the crisis.

The governmental role in the crisis was also apparent in the way in which
congressmen of both parties bought into the argument that everyone, regardless of individual circumstances, *must* own a home, thus encouraging the
profligate spread of sub-prime mortgages that inflated the housing bubble
with what would become toxic assets. Instead of creating a house-owning
democracy, these fantasies created an inevitable crash that imperilled the
economy.

Columbia Law School professor Harvey J. Goldschmid, who served as an
SEC commissioner, has talked about the plethora of mortgages hawked by
unscrupulous, unqualified agents whose sleazy courtship of naïve clients
largely replaced the conventional, careful evaluation of servicing ability of
prospective homebuyers by small bankers: it was as if you were travelling in
planes flown by untrained pilots and owned by profit-seeking airlines that
sold seats to people who could hardly afford subway fares.

The packaging of these sub-prime mortgages into collateralised debt obligations called mortgage-backed securities (MBS) was married to the credit
default swaps (CDS) invented by J P Morgan bankers, which got third parties
like insurance giant AIG to assume the risk of default on these securities in
exchange for regular payments resembling insurance premiums. The MBS
were expanded massively, because it was assumed that the risk of default in
the underlying mortgages was minimal because not everyone would default
together. The massive exposure created by those who blithely issued CDS
but did not set aside adequate reserves to guard against a possible financial
tsunami guaranteed the collapse of the financial sector.

In short, few on Wall Street caught up in the euphoria over these financial innovations allowed for the reality of huge potential downsides that
should have required prudence and safeguards. All economists and policy
makers know about what Joseph Schumpeter called the 'creative destruction'
of capitalism, but the invention of these new financial instruments had a
wholly different downside possibility, one capable of bringing about what I
have called – and journalists such as Gillian Tett and Thomas L Friedman
have since called – 'destructive creation'.

This potential requires that innovation in the financial sector be dealt with
differently from other innovation. I have therefore argued that we need an

independent set of experts, who are familiar with Wall Street but are not part of it (or of the Wall Street–Treasury Complex), to evaluate the downside of new instruments, and to make that informed analysis available to regulators, who, after all, cannot regulate what they cannot understand.

Such a committee would not necessarily solve all problems lurking in our economic future. As Keynes once remarked in a letter to Kingsley Martin, editor of the *New Statesman*. 'The inevitable never happens. It is the unexpected always.' But such a committee, which in different versions is part of the new financial regulatory architecture now being discussed, might be able to make the unexpected a little less inevitable.

Need I argue further that the notion of capitalism as a collapsed system requiring invasive surgery is far from compelling? I hope not. But one observation must be made regarding what exactly needs to be done to strengthen capitalism today. Capitalism works best when those who do not succeed, and are buffeted by the vicissitudes of life, still believe in success – believe that those who do succeed put their wealth to good use, and do not merely engage in self-indulgence. Remember that the Calvinists and the Jains of Gujerat accumulated wealth but spent it not on themselves but on promoting social good.

Capitalism works well when those who lose feel that one day they might also win. This is the great American dream: even when mobility has been less real than imagined, the belief matters.

Today, in the United States, both 'stabilisers' of capitalism have taken a hit. There has been far too much flaunting of wealth, even as working-class incomes have stagnated, with magazines on 'How to Spend It' in the *Financial Times* and displays of the insufferably rich glitterati in the 'Style' section of the *New York Times*. These are among the countless examples of a compliant, complacent, profit-seeking media establishment giving such displays wider circulation even as they occasionally condemn the return of the Gilded Age.

CEOs in the manufacturing sector hit a nerve when they were seen cashing in stock options as their firms were failing, leaving their workers and shareholders with defunct stock options and stock. I believe that the condemnatory reaction arose not from the sums involved and notions of 'justice' and 'fairness', but from the fact that this phenomenon deeply offended the cultural and ethical sensibilities of Americans. Instead of standing at attention on their sinking ships while the passengers got out, CEOs commandeered the lifeboats and left those who depended on them to drown.

The concern with high pay is not an answer. American society, after all, tolerates extreme inequality in pay – college presidents, the critics of capitalism on campuses and on Wall Street; media anchors – in fact, virtually everyone enjoys salaries and emoluments that appear outrageous to someone else. In

India, when we espoused socialism, the cynical definition of outlawed luxury was goods that the socialists did not (presently) consume. Once I was at a Planning Commission seminar and a socialist planner said we should not spend scarce foreign exchange on importing lipstick. Instead of arguing the economics of what he had said, I simply said that, even as he spoke, I could smell the imported Brylcreem in his hair.

We need to take a different turn. Bill Gates and Warren Buffet offer splendid examples of great, capitalist fortunes put to social use, making the capitalism they exemplify more palatable. When modern corporations do this, we call it corporate social responsibility. More of this will clearly have to be done. But we also need to respond to the steady erosion of the American myth of mobility. Today, after nearly a quarter-century of wage stagnation, and growing evidence that educational access for the poor has also declined, that myth is in a disastrous decline. We have to respond by improving education and by relieving anxiety through reforms that make health care part of a basic provision for the poor. These reforms strengthen capitalism. Without them, the economic populists will enjoy a success that they do not deserve.

DAVID BLANCHFLOWER [1]

The current recession reflects more than just cyclical movements in consumer spending or investment. Rather the UK economy has been hit by the greatest financial crisis of our lifetimes. In the medium term the prospects for the UK will be dependent on a healthy financial sector and unless the problems in the financial sector can be successfully addressed, growth in the UK economy is unlikely to return to its potential rate in the near future.

Furthermore, conventional monetary- and fiscal-policy stimuli can only provide an accommodative background for structural adjustments within the financial sector. They cannot solve them per se. This has been more than evident as a range of initiatives, such as the bank recapitalisation scheme, have been necessary to prevent the collapse of the UK financial sector.

We need to clearly identify the structural problems in the financial sector and solve them. In short, a large part of our financial infrastructure remains dysfunctional because of the difficulties in valuing complex assets and derivatives, for which there is little investor appetite as a reappraisal of risk is taking place within the global economy. That these assets remain on banks' balance sheets has increased uncertainty about our banks' capital adequacy and remains a barrier to private investment.

A range of solutions has been proposed to solve this problem. For example, public purchases of 'troubled' assets, the creation of a 'bad bank' to purchase 'troubled' assets from financial institutions and, finally, outright nationalisation of our banks. In the UK we have concentrated on providing insurance against future losses from these assets, amongst other measures, to improve confidence in the capital adequacy of our banks. But it is possible further action may be necessary to bolster confidence in our financial institutions.

Indeed, further falls in asset and house prices will raise questions regarding the capital adequacy of the financial sector. Ben Bernanke has suggested in the US context that 'efforts to reduce preventable foreclosures, among other benefits, could strengthen the housing market and reduce mortgage losses, thereby

[1] This entry was taken from an open lecture given at the University of Stirling, 25 February 2009.

increasing financial stability'.[2] Alternatively, public-policy initiatives focused on maintaining employment and stimulating the economy more generally may help to prevent a new round of falling house prices and constrained credit.

In this vein the Bank of England is planning to engage in measures to maintain the flow of lending within the economy. Under the Asset Purchase Facility (APF) the Bank of England has the ability to buy a range of assets to provide an effective stimulus to the economy as an instrument of monetary policy. These assets include commercial paper, corporate bonds and similar securities. The aim is to reduce the cost of finance for firms by providing liquidity to the market and encouraging debt issuance.

These measures are intended to improve conditions in money markets. But it may be some time before there is a marked improvement in overall credit availability. This could imply there is now a case for a large fiscal stimulus, concentrated on employment, to allow time for the adjustment within the financial sector absent of a downward spiral of house prices and negative equity. Indeed, the impairment of monetary policy raises questions about the appropriate policy mix between fiscal and monetary tools to stimulate the economy. Many commentators have noted that the distinction between fiscal and monetary policy becomes blurred as interest rates move closer to the zero bound and central banks engage in policies labelled as 'quantitative easing'.

In the United States context Professor Martin Feldstein has commented: 'It has become clear that the current downturn is different from previous recessions and that monetary policy would not be effective in bringing us back to full employment.'[3]

Similarly, the San Francisco Federal Reserve chairman and distinguished economist Janet Yellen has commented:

In ordinary circumstances, there are good reasons why monetary, rather than fiscal, policy should be used for stabilisation purposes. But we are in extraordinary circumstances, and the case for substantial fiscal stimulus over the next few years is very strong. First, as I have indicated, with the economy contracting significantly, it is time to 'pull out all the stops' – that is, to deploy both monetary and fiscal policy – to avoid a deep and lingering recession. Second, the case for fiscal stimulus is strengthened by the fact that monetary policy has already moved its short-term interest rate essentially to zero.[4]

[2] Bernanke, Ben, 'The Crisis and the Policy Response', Stamp Lecture, London School of Economics, 13 January 2009.
[3] Feldstein, Martin, (2009), 'Rethinking the Role of Fiscal Policy', NBER Working Paper No. 14684.
[4] Yellen, Janet, (2009) 'The Outlook for 2009: Economic Turmoil and Policy Responses' presentation to the Financial Women's Association, San Francisco, CA, 15 January 2009.

Of course, we are largely returning to the ideas attributed to Keynes. That is, when monetary policy becomes ineffective because financial markets have become dysfunctional, it is left to fiscal policy to provide an effective stimulus to the economy. That said, I would echo Ben Bernanke's view that 'fiscal policy can stimulate economic activity, but a sustained recovery will also require a comprehensive plan to stabilise the financial system and restore normal flows of credit'. In the US the planned fiscal stimulus of just under $800 billion, currently being implemented by President Obama's administration, is planned to provide around 4 million jobs. In the context of the UK this would be comparable to a stimulus of around £90 billion or 750,000 jobs.

It is clear that the UK is now taking action on both fronts, monetary and fiscal, to stimulate the economy and solve the specific problems in the financial sector. I will not speculate on the size of the fiscal stimulus that is being planned in the budget. Rather, I would like to discuss how any fiscal stimulus that is being planned can be best focused on the labour market with the goal of sustaining employment.

The Costs of Higher Unemployment

In the three months to December 2008 the deterioration in labour-market conditions continued. Employment fell by 45,000 in the final quarter of the year. In the final quarter of 2008 the unemployment rate stood at 6.3 per cent, its highest rate since 1998. There are now almost 2 million persons unemployed in the UK.

In 2008, we witnessed the deterioration in labour-market conditions. Early in the year, a broad range of firms across each economic sector had already begun to cease net recruitment of employees. As the year progressed and economic conditions deteriorated, an increasing range of firms considered significant cuts in their employment.

The very latest survey measures of firms' employment intentions continue to deteriorate to historic lows. Indeed, the media have reported large employment reductions planned for a range of firms in the UK. In my view the unemployment rate is set to rise further, probably to close to 10 per cent by the end of 2009. This could imply there will be over 3 million unemployed by 2010. The ITEM club predicts that overall UK unemployment will reach 3.4 million in 2011.

In past recessions the deterioration in labour-market conditions has been severe, typically lagging behind the contraction in actual economic output, and then taking a number of years before unemployment begins to fall back. This time there is some limited evidence (it is too early to say for sure) that the reduction in employment may have followed the contraction in output more quickly than usual and is a big a deviation from past trends. This could imply that employment will pick up more quickly when the recovery in output emerges. But this is far from certain, so we must not be complacent. As for economic output, Reinhart and Rogoff (2008) find the rise in unemployment tends to be particularly severe during financial crises.[5]

Rising unemployment may lead to a reduction in the supply capacity of the economy. If workers remain unemployed for sustained periods they may lose their skills, thus reducing their human capital. High rates of long-term unemployment in the economy may mean there is a mismatch between those skills that workers possess and those for which there is demand. People may also be less likely to participate in the labour market the longer their spell of unemployment persists.

Unemployment has undeniably adverse effects on those unfortunate enough to experience it. A range of evidence indicates that unemployment tends to be associated with malnutrition, illness, mental stress, depression, increases in the suicide rate, poor physical health in later life and reductions in life expectancy. However, there is also a wider social aspect. Many studies find a strong relationship between crime rates and unemployment, particularly for property crime. Sustained unemployment while young, especially of long duration, is especially damaging. By preventing labour-market entrants from gaining a foothold in employment, sustained youth unemployment may reduce their productivity. Those that suffer youth unemployment tend to have lower incomes and poorer labour-market experiences in later decades.[6] Unemployment while young creates permanent scars rather than temporary blemishes.

Intervening in the Labour Market

What should we do about rising unemployment?

There has been a range of approaches to address rising or long-term unemployment in the past. First, *passive* policies such as automatic cash payments to the unemployed. Second, *active* labour market programmes (ALMPs) to improve both the supply and the demand for labour. Supply-side measures have included training schemes, providing job seekers with

[5] Reinhart, C M and K S Rogoff (2009), 'The Aftermath of Financial Crises', NBER Working Paper, No. 14656.
[6] See Gregg, P A and E Tominey (2005), 'The Wage Scar from Male Youth Unemployment', *Labour Economics*, 12, pp. 487–509, or W Arulampalam (2001), 'Is Unemployment Really Scarring? Effects of Unemployment Experiences on Wages', *Economic Journal* (111), November, pp. F585–F606.

information and guidance on how to find employment, providing services to match job seekers with existing vacancies, and implementing sanctions and incentives to encourage job seekers to find employment. Policies to improve labour demand include subsidies for employers to maintain or increase their employment, in addition to job-creation schemes.

Within the UK government's overall expenditure on labour-market initiatives a high proportion is spent on ALMPs, reflecting a view among policy makers that they are at least partially effective. Assessing the effectiveness of these schemes has become a cottage industry within the academic community. ALMPs have been subject to more rigorous scrutiny than most economic policies. That said, care must be taken in generalising from such studies. The results may be specific to particular groups within the population, the long-run results may differ from the short-run, differences in institutional structures may reduce the applicability of studies from one country to another, and the evaluations themselves rarely take account of the general equilibrium consequences of policy intervention.

Nevertheless, most studies, from a large range of countries, indicate there are little apparent tangible returns from ALMPs. Asked by *The Economist* in 1996 how much training schemes in the US help their clientele, Jim Heckman replied that 'zero was not a bad number' (*The Economist*, 6 April 1996).

In contrast to the international trend of poor evaluations of ALMPs, there have been more positive results from evaluations of recent initiatives in the UK. The New Deal for Young People (NDYP) was established in 1998 aimed at people aged eighteen to twenty-four. Since the introduction of the NDYP, a range of other New Deal programmes have been established aimed at improving the employment prospects of specific groups. Blundell et al. (2001) found that participation in the NDYP raised the probability of employment by around 5 per cent in the short run. Recent evaluations of the NDYP have been the most positive, consistent with a continuing process of improvement in implementation and delivery. For example, Beale, Bloss and Thomas (2008) suggest that those who participated in the New Deal for Lone Parents (NDLP) scheme spent sixty-four days less on average on benefits than similar individuals who did not join the NDLP programme.[7]

So recent labour-market interventions in the UK appear to have achieved some success. However, the positive findings for the NDYP are drawn from a period – 1998–2007 – when unemployment rates averaged below 6 per cent. A key ingredient in their success was buoyant labour demand within the UK

7 Blundell, R, M C Dias, C Meghir, J Van Reenen, (2001), 'Evaluating the Employment Impact of a Mandatory Job Search Assistance Program', Institute for Fiscal Studies, WP01/20. Beale, I, Bloss, C, and Thomas, A, (2008), 'The Longer-Term Impact of the New Deal for Young People', Department for Work and Pensions Working Paper No. 23.

economy. Past positive evaluations of the NDYP (and related schemes) do not imply that these programmes are likely to have a material effect during a recession when vacancies dry up and redundancies rise. ALMPs will have to be supported by other labour-market policies, in particular those to support labour demand and the broader UK economy, if we are to be successful in addressing rising unemployment.

Proposals to Deal with Rising Unemployment

I would like to outline some proposals. These proposals have not been costed, so they are intended as options for policy makers to consider. I hope they may be helpful in starting a national debate on what to do about rising unemployment in general, and youth unemployment in particular, where the long-run costs may be greatest. However, as I have argued, these measures are no substitute for guaranteeing the medium-term prospects for the UK economy by addressing the problems in the financial sector – though these measures may help that adjustment.

1) Introduce a substantial short-term fiscal stimulus focused on jobs

If we use the metric of the Obama package, that would imply a fiscal stimulus in the UK of around £90 billion, which would translate to creating 750,000 jobs. This number is a good starting point for discussion.

Tax cuts and reduced National Insurance contributions aimed at the low-paid and the young would likely provide a stimulus to the economy because these groups tend to have a high marginal propensity to consume. Similarly, temporarily increasing unemployment benefits as well as their duration may be appropriate at a time when there are large-scale redundancies in the economy.

2) Raise the education leaving age to eighteen

In the final quarter of 2008 there were 700,000 young people under the age of eighteen who were economically active, and of whom 184,000 were unemployed. In an advanced society all these youngsters should be in full-time education, jobs with significant elements of education or training schemes such as apprenticeships.

The OECD has found that the UK is significantly worse than other countries at improving skills after the age of eighteen. My own analysis indicates that the proportion of eighteen-to-twenty-four-year-olds with no qualifications has changed little since 1993. The Economic Affairs Committee of the House of Lords recently concluded:

Many school leavers in the UK have not acquired the minimum level of functional numeracy and literacy and social skills necessary to benefit from apprenticeship training. In our view, the improvement of levels of functional skills in mathematics and English is fundamental and should be given much higher priority in schools.

I agree.

International evidence indicates that there are tangible returns from raising the education-leaving age. Oreopoulous (2009) found the introduction of a higher school-leaving age in the US had significant benefits by reducing the school drop-out rate, increasing college enrolment and reducing the probability of future unemployment. Those who were compelled to remain in education were less likely to claim unemployment benefits and their future incomes were higher. Harmon and Walker (1995) found a positive effect of 14 per cent on future earnings from school compulsion and Oreopoulos (2009) an average effect of 12 per cent. Other studies find additional education lowers the likelihood of committing crime and teen pregnancy, and raises life expectancy. Additional years of schooling raises happiness.[7]

To achieve the aim of improving youth education I am not suggesting we need to employ an army of truant officers to haul unwilling adolescents back to the classroom. A more subtle approach is required. First and foremost, the way to raise education standards is to keep existing students in school. There are a number of ways to achieve this. Any new policy to raise the education-leaving age would need to be accompanied by initiatives to widen the range of available courses and training. There could be some small room for exceptions such as work-based apprenticeships with college-based training.

One possibility worth considering is to give students a monetary incentive to stay on at high school and obtain a qualification. Such a scheme is already in operation in the UK. The Education Maintenance Allowance (EMA) offers large financial stipends to children from low-income families for every week of high school they stay beyond the minimum leaving age. Students that receive the EMA could gain more over their lifetime than the cost of the EMA itself if the additional schooling generates reasonable returns. One way of doing this is to increase the leaving age while continuing to make EMA payments to families with low incomes.

[7] Oreopoulos, P (2009), 'Would More Compulsory Schooling Help Disadvantaged Youth? Evidence from Recent Changes to School-leaving Laws', forthcoming in *An Economic Perspective on the Problems of Disadvantaged Youth*, edited by Jonathan Gruber, University of Chicago Press and NBER. Harmon, C and I Walker (1995), 'Estimates of the Economic Return to Schooling for the United Kingdom', *American Economic Review*, December, pp. 1278–86.

3) Provide further encouragement for youths to undertake further and higher education

With unemployment rising sharply, demand for places in higher education is likely to rise. Indeed, the figures from UCAS earlier this month showed a 7.8 per cent increase in the number of applications to higher education. Young people who otherwise would have entered the labour market may decide to delay their entry by participating in higher education courses and adding to their human capital. Government policy could attempt to encourage this by providing additional higher-education courses. One interesting way to attempt to increase participation in higher education is to require that every student go through the post-secondary-school application process, even if they don't initially intend to go. Recent work in behavioural economics suggests this could be an effective and cheap way of encouraging students to engage in higher education. Making it easier to apply and become eligible for student aid would probably have a similar positive effect.

Monetary incentives for students to participate in higher education may also be appropriate. With approximately 800,000 people attaining age eighteen in the UK, the fall in student support will act as a major disincentive for applicants from low-income backgrounds. Targeted support, aimed at increasing take up of foundation degrees and 2 + 2 full-time routes could be expanded via selective support mechanisms. More general types of support, encouraging higher-education institutions to increase their intakes whilst providing more support for those on low incomes (e.g. full grant and fees) could form the 'top end' of a package designed to encourage sixteen-to-eighteen-year-olds to stay on in education as they prepare for higher education. These would be temporary measures.

4) Expand the number of teacher-training places

If youth education is to expand, there will have to be an expansion of teacher training. Conveniently, the number of people considering teaching as a career appears to be rising. The number of hits on the website of the Training and Development Agency for Schools (www.teach.co.uk) had increased by almost 35 per cent in the period March to September 2008, compared with the same period in 2007. In the past the UK has struggled to attract graduates into the teaching profession. It might well be expedient for government to take advantage of the current weakness in labour-market conditions and expand teacher training.

5) Create jobs through investment in infrastructure with particular emphasis on shovel-ready projects that could can be started quickly

Local authorities, health authorities, universities and housing associations have construction projects ready to be implemented. Likewise, further investment in social housing could take advantage of spare capacity within the construction sector, where the downturn has been particularly severe. It is essential that the planning system should not obstruct such initiatives. It may be necessary to expedite planning processes that hold up major investments in infrastructure.

6) Allow public-sector and non-profit organisations to fill available vacancies by providing increased funding for two years

Provide funds directly to public-sector organisations such as local authorities, health authorities and universities to fill the vacancies they currently have. The idea is that if the budget constraint were lifted – at least temporarily – many more teachers, police, youth workers and social workers could be hired. The second stage would be to have them prepare claims for further money for short-term job creation with subsidies for the unemployed and training for the young. A further possibility is to fund public works programmes that would have the added bonus of providing work for unemployed construction workers.

7) Implement a temporary, limited and targeted expansion of Active Labour Market Programmes

We should avoid the mistakes of the past, when large-scale costly schemes such as YTS and YOPS failed to have material positive impact on employment prospects. Nevertheless there may be room for a limited expansion of existing schemes, particularly for those schemes clearly targeted at the young. It is important these schemes should be piloted carefully and re-evaluated, checking to see if they yield positive outcomes for participants in the context of an unfavourable labour market. However, we are only advocating small, narrowly focused schemes, not broad-based schemes such as YTS and YOPS, which were so ineffective in the past.

8) Provide incentives to encourage the use of short-time working and job sharing; these might take the form of time-limited tax incentives

One possibility suggested to us by Paul Gregg, which I support, would be to temporarily reduce the 'hours rules' for tax credits. Currently, with the exception of lone parents, people have to work thirty hours to claim tax credits. His suggestion, which we think is a good one, would be to reduce this to sixteen or twenty hours for two years. Some people will lower their hours of work (e.g. go part-time or share their jobs) to take advantage of this and so release hours of work for others.

Conclusions

As bank rate has been cut towards zero the transmission of monetary policy
has become impaired precisely because of the dysfunction of financial institutions and money markets. In large part this problem relates to the difficulties in valuing a large range of complex, mortgage-backed securities,
derivatives and related assets. To deal with these problems the Bank of England
is ready to implement a range of new measures to support lending to households and firms. However, it is unclear when overall credit conditions will
begin to improve significantly. At a time when monetary policy is impaired,
it may be appropriate for fiscal policy to provide an effective stimulus to the
economy. Such a stimulus would provide time for the appropriate adjustment
within the financial sector to occur.

Given the risk of higher unemployment coupled with negative equity in
the household sector, fiscal stimulus should be focused on sustaining labour
demand, on adding to the human capital of youth, and on sustaining labour
demand through shovel-ready infrastructure projects and expanding public-
sector employment where appropriate.

Assuming that the world is not plunged into global war, I believe there will be a new world order in the twenty-first century. This will not happen out of dewy-eyed idealism or out of a belief in the inherent brotherhood of mankind, but because a new world order will be necessary if we are to have the predictability we need to perform basic economic and social functions in a globalised economy.

Nowadays, no aspect of our lives is untouched by global forces. Our health is at risk to global epidemics. Our physical security is at risk from accidents on international flights, from crimes fed by the international drugs trade and from multinational terrorism. Our economic security is at risk from international financial collapses or from possible closures of international trade routes. The environment we live in is an international one, so we need international standards for water and air pollution. None of these elements can be confined within national boundaries. The Internet has abolished international boundaries in communications. Interconnectedness creates interdependence, and interdependence requires mutually understood rules.

Since the mid-nineteenth century and before, international rules have been devised and agreed to govern global issues. International rules were agreed on the postal service. International rules were devised on the conduct of wars, and these have been respected since in varying degrees. The laws of the sea, and laws governing the international slave trade are other examples. Hugo Grotius published his argument for the principle that the high seas were international territory and should be governed by international law as early as 1609. So the idea of a world order was not invented yesterday!

In practice, international laws, codified in treaties, had to take precedence over national laws, where there was a conflict in a national court. If national rules were given precedence, the basis for international law would simply disappear because no one would be able to know whether or when the international rule would be followed in the courts of another country.

This network of international treaties, rules and understandings has multiplied exponentially in recent times, as cheaper communications have made us all more interdependent on one another, no matter where we live. But there is something essential missing in all of this: democratic participation. National laws have legitimacy because people elect the public representatives who devise and make them. Electorates may disapprove of some of the national laws made in their name, they may even be ignorant of the laws' content, or of how it was made, but they do know that on election day, they can throw out the public representatives who have made bad national laws.

The same does not apply to international treaties and rules. A national law maker who is criticised for ratifying an international treaty can legitimately respond that he personally had little input to the content of the treaty – that was devised by diplomats in secret negotiations – and that when the treaty came before his parliament for approval he could not amend it – he could only vote 'Yes' or 'No'. And voting 'No' might have meant losing some of the good aspects of the treaty, making his country into an international pariah, feiting the goodwill it needed for other even more important projects.

How then can one introduce more democracy into international law making? The answer to that question will determine the nature of a new global order in the twenty-first century. If we do not find an answer to it, I fear we will see an erosion of support for international rules on the basis of a claim that they lack adequate democratic legitimacy.

I believe that the European Union provides an, albeit imperfect, model for resolving this dilemma. The European Union is in fact the world's only multinational democracy in the sense that:

1. It makes rules that apply to twenty-seven sovereign nations that, in case of conflict, override the rules those nations themselves make.
2. It makes these rules partly through traditional diplomatic negotiation in its Council of Ministers, but
3. more importantly, EU rules also have to pass a democratic test. As well as being approved by the Council of Ministers, they have to be approved by a directly elected European Parliament.

No other international organisation has a directly elected parliament involved in its rule-making process.

Eurosceptic MEPs may complain about the procedures of the European Parliament, but at the end of the day they each have a vote and they each can use it to try to block any EU rules they do not like. They do not have that opportunity in organisations like the United Nations, NATO, the World Trade Organization, the World Intellectual Property Organization, or any of the hundreds of other international organisations that do their business by diplomatic means only and without any directly elected democratic parliamentary involvement.

Of course, the job of making rules democratically for twenty-seven EU states is not easy. As yet, there is not a fully formed EU public opinion and there are no EU-wide media to shape it. But that is evolving gradually. British media in particular – the BBC and the *Financial Times* are examples – are increasingly creating and shaping EU-wide opinion.

Processes are also being developed to allow early drafts of proposed EU laws to be debated in the twenty-seven national parliaments before they are considered by the European Parliament or the European Council of Ministers. That will give more time for discussions to take place both within and between countries, and for an EU-wide public debate to develop on the merits of particular proposals. That will be much better than the process for other international rules, which are presented as faits accomplis at the end of years of secret negotiation.

I believe that the EU democratic model could be extended on an experimental or case-by-case basis to other international organisations. A worldwide directly elected parliament may seem fanciful, but one could begin at regional level, as has been done in Europe. One could also change the procedures of the existing Inter-Parliamentary Union to provide for the direct election of some of its membership. If this is done, we can avoid a crisis of legitimacy in globalisation. But if we do not address the issue, we should not be surprised if there is an intensification of riotous behaviour in the margins of international gatherings – behaviour led by people whose own ideas may be entirely nihilistic but who have cottoned on to the fact that there is something very important missing at the heart of globalisation: democracy!

Peak Oil or Peak People?

As we drive up to gas stations to fill up our tanks and dump out our wallets, the headlines proclaim PEAK OIL. According to this hypothesis, the earth is running out of dead dinosaur detritus and oil prices must go up. 'We cannot drill our way out of the mess,' goes the refrain. Even billionaire tycoon T Boone Pickens turned in his oil-drill bit for a windmill and bought full-page ads proclaiming the end of fossildom.

Since soaring oil prices in 2008 coincided with soaring cotton, copper and corn prices, 'peak oil' pundits might extend their argument to all commodities. Forget 'peak oil', it's 'peak *everything*', including cocoa beans, which jumped 50 per cent in 2008. Had a billion Indian and Chinese workers toiling in the summer sun traded in their afternoon tea for steaming cups of hot cocoa?

Oft-quoted 'experts' apparently believe that the world is not just flat, it is also hollow. They contend that our resources are gone. But the stumbling block to tamer pricing is not geologic – nor even environmental – it is a lack of talent. *We are not suffering from peak oil – we are suffering from 'peak people'*. The US graduates only 10 per cent of the numbers of petroleum engineers it did twenty-five years ago. Cheap oil in the 1980s and 1990s led the oil-rig count to plummet from 4,500 in 1981 to 636 in 1986, and lay-offs followed.

The rig count is climbing again, but stymied by the lack of manpower. Community colleges and foundries in Houston are furiously training machinists who can handle pipes and valves without tripping into the gears like Charlie Chaplin in *Modern Times*. West Virginia has a shortage of coal miners because that coal miner's daughter does not want to don a headlamp and push the 'down' button in the elevator shaft. Moreover, today's miners must learn how to wield sophisticated equipment.

We see the same pattern across commodity markets. When steel prices have rocketed up, we do not have metallurgical engineers. We cannot harvest enough soybeans, and we do not have agricultural engineers. The US has only 33,000 agricultural scientists. That number has not budged in the past decade.

Today in the US, we have more dance choreographers than metal casters. That makes it easy to put on a high-kicking production of *Oklahoma*, but a lot tougher to erect an oil rig in Tulsa.

What can we do as China and India industrialise? Higher prices will undoubtedly draw more people into commodity disciplines, but universities and community colleges should help by launching commodity majors – not to train 'make a fast buck' speculators in the trading pits of Chicago, but to figure out how to get more stuff out of the ground.

Wealthy universities should take the lead. Princeton's faculty may be more excited by Camus than by manure, but with a $14 billion endowment, a little can be allocated to getting more stuff to grow in dirt. In the past year, fertiliser prices have rallied even more than gold. The heroine in Thornton Wilder's *The Matchmaker* says: 'Money is like manure; it's not worth a thing unless it's spread around encouraging young things to grow.' The commodity boom has erased any difference between the two.

Reactionary attitudes in the rest of the world must change. Monsanto is pledging to double the yield of corn, cotton and soy by 2030, using 30 per cent less water and energy. But instead of applauding, extremist environmentalists attack the company for creating genetically modified 'Frankenfoods'. They ignore the billions of lives saved from starvation during the agricultural revolution by scientists like Nobel Peace Prize winner Norman Borlaug, who figured out how to genetically modify wheat and corn to create thicker stalks and larger heads. Through Borlaug's efforts in the 1960s, Mexico turned into a wheat exporter, while India and Pakistan doubled their wheat output. And yet Borlaug often found himself attacked by environmental lobbyists who, he said, 'never experienced the physical sensation of hunger. They do their lobbying from comfortable office suites in Washington or Brussels. If they lived just one month amid the misery of the developing world, as I have for fifty years, they'd be crying out for tractors and fertiliser and irrigation canals and be outraged that fashionable elitists back home were trying to deny them these things.'

Though I disagree with peak theorists, I cannot deny that oil and some other commodities are harder to reach than they used to be. One of my mentors, legendary investor Julian Robertson, used to say that Saudi Arabia could tap oil just by sticking a straw in the ground. Now they need a pipe at least as long as a hookah. But that's why people matter more. After years of planning, Exxon is pumping oil off the coast of Siberia. The barrier wasn't the foul weather nor the foul temper of the Kremlin. The barrier was brainpower.

Until recently no one could figure out how to drill down seven miles horizontally through icy water.

If you scroll back to the 1980 presidential debates, you will hear peak-oil arguments from President Carter, who scoffed at Ronald Reagan's claim that the earth's oil and gas reserves were not yet tapped out. Hadn't the old actor read the papers? Only an intellectual dinosaur could still believe in dinosaurs. What happened? Following deregulation of domestic prices, oil prices began a twenty-year cascade downward.

The Malthusians portray a global nightmare of too many hungry people chasing too few tortillas and chickens. Is the world hollow? Only if our minds are.

PETER COSTELLO [1]

It is worth remembering that Labor's first [Australian] budget, the budget that was brought down twelve months ago, in May 2008, forecast an economy which would grow at around 2.75 per cent. When Mr Swan, the treasurer, brought down that first Labor budget some twelve months ago he said in his speech: 'We are budgeting for a surplus of $21.7 billion . . . 1.8 per cent of GDP, the largest budget surplus as a share of GDP in nearly a decade.' He went on to claim that it was a 'surplus built on substantial savings' and, further, a 'surplus built on disciplined spending'. When he brought down the first Labor budget in May 2008 what Mr Swan was saying was that he was no girly-man; he was going to produce a huge budget surplus – none of these wussy coalition budget surpluses of 1.5, 1.3 or 1.4 per cent. He was going to produce a budget surplus of 1.8 per cent of GDP. Now, of course, none of what he forecast came to fruition – none of it. As I said at the time, the 2008 budget is best filed in the fiction section of the Parliamentary Library because the forecast could not be held from May 2008 to May 2009. And when he came back here in May 2009 he adopted a somewhat different approach. He had had no trouble telling us about the bottom line in May 2008, but in May 2009 he was strangely silent about what the bottom line of the budget would be.

A budget is a statement of how you are going to manage expenditures and revenues over the course of the year. The most basic, fundamental thing about a budget is what you are budgeting for. It makes no sense to say: 'I'm budgeting for an undisclosed bottom line. I can't tell you whether I'm budgeting for surplus or deficit. I can't tell you how much it's going to be.' The crucial thing about a budget, particularly a Commonwealth budget, is to actually inform the nation what the budget is. Is it for a surplus? Is it for a deficit? Is it for X billion dollars or is it for Y billion dollars? We had the extraordinary situation on budget night this year where the one critical fact that governs the parameters of any federal budget was actually omitted from

[1] This entry was taken from a speech given to the Australian House of Representatives, 26 May 2009.

the speech because apparently, we are told, the spin merchants of the Labor
Party had said to the Treasurer, 'You cannot utter those words in the parliament; it will go on film and it could be used against you.' Chalk one up for
the spin-meisters; chalk one down for accountability and transparency in
public debate in this country.

The $22 billion surplus which was forecast in May 2008 came in as a
$32 billion deficit. I want to make this point: that was driven by policy decisions.
Do not let anybody claim that the failure of the government to deliver its forecast in 2008–9 was driven by revenue downturns. As this year's budget papers
make entirely clear in table 5 of budget statement No. 3, it was policy measures, new spending of $33.3 billion, that turned that forecast surplus into a
deficit. In addition to that there was a parameter change. But it was not the
parameter change that drove the budget into deficit, it was the new spending.
In October, there was the spending on the Economic Security Strategy. In
December, there was the spending on the Nation Building Strategy. In February,
there was the spending on the Nation Building and Jobs Plan. It was policy
measures that drove the projected surplus of 2008–9 into deficit. As table 5 of
budget statement No. 3 shows, again in this fiscal year $32 billion of new spending,
of new policy measures, will drive the budget into deficit. In addition to that
there are parameter changes of $45 billion which will drive it into a deep deficit.

Discretionary policy measures drove the budget into deficit in 2008–9, as
they will drive the budget into deficit in 2009–10. Why do I emphasise the
failed forecasts of last year's budget? Only to make this point: if the government's budget forecasts between May 2008 and May 2009 were interrupted
by new discretionary policy spending, we should take with a grain of salt the
forecasts and projections which it now wants us to believe in this document
out over the next seven, eight and in some cases thirteen years. Because this
government would have you believe that, even though it was wildly inaccu-
rate between May 2008 and May 2009 on growth forecasts, and indeed on
policy measures, you can believe the projections that it gives for six years of
continuous growth to bring the budget back into balance in 2015–16, and,
what is more, you can believe the projections for another seven years of
continuous growth after that to retire in 2021–2 the debt they are building up.

Let us just consider this for a moment. The government would have you
believe that for seven years, from now until 2015–16, we will have: a contraction of 0.5 per cent this year, followed by 2.25 per cent growth, 4.5 per cent
growth, 4.5 per cent growth, 4 per cent growth and 4 per cent growth out
to 2015–16, which will bring the budget back into balance. The government
is very confident, apparently, in growth figures between now and 2015–16. It
then says there will be above-trend growth after that, and then returning,
once we have got to full employment of 5 per cent – interestingly defined as

5 per cent in the budget papers – to continuous growth to 2021–2. That will be in 2021–2, as we heard from the Prime Minister in question time today.

And what will be the great achievement by 2021–2? We will be back where we were in 2006. The Prime Minister says that he has a plan to get us back, by 2021–2, to where we were in 2006, which is debt-free. Maybe this is what Labor meant by its education revolution. Think of those tiny tots who started school this year. After they have done seven years of primary education, the budget will just be getting back to balance. After they have finished all of their primary education and all of their secondary education, according to the most optimistic forecast in this budget, just as those tiny tots who started school this year are coming out of the education system after thirteen years of education in 2021–2, we will be coming out of temporary debt. I wonder if those kids who are going into thirteen years of education regard it as a temporary education. I wonder if those kids who are going into primary education regard seven years of primary education as a temporary period. That is how this government regards it. It regards it as a temporary deficit, just as it regards thirteen years of debt as temporary debt. That is even on the most optimistic of assumptions – that is, two years of growth at 4.5 per cent followed by four years of 4 per cent followed by trend growth, with no interruption over that period. Let me say this to the House: it just will not happen.

The Treasurer said today in question time that he has put a ceiling on the growth of outlays. Has he? What has he actually done? Has he legislated a ceiling on the growth of outlays? No. What he means by saying that he has put a ceiling on the growth of outlays is, in order to make his figures add up, he intends that there will be no more than 2 per cent growth in outlays over all of those years, just as he intended in May 2008 to produce a budget surplus. And there is no reason to believe this intention will come into reality any more than his intentions of last year came into reality in the past twelve months. 'That fixed that,' he said. 'I've put a cap on outlays; 2 per cent real growth every year.' If only it were that easy; if only you just had to say it for the word to become a deed. This is a treasurer whose one and only budget had an increase of outlays of 13.5 per cent and who now says, 'Over a period of seven years I'll restrict it to 2 per cent per annum. And I'll restrict that through the election in 2010 and 2013. And then, in order to pay off debt, we'll go through the election of 2016 and 2019 and we'll be back where we started in 2021–2.'

Of course, all of the assumptions in relation to that assume that there will be no tax cuts, that inflation will take off again as the economy grows and the revenues will come back through bracket creep. Before the 2007 election, I recall the now Prime Minister saying, when he refused to follow the full coalition tax plan, which was to cut the top marginal tax rate from 45 to 43 to 42 per cent in this term, that in his next term, if he were re-elected, he would be looking at bringing the top marginal tax rate down to 40 per cent. But of course there is no capacity to do that in these budget papers. These budget papers assume getting the budget back into balance without tax cuts and without indexation – bracket creep.

It is sometimes claimed that all of this is the result of some kind of collapse in the terms of trade. Well, the terms of trade are forecast to fall 13.25 per cent this year off the all-time record of 2008, when the Labor Party was in government, and it will take those terms of trade back to 2007 levels. But they will still be substantially higher than they were under the coalition government. There has been no collapse in the terms of trade. In fact, the budget papers themselves say on pages 2–30: 'Even after this fall, the terms of trade would remain around 45 per cent higher than the average in the decade prior to the commodity boom . . .' So it is not as if the terms of trade are going to be at some historical low. They are going back to 2007 levels as a result, higher than what they were when I was treasurer from the period of 1996 to 2007 – much higher, in fact. And this government is blessed, according to these forecasts, by terms of trade which will be much higher than they were during that period.

In fact, this is where the budget story becomes very puzzling indeed. On the one hand we are told this is the greatest downturn since the Great Depression and yet, on the other hand, the budget forecasts a contraction of 0.5 per cent of GDP. In the year to June 1983, in that recession, there was a contraction of 3.4 per cent. In the recession to June 1991, there was a contraction of 1.5 per cent, so the government is in fact forecasting a much milder recession than 1991 or 1983. It is forecasting in this recession that unemployment will rise to around 9 per cent compared to 10 per cent in 1982 and 11 per cent in 1991. When the Treasury does its analysis of how we will come out of this recession, it does its analysis comparing the experience of 1982 and 1991, not the Great Depression, when unemployment peaked at around 20 per cent. The Treasury is comparing this with 1982 and 1991, and indeed forecasting that it will be milder than both of those recessions. The only thing that will be greater coming out of this recession is the budget deficit, because in neither of those recessions did the budget deficit ever blow out to 5 per cent of GDP. So, on the indicators of growth and employment, this will be a milder downturn than 1982 and 1991, and bear in mind we have had many recessions over the last fifty years, but the budget deficit will be of a greater dimension. Indeed, the debt build-up will be of a greater dimension. From trough to peak, debt will build up about 18 per cent of GDP compared to the Keating recession where, from trough to peak, it built up about 14 per cent of GDP.

And when the government says, incidentally, that Australia will have a debt-to-GDP ratio that is far better than those of comparable countries around the world, it is not because of anything this government has done. This government is building debt to GDP up by about 18 per cent of GDP. It is because it started from a net asset position. It is because the coalition paid off all debt and established the Future Fund and had a negative net debt of about 4 per cent of GDP. Countries like the US and the UK started with debt-to-GDP ratios of about 50 per cent. While the coalition was delivering surplus budgets through the late 1990s and early 2000s, in the UK and the US they were running up deficits. While we were paying back debt, they were building debt up. The strength of the Australian position comes not from anything the Rudd government has done, but from its strong starting point – and it would be an honest thing for Mr Rudd to actually acknowledge that. If we had gone into this down-turn with a debt-to-GDP ratio of 50 or 60 per cent, we would have built it to 80 too. But we went in with a negative net debt and asset position because we had sat here and retired debt and built an asset position without the help of the Labor Party through those periods when comparable countries, such as the US and the UK, were running deficits and building up their debt position.

Undoubtedly there has been an international downturn, but the government's response here in Australia reminds me of the statement of Rahm Emanuel, chief of staff to President Obama, who said that you never want a serious crisis to go to waste. This government has not let this crisis go to waste – dusting off spending proposals which we could not afford when we had the money and introducing them now that we do not. These are spending proposals like giving out cheques, as the government did before Christmas; spending proposals such as insulating houses, a spending measure which was rolled up to me which I did not believe we could afford when we had the money, but the government believes we can afford it now that we do not have the money. It is funding projects which it hopes will boost its election prospects. Mr Deputy Speaker, you would have heard in question time the Prime Minister, equipped with graphs and pictures, talking about projects he is funding with borrowed money in order to try to buy electoral appeal.

This is the biggest increase in outlays that this country has seen since Gough Witlam. Whitlam increased outlays by 15.7 per cent in 1975–6 and Rudd increased them by 13.5 per cent in 2008–9. But I will say this for Whitlam: Whitlam at least did not flood spending out into the community from borrowed money. Under Whitlam we had no net debt. The difference between Rudd and Whitlam is that Rudd is borrowing the money that he is flooding out into the community – much more Peron than Whitlam, this approach, to borrow money and flood it out into the community in an effort to try and buy votes. Let us be honest about this. Under the cover of the global financial crisis, a whole host of policies were advanced for political gain. These debts will be with us for twenty years at least – maybe for ever. The Australian public will pay for this recklessness.

MARTIN FELDSTEIN [1]

Three housing-sector problems discussed at the Jackson Hole conference in 2007 pointed to a potentially serious decline in aggregate demand and economic activity. What are the implications for current Federal Reserve policy?

It was widely agreed that neither the Federal Reserve nor the government should bail out individual borrowers or lenders whose past mistakes have created losses. Doing so would simply encourage more reckless behaviour in the future. But it would be a mistake to permit a serious economic downturn just in order to avoid helping those market participants.

But what should be done about the frozen credit markets and insolvencies that result from mortgage defaults? The Fed and other central banks have correctly stressed their roles as lenders of last resort, providing liquidity to member banks against good collateral at rates that exceed the Federal funds rate. There are of course many important financial institutions – including the investment banks and large hedge funds – that do not have access to the Fed's discount window. The Fed has appropriately encouraged the commercial banks to lend to them against suitable collateral with the ability to rediscount that collateral at the Federal Reserve.

It is not clear whether this will succeed, since much of the credit-market problem reflects more than a lack of liquity: a lack of trust, an inability to value securities and a concern about counterparty risks. The inability of credit markets to function adequately has weakened the overall economy. And even when the credit-market crisis has passed, the wider credit spreads and increased risk aversion will be a damper on future economic activity.

Even with the best of policies to increase liquidity, future aggregate demand is likely to be depressed by weak housing construction, depressed consumer spending and the impaired credit markets. Although lower interest rates cannot solve the specific problems facing credit markets, lower interest

[1] These comments are drawn from 'Housing, Credit Markets and the Business Cycle', presented at the August 2007 Kansas City Federal Reserve Conference and published in the conference volume, *Housing Finance and Monetary Policy* (Kansas City Federal Reserve, 2008).

rates now would help by stimulating the demand for housing, autos and other consumer durables by encouraging a more competitive dollar to stimulate increased net exports, by raising share prices that increased both business investment and consumer spending, and by freeing up spendable cash for homeowners with adjustable-rate mortgages.

But the Fed must also focus on inflation. There remains a risk of rising inflation because of slowing productivity growth (unit labour costs are up 4.5 per cent from the second quarter of 2006 to the second quarter of 2007), the falling dollar and higher food prices that have pushed market-based consumer prices up at a 4.6 per cent rate to September 2007. How should the Fed now balance these two goals?

We know there is no long-run trade-off between price stability and achieving full employment and growth. But how should policy makers interpret the short-run relation between price stability and employment?

One view is that monetary policy should focus exclusively on achieving price stability because that is the best way to achieve full employment and maximum sustainable growth as rapidly as possible. If that view is correct, there is no reason to change current monetary policy. The 5.25 per cent nominal Federal funds rate was relatively tight in comparison to the historic average real Fed funds rate of about 2 per cent. The housing and credit-market problems that I have discussed will simply reinforce this tight monetary policy and speed the decline in inflation.

But there is an alternative and more widely held view that the Federal Reserve should give explicit weight to unemployment or unused capacity in the short run as well as to inflation. That is the view that underlies all variants of the Taylor Rule. If that view were accepted, there would be two reasons for a major reduction in the Federal funds rate – possibly by as much as 100 basis points.

Experience suggests that the dramatic decline in residential construction provides an early warning of a coming recession. The likelihood of a recession is increased by what is happening in credit markets and in mortgage borrowing. Most of these forces are inadequately captured by the formal macroeconomic models used by the Federal Reserve and other macro forecasters.

Even if all the evidence does not add up to a high probability of an un-acceptable decline in economic activity, the Fed could adopt the risk-based 'decision theory' approach in responding to the current economic environment. As the triple threat from the housing sector materialised with full force, the economy began to suffer a very serious downturn. A sharp reduction in the interest rate – in addition to a vigorous lender-of-last-resort policy – served to attenuate what otherwise could have been a worse outcome than what we have experienced so far.

But what if the outcome in the absence of a substantial rate cut were more benign and yet the Fed nevertheless cut the Federal funds rate? The result would be a stronger economy with higher inflation than the Fed desires, an unwelcome outcome but the lesser of two evils. If that happens, the Fed would have to engineer a longer period of slower growth to bring the inflation rate back to its desired level. How well it would succeed in doing this will depend on its ability to persuade the market that a risk-based approach in the current context is not an abrogation of its fundamental pursuit of price stability.

TONY FERNANDES

Bouncing Back?

As I write this in the fall of 2009, there is much talk that the worst seems to be over. The global economy appears to be stabilising, stock markets seem to have stopped swooning and regained an upward momentum, 'green shoots' has become a much-touted phrase and the global financial architecture seems on the way to being patched up.

That's the good news from a bird's-eye perspective. But out there in the streets and suburbs, the worm's-eye view remains dim. Job losses may be slowing, but workers are still being laid off. Some corporations are cautiously considering hiring, but the number of applicants for each job tells its own story (in some areas in Great Britain, eight times as many as would have been expected before apply for each posted job). Unemployment is either rising or stays stubbornly high in Europe and the United States. Consumer confidence, as measured in monthly surveys, yo-yoes up and down. In short, recovery – if one can call it that – seems uneven not just between nations but even within nations – varying from region to region, from industry to industry. Pessimistic optimism appears to be the order of the day.

Before trying to predict what lies ahead, perhaps we ought to recap how we got here. The recovery strategy adopted by most nations has followed a standard path: first, measures for damage limitation, with emphasis on the reconstruction of the banking system and the introduction of new guidelines to govern the financial system, and second, the introduction of stimulus packages and a revision of fiscal and monetary policies to promote expansion. Each stage of this strategy has its own set of risks.

- Stimulus packages boost output and create jobs in the short term. But they also contribute to budget deficits, suggesting that at some point in time there will be a need to raise taxes or cut spending to finance the deficit. So there is no free lunch here.

- Governments want to push demand up and go for growth. Tax reductions and interest-rate cuts can help to do this. But if these measures succeed and economic activity is raised to a new level, prices will also tend to rise, and so will wages. The threat of inflation then becomes real. Can this be handled?
- In countries like the United States where the wealth of households has been substantially reduced by the crisis, there will be less money to spend and the need to save is urgent. Can a higher savings rate be sustained in societies where spending is a way of life?
- To reduce trade deficits, countries need to increase exports and reduce imports. If they are unable to do this foreign capital will be needed to fund domestic investment. Will such funds be forthcoming? In the case of the United States, where the deficit is forecast to continue for many more years to come, will its traditional banker, China, continue to finance its deficits?
- If demand from the West remains dim, Asian economies will have to look for new sources of growth. Where will these be? Can domestic demand increase sufficiently to compensate for the reduction in exports to traditional markets? Or can the new China be the replacement market for the industrialised nations of the West?

Social and Political Impact

There is a need also to consider the wider social and political impact of the crisis and how it will affect the shape of the new world economy. This discussion can be framed in terms of a discussion of three dichotomies:

Globalisation: protectionist or market-driven

Trade is the key driver of globalisation and has been responsible for the growth of economies everywhere. The use of modern technology has also increased the speed and volume of communications between participants of the global economy. I have no doubt that the development of many countries will depend on the continued free flow of trade in its various forms between countries.

However, the current economic crisis has caused some countries to question the validity of this argument. They have instead argued that countries need to protect themselves against the ravages of the world and if this requires them to adopt protectionist measures to save jobs and support companies at home, so be it.

It is not a path I would support. As an entrepreneur, my experience has been that the important question to ask in such circumstances is not what impact a protectionist measure will have on a particular industry or company, but whether it will add to or detract from the overall contribution to value creation in terms of jobs, wealth and opportunities. In every case that I have encountered, the argument for protectionism has failed to pass this test.

Capitalism: free market vs regulation

The housing bubble and the shadow banking system that sustained it did not develop behind the backs of regulators. Its lack of discipline and its excesses were well known to the authorities. The greed of homebuyers and lascivious bankers doesn't have to be condoned, but ultimate responsibility for the crisis has to be laid at the foot of regulators who chose not to intervene.

Indeed, the failure of the housing market has more to do with corporate governance than with the price of the bricks and mortar that went into the building of the homes, or the earnings of investment bankers who traded in mortgage securities.

Much has been written in recent times to try to explain this failure of judgement on the part of regulators. As I have said earlier, some have attributed their reluctance to intervene in the marketplace as reflective of a conservative mindset in the American psyche that would rather have problems of the market sorted out by free-market forces than by direct government intervention. This hands-off approach has manifested itself in various facets of American life, and arguably has contributed to the growth of a culture of excess that has dominated Wall Street and corporate America in recent times.

Americans are paying a heavy price to indulge in this debate. In a way, one can say that America has not learned from its past. In the 1980s, the country experienced what was then the greatest collective failure of financial institutions since the 1930s, known as the Savings and Loans Crisis. The causes of that crisis are not entirely on all fours with those of the present, but the similarity in one respect stands out: the failure of regulators to do what they needed to do.

Western domination vs Asian ascendancy

Two dominant impressions have emerged from the global economic crisis. The first is that American dominance of the world economy has been damaged. While the American economy will continue to be the biggest in the world for quite a while yet, it has lost the authority associated with a system that functions effectively, supports growth and brings out the best in its people.

The second dominant impression is that China is now on the rise, both economically and politically, and although it has some way to go to be the dominant economy on the planet, it is clearly in the ascendant. If India regains the same trajectory as it was on before the crisis struck, the two Asian giants that account for one-third of the world's population are likely to also account for a much higher share of the world's economy.

These developments will clearly have implications at a number of levels. First, at the level of global governance. What will be the roles of the World Bank and the International Monetary Fund in the future? How will they be managed and who will manage them? What will be the balance of power and influence in other world bodies like the United Nations and the World Trade Organization?

One can also expect that, with time, bilateral relations with China and India for many countries will be adjusted to a different level. It will not be a case of downgrading relations with the industrialised West, but one of raising relations with China and India to a higher level.

But for the foreseeable future, neither China nor the United States – and certainly not India – is large enough or strong enough to exercise global leadership on its own. They will have to live with each other and agree on a modus vivendi that will give both room to assert themselves.

WOLFGANG FRANZ

There is wide disagreement on the question whether our use of natural resources is endangering future economic possibilities. Global industrial output increased forty-fold and world population grew three times as large in the last 100 years. Economic growth is clearly related to air and water pollution, resources depletion or global warming. Without changes in the structure and the technology of the economy, increasing economic activity would require more energy and material inputs and generate additional waste by-products. Energy use has increased by a factor of sixteen, global carbon dioxide emissions grew tenfold from 1900 to 2000. On the one hand, degradation of the world's resources eventually limits economic growth. Economic growth and sustainable development are conflicting goals from this point of view. However, on the other hand, economic growth and environmental improvements are often complementary, as economic development generates technological progress: resources are used more efficiently and new abatement technologies are developed. Economic growth provides additional resources to tackle environmental problems and generates a demand for a cleaner environment: people are less willing to accept environmental damage in order to increase their own income. The environmental Kuznets hypothesis suggests that environmental degradation and pollution increase in the early stages of economic growth, but economic growth leads to environmental improvement at high-income levels. There is empirical evidence that water and air pollution is indeed reduced as income per capita increases.

Europe's environment has improved in many areas. There has been a relative decoupling of resource use – materials and to a lesser extent energy consumption – and economic growth in Europe. At the same time environmental impacts of energy use – except for carbon dioxide – have been reduced, mainly through the use of end-of-pipe technologies. Local air and water pollutants have therefore fallen considerably in the last decades. However, some pollutants continue to increase on a global level. China's strong economic growth, for example, has created serious concerns about local air pollution and water pollution. Air pollution from motor vehicles, power plants and industry harms human health, buildings and natural resources, especially in large cities. Water pollution is a significant health risk in rural areas. The OECD estimates that 190 million people are suffering from illnesses due to contaminated water each year; 20 million cases of respiratory illness a year are expected within fifteen years if air pollution is not controlled. According to the World Bank, the costs of environmental degradation and pollution amount to the equivalent of 8–12 per cent of China's GDP annually. This illustrates the benefits of stronger interventions to improve the environment. Treating the environment as a free good gives a wrong signal for the direction of future growth. Without further air-pollution-control strategies, for example, the negative impacts on human health and vegetation will not decline in the coming decades. Pricing the environment directs producers and consumers to sustainable growth in the long run. However, the pollution-control strategies have to allocate specific reduction measures across economic sectors, pollutants and regions in a cost-effective manner. It is not future economic growth per se that endangers the environment, but missing environmental policy to incentivise producers and consumers and lags in environmental enforcement.

The burning of fossil fuels – like coal, oil and natural gas – not only causes air pollution, it also has a major effect on our climate. Climate change is probably the most pressing environmental challenge for the future. If unchecked, climate change will damage the economy in the second half of the century through an increase in global temperatures, changes in rainfall patterns and an increase in the number of extreme weather events like severe floods and droughts. A temperature increase of three degrees might result in GDP losses of around 3 per cent. The Stern Review even argued that the costs of doing nothing at all would be between 5 per cent and 20 per cent of GDP for ever. However, the scale of future climate impacts will vary between sectors, between regions and over time. While developed countries might even benefit in the first half of the century, climate change will have a disproportionately harmful effect on the overall economy of developing countries, especially in the second half of the century. The poor are much more vulnerable to climate change because of their low physical and financial capacity to cope with economic shocks and their heavy dependence on natural resources and climate-sensitive sectors such as agriculture. Economic growth and development reduce the exposure to adverse climate-change risks in developing countries. Growth also generates resources available for adaptation to climate change, which will be essential as the adverse effects of climate change unfold in the next decades. Developing countries might hence be better served by continued advances in income, health and education than by abatement of greenhouse-gas emissions. Technical and financial assistance with adaptation, from developing countries, is necessary to alleviate damage to the economies of poorer countries.

Global policies to fight climate change are indispensable. In order to determine the economically optimal level of greenhouse-gas mitigation, governments should look at the social costs of carbon, i.e. the global damage done by the emission of one extra ton of carbon today – and therefore the benefit of abating this extra ton. Owing to scientific, economic and political uncertainties and the ethical value judgements involved in discounting future climate-related damage, the range of estimates for the social costs of carbon is enormous. However, under standard assumptions the marginal damage costs might be around US $50/tc. Appeal to risk justifies higher abatement costs, as economically reasonable policies to fight global warming are a desirable risk-management strategy. As a consequence, a comprehensive post-Kyoto climate agreement has to be adopted soon with a global carbon tax or a permit price in a global-emissions trading system that takes into account the social costs of carbon. A global emissions trading system based on equal per capita emission rights can provide the necessary incentives for the emerging economies to join the agreement: emissions trading results in a significant transfer of resources from developed countries to developing countries. Climate change would then still reduce future growth, but the harmful effects would be minimised.

STEPHANE GARELLI

The World the Day After

The French writer Paul Valéry summed up the present situation rather well: 'The problem with our times is that the future is not what it used to be.' And indeed, as the world emerges from the most severe recession of the past fifty years, the new rules of the game are more uncertain than ever. There are, however, a number of issues that will define the business context during the next few years and that will drastically affect the competitiveness of enterprises.

As governments struggle with their exit strategies from the crisis – which basically implies retrenching from an excessive ownership of the economy – the most serious problem remains the management of a formidable amount of debt. Between 2007 and 2010, the combined debt of the G20 countries has soared from 76 per cent of their combined GDP in 2007 to 106 per cent, which means an increase of \$9,000 billion. In a financial environment where interest rates will remain low in order not to jeopardise the economic recovery, governments need to find money: after all, printing it is not a long-term solution. Sovereign funds in emerging nations, which appeared at one point to be a possible source of financing both for governments and the private sector, are now increasingly reluctant to invest outside their sphere of influence. Thus, in the long run, there may be only one solution: increasing revenues from taxes . . .

The problem with such a strategy is that, in a modern economy, companies and individuals are highly mobile. They have access to sophisticated financial instruments and they could ultimately decide to relocate elsewhere. Before increasing tax rates, which is a highly visible and potentially a very damaging political strategy, the priority for governments will be to first close the various international tax loopholes. The Obama administration, for example, has launched a series of proposals to increase the tax revenues from American companies operating abroad. The attacks on so-called tax havens, which also took place in the context of the OECD, follow the same logic: ensuring that companies and individuals cannot avoid the pressure of increased taxation by using the legislative differences between countries.

The reform of the tax system will take place within the more comprehensive objective of reorganising the corporate regulatory system worldwide. As a consequence, the amount of legislation and regulation will drastically increase at national and international levels. National governments are at the forefront of this process and have gained more power than ever over the economy. Even if their declared objective is to retreat from an excessive involvement in the economy, national politicians will be keen to preserve a significant amount of authority on economic matters, to the detriment of international organisations (thus increasing the risk of unilateral measures and protectionism).

Besides debt, inflation will be a key concern. The enormous amount of liquidity injected into the economy as well the surge in commodity prices triggered by the demand from emerging economies raise concerns about price stability. Central banks will probably accept a certain level of inflation during the early stages of the economy recovery. Deflation – i.e. a durable fall in prices – delays a decision to purchase a product, since consumers believe that prices will be cheaper in the future. Inflation, on the other hand, incites consumers to buy now because they anticipate a price increase in the future. The anticipation of inflation is thus, traditionally, a significant factor that induces households to resume spending.

In addition, a higher level of inflation depreciates the nominal value of debts. The likelihood of an inflationary environment will force companies to rethink their allocation of assets. For example, cash positions will be less rewarding than investing in tangible and industrial assets. This will reinforce the strategy of emerging nations to invest a more significant part of their financial resources in acquiring tangible assets and companies abroad. It could also induce companies to rethink their outsourcing strategies and to maintain more assets on their books.

As indicated earlier, the third phase of the crisis will be social. After the financial and the economy cycles, the world is now dealing with the aftermath of all recessions: unemployment! The general level of unemployment in most advanced economies is likely to remain high for some time, most probably above 10 per cent, and in certain cases such as Spain may even reach 20 per cent. The social cost of unemployment will not help governments to quickly address their budget deficits. In addition – and as is always the case in the early phase of an economy recovery – hiring is not likely to resume quickly, leading to a so-called 'jobless recovery.' History has shown that companies want to be certain that the economy is back on track before employing people again.

The challenge for companies will be to manage the formidable level of complexity and regulation that now defines the context of business. Interestingly enough, it comes at a period of time when customers are eager to have a much simpler business model. During the past decade, globalisation and more sophisticated management techniques have created an immensely complex environment for companies and customers alike. Processes, such as purchasing orders, and products, such as cellphones, have become increasingly complex without necessarily bringing a proportional added value to clients. As Peter Drucker said: 'There is nothing so useless as doing efficiently something that should not be done at all!' Precisely, the added value of companies in the future may be to absorb the complexity of the business environment and transform it into a simpler model for customers. The success of the iPod nano from Apple, with only four buttons to operate, is a great example of such a simplification.

As a consequence, some 'deglobalisation' may take place, especially in the financial sector. The so-called 'universal banking model' with comprehensive activities in all sectors and affiliates in every country may be revisited. Experience has shown that the advantages of such a model may be annihilated by the amount of management time spent on compliance, market and risk management. As some recent events have demonstrated, even the most sophisticated management model could not prevent an isolated individual putting the entire company at risk with one 'unnoticed' action. The new model may be a 'Facebook' type of approach: managing a network of partner institutions around the world, which would each deal with local compliance.

In the end, the new brave world that emerges from this crisis implies a change in mindset. New rules and legislations will not correct the wrongs of the old system. Despite all the energy shown by legislative bodies around the world and by international organisations, the modern global economy probably will remain too complex to be regulated in its most minute details. Corporate ethics, transparency and a sense of social responsibility are also part of the solution. They will serve to attract the best talents, since the younger generation is increasingly keen to work for companies whose value system is in line with theirs. In short, making a difference will be not only about being good at what you do but also about being good at what you are.

The pressure of public opinion will also force this change towards higher ethical standards. Much more will be expected from companies in the future. Henry Ford said: 'A business that makes nothing but money is a poor business!' Companies will be much more present in society to deal with such issues as the environment or the development of a new business model for the poorer populations of the earth. It will be the ability to think about the future in different terms that will define success. Many decades ago, John Maynard Keynes had already underlined this point after the greatest recession of the past century: 'The real difficulty lies not in developing new ideas but in escaping from the old ones!'

FRED HU

The Western financial system, despite having been dealt a devastating blow during the 2007–9 financial crisis, has by now largely been stabilised. The weak institutions have been bailed out by government and forced to change, however gradually, and the stronger institutions have weathered the crisis and continued to perform well. In all likelihood, the Western financial system will remain the most competitive, dynamic and efficient system in the world, and will continue to dominate the global markets for a considerable period of time to come.

However, a tectonic shift is already under way. China is rapidly emerging as a significant player in the global economy and global financial markets. China's impact on the world economy is no longer limited to its manufacturing prowess, inexpensive exports and voracious appetite for natural resources and commodities. With rapid economic growth, a very high savings rate, persistent current-account surpluses, and substantial accumulation of sovereign and private wealth, China has become an increasingly prominent exporter of financial capital to the rest of the world.

By June 2009, China's official foreign-exchange reserves reached a whopping US $2.1 trillion. China Investment Corporation (CIC), the fledging sovereign wealth fund, has more than US $200 billion to deploy in global markets. Chinese companies, armed with strong balance sheets and record earnings, have been increasingly willing to venture overseas, making cross-border acquisitions or undertaking green-field investment projects. An actual or perceived shift in China's asset allocation tends to impact interest rates, currencies, and equity and commodity prices in the global markets.

China's outbound investment has been greeted by mixed reactions so far. While many nations regard Chinese investment as a welcome source of liquidity and capital, some countries such as France, Italy and Germany have viewed it with suspicion and growing alarm, and have taken steps to curb or block Chinese investment in sensitive industries or companies, or tightened the investment review and approval regimes. There is also criticism of Chinese investment in Africa and other emerging markets for having allegedly neglected the environment or human rights.

China's newly found role as a leading exporter of capital to the rest of the world presents both opportunities and challenges. The world economy will benefit greatly from smoothly and successfully integrating China into the global financial system, just as it has gained from integrating China into the global trade system, culminating in China's accession into the World Trade Organization in 2001. But the process of accommodating a large and rapidly ascending trade and financial powerhouse is fraught with uncertainties, frictions and even disruptions. It requires China to work constructively with her trading partners to create win–win opportunities and keep financial protectionism from becoming a new threat to the stability of the world economy.

The current global financial crisis has brought scrutiny and attention to China's role in contributing to the global economic imbalances. Numerous commentators have cited China's large current-account surpluses as a factor responsible for the so-called global 'savings glut', which fuelled excessive consumption and a high level of household indebtedness in the developed economies, particularly the UK and US. While it is true that Chinese capital has played a substantial role in financing the investment–savings gap in 'deficit countries' such as the US, it is far less clear about the causal relationship between the Chinese thrift and American excesses in sub-prime mortgage loans and the housing bubble.

Regardless, the global financial crisis and the resulting recession have led to a sharp contraction of Chinese exports, thereby sending a clear warning to China about the perils of following an export-led growth model. In response, the Chinese government has aggressively applied fiscal stimulus and monetary easing to prop up domestic demand. In the short term, Chinese policy stimuli have achieved remarkable success and it is clear that China has led the global recovery. The trillion-dollar question remains, however, whether China has shifted to a new and sustainable long-term growth model less dependent on exports and more on domestic consumption.

To be sure, it is no easy task to eschew a successful growth model that has served China well for three decades. Japan perhaps serves as a rather discouraging example. To shift export-led to consumption-driven growth, China must undertake significant structural reforms. China must establish a comprehensive social-security system comprising old-age pensions, unemployment insurance and medical insurance to help mitigate threats to Chinese citizens, reduce precautionary savings and thereby increase private consumption. Furthermore, China must also undertake financial reform.

This latter point is perhaps the least understood both within and outside China. It is well known that the Chinese financial system has weathered the global financial crisis largely unscathed. China now boasts three of the world's five largest banks by market capitalisation, two of the five largest insurance companies, and several big and successful securities firms.

In contrast to massive write-downs and losses in the Western banking sector, Chinese banks generally possess strong balance sheets, with record earnings, good asset quality and an adequate capital base. ICBC, the world's largest bank by capitalisation, is also the most profitable, earning a record of US $16 billion in net income in 2008. With the average loan-to-deposit ratio at 70 per cent, the Chinese banking system is flush with liquidity. A stable and healthy banking system has been instrumental in engineering China's speedy economic recovery since the first quarter of 2009.

If China's financial sector is performing so well, why does it need to reform at all? The short answer is that China's bank-dominated financial system is not conducive to economic rebalancing. China's corporate banking model is geared to serve the country's large state-owned companies, providing a nearly unlimited supply of credit to fund large SOE fixed investment. By contrast, China's small and medium enterprises (SMEs) continue to face high hurdles in accessing credit and capital, limiting their expansion and growth in employment. Similarly, underdeveloped retail banking has also constrained Chinese consumers from increasing consumption expenditure at a faster pace than is the case today. Shortage of consumer-finance options in the form of credit cards, auto loans, student loans, or other consumer credit, and near absence of pensions and private health-insurance coverage is a key factor responsible for high household savings and a low rate of growth in private consumption in China.

In addition to adjusting the banking model to better balance the need of the corporate and household sectors, China also faces significant opportunities to reform and develop its domestic equity and bond market.

The Chinese stock market, less than two decades old, has expanded rapidly in recent years. With a market capitalisation of US $3.6 trillion, it is already the second-largest in the world after the United States. The Shanghai Stock Exchange enjoys one of the largest daily trading volumes, mostly driven by more than 100 million strong retail investors.

While New York and London have been badly bruised by the financial crisis, Shanghai has been aggressively playing the 'catch up and overtake' game. The Chinese State Council has made it a national goal to make Shanghai a leading IFC by 2020. If China makes progress in overhauling its legal and regulatory system, its tax code, and in liberalising its capital account to make the yuan fully convertible, Shanghai's tremendous promise and potential can be realised, and by 2020 the city that once was the pre-eminent financial centre in East Asia could expect to rival London and New York as one of the leading centres of global finance.

In general, the rise of China will probably produce a profound impact on the world economy. As China overtakes Japan in the near term and rapidly closes the gap with the US in economic size, it will be almost certain that it will play a major leadership role in the twenty-first century. China will be a more proactive participant in the reforms of global financial architecture and the international monetary system through its expanded role and influence in institutions such as the IMF and the FSB. The Chinese yuan will also probably assume greater importance in world trade and finance, joining the ranks of the US dollar, the euro and the Japanese yen as one of the leading international reserve currencies.

WILL HUTTON [1]

This was a crisis firmly minted in the London/New York banking system. Bankers acknowledge they 'mismanaged risk'. That is too kindly on assessment. They irresponsibly gamed the system and grossly abandoned their responsibilities to customers and shareholders alike.

There is a now familiar roll call of villains, ranging from irrational bonuses to sleepy regulators – not to forget the extraordinary international financial relationships that created such a formidable build-up of liquidity. All have to be addressed.

Lack of Commitment

For there is one factor that has attracted too little comment. The financial system grew too complex because it actively shirked its responsibilities to committed ownership. Instead it vastly magnified financial transactions, much of whose purpose was to reduce commitment, but whose fees and commissions represented both an excessive tax on the real economy and ultimately a source of instability in its own right. It is vital that this changes. But it is also time to stop kicking the entire banking system, even if some individual bankers deserve excoriating criticism (and perhaps police questioning). For it is vital that the financial system sustains itself and maintains the existing volume of credit, and new credit flows, rather than shrinks them in response to punitive regulation and lectures about returning to less risky traditional banking.

We need our financiers to take risks more than ever, in a regulatory context that encourages more sustainable business models. The gross domestic product (GDP) of each G7 country will decline in 2009 for the first time since 1945. We do not need matters to grow worse.

The heart of the crisis was the mania for securitisation and the false belief

[1] The following entry was originally published in *The Banker* on 5 January 2009.

that risk could be insured against through tradable derivatives – credit default swaps (CDSs). As securitisation became more and more fashionable and the credit-rating agencies got ever more ready to award high credit ratings to structured investment vehicles holding tranches of ever more dubious debt, so the financial system became ever more vulnerable to a decline in underlying asset prices.

Collapse of Trust

When the decline struck, nobody knew who held how many risky securities and how good the insurance via CDSs was. Fear struck and trust collapsed. In the event, the system has accepted $2800 billion of mark-to-market losses in the debt market, according to the Bank of England. Interbank lending froze – and it is only just unfreezing, courtesy of government guarantees. Banks have been recapitalised with public funding throughout the G7. Liquidity running into trillions of dollars has been injected into the system. And still it totters. There will be more failures and shocks before the story is over.

But securitisation was not the only culprit. There has been too much leverage against too little capital. The development of a $360,000 billion-plus market in derivatives in the so-called shadow financial system – compared with a world GDP of $60 billion and world share value of $40,000 billion – has also been a source of instability. It has caused violent movements in share prices, currencies and commodity and bond prices as the bets on these real financial variables dwarfs the turnover in the assets themselves. This is mayhem.

I agree that securitisation at its best is a technical way in which the owner of assets can hedge the risk by selling some of them on and assuming different ones to get a more even balance of risk. In this sense, securitisation is an important innovation, as is the capacity to extend insurance into banking and lay off loan-default risk. Any reform now needs to respect and retain these innovations.

What went wrong is that financiers went wild. Securitisation passed from being a means for owners to legitimately hedge risk to a more general retreat from any of the responsibilities of ownership. A bank owns a relationship with its borrowers. But banks began to think less of the 'owned' relationship and more of how they could generate fees from commoditising the relationship into a tradable transaction: securitisation. And worse, squaring and cubing the income streams in collateralised debt obligations not only made the securities harder to value, they also became a means of smuggling low-value income streams into higher-rated ones.

The lack of ownership commitment has become an epidemic. It manifests itself as the practice of lending shares in exchange for a fee to short sellers. It is the practice of 'rehypothecating' assets bought with loans that a bank has provided a hedge fund in order to lend against them again. It is contracts for difference. It is tradable CDSs. It is the mania for bids and deals in which the wider public is told that 'ownership does not matter'. It is the private-equity industry regarding companies as vehicles for leverage and mountainous returns to private-equity partners. It is a financial system that focuses entirely on transactions, leverage and deal flows – and not the needs of the under-lying real economy it exists to serve.

Reintroduction of Ethics

There are many dimensions to reform, which I will not rehearse here once again; but the prime objective has to be to reintroduce ownership and the accompanying ethics of responsibility, commitment and trust back into the system. It has been allowed to become overly transactional. It must be rebiased towards committed ownership. There are pros and cons to any reform, but some that must be considered include: loans and shares should not be lent to third parties for fees; unless proof of long-term ownership can be demon-strated, the dealer should forfeit rights to any sales proceeds. Short selling and rehypothecation should be banned. Owners of contracts for difference should have to declare their identity and purpose in buying assets indirectly; short-term trading should be subject to a transactions tax. Organisation for Economic Cooperation and Development (OECD) governments should declare that the same disclosure rules and requirements will be made of all tax havens. The presumption should be that non-compliance implies guilt. All bonuses in financial services should be paid on the basis of five-year perform-ance – long enough to see if performance is genuinely 'alpha'. One-year bonuses should be subject to severe marginal tax rates.

Resist Revenge

Above all, we have to be generous to a stricken financial system. It grew too large. It paid itself too much. It became a tax on the real economy. It neglected its ownership responsibilities and insisted it should be lightly regulated. It has brought the world to the edge – and the instinct for revenge, as with reparations from Germany after the First World War, is powerful – thus the language of salary caps, punitive dividends on preference shares and regula-tion to deliver high-risk aversion.

But it must be resisted. Our attitude should be very much more like the Americans and the Marshall Plan post-1945. We need to rebuild the financial system and it cannot be done without the state and taxpayers' money. It may be necessary to arrest some leading financiers and organise some show trials; but just as after the Second World War it was in our self-interest to be generous to Germany, so we must now be generous to finance. We need credit and finance to take risks, and we need to sustain some of the innovations of the past few years. The alternative is the all-too-real prospect of a world recession, even depression. And there are only months left in which to act.

A N D R E W   K E E N

Asking if there will be a new world order in the twenty-first century is like wondering if the sun will rise tomorrow. And just as the sun always shows up every morning, so every century inevitably witnesses the birth of a new world order. In the nineteenth-century world of nation states, this new order was an industrial entrepreneurial elite of robber barons. In the twentieth century, it was an organisational corporate elite running an Americanised world order in the sanitised name of economic efficiency and mass democracy. And in the twenty-first century, it will be a globalised informational elite, a 'numerati' whose mastery of new technology will define a geographically dispersed yet intellectually and financially concentrated new world (dis)order.

In *The Rise and Fall of Elites*, the early twentieth-century Italian economist and sociologist Vilfredo Pareto argued that 'except for short intervals of time, peoples are always governed by an elite. I use the word elite [*aristrocrazia*] in its etymological sense, meaning the strongest, the most energetic, the most capable – for good as well as evil.' The refreshingly unsentimental Pareto was right. But strength, energy and ability (as well as good and evil) are always defined and limited by the social, economic and technological realities of any age. Dale Carnegie or William Randolph Hearst didn't have the organisational skills to run IBM. The obstinate Henry Ford would have failed miserably in Silicon Valley. And the young mathematical wizards at Google couldn't have run a hierarchical railway or shipbuilding company.

Of course, the rise of a new world order also presumes the decline of an old world order. As Pareto argued, 'Due to an important physiological law, elites do not last. Hence, the history of man is the history of the continuous replacement of certain elites; as one ascends, another declines.' This ascent and decline of elites on the up and down elevators of history is a favourite parlour game of Hegelians, always sniffing around for that symbolic moment in history when one great world order is replaced by another. And I suspect that the great economic crisis of the early twenty-first century will eventually be seen as one of those watershed moments – when a new *aristocrazia* of the strongest, the most energetic and the most capable replaced the tired old twentieth-century elite.

The seeds of meta-historical change can be found in every twist and turn of the crisis. The surreally managed Wall Street meltdown, the shrinking of the US dollar, the expansion of the Federal debt and even the prematurely celebratory election of the woodenly populist Obama are all undeniable evidence of the decline of the United States as both a great economic and cultural power; while the failure of the crisis to really impact China, India and even Brazil reflects the rise of these new powers in great-power economics and politics.

But rather than a relatively superficial shift of geo-strategic and economic power from one set of nation states to another, I suspect that the early twenty-first-century crisis represents a watershed of a much more profound change in the nature of things. It's no coincidence that the economic crisis occurred in the midst of the continued withering away of industrial production in the West and the rise of revolutionary technologies, particularly on the Internet, that are challenging the hierarchical organisational structures of twentieth-century companies. Nor is it a coincidence that the blinding electronic speed of the crisis and the inhumanely sophisticated financial algorithms that caused the crash in the first place reflect the increasingly central role of digital technology in the post-industrial world.

As the *Business Week* journalist Stephen Baker argues in his 2008 book *The Numerati*, the masters of the new universe are the PhDs in mathematics, best able to exploit the power of the digital revolution. And these numerati work at companies like Google – an eleven-year-old knowledge company now with a market cap of over $160 billion. In his 2009 book entitled *What Would Google Do?* Jeff Jarvis argues that Google's flat organisation and its endless innovation are the model not only for twenty-first-century media but also for business, education and politics. Many other futurists also see the birth of a new digital order in which power and wealth will be more equally distributed. Some, like New York University scholar Clay Shirky even believe that we are on the brink of a post-organisational age in which the Internet will empower everybody to organise themselves outside the formal structures of twentieth century hierarchies.

But I suspect that Vilfredo Pareto would be unimpressed with the idealism of new-world-order apologists like Shirky and Jarvis. In *The Rise and Fall of Elites* Pareto argues that the ideology of the new elites is always shrouded in morality. This elite, he says, 'assumes the leadership of all the oppressed, declares that it will pursue not its own good but the good of many; and its goes to battle, not for the rights of a restricted class, but for the rights of almost the entire citizenry'. Pareto is, of course, correct. For all the altruism of Google and the other 'do no evil' juggernauts of the revolutionary digital economy, the new world order of the twenty-first century is no less self-interested than the elite of any previous epoch. What's different, however, is the new skills that will gain entry into the new world elite. Mirroring the borderless technology of the contemporary age, the key attributes of the twenty-first-century global elite are infinite flexibility, creativity, innovation, mobility, unpredictability, irreverence and rebellion. The industrial assembly line has been replaced by the start-up whiteboard. As the iconic advertisement for Apple computers advised us: 'Be different.'

What will also be different about the new new world order is the anarchic uncertainty of the global environment. The twenty-first century will be shaped not only by viral digital technologies, artificial intelligence and nanotechnology, but also by more and more sophisticated terrorism, medical pandemics both real and imaginary, and by the contagion of infinite data that will increasingly confuse truth, rumour and fiction. Kissinger Associates' managing director Joshua Cooper Ramo thus christened this new world order in his 2009 book as *The Age of the Unthinkable*. In this epoch, Ramo argues, 'the power of the individuals has never been greater'. But these individuals, he tells us, must continually think and act like revolutionaries if they are to exploit the uncertainty of the age to their own advantage.

The new world (dis)order in the twenty-first century, therefore, is a profound shift from the organisational certainties of the twentieth century. It's a new age of hyperglobal and high-speed capitalism in which, to quote Marx, 'all that's solid melts into air'. Joseph Schumpeter's twentieth-century storm of creative destruction is turning into a twenty-first-century perpetual hurricane. This is Leon Trotsky's permanent revolution choreographed by capitalism's ultimate apologist, Ayn Rand.

The most interesting question of all is what comes after the twenty-first century age of the unthinkable? How much faster and more global can things become? Can human beings catch up with the technology that is so radically transforming their world? Above all, will the sun continue to rise in the twenty-second century?

VACLAV KLAUS [1]

This year we will celebrate the twentieth anniversary of the fall of communism, of our Velvet Revolution, as we used to call it, and we can say with
full confidence that the transition is over. We have become a normal –
whatever that means – European country and, as a consequence of this, we
already have standard 'European' problems, not the specific problems of a
country in transition. This is, however, a mixed blessing.

Gradually adjusting our political, social and economic systems to the rules
and institutions of the European Union, we imported both its positive and
its less positive attributes and features. Even though our post-communist era
was characterised by a complete disbelief in the ability of the government
to intervene in the economy and by a radical deregulation, liberalisation,
privatisation and desubsidisation of the economy, we – with some resistance
– slowly came to accept the very rigid and demotivating European economic
and social system and are nowadays confronted with problems connected
with it. Specific problems resulted from the European unification process
itself. It turned out not to be a slow-going, natural, genuine, authentic,
evolutionary process, as some of you may expect, but a fundamental
change, orchestrated from above, of the whole European institutional
framework.

And this is not the only serious challenge we have to face. Like you, we
also have to deal with the artificially created global-warming problem and
with the consequences of the ongoing economic crisis. I will briefly touch
upon all of these topics now.

First to our European problem. As president of a country currently presiding
over the EU Council, I had an exceptional chance in February 2009 to
address the European Parliament – and together with it millions of Europeans – and used it to make some rather critical remarks on the situation
in Europe. Some of the parliamentarians did not want to hear them, but

[1] The following entry is a transcript of Václav Klaus's speech: 'Europe, Global Warming and
the Current Economic Crisis: As Seen From Prague' as part of the World Leaders Forum
Series, Columbia University, New York, 9 March 2009.

I knew it was necessary to speak them because the ordinary people did want to hear it.

We became EU members in May 2004 because we wanted to participate in the European integration process. We did not want to stay aside, as we were forced to throughout the communist era. However, for many of us in Europe, and especially for those who spent most of their lives in a very authoritative, oppressive and non-functioning communist regime, the ongoing weakening of democracy and free markets on the European continent is a most undesirable development.

This development is not accidental and easily reversible and there are several reasons for it, one of them being the reconstruction of European institutions, which can be summarised as the march towards an ever closer union. This phenomenon has been around for some time, at least since the Maastricht treaty, and became the main idea behind the rejected European Constitution and lately also behind its new version, the Lisbon treaty. For me, it is a mistaken project which – by suppressing the role of nation states – paves the way to a post-democratic Europe.

The other, easily observable and well-documented reason is a gradual shift away from liberalising and removing all kinds of barriers towards a massive introduction of regulation and harmonisation from above, towards an ever-expanding, overgenerous welfare system, towards new and more sophisticated forms of protectionism, towards continuously growing legal and regulatory burdens on business, towards the markets undermining quasi-competition policies, etc. All of that weakens and restrains freedom, democracy and democratic accountability, not to speak of economic efficiency, entrepreneurship and competitiveness.

The Czech EU presidency slogan, 'Europe without barriers', attempts to bring the original ambitions of European integration – liberalisation, opening up, getting rid of barriers and of protectionism – back to our agenda. And rightly so, because this is very much needed.

For me and my country, EU membership has never had any alternative. Yet, saying that does not imply that we are willing to accept that the forms and the methods of the EU institutional arrangements don't have alternatives. To take one version as sacrosanct, as the only permitted and politically correct one, is unacceptable. The right of the people to say 'yes' or 'no' to the European Constitution or to the Lisbon treaty or to any other similar document should be considered sacred.

I said it is not accidental. As usual, ideas have consequences. All of the developments I have mentioned are connected with the currently dominant European ideology I call 'Europeism'. In the last couple of years, this loosely structured, rather heterogeneous, not coherently described, formulated, analysed or defended 'conglomerate of ideas' has achieved an enormous strength, supported by the vested interests of politicians and their fellow travellers. Its main aspects can be summarised in the following way:

- belief in the so-called 'social-market economy' (it deserves to be in German: '*die soziale Marktwirtschaft*') and demonisation of free markets;
- reliance on NGOs, on social partnership, on corporatism, instead of on classical parliamentary democracy;
- aiming at very activist social constructivism as a consequence of the disbelief in the spontaneous evolution of human society;
- indifference towards the nation state and blind faith in internationalism;
- promotion of the supranationalist model of European integration, not its intergovernmental model.

All of this is something most Americans don't pay sufficient attention to. Europe is usually discussed here in the context of European pro- or anti-Americanism, or by means of the now fashionable distinction between old and new Europe. A serious dialogue between Europe and America is long overdue.

As I have already indicated, I see another big problem in environmentalism and in its currently most aggressive form – global-warming alarmism. The problem is not global warming, but the ideology that uses or misuses it. It has gradually turned into the most efficient vehicle for advocating extensive government intervention into all fields of life and for suppressing human freedom and economic prosperity. I will not discuss it extensively here now. I refer to my book *Blue Planet in Green Shackles* and to my keynote address at the 2009 International Climate Change Conference here in New York City.

The problem is that we keep hearing one-sided arguments only. I am frustrated that the global-warming propaganda has not been sufficiently challenged both inside and outside climatology. It should be stressed that the global-warming debate is a complex issue and climatology is only a part of it.

As an economist, I have to claim that there is in this debate a special role for the economics profession, which has been developing its own scientific sub-discipline called 'the economics of global warming'. The economists should come up with arguments about the inexhaustibility of resources, including energy resources, on condition that they are rationally used, which means with the help of undistorted prices and well-defined property rights. They should supply us with comprehensive studies about the costs and benefits of the currently proposed 'green' measures and policies. They should explain – even to non-specialists – the very complicated relationship between different time horizons (discussed in economic theory by means of discounting). They should return to the elementary economic argument about rational risk aversion (which would help to undermine the fuzzy and indefinable precautionary principle, used by the environmentalists), and they should bring back the arguments about the positive role of markets, prices, property rights and about the tragic consequences of the unavoidable government failure connected with ambitions to do such things as controlling global climate. The main arguments are developed in my book.

The last issue, I would like to mention here today, is the current financial and economic crisis. I spent three days discussing this topic with many leading politicians at the World Economic Forum in Davos (2009), and my depressing feeling from these discussions is that both elementary rationality and economic science have been excluded, suppressed or forgotten. The very unpleasant, day by day deeper economic crisis should be treated as a standard, cyclically repeated economic phenomenon, as an unavoidable consequence and hence a 'just' price we have to pay for long-term playing with the market by politicians and their regulators. Their attempts to blame the market, instead of themselves, should be resolutely rejected. Their activities, aiming at 'reforming', which means re-regulating the economic system worldwide, are all very doubtful and, as I said in Davos: 'I am getting more afraid of reforms bringing in more rules and increased international regulation than of the crisis itself.' A large increase in the scope of financial regulation and protectionism, as is being proposed these days, will only prolong the recession.

My country has not, luckily, experienced any financial crisis so far. We had one ten years ago, at the time of the Asian financial disturbances, and it motivated our banks to become very cautious. We did, however, import an economic crisis. This happened partly because of the fall of demand for our exports, and partly because of the behaviour of the foreign banks that own our local banks. Due to the problems in their mother countries, and in the attempts to rebalance their portfolios, they dangerously restricted credit even in countries without apparent financial vulnerabilities. This is the effect of globalisation and of our rapid selling of our state-owned banks after the fall of communism, when there was no domestic capital at our disposal.

Aggregate demand needs strengthening. One traditional way to do this is to increase government spending, mostly on public-infrastructure projects, on condition that these are available and the country is ready to massively increase its indebtedness. The Czech government has not yet decided to do so because we do not believe in this procedure. Not all of us are Keynesians, even now. It would be much more helpful to initiate a radical reduction of all kinds of restrictions on private initiatives introduced in the last half a century during the era of the brave new world of the 'social and ecological market economy'. The best thing to do right now would be to temporarily weaken, if not permanently abolish, politically correct labour, environmental, social, health and other 'standards', because they block human activity more than anything else.

We are looking forward to working with US President Obama. I am convinced his visit to the Czech Republic at the beginning of April will be a good opportunity and we hope this administration will – under his leadership – try to find an optimal mix of continuity and discontinuity both in American foreign and domestic policy. I hope it will include:

- not endangering the basic institutions of the market economy while fighting the current crisis;
- staying involved in international affairs but listening more to friends and partners.

In the moment of the fall of communism, almost twenty years ago, I did not expect to experience such an extent of government intervention into my own life as I see now. I am, therefore, convinced that fighting for freedom and free markets, something we always appreciated here, in this country, remains the task of the day.

F W DE KLERK

The State of Governance in Africa and the Need for Continuing Economic and Constitutional Stability in South Africa

Four years ago, for a brief moment before and after the G8 meeting at Gleneagles, the attention of the world was focused on the plight of Africa. Bob Geldof's Live Eight campaign had sensitised the populations of developed countries to the crisis in Africa. At the insistence of Tony Blair the G8 rose to the occasion and renewed its intention to address the continent's crippling burden of debt. It also promised to give consideration again to the iniquitous impact of OECD agricultural subsidies on the economic prospects of the continent.

In the intervening four years the international media caravan has moved on. The world's attention quickly shifted back to the wars in Iraq and Afghanistan, the increasingly inescapable reality of global warming and more recently the global financial crisis.

But still the crises in Africa persist – regardless of whether or not the world is watching. The conflict in Dafur remains unresolved; famine continues to stalk parts of the Sahel region. Tensions continue to flare in the continent's trouble spots. Somalia is still a failed state; the Democratic Republic of the Congo is still little more than a geographic expression for a state of persisting chaos. In Zimbabwe the wily old President Mugabe continues to hang on to power – despite the welcome advent of the government of national unity with the MDC.

The perception continues that Africa is lagging further and further behind in the global race, despite some quite rapid growth arising from the recent commodities boom. Between 1960 and 2005 the human-development index in the developing world as a whole increased from 0.260 to 0.691 on a scale where 1.0 represents the highest levels of development. However, in sub-Saharan Africa it increased only from 0.2 to 0.493.[1] All of this has led to the development of what is called 'Africa pessimism'.

[1] UNDP *Human Development Report 1993* (New York, OUP, 1994).

However, if we look at Africa with greater discernment we begin realise how unfair this perception is.

There are, indeed, too many countries that continue to conform to the African stereotype of poverty, conflict and tyranny. However, such states conform to the stereotype not because they are African, but because poverty, tyranny and conflict go hand in hand throughout the world and throughout history and not just in Africa. The nine countries in Africa that have experienced the bitterest conflict during the past fifteen years have one thing in common: they are all extremely poor. The average per capita GNP incomes of these countries is less than US $200.

Poverty and the state of political development also go hand in hand: the average per capita GNP income of the sub-Saharan African countries that are classified as 'not free' is US $352; that of the countries that are regarded as being 'partly free' is US $552; and that of the free countries is US $2,115.

The problem, accordingly, is poverty – and not Africa. The challenge for the world – and most notably for Africa itself – is to address the root causes of the vicious cycle of poverty, conflict and tyranny in their continent. It is a challenge that Africa seemed to accept at the beginning of the millennium.

In July 2001, African leaders assembled at the 37th Summit of the OAU, adopted the basic framework document for the New Partnership for Africa's Development. According to them, NEPAD's objective was 'to consolidate democracy and sound economic management on the continent'. Through the NEPAD programme, they made a commitment to the African people and the world to work together in rebuilding the continent. They pledged to promote peace and stability, democracy, sound economic management and people-centred development. They promised that they would hold each other accountable in terms of the agreements outlined in the programme.

Eight years have elapsed since then. The question is: how is Africa progressing with its goals? and – in particular – what is the state of governance in Africa today?

The first goal that the African leaders set themselves was to end the conflicts that afflicted the continent. They commited themselves to strengthening mechanisms for conflict prevention, management and resolution at the subregional and continental levels, and to ensure that these mechanisms are used to restore and maintain peace.

They chose wisely. The reality is that without peace and stability there can be no economic and social development, and without economic and social development it is difficult to entrench viable democratic systems and systems of good governance. Without viable democracies and good governance it is often difficult to maintain peace.

These elements – peace, development and democracy – constitute a virtuous circle in which each element reinforces the others. However, if there is any beginning to the circle, it almost always lies in the need for peace and stability since, as we have seen in Africa's war zones, little can be accomplished without them.

The way to address the vicious cycle of poverty, war and repression is accordingly to promote the virtuous circle – the cycle of democracy and good governance, economic development and the circumstances necessary to enable different communities to coexist in the same societies.

Former South African President Thabo Mbeki deserves praise for his tireless efforts to promote peace in Africa. Considerable progress has been made during the past fifteen years. The devastating wars in Angola and Mozambique have ended. Fragile peace has returned to the southern Sudan. The civil wars in Sierra Leone and Liberia have been resolved. Nevertheless, warfare, hostilities and tension persist in too many areas – most notably in Darfur and Somalia. However, in all these areas the African Union – strongly supported by South Africa – continues to work tirelessly to find peaceful solutions.

The second goal that NEPAD set itself was to promote democracy. African leaders committed themselves to promote and protect democracy in their respective countries and regions, by developing standards of accountability and, transparency and participatory democracy at the national and sub-national levels.

What progress has Africa made with the promotion of democracy? In fact, much of sub-Saharan Africa has, during the past fifteen years, made heartening strides towards democratic government. Freedom House, a New York-based organisation that monitors the state of civil and political rights in countries around the world, now classifies eleven of Africa's fifty-two states as being 'free' multiparty democracies (compared with eight only a few years ago); another twenty-three are regarded as being 'partly free' and eighteen as 'not free'. Interestingly, despotism is not primarily a sub-Saharan phenomenon: four of the five African countries north of the Sahara are classified as 'not free'.

Other aspects of good governance have proved to be more elusive – particularly in the areas of accountability, transparency and macroeconomic stability.

African governments also committed themselves in their NEPAD undertakings to creating an environment in which economic growth could take place. According to Tony Blair's Commission for Africa, African governments needed to improve the integrity of their legal systems and upgrade their physical infrastructure. They had to address problems of poor governance and corruption and had to stop over-regulating the private sector. They needed to stimulate trade through greater regional integration and the lowering of tariffs and non-tariff barriers.

How have they fared? Corruption is still a major problem in most African countries. According to a survey conducted by Transparency International in 2006, 35 per cent of Africans reported that they or someone living in their household had paid some form of bribe during the preceding twelve months. The comparative responses for North America and the European Union were 2 per cent; for Asia and the Pacific 7 per cent; for the newly independent Asian and European countries 11 per cent; and for Latin America 17 per cent. Interestingly enough, the figure for South Africa was only 5 per cent.

Anomalously, 44 per cent of Africans thought that their current government's actions in the fight against corruption were effective or very effective compared with only 18 per cent who had the same view in the European Union! This probably reflects much greater intolerance of any form of corruption in developed countries.

There are also continuing problems with macroeconomic policy and good governance. The Economic Freedom Network carries out an annual assessment of the full range of governance factors in its annual World Economic Freedom Report. The report grades countries around the world according to more than forty-five different factors, including taxation, trade and monetary policies, law and order, labour flexibility, market regulation and the independence of the judiciary. According to the 2006 report Botswana has the freest economy in Africa. Nevertheless, it ranks only thirty-fifth in the world. Only three African countries are listed among the fifty freest economies in the world. South Africa is placed fifty-third. Nineteen of the world's thirty least free economies are in Africa. All this has serious implications for NEPAD's commitment to good governance and to its goal of promoting development.

There are some facets of economic policy that African countries must address as urgently as possible. They must stop the flight of capital from the continent. Although Africa rightly complains about its crippling debt burden, the reality is that US $285 billion left the continent between 1970 and 1996. Each year Africa loses another US $20 billion – which means that for every dollar lent to Africa in recent decades 80 cents has returned to the developed world.

Africa must liberalise its own tariffs, which are among the highest in the world. It must expand intra-regional trade, which now accounts for only 10 per cent of its total trade compared with intra-regional trade in Europe and North America, which accounts for 67 per cent and 40 per cent of their total trade respectively.

At the same time there is a great deal that the international community can do to make the economic playing fields more level. Steps should be taken to increase Africa's diminishing share in global trade – which has declined from 2 per cent in 1980 to 1 per cent in 1999. Although First World nations are quick to give lip service to the need to help develop African economies, they are often ruthless when their own interests are adversely affected. The tariffs that they have imposed on agricultural imports from Africa are four to seven times higher than the tariffs they impose on manufactured exports. The developed countries continue to subsidise their farmers to the tune of US $280 billion per annum. By so doing they make it difficult for Africans to compete in the one area where they have a competitive advantage.

Africa needs two things: a fair break from the rest of the world and the determination to address its own problems. The New Partnership for Africa's Development – NEPAD – is intended to do precisely this. However, greater content must be given to NEPAD's programmes.

- There must be more progress with the promotion of democracy. Although Africa now has eleven fully functioning democracies, the reality is that there are still eighteen dictatorships in Africa.
- The Peer Review mechanisms must be more fearlessly applied. This will not happen if African leaders continue to avoid criticism of countries like Zimbabwe that are in clear breach of everything that NEPAD proclaims.
- NEPAD's goals will not be achieved unless African governments adopt policies that will liberate and energise their economies and that will lead to much greater intra-regional trade.
- Neither will they be achieved if basic standards of governance are not maintained and if corruption is not tackled.

Perhaps the African Union should have followed the example of the European Union and admitted to membership only those states that clearly comply with basic democratic, fiscal and governance standards. This would have entailed a much smaller organisation to begin with – but it would have set clear standards and would have helped to eliminate the gap between real content and hopeful rhetoric.

NEPAD must not become yet another empty acronym. The future of the continent depends on the ability of Africans to establish peace and stability; to promote genuine democracy and to ensure basic standards of good governance.

Another factor that will undoubtedly have an enormous impact on Africa's future will be the continuing success of South Africa's free-market constitutional democracy. This is because South Africa is by far and away the continent's most significant economic power. Its GDP – measured on a purchasing-power-parity basis – is about US $600 billion – about the same size as the Argentine and Polish economies. With only 6.5 per cent of the population of sub-Saharan Africa, South Africa produces a third of its gross economic product and generates two-thirds of its electricity. South Africa's predominant position in Africa – together with its internationally applauded democratic credentials – helps it to punch well above its weight in the international arena. It is a member of the G20. It plays a leading and constructive role in Africa and it enjoys good relations with other leading emerging economies. Accordingly, the future success of much of the continent is inextricably interwoven with the future success of South Africa.

South Africa has made significant progress since 1994.

- It has held four free and fair democratic elections since then.
- Until last year it had experienced fourteen years of uninterrupted economic growth facilitated by sensible macroeconomic policies that the ANC government had implemented – despite its socialist rhetoric. Like the rest of the world, South Africa is wrestling with the fall-out from the global financial crisis. Although the economy will shrink by 1 per cent this year, South Africans are confident that they will be less severely affected than most countries.
- South Africa has become an increasingly popular tourist destination – and tourism now contributes more than 8 per cent to our GNP – more than gold. Some of its restaurants and hotels are counted among the best in the world in international surveys.
- The car and truck industry also contributes about 8 per cent of GNP – with exports of the highest-quality Mercedes-Benz and BMWs to countries all over the world. Last year South Africa produced 600,000 motor vehicles.
- More importantly, life is getting better for more and more South Africans. Since 1994 millions of black South Africans have joined the middle class, enlarging our consumer market and contributing to societal stability.
- However, it is not only the black middle class that has benefited from the new South Africa. Since 1994 the government has built more than 3 million houses for disadvantaged communities. It has also extended water and electricity services to more than 70 per cent of all our households; and 13 million children and old-age pensioners now receive state allowances.

These are all positive aspects of the new South Africa. But there are also the well-known negatives:

- South Africa has the highest number of HIV-infected people in the world.
- Almost 50 per cent of South Africans live in poverty. The country remains one of the most unequal societies in the world – despite the ANC's

commitment to the promotion of equality and despite the fact that the achievement of equality is one of the founding values in our Constitution. South Africa's GINI coefficient – which measures inequality in societies – has remained virtually constant at 0.66 since 1994.

- One of the main causes of poverty and inequality is the very high and persistent unemployment rate. At least 30 per cent of black South Africans are unemployed or have given up looking for work. Unemployment, in turn, has its roots in the dismal failure of our education system to prepare entrants for the labour market; in the effects of global competition; and in our rigid labour laws. All this has been aggravated by the influx across our porous borders of uncounted millions of economic refugees from other African countries.
- Unemployment and poverty are, in turn, among the main causes of the unacceptable levels of violent crime that we experience.

So, South Africans finds themselves after fifteen years of constitutional democracy balanced between justifiable pride over our significant achievements and deep concern over our unresolved problems.

The question that engages observers now is how the new government of Mr Jacob Zuma will affect this balance: will he continue to build on the constitutional and economic progress that we have achieved? Will he be able to address the enormous societal problems that continue to confront us?

A great deal will depend on the role that Jacob Zuma will play. He has no pretensions to being an intellectual of the Mbeki genre. He is pragmatic and does not seem to have any ideological preconceptions. He is a good listener – and much will depend on the quality of the advisers that he selects. Also, unlike Mbeki, he is charismatic and a man of the people. He makes no secret of the pride he takes in his Zulu heritage and enjoys performing in traditional Zulu regalia, dancing and singing at public gatherings.

Zuma's close identification with his traditional culture is one of the main sources of his political success – because at the end of the day South Africa is an African, and not a Western, country. However, South Africa operates within a global context in which the rules are not set by Africa but by a global consensus on how states should manage their economic and constitutional affairs. That consensus requires constitutionalism and the rule of law, uncorrupt administration, free markets and responsible macroeconomic policies.

This, in essence, is the dilemma that President Zuma will face: he will have to straddle the divide between the populist demands of his left-wing alliance partners and the macroeconomic dictates of the global economy, between the collectivist traditions of Africa and the individualist freedom and constitutionalism-based values of the mainstream international community.

The next five years may well determine the future of South Africa for the coming century. They will reveal whether the constitutional democracy that South Africa established with so much optimism fifteen years ago will continue to flourish; whether its economy will continue to grow; and whether it will be able to address the serious societal challenges that confront it on all sides.

South Africa's future success will, in turn, be a major factor in determining the future success of the rest of sub-Saharan Africa.

RICHARD KOO

The most significant feature of the post-crisis world is likely to be a much expanded role for the government in both macro and banking fields in those economies that suffered balance-sheet recession. On banking, it is clear that no quick resolution of the non-performing loan (NPL) problem is possible when so many banks are having the same problem at the same time. In such a systemic crisis, where the number of financiers or purchasers of distressed assets is dangerously insufficient compared to the number of sellers, the government regulators must *go slowly*. In such circumstances, what is needed is a credible ten-year NPL amortisation programme where, under strict government supervision, banks are given a realistic time frame to write off their problem assets using their earnings. Government supervision is needed to assure the outside world that the problem will actually go away in ten years. Once a credible scheme is in place, the market will no longer worry about the banks, which will allow these banks to then conduct their lending activities without worrying about sudden disruption in their funding.

This is the essence of the scheme Paul Volcker, the then chairman of the Federal Reserve, put in following the devastating Latin American debt crisis of 1982. Even though the process took nearly a dozen years, no credit crunch emerged while banks quietly wrote off problem loans over that period. Indeed this incident proved that quick resolution of an NPL problem is not a necessary condition for bankers to lend. The key is having a credible NPL amortisation programme, not the speed of NPL disposal. With US taxpayers not disposed towards helping banks with more money, it is also the only realistic option.

For those banks that require additional capital to continue lending, government should provide that capital on the condition that it will be used to support lending and not to write off problem loans. This is the understanding upon which the Japanese government provided capital to the banks in the 1998–9 period, which succeeded in eradicating the credit crunch that emerged in late 1997.

On the macro front, I have already argued in the previous section that government must maintain fiscal stimulus until the private sector has finished repairing its balance sheets; however, a new challenge awaits the government: many years of debt repayment under painful recession is likely to have made the private sector extremely wary of taking on new debt even after its balance sheets are repaired. Many may become completely averse to borrowing. It is said that those Americans who lived through the Great Depression never borrowed money until they died. The same phenomenon is currently observed in Japan. After paying down debt for nearly fifteen years, Japanese companies are now extremely debt-averse, even though their balance sheets had been cleaned up by 2005 and with interest rates still near zero. But that means the government must continue playing the role of the 'borrower of last resort' until private-sector aversion to lending is overcome.

The government will face two challenges at this juncture. First, it must do everything possible to help the private sector overcome its trauma by offering big incentives to borrow money. These may include generous investment-tax credit or depreciation allowances. Japan under Prime Minister Taro Aso was about to embark on this path when the Lehman fiasco resulted in the collapse of global demand for Japanese exports. These incentives, if successful, should be removed promptly so as not to encourage another irresponsible borrowing binge. However, there is a real possibility that those traumatised individuals will not return to borrow money for years even with those incentives in place, as the above post-Depression American experience indicates.

That raises the second challenge for the government: should it continue to borrow the remaining excess savings in the private sector and invest those savings in the country's future, such as education and research, or allow the private sector to seek investment opportunities knowing that the demand for funds from the non-financial sector may be significantly less than supply? This latter option is particularly problematic because one of the reasons for bubbles is that too much capital chases too few investment opportunities.

In the past, economies seldom faced a predicament of too much capital. When many new and revolutionary products were being invented, ranging from railways to television sets, capital was needed to put those products into production. In the aftermath of wars or natural disasters, capital was not only needed but was extremely scarce. Whatever capital was available under those circumstances was usually put to good use.

But in recent decades, the savings generated by the private sector seem to be far greater than the capital requirement of the non-financial sector, resulting in a bloated financial sector looking for opportunities that do not actually exist. In such a world, investment funds are prone to jump into bubbles because only bubbles seem to offer above-average returns. Even though many fund managers are aware of the risks involved, they cannot easily disengage from a bubble because early withdrawal almost always means achieving less return than realised by the competitor who stayed on. In turn, this means those who withdraw early will have a poorer investment record and fewer funds to manage in the following period. When everybody waits until the very last moment for a sign to sell, there will be no buyers when the bubble finally bursts. The resulting price collapse decimates these funds, as countless bubbles have done in the past.

If there is indeed a dearth of investment opportunities in the non-financial sector relative to funds available, the unpleasant choice for policy makers is to either let the government borrow and spend the excess savings in the private sector or let the private sector continue to squander away their funds in bubbles. Although both are undesirable at some level, the former may still leave something valuable at the end. For example, if the US government borrowed and spent the excess savings in the private sector to teach Chinese or Hindu to the American people, the US competitiveness vis-à-vis China and India would improve. If the same funds were gambled away in bubbles, the chances are high that those funds would have lost a large sum at the end. A large taxpayer fund may also be required to bail out the economy and financial institutions, as demonstrated in the recent episode. Given the choice, it is worthwhile to think about what the government should do if it is indeed the case that, even with generous incentives, the non-financial private sector cannot absorb all the capital generated in the economy.

The idea of government borrowing and spending money was always viewed with suspicion because it was assumed that the private sector could use the money better. And that was indeed true for most periods in the past. But recent experiences, starting with the Asian bubble of 1997 followed by the IT bubble of 2000, the housing bubble of 2006 and the commodity bubble of 2008 suggest that the private sector has not been good with its money, that there is too much financial capital chasing too few opportunities in the non-financial world. The aversion to borrowing at all levels, which is likely to increase after the current crisis, will widen the gap between the supply and demand for funds even further. If that is the case, until technological breakthrough or scientific discovery makes capital scarce again, government should consider borrowing and investing excess savings in the private sector in education and research for the future.

NORMAN LAMONT

The Future of the Global Economy

What lies ahead?

Despite the severity of our current problems, eventually the recession will end, recovery will begin and world trade will recover. One of the key objectives must be to see that the free-trading liberal system that created so much of the prosperity in recent years is maintained. This is particularly important for poorer countries. At the moment, in the middle of the world recession there are undeniable pressures towards protectionism and the unwinding of globalisation.

All my political life, politicians, not least in America, have made noises, but only noises, about protectionism. I remember so vividly how Bill Clinton, in his first presidential election, hinted that he might repeal NAFTA. Barack Obama also made protectionist noises during his election campaign. But this time, the move towards protectionism, not just in the United States but everywhere, seems more serious. Indeed, the line between so called 'stimulus measures' and pure protectionism has become blurred. Politically, the climate has moved against free markets towards big government.

My own country, the UK, is particularly vulnerable. We have an open economy where exports represent one-fifth of GDP. Thirteen per cent of the labour force is foreign; 40 per cent of shares on the London Stock Market are owned by foreigners.

Everywhere I see creeping protectionism and the reversal of the process of liberalisation, not just in trade but in labour markets, capital markets, banking, public procurement and industrial policy. There are indeed many forms of protectionism other than the imposition of tariffs. Take labour markets: it was, surprisingly, the British prime minister, Gordon Brown, who talked about 'British jobs for British workers'. Predictably, this led to an awkward strike at an oil refinery on the Humber as workers took him at his word. Such slogans are neither realistic nor sensible. How can we afford not to learn from other people's skills? If business is to survive, we need to recruit people with the right skills. In 2009, according to the WTO, trade was estimated to fall something like 9 per cent. That, in itself, is a process of deglobalisation even though it may just be temporary.

In public procurement, there is more and more evidence worldwide of protectionism. Everyone was aware of the 'buy American' clause in the original stimulus legislation. There is a widespread but mistaken impression that it was removed from that legislation although in fact it continues. But there is also similar legislation in many other countries. There is 'buy Malaysian' legislation, 'buy Filipino' legislation and even in the EU the Spanish industry minister Miguel Sebastian has talked about a 'buy Spanish' policy. Perhaps the most subtle and dangerous form of protectionism has been industrial activism. Lord Mandelson has claimed that the government's industrial policy is not about picking winners, though he has not been very clear what it is actually about.

Much industrial aid is protectionism by another name. Take the automobile industry, which is as globalised as any industry gets. Yet we had Germany trying to separate Opel from the rest of the industry and to reverse a long-standing, global integration of the industry. The same might be said of the British government's attempts to rescue Vauxhall. And President Sarkozy of France has said, 'If we are to give financial assistance to the auto industry we don't want to see another factory being moved to the Czech Republic.' In the United States, the Washington rescue package for the automobile industry covered the big three, but not a cent went to Toyota or other Japanese or foreign manufacturers.

Much the same applies in banking. In bank rescues, priority is given to maintaining domestic lending. Cross-border bank lending declined by over $4.8 trillion in 2008. The emerging markets of the former communist countries in Eastern Europe have been the hardest hit. In these countries the banking system has been foreign-owned, particularly in Austria.

There is a lot of talk that in future we must correct the so-called 'global imbalances' between the lending countries of Asia and the borrowing Anglo-Saxon countries like the United States and Britain, of course. We do not want to go back to a world of massive borrowing and an unsustainable boom, and it is true that the huge surpluses of China, Japan and Germany, being invested in US assets, particularly Treasury bills, inflated prices and drove down yields. I would argue that these imbalances are not inherently so different from the imbalances within individual countries, where some regions may be saving areas, some consuming areas. What is important is that capital is allocated in an efficient way to the most worthy projects. We must be careful that we do not destroy the interdependence of the global economy and attempt to substitute national self-sufficiency. There will always be a mismatching of savings and investment between countries, and attempts to prevent this could leave us poorer.

So far, I have listed the things that are going wrong – the slide towards protectionism and the unwinding of globalisation. But this, I hope and believe, must be only a temporary phenomenon in response to the recession. The most important point is that we should get back to the dynamic growth of trade that has served us so well in the past. As Gordon Brown has rightly said, 'In the end, protectionism protects no one.' It is up to him to show he means what he says.

MAURICE LEVY

When leaders from all sectors and regions of the world met at the global summit of the World Economic Forum at the beginning of this year, they resolved to 'reboot' the world economy so that important principles be taken into account in ways that 'business as usual' did not allow in the past.

So they were resolutely positive in arguing that it is in times of severe systemic crisis that major new priorities should be built into the policies and foundations of the world economy as it is reset. These include such generally globally shared values as environmental protection, education, health, gender equality and human development through better sharing of scarcer resources. This will require new financial rules, technologies, and social change. Can we have faith in our current world leaders – and the system of world leadership – to attain these objectives?

When we look rationally at the world leaders gathered at the G20, one can have doubts on what of importance and significance can be decided and then implemented by all of them. World leaders have different interests, different agendas, and different economies. I am not optimistic that the G20 leaders will see beyond these differences to agree to the significant responses that are required to re-establish a healthy system and thus restore public confidence.

Processes will not automatically re-establish the system; they will need to be accompanied by a reassertion of ethics and values. This is shown by recent financial-sector history: The Enron, Adelphia and Worldcom financial scandals in the US led to the tough Sarbanes–Oxley financial and management regulations. Yet this did nothing to prevent Madoff and his incredible Ponzi pyramid scheme nor the collapse of the financial system.

I do think that we will soon see some minor changes in financial regulation and, if we are lucky, maybe even a loose coordination of financial regulation at global level with some additional reforms. I think we will see somewhat more change in the private sector. I believe that corporate boards will be more cautious, particularly those in the financial world, where they will be more cautious, more risk-averse and will demand more ethical behaviour. I also believe that the boards will be more questioning and more powerful.

If something changes in the near future, it is clearly the fact that business will be led by more ethical leaders. Cynicism will be rejected both by employees and consumers. And probably investors will have to follow. They will have to take into account the *values* around their investments as well as around their own behaviour, and not only the *value* of their investment.

Concern for sustainable development will probably lead to green or 'true-blue' economies. There will be innovations which will help create new industries, new jobs, and new businesses.

Ageing will also be a major factor of the future and some countries will have to massively open their borders to immigration, significantly changing the composition of the population as well as the cost of production of their manufactured products.

Innovation in genetics as well as new health technologies also will create new enterprises. These will not only be new kinds of cellphones or Internet computers but certainly totally new products that cannot yet be imagined today. And, obviously with an ageing population, services to the person will boom.

Scarcity of resources will make basic raw materials more sought after, more necessary and, of course, more expensive, changing again the balance of power.

Globalisation, a continuing shift in wealth thanks to basic resources, as well as innovations, will create new divisions in the world.

It's not only private-sector company boards and managements that will need to manage innovation; political leadership will need to stay on top of these changes to make public policies relevant. By working together, they will need to restore public confidence in the post-crisis world.

AUGUSTO
LOPEZ - CLAROS

The key lesson to emerge from the financial crisis is that we have global financial markets but no global rule of law. In the past thirty years the global economy has become both more complex and more interconnected, but the mechanisms and institutions that we have to deal with crises have not kept pace with the tempo of change and what has emerged is a 'governance gap', an inability to cope with complex global problems either because the institutions we have are woefully unprepared or, in some cases, because we do not even have an institution with relevant jurisdiction and adequate resources to address the problem in question (e.g., climate change).

The process of globalisation is unfolding in the absence of progress in the creation of an international institutional infrastructure that can support it and enhance its potential for good. There is no global environmental authority; policy in this area is being done via ad hoc approaches involving elements of international cooperation, voluntary compliance and large doses of hope. In the absence of a body with jurisdiction over the global environment and the associated legal-enforcement authority, de facto the international community has abdicated management of the world's environment to chance and the actions of a few well-meaning states. The global economy has no lender of last resort – there is no reliable, depoliticised mechanism to deal with financial crises. Whether a country gets an IMF bail-out or not in the middle of a financial meltdown used to be a function not of a transparent set of internationally agreed rules, but rather several other factors, including whether the IMF's largest shareholders might consider the country to be a strategic ally worth supporting. There is no agency charged with the responsibility for giving legal meaning to the noble principles enshrined in the Universal Declaration of Human Rights. According to the US State Department, there are forty-four nations with the capacity to build nuclear weapons – nuclear proliferation remains yet another example of global institutional failure. Major planetary problems are being neglected because we do not have effective, problem-solving mechanisms and institutions strong enough to deal with them. What the latest developments in the financial markets show with sobering clarity is that global crises cannot be solved outside a framework of global collective actions involving supranational cooperation and a fundamental rethinking of the 'national interest'. Clearly, an integrated global community of nations needs to lay the basis for effective mechanisms of global governance.

Albert Einstein, who together with Bertrand Russell and others gave a great deal of thought to political requirements in the new climate created by the arrival of nuclear weapons, believed that one way one could address the evident failings of the international institutional framework was to create truly supranational organisations. In 1946, soon after the creation of the United Nations and very much aware of this organisation's limitations, he wrote:

> The development of technology and of the implements of war has brought about something akin to a shrinking of our planet. Economic interlinking has made the destinies of nations interdependent to a degree far greater than in previous years . . . The only hope for protection lies in the securing of peace in a supranational way. A world government must be created which is able to solve conflicts between nations by judicial decision. This government must be based on a clear-cut constitution which is approved by the governments and the nations and which gives it the sole disposition of offensive weapons. A person or a nation can be considered peace-loving only if it is ready to cede its military force to the international authorities and to renounce every attempt to achieve, or even the means of achieving, its interests abroad by the use of force.

Russell held similar views:

> A much more desirable way of securing world peace would be by a voluntary agreement among nations to pool their armed forces and submit to an agreed International Authority. This may seem, at present, a distant and Utopian prospect, but there are practical politicians who think otherwise. A World Authority, if it is to fulfill its function, must have a legislature and an executive and irresistible military power. All nations would have to agree to reduce national armed forces to the level necessary for internal police action. No nation should be allowed to retain nuclear weapons or any other means of wholesale destruction . . . In a world where separate nations were disarmed, the military forces of the World Authority would not need to be very large and would not constitute an onerous burden upon the various constituent nations.

In the aftermath of the chaos and destruction unleashed by the Second World War Einstein, Russell and others laid out an important argument in favour of the creation of an international authority, explaining that the time had passed when military conflicts and their associated damage could be reasonably contained. In earlier times, because of the limited destructive power of weapons, a war between, say, France and Germany, did not, on the whole, have global implications. In the nuclear age, however, war had become unthinkable and its consequences universal. National sovereignty, which had always been understood to mean the right of a country to defend its interests by the use of force if necessary, but the exercise of which had assumed that conflicts would remain largely confined to given geographic areas, no longer served the interests of anyone. On the contrary, thus understood, national sovereignty cast a dark shadow over the future of everyone. Hence the notion eventually emerged that lasting international peace would be feasible only in the context of the creation of a global institution based on the principle of collective security.

An additional argument supporting the creation of global institutions stems from the flowering of science and technology. Since this is irreversible and no longer under the control of any one government or power, the process of global integration and interdependence – what we now collectively call globalisation – will continue to bring nations and peoples together and will increasingly expose the weaknesses of prevailing international political arrangements. As problems became more global in nature – from the environment to the functioning of the international economy – situations could emerge where important areas of human endeavour no longer receive adequate attention, creating the risks of ever more intense crises. Thus the creation of supranational institutions can be seen as fundamentally a preventive measure, designed to bring into being bodies with the appropriate jurisdiction over problems no longer under the control of today's sovereign states.

The above notwithstanding, I think it is unlikely that the next decades will see a quick move towards the establishment of an international institutional infrastructure, which is most often associated in people's mind with a world government. I think what may be necessary first is for us – the human family – to collectively experience the limitations imposed on human welfare and prosperity by our current economic and political arrangements, which are dysfunctional at best. It is regrettable, but the twentieth century taught us that major initiatives of global cooperation (e.g., the League of Nations, the UN, the creation of the European Union) seem to emerge in the wake of much pain and destruction. At the height of the crisis in 2008 I had thought that maybe our leaders would seize the opportunity that the crisis provided to begin to move us in the direction of better mechanisms of governance. However, at the moment, much of the policy effort seems to be focused in recreating the conditions of the early part of the decade, which, in many ways, bore much of the responsibility for the crisis itself. Yes, in time there will be a new world order. There might even be such a new order in the twenty-first century. But it is difficult to see this happening on present trends. On the other hand, the future may have for us several surprises in store (e.g., as yet unknown consequences of climate change) and it is conceivable that, under some circumstances, these could precipitate major changes in human priorities, values and consciousness.

GERARD LYONS

Shift in the Balance of Power

A profound change is under way in the world economy. The balance of economic and financial power is shifting from the West to the East. This shift could usher in a super-cycle of strong, sustained growth for those economies best positioned to succeed. The successful countries will fall into one of three categories, being those with strong financial resources, those with natural resources such as energy or rich in commodities, and those with the ability to adapt and change.

The recent financial crisis shows that economic-growth models need to change. The crisis was triggered not only by a systemic failure of the financial system in the West but also by an imbalanced world economy. Savings flowed 'uphill' from regions running current-account surpluses, such as the Middle East and Asia, to deficit countries in the West, such as the US, UK and Spain. Some blame the savers, not just the borrowers. This is harsh. Although the surplus countries provided the savings to fuel the global boom, they were not the main problem, but they are central to the solution if we are to ensure a future balanced global economy.

Another important aspect of this shift is already being seen, with a change in global policy forum. The Group of Twenty (G20) has now assumed the role of the major policy forum, thus giving a voice to emerging economies. Also, the Financial Stability Board, again with a large number of emerging economies, has assumed a key role in addressing issues arising from the financial crisis.

Although the 1944 Bretton Woods agreement is no longer in place, it has continued to drive much monetary and financial thinking. In particular, no obligations were placed on savers to correct global imbalances. The onus was put on countries with deficits to take corrective action. This has to change, and the signs are this will happen. To achieve future balance, the West should spend less and save more, and in the adjustment phase become relatively poorer. The Middle East and Asia should do the reverse. This, however, is not something that can happen overnight and will not be easy. Not only is it likely to take years, but it will require a shift in the policy environment to make it happen. This is highlighted by the extent to which many emerging economies have a growth model that is heavily driven by what happens in the West. If the West is not booming, Asia and many other emerging economies cannot boom. But, as the shift in power takes place, more of the growth across emerging economies will be driven by what happens about domestic factors and will become self-sustaining. In the process, money and savings will flow eastward as multinationals and pension funds invest in markets with higher growth and rising incomes.

At the 2009 annual Asian Development Bank meeting in Indonesia, there was a determination to put steps in motion to achieve this. One focus will be on boosting social safety nets in order to discourage precautionary saving. The other key focus will be for Asia to deepen and broaden its capital markets to allow firms to raise funds, invest and generate jobs. In the process, one should expect to see growth across the small and medium-sized enterprise (SME) sector and more Asian companies becoming global in their outlook, including using a strong domestic and regional footprint to make international acquisitions. Expect to see more global brands from Asia.

If this shift takes place, the implications are huge. In particular, there will be the emergence of a huge middle class. Demographics is not destiny, as China and India demonstrated over the last hundred and fifty years; having a large population does not guarantee economic success. But if the right policies are in place, then the shift to domestically driven growth will see more jobs, increased spending and a huge market that, in turn, attracts more investment. Over the next decade, Asia needs about 750 million extra jobs for its young, growing population. Although much attention in recent years has been on China and India, the pace and scale of change on the ground across a multitude of countries is breath-taking, whether it be in Indonesia, with over 223 million people, or Vietnam, rapidly opening up, or even Brazil, where in the space of a decade expectations about that country's future potential have been transformed. The catch-up potential of all these economies, and many others, is huge.

This has already fuelled a huge infrastructure boom. Although the financial crisis has dampened this, the underlying need and desire to invest more in infrastructure have not receded. This creates concern, particularly about the environment. There are serious implications for commodities, trade and financial flows. Already China accounts for one-third of global demand for metals, and this is rising. India could follow suit, not just in metals, but in food as well. The outcome will be higher commodity prices, increased investment

in countries rich in resources and in water, and a growing need for technological solutions.

It has also, in recent years, exerted upward pressure on commodity prices.
Yet, when commodity prices were rising sharply, it draw attention to the lack
of previous investment in many of the commodity-producing countries,
whether in Africa or elsewhere. As financial conditions normalise and world
growth recovers one should expect to see, in the future, increased investment
in the commodity-producing regions. This is a tremendous positive for Brazil
and for many countries across Africa.

The Middle East, too, which alongside Asia enjoyed high savings and large
current-account surpluses, has a need to diversify its region. Demographics,
diversification and the dollar dominate prospects for the Middle East. Although
energy is always likely to dominate the region, there is a need to diversify
into other areas, in order to generate jobs for young, growing populations.
This, too, requires monetary policy to be set to suit domestic needs, and the
Middle East, like many other regions, may shift in coming years away from
the dollar.

As emerging regions boost domestic demand and grow, it is likely that
trade flows between these areas will increase. New trade corridors are being
seen. Intra-Asian trade is rising sharply, as too is trade between Asia and Latin
America, Africa and the Middle East, often with China at the centre. Still
much of Asia's exports eventually satisfy demand in the West, but the underlying increase in 'South–South' trade cannot be ignored. This will continue,
particularly as domestic markets grow and as more companies from the West
invest in the emerging regions to sell to the bigger domestic markets. Furthermore, if India continues to open up, then it could do for South Asia, the
Middle East and East Africa what China has done in recent years for East
Asia, boosting regional trade flows.

China is still a poor country with huge imbalances, yet its rise over the
last three decades has been phenomenal. Now, China is heading into a new
development phase, building its infrastructure to compete at every level.
China's huge stimulus package over this year and next is supplemented by
two profound measures – one aimed at building a social safety net and the
other at helping farmers to buy consumer goods. China's growth is forcing
others to step up a gear, too. India's recent election could usher in a period
of reform, boosting investment and innovation. With 600 million people aged
under twenty-five, the potential for India, if it gets this right, is huge.

This will continue, and as it does, it will spell problems for the dollar.
There is a slow-burning fuse underneath the dollar. A decade ago, Asian
central banks held one-third of global currency reserves, and this has now
risen to two-thirds, the bulk in dollars. Although this has been called the

'dollar trap', the reality is that countries do not want to sell the dollar actively. Instead, passive diversification is under way. As reserves build, fewer are put into the dollar. China has already raised questions about the dollar's role as a medium of exchange and as a store of value. Brazil and China recently discussed paying for each other's trade in their own currencies, not in dollars, as is the norm. As trade flows change, expect more countries to manage their exchange rates against baskets of currencies with which they trade. This points to alternatives to the dollar.

Emerging countries are accounting for an increasing share of global growth. As they do, this will naturally raise questions about the most appropriate business model. Expect to see more focus on state capitalism, as governments play a more important role, as seen in recent years with the increased focus on the activities of sovereign wealth funds. There will be increased competition, as countries compete not just on price, but by trying to move up the value curve, innovating and investing more in research, design and development and in education. All of this will pose increasing challenges for countries in the West, many of whom will have to adapt and change to compete.

The shift of economic power from the West to the East will create profound challenges for many economies, not least the US. It will create huge opportunities for emerging economies, especially those that can position themselves to benefit from the new reality. Regardless of the winners and losers, this shift is inevitable, and it is crucial to correcting the imbalances in the global economy.

The twenty-first century will be a multipolar world. The gradual shift of economic power from the 'old' developed world, or Europe and North America, to the 'new', emerging world of Asia, Africa and Latin America that is already evident now will carry on relentlessly. The shift of power will be as significant for the world as the shift that took place as a result of the Industrial Revolution. Indeed in a way it will be a reversal of the shift of the Industrial Revolution.

Back in 1800 the world's largest economy was China, the world's second-largest India. That balance was changed radically by the early industrialisation first of Britain, then of Europe and then of North America. The balance of probability is that by the middle of this century (and probably much sooner) China will again be the world's largest economy, while India may well be as large, or nearly as large, as the United States.

The possible path of growth has been well charted by the investment bank Goldman Sachs. It has developed the concept of the BRICs versus the G7, BRIC being a clever acronym for the four largest economies of the emerging world: Brazil, Russia, India and China. The bank developed an economic-growth model, with variables including the size of the working population and assumptions about technology transfer, that has so far proved remarkably accurate. Indeed the shift of economic power to the BRICs is working rather faster than early versions of the model suggested. In brief, it suggests that China will pass the US to become the world's largest economy some time in the late 2020s, while India may pass the US in the 2040s. China will probably have passed Japan to become the world's second-largest economy by the end of 2010.

The purpose of any economic model is not to say what will happen but rather to give an intellectual framework for people to think about what might happen if present trends continue. My own view is that the BRIC progress will prove very broadly right, at least for the next generation. There will be grave setbacks, of course. History teaches us that. It is impossible to chart accurately the time scale over which the shift of power will occur. And there will be grave problems confronting the entire world economy, including environmental challenges. But it is hard to see the big picture changing in any radical way. There will be a new order and we can sketch its outlines now.

First, there will be, as noted above, a more balanced world. The present G7 economies, most particularly the US but also to some extent European nations, will still retain technical, scientific and educational leadership for many years to come. The principal military power will remain the United States. The dollar, with the euro, will remain important currencies. The 'old' world will retain social leadership, as many aspects of the way it organises its societies are extremely attractive to the 'new' world. But gradually the balance will shift, much as the balance shifted from Europe to the United States during the twentieth century.

Second, the ideas of the new world, the universities, the publishing empires, the entertainment enterprises and so on will start to affect the old. Chinese and Indian notions of family life will start to shape European and North American notions. Latin America will change the United States and Canada. We can see the start of this process now, particularly in the entertainment fields, but we should expect it to go much further. This does not mean that, for example, the great universities of the US will soon be challenged by those of China, reversing the present pathway for Chinese students to come to the US. It will be a while before Americans and Europeans flock to China to get a better university education. But it does mean embedded assumptions of Western academic superiority will increasingly be challenged. Soon the West will find itself learning as much as it teaches.

A third area of change will be in business and finance. One shift will be in money. Other currencies will join the US dollar and the euro to fulfil the classic functions of money: to be an internationally accepted medium of exchange, unit of account and store of value. It may eventually be that some kind of world currency will be adopted and there will certainly be pressure for that. Meanwhile a multicurrency world will suffice. Just as important, Asian ideas of company organisation and management will influence European and North American ones.

There will be convergence. Just as we can see elements of Western market capitalism being adopted in the rest of the world – for example, Shanghai has Asia's largest stock-market trading floor – so elements of the structures of the emerging world will start to shape our own corporate models. One particular one may be a quest for companies to take a long-term view of their aims and aspirations. Another may be that Western attitudes to corporate governance will be less relevant when Western companies no longer dominate the global corporate arena. Chinese and Indian approaches to corporate organisation and governance will by contrast become much more significant.

None of this should be taken to suggest that Europe and North America will suddenly become much less important in the world. We will not wake up one day to discover that a new world order has suddenly overthrown everything we understood about how the world was run.

Change will be gradual and incremental. There will be periods when it speeds up. We are just going through one at the moment, symbolised by the elevation of the Group of Twenty, which includes the largest emerging nations alongside the so-called 'advanced' economies of the Group of Seven. The G20, not the G7, has now become the main forum for international economic coordination.

There will be periods when the shift slows, maybe even reverses for a while. But by the middle of the century the world economy will have achieved a new equilibrium. No single country will dominate the globe, either in economic or political terms and maybe not in military terms either. What we have to do is learn how to manage a multipolar world to the benefit of all its citizens.

Periods of great economic and financial stress inevitably focus attention on cyclical issues and policies. However, they also force us to focus on more secular and structural issues, which we either neglected in the preceding boom, or which suddenly assumed an importance we did not recognise before. The financial and economic crisis of 2007–9 can be expected to leave us with an uncomfortable legacy of anaemic growth, high unemployment and bloated levels of public debt, and with large ideological issues about the role of government in the economy. Quite how we respond is of course unclear, but the following list of six developments may figure prominently on our post-crisis world agenda.

First, financial stability should and probably will remain an enduring goal of public policy. It is possible that we will over-regulate, and stifle the capacity of banks and businesses to innovate and become more productive. It is also possible that the momentum for reform will succumb to inertia and political acrimony. However, the likelihood is that over time financial re-regulation will lead to changes in the way banks and other financial entities operate and behave. The role of the financial-services sector, measured by the growth of bank assets and profits, and its contribution to GDP and employment, will probably diminish. The ease of access to credit and the terms under which it is acquired will both become more restrictive.

Second, the use of leverage, therefore, to drive economic growth will decline. Banks, as suggested above, will eventually resume normal credit-intermediation functions, but normal will not be the same as it was in the ten to fifteen years leading up to the bust. However, households will also spend some time rebuilding the liquid savings pools that were run down during the last decade or so, and or paying off mortgage and consumer debt. The cult of debt-financed consumption that became deeply entrenched in some economies, such as the US, UK and other parts of Western Europe appears to be giving way to the need for greater financial security, and higher levels of personal savings. This suggests a more cautious and restrained environment for personal consumption and for home prices.

Third, there will come a point, perhaps in 2010 or later, when governments and central banks will reverse and withdraw the exceptional measures they have adopted to stabilise the financial system and the economy. These so-called 'exit strategies' will be awkward and could lead us towards new turbulence. If implemented too early, these policies could tip us back into recession. If implemented too late, they could invite another financial crisis that might be associated with alarming levels of public borrowing and debt or, possibly, with rising inflation. In any event, the next several years are almost certainly going to be characterised by overt restraint in the conduct of monetary and, more importantly, fiscal policies. The latter will emphasise a durable decline in real terms in aggregate public expenditure, even if some programmes are kept off-limits; a broadening of the tax base, for example, removing exemptions from VAT or, in the US, the introduction of a VAT; and higher tax rates on individuals, companies and capital. These will act to restrain or lower economic activity, while hopefully causing governments to emphasise employment-generative programmes geared towards future growth.

Fourth, the crisis has increased the profile and perceived significance of demographic change, specifically the unique change in age structure that is now occurring in earnest. To a significant degree, the immediate focus is on the destruction of pension asset values, on rising unemployment or under-employment. But these issues dovetail perfectly with the structural issues associated with rapid ageing. The baby-boomers that were the rocket fuel of the boom of the last twenty-five years are now starting to retire in droves, their life expectancy in retirement is higher than ever before and rising, and they will not be replaced fully or at all by their progeny, thanks to the decline in fertility rates. The worst affected economies are those of Japan and both Western and Eastern Europe. The US, UK, Scandinavia, Australia and Canada are in a slightly better position, having somewhat higher fertility rates, but all will experience a marked increase in the dependency of their booming over-sixty-five population on a stagnant or declining productive labour force.

This phenomenon is only partly about quality-of-life issues for older citizens, which is already a significant public-policy focus. Fundamentally, it is about the macroeconomics of increasing the capacity of the labour force to support and pay for ageing societies. This leads to the conclusion that we have to rethink radically the ways in which we think about the participation of older workers and women in the labour force, the role that education and training can play in raising employment rates and productivity throughout working lives, the deployment of phased retirement and flexible working practices for employees, how and how much people should save for retirement, and acceptable levels of immigration. But it goes even further. Demographic change, as described, is changing family structures, with rising proportions of childless and one-child couples, single-parent families and units with two or three generations but few siblings and cousins. These family structures generate a greater dependency burden on single children or the state, and especially on women upon whom the bulk of care responsibilities falls. This might then exacerbate problems associated, for example, with suitable employment and working practices. In short, the post-crisis world is likely to see governments, companies and the charitable sector paying much greater attention to policies and products designed to facilitate the demographic transition.

Fifth, we may find a rising interest in innovation as a source of future growth and prosperity, bearing in mind that the factors listed above will all be weighing against it. Technical progress and human ingenuity have traditionally combined historically to advance our well-being, and often during times of crisis. Scientists and economists see great possibilities in the fusion of new technologies, specifically info-, bio- and nano-technologies. While largely focused on medicine, these technologies could revolutionise and help to 'green' an array of products and processes in a large swathe of sectors, including energy, food production and agriculture, transportation, manufacturing and construction. None of this is going to happen soon, unfortunately, but it is quite likely that innovation will become the mantra in the coming decade.

Sixth, there is a vital international dimension too that should not be obscured but that is tough to predict. With luck and good sense and international governance, the economic troubles in advanced nations might be allowed time to mend, while China, India and other emerging markets continue to pick up the baton in the global economy by relying more on domestic demand and income expansion in their own economies and regions. Regardless, the overwhelming consensus about the inevitability of the decline of the West and the rise of China, India and others may end up being flawed or at least a half-century premature. If technical progress and innovation are the prized assets of the next two decades in this century, who is to say that the US and some other developed nations won't scoop the pool?

On the other hand, lack of international cooperation, and disputes between the West and major emerging markets over trade, capital transactions, access to resources and climate change could end up with rising levels of protectionism that threaten to reverse what is already a slowing process of globalisation. This would undoubtedly to be to no one's benefit, least of all the emerging nations or the poorest countries in Africa and Western Asia. Uncertainty, alas, will be the dominant feature of the post-crisis world as far as international relations are concerned.

The global crisis has made it clear that we live in a world of 'permanent impermanence', largely because globalisation (more precisely interconnectivity) exponentially increases uncertainty and as a result favours the occurrence of black swans: very low probability – very high impact kinds of events, such as most of the global risks mentioned above: terrorism, pandemics, financial crises or extreme weather events. This draws the contours of a world that requires more resilience and adaptability.

A significant and growing number of opinion and policy makers believe that the current crisis represents something much more fundamental than a simple and deep recession – some even call it 'The Great Disruption', arguing that our existing growth model has simply become unsustainable. Why? For the sake of simplicity, let's just imagine what happens if the billion plus people in Asia who are about to become the 'new middle class' start consuming in the same proportions as the Americans and Europeans have done until now. In such a scenario, resource constraints become of an order of magnitude difficult to fathom and life on earth becomes unbearable. A Chinese, for example, currently consumes on average 50 kilograms of meat per year, versus 220 kilograms for an American. To put this into perspective, the production of 1 kilogram of beef requires an average of 15,000 litres of water and releases greenhouse gases with a warming potential equivalent to 36.4 kilograms of carbon dioxide (the rough equivalent of a three-hour drive while leaving all the lights on at home). How will that affect water scarcity and air pollution? Need another example? In India, there are currently ten cars for thousand people versus a ratio of 700 per thousand in the Western world. What world will we be living in when there are seventy times more cars on Indian roads? This is not to suggest that 'new consumers' in emerging markets should refrain from consuming the way we have done in the West until now, but these two basic examples simply beg the question of whether the world can afford it. No matter what happens, where and when, consumer behaviour will have to adjust, either willingly – as shown by the 'smart planning' movement in the most affluent societies – or by regulation. As Chandran Nair, the founder and CEO of GIFT (the Global Institute for Tomorrow, based in Hong Kong), puts it: 'If we don't change, change will visit us and it will be painful.' This is why we might progressively move away from a disposable society to a much more 'responsible' one, which will favour entrepreneurs with bold ideas and social entrepreneurship (such as an individual who has made some good money by selling water in biodegradable bottles produced from maize instead of oil). Long-term, this is hugely positive for all investors positioned in industries and goods that can mitigate the over-consumption risk: water scarcity, energy efficiency, renewable energy, pollution and waste, CO_2 emissions, disappearing ecosystems etc., but the social and geopolitical costs of adjustment in the short and medium terms are monumental.

A similar debate (about a long-term issue that is going to redefine the way we live) concerns health and ageing. The debate about the reform of the health system in the US is a potent reminder that these issues are two of the most prominent of the twenty-first century. This is, by the way, true for both developed and emerging countries, where the rapid increase in ageing (twenty years from now, just in China, India and Indonesia alone, 600 million people will be beyond retirement age) will exacerbate social and fiscal problems. There is an urgent need for new solutions, particularly vis-à-vis the capability of our current policies to address these issues and in terms of redistributive policies. In the field of finance, the much respected head of the FSA – Adair Turner – has already broken the taboo by asking whether 'more market is always better'. The uproar caused by his suggestion that it might be worthwhile considering a Tobin tax shows that the much-needed reform of the financial system is held hostage by potent vested interests and beset by collective action problems (the financial-industry lobby is now more powerful than the defence industry used to be twenty years ago – shaping the intellectual and regulatory debate in its favour).

A few predictions to finish:

We all know that, in the words of Niels Bohr the Danish physicist, 'Prediction is very difficult, especially about the future.' Indeed! But the constant need to form an opinion about the future every time we make a decision is inherent in our human condition (whether it is to marry, to invest, to go on holiday, to accept a job . . . or anything else). To that effect, we make below a few macro predictions.

Economics

- Governments, as spenders of last resort, will be forced to run deficits. A vast majority of people will be condemned to a lower standard of living. So will their children.

- The global crisis will generate a new system with greater stability, which will come at the cost of productivity and flexibility.
- Inflationary trends will prevail over the medium and long term. Higher interest rates are almost certain.
- The era of 'leave it to the markets' is over – 'the grab-bag of ideas based on the fundamentalist notion that markets are self-correcting, allocate resources efficiently and serve the public interest well' (Joseph Stiglitz).
- The entrepreneur (whose main function is to create value in the real economy) will replace the speculator (whose main function is to provide liquidity to the markets) as the new 'master of the universe'.
- Increased correlation in the financial markets will become the norm (the world is 'concatenated'; so are the markets). The principle of diversification (instruments, strategy) is losing ground. Only 'diversification of behaviour' matters.
- As distrust of large institutions is growing, small will again become beautiful. Independence – of opinions and decisions – will come at a huge premium.
- The days of opacity are over. Simplicity will prevail. Quantitative models will be disregarded. Experience will be valued again. Oversight will become as important as insight.
- The most talented graduates will stop going to investment banking. Instead, they will go towards regulation, accountancy, tax inspecting, journalism and engineering, and maybe even NGOs and philanthropy!
- Like everybody else, they'll live in a world of much greater regulation and higher taxation. In addition, they may become one of the prime targets of the backlash against globalisation.
- Offshore locations will come under increasing pressure. Invasion of wealth privacy may become the norm.
- Conscious consumption will progressively replace conspicuous consumption. Inexpensive pastimes will become ever more popular. Small (important!) pleasures will be back in vogue. New, different forms of social bonds may be forged. Bling will go out of fashion.

Geopolitics and Society

- More and more, we will live in a permanent contest between the centrifugal impulse inherent in a multipolar system and the centripetal force of interdependence, which some call an 'interpolar' world. It is a world in which it is impossible to tell whether competition will prevail over cooperation or vice versa.

- The 'great reconvergence' between the East and West will speed up. The shift to an Asian-centric world may accelerate. Asia will favour a statist – possibly autocratic – model of development.
- The large – and economically promising – segment of the middle class (both in developed and emerging countries) will enter an era of 'affluent deprivation'. A large majority of their population will remain relatively wealthy but will feel relatively poorer. The sentiment of frustration and resentment will grow.
- Emerging economies will do their utmost not to depend on foreign capital. Controls of capital flows will be reintroduced.
- The world will become more 'local'. As we are entering an era of suspicion (about the markets, governments, institutions), we'll consequently fall back on our family, village, clan, tribe or religion.
- Will the global balance of power be shifting? Too early to tell, but end of 'Chimerica'.
- 'Locational privacy' (the right to keep information about where we are to ourselves) is gone, as it is now collected automatically and stored indefinitely by mobile-phone operators. Soon, the notion of privacy itself will disappear too.

MIKE MOORE[1]

How have the rules, customs and habits that govern successful countries evolved? The big ideas of history – democracy, the separation of Church and State, property rights, independent courts, a professional civil service, the civil engagement that drove reform to widen the franchise and promote social mobility, the civil rights movement, the women's and the environmental movements – have all played their part in the creation of our successful modern societies. Far from being pessimistic about the state of the world, I am always recklessly, even dangerously, optimistic.

When I was first active in politics, I wanted to understand how to do things, but as I've grown older my emphasis has shifted somewhat and I've become fascinated by the question of why we do things and where our beliefs and ideas come from. We are what we have learned. In my new book, *Saving Globalisation*, I've set out to praise the people, principles and institutions that have helped shape my belief that we can make this world a better place, and to explain some of the historical follies that continue to impede progress towards that goal.

While writing my earlier book *A World Without Walls*, which dealt with the economic and social consequences of globalisation, I was struck by the overwhelming evidence that open democratic societies, run by the rule of law, with accountable leaders, honest public servants and an engaged civil society, produced the best results. Human rights, labour standards and environmental outcomes all improved under such conditions. The Kuznets curve famously shows that as average income stabilises over the course of a nation's economic development, economic standards eventually equalise, with environmental outcomes improving as living and educational standards are lifted. Just as a free economic market corrects imbalances and provides more effective and prudent use of resources, so a free political market corrects injustices with an engaged civil society and accountable and responsive leadership. The

---

[1] This entry previously appeared in *Saving Globalization: Why Globalization and Democracy Offer the Best Hope for Progress, Peace and Development* (Singapore: John Wiley and Sons (Asia), 2009).

environmental movement, the women's movement and the civil rights movement all mobilised opinions that shaped the agenda to which legislators and
businesses responded.

As globalisation has lifted hundreds of millions out of extreme poverty,
this should be a time of hope; yet the enemies of reason, with their dark
destructive messages of doom and hate still have a constituency and gain
much media coverage by selling the old-time religion of protectionism,
anti-enlightenment and anti-modernity. The iron reality is that no nation,
any more than any individual, can hope to prosper isolated and cut off
from others. History has shown that isolation is no defence from the drama
of international events. Just as the world's economy has globalised, so have
its problems and solutions. From whaling to child labour, terrorism to
climate change, no nation can hope to achieve peace and progress alone.
It is of no use if one nation cleans up its own environment if its neighbours do not. HIV/Aids cannot be cured or contained by any individual
nation's actions. These days, no single economy can even run a tax system,
fight drugs or run an airline without the cooperation of others. Nor can
any one domestic response reasonably encourage confidence back into
faltering global markets. Few of us are isolationist or protectionist when
our children are ill or want a first-class education; instead, we seek the
world's best for them. So too should we seek the best for our respective
countries.

Security, stability, sustainability and economic growth, the fight against
terrorism, organised crime, and the struggle for human rights – all of these
challenges need international solutions. No nation, grand or modest, can ever
hope to assist with or be the beneficiary of the solution of the great issues
of our age without the cooperation of others.

A study conducted by the World Bank's environmental department began
by defining natural capital as the sum of non-renewable resources (including
oil, natural gas, coal and mineral resources), crop land, pasture land, forested
areas and protected areas. Many of us think of capital, produced or built, as
the sum of machinery, equipment, and structures (including infrastructure)
and urban land. The study concluded: 'Human capital and the value of institutions (as measured by rule of law) constitute the largest share of wealth in
virtually all countries.' The rule of law is the basis of 57 per cent of a country's
intangible capital. Education accounts for 36 per cent. 'Rich countries are
largely rich', the report said, 'because of the skills of their populations and
the quality of the institutions supporting economic activity.' Taking into
account all the world's natural resources and produced capital, 60 per cent of
the wealth of poor nations and 80 per cent of the wealth of rich countries
can be classified as 'intangible wealth'. What was particularly new in this

World Bank report was the inclusion of a rule-of-law index, devised using several hundred individual variables measuring perceptions of governance, drawn from twenty-five separate data sources constructed by eighteen different organisations that included civil society groups, political and business risk-rating agencies, and think tanks.

Switzerland scores 99.5 out of 100 on the rule-of-law index and the United States hits 91.8. Contrast these figures with Burundi's 4.3 and Ethiopia's 16.4. The thirty wealthy, developed nations comprising the Organisation for Economic Cooperation and Development (OECD) have an average score of 90, while sub-Saharan Africa's is just 28.

The natural wealth in rich countries like the United States is a tiny proportion of their overall wealth – typically 1–3 per cent – yet they derive more value from what they have. Crop land, pastures and forests are more valuable in rich countries because they can be combined with other capital, like machinery and strong property rights, to produce more value. Machinery, buildings, roads and so forth account for 17 per cent of the rich countries' total wealth.

Overall, the average per capita wealth in the OECD countries is $440,000, comprising $10,000 in natural capital, $76,000 in produced capital and $354,000 in intangible capital. (Switzerland has the highest per capita wealth, at $648,000. The United States is fourth, at $513,000.) By comparison, the World Bank study found that total wealth for the low-income countries averages $7,216 per person – $2,075 in natural capital, $1,150 in produced capital and $3,991 in intangible capital.

Protectionism in all its forms retards progress by suffocating change and slowing down our ability to learn, adapt and improve. Essentially, it is a contest over which country has the most money to waste on subsidies to ignore and postpone the harsh realities of the world.

All progress is originally hard won. These days, those who resist progress oppose imports that threaten the privileged status quo, they oppose immigration and offshore investment, the WTO, the World Bank, and multinational companies. Fear, self-interest and a looming election are great motivators for change, as is a global crisis such as climate change or recession. These perils could well unite us.

There have been three great waves of change in world history: the agricultural revolution, which took thousands of years to play itself out; the industrial revolution, which took a mere 300 years to evolve and, third, the information age, which has taken just a few decades to develop.

The new information age means that electronic-based grassroots pressure groups and the media have more power than most politicians to influence the people. It's a talkback, telecratic democracy. How we learn, what we eat, our values, our votes and our ethics are increasingly influenced by forces outside our homes, our workplaces, our country.

Western societies have done better in terms of wealth, health and general well-being for the past two centuries, in the main because they have embraced the insights of the Enlightenment, out of which human rights, freedom of religion and freedom from religion, equal rights under the law and, eventually, formal democracy evolved.

These were big ideas that shaped the world for the better. Others, such as property rights and the genius of the 'limited liability company', which gave life to the notion that a commercial entity existed beyond the life of its creators, protected families from the threat of imprisonment for commercial setbacks, changed the concept of inheritance and fundamentally altered the way we managed risk. Fancy being able to borrow against an asset codified by a piece of paper! These commercial developments gave the Dutch and then the English a trading and commercial edge. They worked best only in an environment where the rule of law could be trusted, and where the king or the man with the sharpest sword didn't win every argument.

Commerce and trade, underpinned by predictable rules of engagement, have lifted living standards. The reintegration of China and India into the world economy has changed everything, except our global governance, and has instigated practical debate as to how our international architecture should reflect this new reality. We must now promote an agenda of inclusion to ensure that the backlash against change does not ignite another period of deglobalisation. We must ensure the world's poor are able to continue to rise to better economic circumstances. But without adequate domestic policies of adjustment such contrary reactions are predictable. New forces of reaction, the new enemies of reason, gain strength because of the failure of governments to promote domestic policies that consider the marginalised. We must not fear our future; we must face it optimistically.

I finished my first essay by raising the question as to whether this crisis might lead to some good. Certainly when it comes to the fundamental international economic concern of the pre-crisis era, namely the large and persistent US current-account deficit, the associated low level of personal household savings, the extraordinary amount of capital going to the US from the rest of the world and, of course, the steady build-up of current-account surpluses in China and beyond, the crisis appears to be dealing with those problems!

Recent data show the US current-account deficit back below 3 per cent of GDP, the US personal savings rate, up to 3–4 per cent, more than in Japan, and signs that China's current-account surplus has peaked. Perhaps the future for the US is as an Asian-style exporter and for much of Asia the opposite!

Of course, linked to some of this is the remarkable emergence of China, and other large nascent economies around the world, as symbolised by our infamous BRICs. Back in 2001, when I first mentioned the phrase, I argued that the world needs better 'economic BRICs' in a paper I published. Two years later, in 2003, two of my colleagues outlined in another paper what the world might look like by 2050, and we showed that it was possible that the combined GDP of the four BRIC economies might be bigger than that of the G7 developed countries by 2037, and China might be as big as the US.

For a brief period during this crisis, especially when world trade slowed dramatically after the Lehman collapse, it became fashionable to suggest that the whole 'BRIC' dream was over; but this, in fact, is far from the case. Looking at our latest forecasts for both 2009 and 2010, most of the positive growth that the world gets is going to originate from the BRIC and other large emerging economies. China reported GDP growth of 8.9 per cent for its third quarter of 2009 – not bad, given its severe export slowdown. We think for the full year, growth will be above 9 per cent, and next year, close to 11 per cent. I find myself arguing that China is actually having a 'good' crisis, as policy makers realised as long ago as last November that they would need to do something to offset a severe export slowing. In addition to a massive monetary and fiscal policy, the authorities have also embarked on the beginning of social-security reform, and it seems to us that China has entered a new, healthier stage of economic development led by domestic demand and consumption.

If you look at the reported retail sales data for both the US and China since the start of 2007, and adjust them to be in the same currency, remarkably the increase in Chinese retail sales has been about the same as the decline in the US. And some people claim decoupling can't happen! What better evidence do you want? Because of this kind of forces, we have been arguing since summer 2008 that in fact our BRIC 'dream' of those countries becoming potentially bigger than the G7 might now happen by 2027 – about eighteen years' time.

Much focus is, and should be, on China, but what about India? It looks as though this year and next India could grow by 6 per cent. For a country that only managed around half that during the 'Hindu growth' years of 3 per cent growth, and at a time when the developed world is going through its most severe recession for decades, this is remarkable. And of course, with an election behind it and India's fantastic demographics, it is conceivable that India might start to show Chinese-type double-digit rates of growth in the next decade.

And what of Russia? Many suggest it doesn't deserve its place at the BRIC table. Russia has certainly suffered badly from the world crisis, but from 2001 to 2008, Russia's growth was well ahead of our assumptions. Even, in fact, with the 7.5 per cent we currently pencil in for 2009, Russia will manage to have grown about the same as we assumed in our 2003 projections for this decade, and above that assumed in our 2001 initial paper.

Brazil is often the under-discussed one, but in my book President Lula should probably go down as the most successful policy maker in a major country this decade. Widely expected to fail and lead Brazil to default in 2001, in fact Lula has given that nation stability it hasn't seen for decades, allowing it to even weather this crisis pretty well. Over the next decade, it is likely that the middle classes will balloon in Brazil, allowing for a vast improvement in that country's wealth and position in the world.

Beyond the BRICs, other large emerging economies are also coping with life. Indonesia, while troubled with terrorism intermittently, is showing strong signs of reform and domestic demand growth. In 'new' Europe, while there is huge focus on the troubled Baltic states and some others, the two most populous nations, Poland and Turkey, have coped with the crisis reasonably well.

Indeed, considering these countries and the BRICs, which have strong demand, around 3 billion people in large-population emerging economies appear to be coping with this crisis pretty well – something that appears to be lost on many.

This is the way for the future, and with it we clearly need a new world order of governance. The G20 advent is perhaps a start, as most of these countries are in there. What is clear is that the G7, the G8, perhaps even the UN, certainly the IMF need to either radically overhaul or disappear. Why are France, Germany and Italy still participating in the G7 and G8 separately? They share the same currency and claim they plan to indefinitely. All three have been overtaken in size by China and Italy will soon be challenged by the other BRIC nations. What is the purpose of them being in the world's leading club? They should be represented by the EU or the euro group leader, if that is what they want to dominate their economic affairs. Without the BRIC nations, we can't get adequate representation of the world economy, nor can we solve the future challenges that are clearly looming, such as energy security and climate change, as well as providing more competition for the dollar.

The world will recover from this crisis, and it looks like it is going to be a more balanced and different place for us all to enjoy as a result. There are, nonetheless, plenty of challenges ahead.

MICHAEL O'SULLIVAN

'To be rich is glorious.'
Deng Xiaoping[1]

The credit crisis has shattered the apparent certainty of many worldviews and over the next ten years at least will inspire a radical overhaul of the most basic assumptions we have held true. In particular, the crisis has upset the familiar geometry of many established socio-economic models and will inevitably lead to a reordering of the way in which countries seek to marshal resources and build alliances with each other.

Economic crises often beget profound changes in thinking about socio-economic models as the pendulum of received thinking swings from old ideas towards new ones (for example, France in the 1720s, Meiji Japan in the 1860s or China in the 1980s). This was also the case in the 1970s, when economic crises throughout that decade and growing geopolitical strains led to the political emergence of Margaret Thatcher and Ronald Reagan in the UK and US respectively. Together, their very similar policies came to be known as 'the Anglo-Saxon socio-economic model'.

This model has dominated the practice and debate of economics since the 1980s but has been severely undercut by the credit crisis. In brief, the Anglo-Saxon model rests on a belief in free trade, the primacy of markets over more controlled or regulated exchanges of goods and services, a small role for the state in the economy (e.g. tax revenues as a percentage of GDP (2006) were 44 per cent in France, 49 per cent in Denmark but only 28 per cent in the US) and in general a deregulated and low-tax business climate (Heritage Foundation).

The Anglo-Saxon approach has been particularly remarkable for the way in which it has become diffused through international policy making, through the 'Washington Consensus' policy package, through the corporate world in terms of the advance of the US multinational corporations ('B-52s of globalisation'[2]) and the rise of the finance industry, as well as the spread of the Anglo-Saxon language, laws and education standards (i.e. the MBA).

---

[1] Quoted p. 55, in Mahbubani, K, *The New Asian Hemisphere* (New York, Public Affairs, 2008).
[2] Bhagwati Jagdish, *In Defense of Globalization* (Oxford, Oxford University Press, 2004) p. ix.

There are two competing models within the Anglo-Saxon approach: the European and the Asian. Broadly speaking the European model is one where government finance and policy play a central role in economic development, and in the case of Germany and France from the 1950s to the late 1980s it had a good track record.[3] in generating growth (real GDP in Germany over this period was 1.5 per cent greater than that of the UK).

The European model has several strands. Ireland and the UK follow the Anglo-Saxon approach, but Germany and France follow the Rheinish stakeholder model, where companies are funded relatively more by long-term bank loans, and where workers and other stakeholders are involved in corporate supervision. Ownership structures are more complex and involve much greater family influence, for example.

Spain, Italy and Greece follow the relatively unsuccessful Mediterranean one that involves heavy social-welfare protection (in Italy social expenditure as a percentage of GDP was 26 per cent in 2005, compared to 15.9 per cent in the US), inflexible labour markets and a relative lack of economic dynamism. The most admired socio-economic model is the Nordic one (Nordic countries plus Netherlands and perhaps Switzerland) which is seen as combining innovation and strategic economic strengths with social cohesion.

The alternative model is that of the now highly globalised Asian Tiger economies and China. What these countries have in common in the way in which they have developed is heavy government control, high levels of investment and savings and a passing interest in the idea of an open society.

The Great Transformation

One of the crucial implications of the credit crisis is that it challenges the assumptions behind the Anglo-Saxon model in particular, questioning its competence and balance (i.e. in that it leads to high inequalities). Even though the relative wisdom of the Asian and European models is somewhat clearer now, policy makers in small and developing countries, amongst others, may well be asking: 'What model should we follow now?' Interestingly, in the early part of the twentieth century there was a similar shift in models with government spending as a percentage of GDP in developed countries ranging from 12 per cent (in the US in 1912) to closer to 31 per cent by the 1930s.

While changes in these socio-economic models take place slowly, some forces for change are becoming clearer. As countries at the epicentre of the credit crisis go though the necessary phases of rescue, recovery and reform,

[3] Landier, A, & D Thesmar, *Le Grand Méchant Marché* (Paris, Flammarion, 2007).

we may well see the role of governments in economies grow, the regulatory pendulum swing towards over-regulation from low regulation, and as in many previous bubbles the use of leverage will be reined in, at least in the short-to-medium term.

As capitalist economies need to lean more on governments and as government-run economies seek to return to capitalist levels of economic growth, the overall near-term trend is likely to be one of 'managed capitalism', along the lines of the 'managed democracy' process described by Vladimir Putin in Russia.

Capitalism itself, as understood by the relationship between producers and consumers of goods and services, is unlikely to change, though the speed at which it takes place could change as leverage is restricted and regulation heightened. The ability to take financial risks will most likely be curtailed, and the scope to bear them will be broadened. Work patterns may reflect and reinforce this.

Economically, one open question is whether the fault lines of the credit crisis were caused by too much competition (open markets) or too little competition (oligarchy and the lack of transparency that goes with it). A related issue is whether the state, together with national-champion-type economic actors, or open markets are best able to create organic economic/profit growth in the long term.

One trend that may support a move towards managed capitalism is that households in Anglo-Saxon countries may discover the costs of low levels of investment in public goods (France and Switzerland spend about 11 per cent of GDP on healthcare as opposed to 8 per cent for the UK) and high inequalities (the Gini inequality coefficient for Denmark is 0.23 but 0.37 for the UK), and that households in Europe and Asia may have their aversion to unfettered capitalism reinforced by the experience of the credit crisis.

In the political arena managed capitalism in its various cultural forms could evolve towards a common model where individual nation states resolve the best way to protect themselves against the side effects of globalisation while fostering prosperity is to adopt a traditional republican model based on strong institutions and skilled technocrats, which mixes the best elements of each regional model – equality (Nordic), fraternity (Asian) and liberty (Anglo-Saxon).

The idea here is that nation states, especially those that are smaller and more open, think more strategically about the effects of outside forces such as international trade, financial markets and global organised crime/terrorism, and then act to construct buffers to limit the effects of these on their economies and societies. This could intensify the pattern whereby more open, successful developed economies have a relatively high degree of government involvement in economic management. In turn, this kind of 'buffer' or republican form could be a guide for the GCC nations or developing countries in Eastern Europe and beyond.

The friction caused by tectonic moves in these socio-economic models also has the potential to open up new political spaces, both within nation states and beyond them as countries vie for influence within multinational bodies and try to build their 'soft power'.

Boston, Berlin, Beijing

At a level above nation states, the desire to curb but not stop the influence of markets, open trade and the power of corporations could lead nation states to place a greater emphasis on the role of multinational institutions and also fuel the growth of regionalisation.

Individual models could adapt towards each other and we may well see a tri-polar world form along the lines of three chief regions incorporating the EU, the Anglo-Saxon world and Asia (led by China), or, as George Orwell named them in *Nineteen Eighty-Four*: Oceania, Eurasia and Eastasia.

Growing regionalisation could lead to a new form of balance of power politics, just as the emergence of a larger Germany at the end of the nineteenth century led to coalitions between other European powers (back then America, like China is now, was the emerging power). The extent to which this will happen is a matter of speculation, but the key lesson from the first wave of globalisation is that a mixture of nationalism, balance-of-power rivalries, financial market imbalances and creeping protectionism led to the end of globalisation.

The next few years will the years of rebuilding after the earthquake, years of hangover after drunkenness. The years beyond, provided regulations are tighter and really implemented, should be slower in terms of growth than 2004–7 but also more stable and predictable. This should be good news for business. For regional managers in charge of various regions of the world, this is the time of managing expectations of the CEO who is asking for more based on some encouraging headline news recently. The reality of recovery is worse than those headlines might suggest.

Initially, we will have jobless recoveries in most markets, tighter credit, less risk taking, continuing clearance of toxic waste from bank balance sheets, more protectionism and continuing fears about unemployment. In such an environment, there can be no faster growth in most markets at least until 2011–12.

We cannot expect that the super-cycle will return even if mini bubbles do. Even if regulators screw up everything, it will not be easy to sell garbage to unsuspecting buyers any more. Banks will continue to improve their balance sheets, which will reduce their ability and appetite to lend. They also need some time to recover from rising bad-loan portfolios and in general they usually dislike lending into a weak economic environment. For business people reading this, it basically means that particularly your distributors, partners and customers will have more difficult access to financing in the future. Households need to restore their balance sheets too, particularly in the Anglo-Saxon world, and companies will be doing the same. More debt will be repaid than demanded.

Memories of the crisis will last a long time. Living within our means will drive decision making at government, household and corporate level. Particularly, many governments will have to squeeze their spending for years to come as they recover from fiscal stimulus and lack of income resulting from the crisis. Any companies dependent on government spending should be rethinking their strategy going forward. There should be fewer commodity and inflation spikes as leverage speculation becomes more subdued.

There will also be differences in growth rates in the developed world vs emerging markets. The power and rise of emerging markets will be unstoppable. As of 2011, they will produce half of the world's GDP at purchasing-power parity – for the first time in over 150 years. They will outperform the USA, Western Europe and Japan in terms of growth by a margin of at least three to one. Emerging markets that have sound economic fundamentals will do better than those who lived for so long beyond their means.

Companies should treat emerging markets as seriously as the developed world. If they do not, they will disappear over time. Over the next decade many emerging markets will become less dependent on the developed world, putting them on a path of more sustainable and even faster growth. There will never be real decoupling (it was always a strange theory), but it will increase as time goes by. In terms of long-term competitiveness, emerging Asia should do best, followed by Eastern Europe and then Latin America, the Middle East and Africa. In the short term, emerging Asia together with the Middle East is in best shape in terms of economic fundamentals and available financial buffers and reserves. Companies should shift more focus to those areas for short-term gain. Others will take longer to recover. Many countries in Latin America and Africa are too dependent on commodity exports (prices of which are uncertain going forward) and Eastern Europe will do well only after it grows out of its debt problem (not all countries are affected). In Eastern Europe the bounce-back potential is best in Poland, the Czech Republic, Slovakia, Slovenia and Russia. Elsewhere, there is little doubt that the likes of China, India, Brazil, Turkey, Egypt, Indonesia, Mexico, Nigeria and others will continue to offer tremendous opportunities for companies who take their business development in those markets seriously.

As economic power shifts to emerging markets, and global multipolarity deepens, it will be necessary for companies to look at their global strategies in a different way. Key success factors of the past can still be deployed, but new ones are emerging all the time and I see them in my advisory practice daily. Just one thing to keep in mind is that in the world of lower growth there will be a tremendous rise of multinationals which will treat international business more seriously. At the same time there will be a continued rise of emerging-market multinationals which will continue to challenge the big ones not only in emerging markets but also in their home markets. This is an unstoppable process that no one should underestimate and it will shape business strategies for decades to come.

Executives running international firms should therefore ask themselves the following questions: how do they intend to lead differently? how will they secure the long-term profitability of the firm? how will they protect themselves against competitors with unpronounceable names? how will they entrench creativity and innovation in the entire organisation? and how seriously will they treat their business development in the international arena?

If this crisis and its subsequent clean-up produce a slower but more stable world, this will be good news for everyone.

EDMUND PHELPS [1]

The justice of a well-functioning capitalism and the reforms that will realise it, not kill it

I believe that countries cannot afford to jettison the innovative activity of entrepreneurs, investors, pioneering managers and their employees that – for two centuries now – has been drawing an ever-widening share of people in an ever-growing number of nations into engaging jobs, exciting explorations and remarkable commercial advances. I will try to explain, getting finally to issues of instability.

What is capitalism? Any concept of a capitalist economy must include private wealth owning. Yet that private wealth must extend to ownership of all or most of the economy's business capital – not merely cars, homes and debts of the state and state enterprises, as under market socialism. It is also necessary that private owners of businesses be accorded control over where to invest – not just along the narrow lines assented to by managers, guilds or unions, as in corporatism, or in ways dictated by the state or oligarchs. But these wealth-centred features are insufficient to capture the character of capitalism in the modern age.

The spirit of capitalism took form in the nineteenth century. With the development of company law, corporate finance, investment banking and patent law, the way was opened for a process of innovation: the conception of novel commercial ideas; the selection by financiers of some of these ideas for development, the realisation by entrepreneurs of the envisioned products or methods, and the adoption or rejection by managers or consumers of some of the new products reaching the market. In this process, private ownership is typical at every stage, required or not. Laissez-faire – a free market of low taxes, tariffs and regulation – is *not* required; it may undermine capitalism's functioning.

[1] This paper expands upon a dinner speech at the 7th Annual BIS Conference on Monetary Policy, Luzern, 26 June 2008, and a lecture at the Borsa Italiana, Milan, 11 June 2008.

Note that a new commercial idea in a country may be an application of an invention or discovery made by scientists *outside* the economy or an innovation made by a business in *another* economy. That was Josef Schumpeter's early view of how commercial ideas arise in a country.[2] (He wrote that developing a new idea into a new product at an economical price required the skills of a savvy entrepreneur.) Instead, the new idea might come from *inside* the nation's economy: an original idea inspired by the observations and imagination of producers, employees, managers or consumers – people 'on the spot'. This was the view of Friedrich Hayek.[3] It is the view of most experts today.[4] If innovation were mere Schumpeterian application or imitation, a socialist system could approximate the results of a capitalist system.

What is the distinctive merit of capitalism? For many, capitalism's main merits are the wealth accumulation it fosters and the individual freedom it helps to protect. Referring to capitalism in his Inaugural Address, President Obama said, 'Its power to generate wealth and expand freedom is unmatched.'[5] For me, that does not capture the value of a well-functioning capitalism. As for wealth, it may be that the challenge of attaining greatly increased wealth in one's young or middle years is absorbing and fun: as Nietzsche and Frank Knight might have remarked, it is like participating in a sport. Yet social observers are right to question whether people find significant satisfaction *beyond some point* from increased *relative* wealth.[6] After you have won the game, what point is there in winning by a bigger point spread? Many entrepreneurs speak of the wealth received as a by-product of what they sought to do or achieve rather than as the goal. In any case, an increase in some people's relative wealth means a decrease in some others' relative wealth. The value of *nationwide* advances in wealth might seem to be on more solid ground. It *is* better to have more wealth in a city or nation where most others have more wealth too: possibilities of a richer and more rewarding life result.

The fault in this view is that the relatively capitalist countries are *not* distinguished by high wealth levels. The somewhat more socialist economies

---

[2] Schumpeter, *Theorie der wirtschaftlichen Entwicklung* (Leipzig, Duncker & Humblot, 1912).

[3] The earliest example is F A Hayek, *Collectivist Economic Planning* (London, Routledge, 1935). See also Hayek, 'Competition as a Discovery Procedure [1968]', in Hayek, *New Studies in Philosophy, politics, Economics, and the History of Ideas* (Chicago, Univ. of Chicago Press, 1978).

[4] It is the view of Alfred Chandler, Peter Drucker, Richard Nelson, Sidney Winter, Giovanni Dosi, Roman Frydman and Andrzej Rapaczynski, Virginia Postrel, Amar Bhide, John Kay and my view too.

[5] Barack Obama, Inaugural Address, 20 February 2009.

[6] I am thinking of attitude surveys and commentaries by Bruno Frey, Richard Layard and Andrew Oswald, to name just those that immediately come to mind.

and more corporatist economies of Western Europe reach wealth levels exceeding the levels in the capitalist economies. The reasons are familiar. One of the major drivers of wealth, the propensity to save, is higher in Luxembourg, Switzerland, Belgium, France and Germany than in the US, the UK and Canada – despite the high security offered by the continental welfare system.

The other driver of private wealth, namely, the level of productivity, is also equal if not greater in the former group of countries than in the latter group. A proposed explanation is that while those capitalist exemplars may be at or close to the 'technical frontier', thanks to their lead in cutting-edge innovation, they waste much of their output potential in false steps, in the costly processes of marketing, and an over-investment caused by the winner-take-all competition of costly R & D projects.[7] Furthermore, the top-down techno-nationalist projects that some relatively corporatist nations have substituted for discoveries bubbling up naturally from the business sector may do well on that score thanks to the resources saved by avoiding wasteful competition for new products involving parallel development work and marketing efforts. One has to conclude that generation of wealth is not special to capitalism. Corporatist economies are as good at that.

As for freedom, it has been argued that a capitalist economy far more than a socialist or a corporatist economy offers help to buttress people's personal and political freedoms against the tyrannies of the state, communities and the culture. Owners of a firm in a capitalist economy would feel it in their pocket book if employees were hired or fired on the basis of their beliefs rather than the firm's profits.[8] Yet the evidence is mixed: some of the relatively socialist and corporatist economies of Western Europe appear to be extraordinarily tolerant of deviance from the mainstream.

A merit of a well-functioning capitalism – I do not mean free-market policies, but low tax rates, etc. – is the economic freedoms it provides entrepreneurs, managers, employees and consumers that socialist or corpo-

[7] Historically, some corporatist economies have sought to substitute a top-down 'scientism' for the discoveries bubbling up naturally from the business sector. Of course, the techno-nationalist projects undertaken in corporatist economies may produce some productivity gains. Yet the selection among these projects and the development decisions along the way are not immune to mis-steps. And techno-nationalism is prone to flaws of its own, such as a tendency to the grandiose and to over-engineering. So it is doubtful that industrial research policy can be creditedfor the good productivity levels exhibited in some corporatist economies.

[8] See for example Henry C Wallich, *The Cost of Freedom*, (New York, Harper, 1960). Somewhere Wallich wrote that 'power is the great enemy of freedom'.

ratist systems do not provide.[9] In Friedman's work, the 'freedom to choose' derives its value as a means to *income*.[10] He suggests that incomes will be higher when participants are free to move over a wide range of regions, occupations and industries and when individuals and enterprises are free to collect microdata on which to make decisions. But that is a thesis that well-functioning capitalist economies, owing to their freedoms, are better at producing income and wealth than more corporatist systems (and socialist ones). As noted earlier, the best corporatist economies tend to exhibit comparable productivity.

The work of Hayek from his *Road to Serfdom* onward suggests another kind of value in economic freedoms.[11] In any real-life economy (not theoretical models in which everything in the present and the future is known), actors may sense or conjecture opportunities or dangers about which there is little or no public knowledge while the individual has significant *private* knowledge about possible benefits or costs as well as imagination and personal experience. Individuals' freedoms to act (or not act) on their unique knowledge, intuition and judgement may be indispensable to people's sense of self-worth and self-reliance. In this view, it would be inadequate to gauge the value of freedom by its contribution to income, consumption, investment and even to the pragmatists' 'expansion of talents' and 'capabilities'. The freedom to act on this basis – to take charge of one's own heading and make one's own mistakes – is a primary good in itself, one of huge importance. Is there evidence of greater economic freedoms in capitalist economies than in the more socialist or corporatist economies?[12] My research using survey data supports the widespread impression that, in the relatively capitalist economies, people in ordinary jobs have freedoms they value – more than workers in the relatively socialist or corporatist economies. In the former economies more

---

[9] Some of the public discussion here looks convoluted. It makes no sense to say that a merit of such a system is that it provides freedoms without which the system could not function. It is necessary to explain what the value to people of such freedoms might be.

[10] Friedman, Milton, *Capitalism and Freedom*, (Chicago, University of Chicago, 1962) and Milton & Rose Friedman, *Free to Choose*, (New York, Harcourt, 1980).

[11] Hayek, F A, *The Road to Serfdom*, (London: Routledge, 1944). See also the commentary in Amartya Sen, 'An Insight into the Purpose of Prosperity', *Financial Times*, 20 September 2004.

[12] Jeffrey D Sachs says no in his 'Response to Easterly on Hayek', *Greg Mankiw's Blog*, Monday, 27 November 2006. He notes that the Heritage Foundation / *Wall Street Journal* Index of Economic Freedom ranks Finland, Sweden and Denmark as 'free economies', with Denmark ranked ahead of the United States – and this in spite of their high rates of taxation, which counts heavily in the Heritage index. This is undeniably interesting, since those three countries are widely regarded as pretty corporatist as well as somewhat socialist. However, the Heritage indicators of 'freedom' largely differ from the individual freedoms in the workplace, financial markets and product markets that I am clearly referring to.

than in the latter, workers say they want jobs offering chances to take initiative and responsibility, which reveals that they know such jobs are available, while acknowledging also the value of teamwork – thus the need both to give orders and take orders.[13]

It is important also to make explicit what Hayek must have believed but did not say. As a long line of Western humanists and philosophers propounded, from Bergson, James and Hume back to Cervantes, Cellini and Virgil, in a significantly unknown world, an individual's freedoms to experiment, to learn, to explore, to act on impulse and to test ideas offer personal benefits in another category under the heading of *personal growth*: expansion of 'talents' and 'capabilities', widening experience and self-discovery. In my work I suppose that all or most people are capable of finding such satisfactions from taking part in the innovation process of a capitalist economy: examining untried ways of producing something, conceiving and developing an innovative product or method and pioneering the adoption of a new product or method.[14]

In this view, the dynamism of a well-functioning capitalism has a fundamental merit. Ordinary people, if they are to find intellectual growth and adventure, have to look outside the home: these rewards can only be found at work, if anywhere. And for these rewards to be available for large numbers of people, the economy has to be based predominantly on a well-functioning capitalist system. Thanks to the grassroots, bottom-up processes of innovation, it can deliver – far more broadly than Soviet communism, Eastern European socialism, and Western European corporatism can – chances for the mental stimulation, problem-solving, exploration and discovery required for a life of engagement and personal growth.[15]

Can dynamism justify capitalism? Could it be that a well-functioning capitalism's value in providing opportunities to act on their own knowledge, intuition and judgement and its value in providing opportunities to be engrossed and to flourish serve to *justify* that capitalism? It is clear how that might be argued: 'If a well-functioning capitalist system offers broad numbers in society chances for a life of initiative and discovery while the other systems deprive people of that experience, then imposing the latter systems on society would be terribly unjust.' The answer would appear to be yes.

---

[13] Phelps, 'Economic Culture and Economic Performance: What Light is Shed on the Continent's Problem,' 3rd Annual Conference of the Center on Capitalism and Society, Venice, July 2006.
[14] See my Prize Lecture, 'Macroeconomics for a Modern Economy,' Stockholm: Nobel Foundation, 2007, and papers of mine going back at least to 2003.
[15] My argument can be sampled in my paper for a 2003 Baumol conference and my June 2006 speech at Sciences-Po as well as the Venice paper and Prize Lecture cited above.

A plausible objection is that even a well-functioning capitalist system would not be just if it failed to strive for the largest possible inclusion of the productive population in that system. It can be accepted that such a system is not fully just, thus unjust. (I certainly agree.) But that does not imply that dynamism cannot be just until a just level of inclusion is sought and achieved. Moreover, it is not capitalism that stands in the way of inclusion; it is the inadequacy of wage subsidies.

Taking instability and crisis into account When President Sarkozy spoke of a 'refounding' of capitalism I wondered whether he had in mind what might be termed a capitalist reformation that would be analogous to the Protestant Reformation in the 1500s. There is the appearance of a parallel between the Church's creation in medieval times of lucrative indulgences, which national governments did nothing to stop, and the banking industry's sale in recent years of overvalued packages of mortgages, called CDOs, which governments did nothing to stop. But the banks held such CDOs on their own account – they did not only sell them to naïve buyers. The moral shortcoming in the banks, it appears, was that the leaders did not have the moral strength to protest the rise of leverage and the deterioration in the quality of the securitised assets to which they gave their seal of approval. With varying discomfort, the CEOs seem to have felt too weak ever to try to call a halt to further expansion of credit – to 'get off the merry-go-round', in the famous words of Charles ('Chuck') Prince, former CEO of Citigroup.

I feel that in combating this part of the problem in the financial sector the first line of defence ought to be laws and regulations. Altruism is a valuable resource but we do not want to risk causing havoc with it by appealing to it in a comprehensive way at all levels of life. There must be social responsibility at some critical points but we cannot afford to overuse this resource lest we find ourselves with too little of it left when we need it most. How does the element of *instability* in capitalist systems affect the argument for continuing with capitalism? One's first reaction, especially if one has high appreciation for capitalism, might be to say that the big swings to which capitalist systems are inherently prone, should not stay society's hand in creating and maintaining a system that is so essential to engaging work and personal growth. The instability experienced does diminish our satisfaction as participants in the economy, but it does not diminish our thirst for the good life.

On reflection, there are valid points in favour of regulation aimed at reducing vulnerability to severe fluctuation. First of all, the good life is not a binary variable: you have it or you don't. A capitalism system dogged by frequent crisis and fears of crisis may levy a toll not only on people's comforts and sense of security but also on the generation of innovation itself. So there may be a gain in the degree of dynamism to be obtained by fortifying the financial system from speculative crises. The second point I would make involves another dimension: No human system can be expected to be innovative all the time, just as no composer would be expected to be in the heat of creation all the time. It is possible, then, that a financial system that is more robust in the face of speculative movements will exhibit dynamism a greater *proportion* of the time – thus, innovation smoothing. So, in principle, creating a financial sector that is less vulnerable to speculative shifts might not be harmful to dynamism.

Indeed, most economists discussing needs for financial reform appear to believe that better alignment incentives and serious regulatory restraints on ruinous competition for profits, though aimed at economic efficiency and maybe increased returns to shareowners, will cost the economy nothing in innovation and employment. But this sort of theorising, though well intentioned and even useful in exposing the perils of excessive gearing of pay to crude measures of performance, is itself dangerous in leaving the impression that, after reforming bonuses, asset markets will no longer be susceptible to huge asset-price swings that are driven only by 'speculative excesses' (to use Spiethoff's convenient shorthand).

Unambiguously good reforms Do there exist reforms that address speculative swings while causing little or no damage to economic dynamism and inclusion? There are ways of fortifying the financial sector against the speculative fever of investors and entrepreneurs in the business sector without obstructing the speculative investment waves that are emblematic of a healthy capitalism. One suggestion, which comes from my colleague Richard Robb, calls for a small tax on the short-term indebtedness of financial companies, including the banks. So many of the banks' problems came from excessive short-term borrowing of little or no social utility. Let us tax that in order to force banks to finance their lending with long-term borrowing instead. There are also ways of tempering the speculative swings themselves without suppressing the spirit of capitalism. A suggestion from my long-time collaborator Roman Frydman calls for the introduction of a band around the index of housing prices, a band around the main index of stock-market prices and so forth. When the index rises or falls outside the band, the government will increase margin requirements, short-selling requirements, and various other costs so as to dampen – but not outlaw – speculation on a further move of the asset-price index.

Do there exist reforms that would address the decline of economic dynamism in the past decade while causing little or no increase in instability? I have been moving towards a proposal to establish new banks of a new kind.

It is not uncommon to see financial entities in a country that are dedicated to residential construction or to agriculture or to exports and so forth. This is curious and disturbing, since little or no economic dynamism comes from our stock of housing as against, say, our stores of clothing and from producing for export rather than home use. (The agricultural sector too has not been celebrated much for its dynamism, however unfair that may be in some cases.) There is no awareness among the general public and its legislatures that most of the economic dynamism inherent in the structure of a country's economy comes from the innovative inclinations of the ordinary people making their careers in the business sector! To right the balance, I suggest to every country that its government establish a corps of banks that are dedicated to lending to – or investing in – companies in the *business* sector. This is not really new. I like to remind audiences that Germany, with its famous Deutsche Bank, had just such a financial institution serving its business sector over the decades of its brilliant economic development – especially in the 1880s and 1890s, when the bank powered the birth of the electrical-engineering industries in Germany. (It also lent to the Edison Company in New Jersey.)

Do there exist reforms that would address the still insufficient levels of economic inclusion without stifling dynamism? Here I would recall the sort of programme that has been adopted to a degree in France, the Netherlands and most recently in Singapore: subsidies to companies for their ongoing employment of low-wage workers. Notwithstanding these breakthroughs, it remains true that the United States has as yet no programme of general subsidies for low-wage employment. And the outlays of this kind in Europe are still under 2 per cent of the GDP.

Yet there is the looming threat that the public, in its understandable desire to keep fluctuations within tighter limits, will push regulations affecting incentives and competition to a point where a trade-off begins: where further regulatory tightening weakens or narrows some of the sources of dynamism. Europeans, in vilifying all hedge funds, all private equity and all short-selling, make it much more difficult than it already was to increase dynamism in their economies – and without getting at the real sources of excessive instability. It is to be hoped that the Europeans will come to see that they are aiming their wrath at the wrong targets.

JONATHON PORRITT

The current world order is, to all intents and purposes, already dead. Its principal driving impulses (the hegemony of the United States, accelerating globalisation, deregulation of capital markets to facilitate that globalisation, and a constant readiness to set aside concerns both about equity and bio-physical sustainability) are all either stalled, collapsed or under unprecedented critical scrutiny. Whether this particular moment in time is seen, in ideological retrospect, as marking the decline and ultimate fall of US-driven neo-liberalism, is neither here nor there: the economic meta-system that has dominated the world for the last thirty years or more is in terminal decline.

To many, that will seem a premature assertion. Now that somewhere between $16 and $20 trillion (depending on how the calculations are done) have been loaned, invested or otherwise 'made available' to bail out the global economy, the working assumption of all those increasingly self-satisfied world leaders is that a return to something resembling business as usual is both available and highly desirable.

Their agenda is at least transparent: strain every sinew (again!) to get the Doha talks on world trade back on track; commit ostentatiously to regula-tory reform in the reassuring knowledge that most of the measures being introduced are manageably superficial; make a serious start on addressing climate change if not in Copenhagen in December, then some time in 2010; and promise more fervently than ever to increase the level of support for the world's poorest countries through some kind of updated Millennium Development Goals.

It's difficult not to be a little world-weary about all this, so comprehensive has been the failure of the current world order that it beggars belief to imagine that people just can't wait to get back to more of the same. The truth, of course, is that the majority of *people* don't want any such return. They *do* want an opportunity to put their skills to good use, to enjoy first-class educa-tional and health services, to feel secure in their homes and engaged in their communities, to have their growing fears about runaway climate change properly addressed by serious policy interventions, to be able to find the right balance between work, family, friends and fun, to manage their debts without feeling crushed by them – and even to start thinking about saving for the future. Nothing terribly dramatic, but something along those lines emerges time after time whenever people and communities are asked to share in 'visioning' exercises.

That's why our politicians *claim* to uphold precisely those goals, on behalf of the people they purport to represent. They then go on to warn people in the very next breath that the only way of achieving those goals is through the self-same economic model that brought the global economy to the edge of total collapse, a model that has exacerbated rather than narrowed the divides between rich and poor (both within many nations and between nations), and has blithely condoned the continuing attrition of the eco-systems and life-support services on which we all depend. If you aspire to a decent life, apparently, you first have to commit to an economic system that undermines pretty much everything that makes for a decent life in the first place.

It is, anyway, a mind-numbingly stupid idea that the current world order is any longer *physically viable*, regardless of how morally repugnant it may be. The government's chief scientific adviser, Sir John Beddington, is spending more and more time warning his political masters that we are heading inexorably into a 'perfect storm', with rising demand for food (caused both by rising population and by better diets in emerging countries like China and India), rising demand for energy (at a time when even the oil companies tell us that the days of 'easy oil' are long gone), and declining availability of water, land and the wealth of biodiversity that underpins all human economies – all compounded by the increasingly serious consequences of accelerating climate change.

Back in August, I saw John Beddington interviewed by Stephen Sackur on the BBC World Service's programme, *Hard Talk*. Sackur came straight out with it and said that some of his colleagues inside government were accusing him (off the record, of course!) of becoming 'an out-and-out neo-Malthusian'. No charge more serious than this, because it is the shade of the unfortunate Thomas Malthus (an eighteenth-century English cleric who predicted that rising human numbers would – at some stage in the future – overwhelm the capacity of the land to feed those increased numbers) that is levelled against anyone perceived to have renounced the cornucopian fantasies on which today's world order is built. (Beddington needn't be too upset. All three of his predecessors in that role were saying exactly the same, and he finds himself now in very good – and increasingly populous – company. For the record, I was first accused of being a neo-Malthusian back in 1975!)

This whole sorry charade (as in humankind acting out a fiction that bears no resemblance to the physical reality of our lives) will, I believe, be brought to a grinding conclusion in the next ten years, come what may. Accelerating climate change is a *current* reality, not a future threat. The lives of millions of people are already dramatically affected by it. That painful physical reality (captured so devastatingly in two new reports, one from Oxfam ('Suffering the Science: Climate Change, People and Poverty') and the other from Kofi Annan's Global Humanitarian Forum ('The Human Impact Report: Climate Change') is simply not part of the current world order largely because it is a reality that currently affects the poor rather than the rich.

Our rich world leaders are now *talking* about climate change. Here in the UK and in a few other countries, we are at last seeing some encouraging signs that the policy interventions now required are going to have to be deep, all-pervasive and potentially controversial. But over the last couple of years, I've come to the regrettable conclusion that our current economy/world order is in fact incapable of bridging the gap between what needs to happen from a scientific perspective (to avoid runaway climate change) and what is 'politically viable'. That system will therefore need to be shocked, as traumatically as possible, as soon as possible, if we are to have any chance at all of avoiding infinitely more traumatic pain in the longer term. Better to experience such climate-induced shocks now rather than drift on and on with today's suicidal complacency.

At which point, the debate about what a future world order will look like is difficult to deal with. Whatever else we know, we know that it will be so utterly different as to make most of today's speculative contributions around some kind of reformed 'business as usual' look frankly ludicrous. Our principal tasks at that point will be to protect our democracies, to defend the rule of law and to empower the United Nations to bring binding – even savage – sanctions against those continuing to take a free 'carbon ride' even as the rest of the world transitions as rapidly as possible from a fossil-fuel economy to a solar economy.

To advance such a position falls outside *any* contemporary political pale. Even the Green Party fears being hammered by straying into such potentially apocalyptic territory. But the truth of it is that we won't actually have any choice. As with Thomas Malthus's projections, it's just a matter of time.

MAMPHELA RAMPHELE

The world is reeling under the impact of a triple crisis. First, we are facing an unprecedented financial crisis that has triggered a worldwide recession. Second, there is irrefutable and growing evidence of climate disruptions that threaten sustainable development, especially livelihoods for the poorest people. Third, there are social crises in multiple places across the globe leading to violent protests and social instability.

South Africa, as a microcosm of the world we live in, is experiencing all three crises with a level of intensity that has attracted the attention of leaders across all sectors of society. South Africa is also unable to escape the impact of the crisis on the rest of the African continent. The impact of the triple crisis respects no boundary. The question facing the global community today is whether we are willing to be bold and use the triple crisis as an opportunity for a major paradigm shift in our approaches to development and social relationships both within and between nations. Let us look at each crisis in turn.

The financial crisis

The collapse of Lehman Brothers in September 2008 was a major wake-up call, drawing attention to a crisis that had been brewing for years under the watch of some of the best brains in the financial-services sector, including regulators of the most powerful nations. The abuses exposed by a series of financial scandals and systemic failures seemed to have failed to convince regulators and taxpayers to demand a shift from perverse incentives in the sector to an environment of accountable stewardship.

Remember the savings and loan crisis under President Bush, Snr in the 1980s? Bail-outs secured a semblance of return to normality, but were the lessons learned? What about the so-called 'Asian flu' of the mid-1990s? The root cause then was the sovereign credit crunch, as many of the Asian 'Tigers' had been overloaded with debt by the financial houses in developed countries that felt protected from reckless trading by the international regime in which the IMF and World Bank were often called upon to organise bail-outs.

The same reckless trading approach and bail-outs were practised with respect to Latin America at huge cost to poor citizens of those countries, who bore the brunt of inflation, devalued currencies and high interest rates imposed as part of the bail-out conditions. Ironically it was Argentina, which had long been propped up by this reckless trading fuelled by perverse incentives, that called the bluff of the international financial community and defaulted on its debt in 2002. There was egg over the faces of all those who had played the reckless trading game of lending into bankruptcy, especially the IMF, which had been feeding the credit-flow frenzy through its provision of foreign exchange to Argentina.[1]

The growing sophistication of financial markets, fuelled by instruments developed by some of the best brains in the world, has spawned monsters that drove Alan Greenspan, ex-Federal Reserve Bank chief, to speak indulgently about irrational exuberance. It could be said that Mr Greenspan was speaking like the parent of a spoilt child who broke rules ever so slightly yet persistently evoked both pride and discomfort in the parent. But this was no innocent negligence by an indulgent parent. The warning signs were ignored, so too were cautionary comments by experts. The Enron and other corporate scandals were also not used to trigger a fundamental examination of the institutions that were meant to form the architecture of propriety and public accountability. The Andersen audit and consulting company could not have been alone in the abuse of public trust. What about the credit-rating agencies that continued to give AAA ratings to assets that turned so sour?

The Lehman Brothers collapse and its aftermath may be the Damascus Road experience the world needed for a fundamental rethink about the management of the financial sector in an interconnected world. No longer can we afford the indulgence that Wall Street and London City players have become so accustomed to. The paradigm shift has to involve key pillars.

First, the much spoken about but not acted upon overhaul of the global financial architecture has to be tackled in earnest. Tinkering on the edges is not enough. Second, reform of the Bretton Woods institutions to reflect the realities of the twenty-first century rather than post-WWII ones is essential. Bringing the new global economic players such as China, India and Brazil into the shaping of the global system cannot be postponed any longer. The voting power on the World Bank and IMF should reflect these realities. Third, the G20 is a much more relevant global leadership forum than the outdated G7. The pretence that the G7 countries have legitimacy as global leaders should be jettisoned and replaced with a mature participatory global order.

[1] See Antony Mueller in 'No Tears for Argentina' at http://mises.org/story/868 for more detailed analysis.

The climate-disruption crisis

The inconvenient truth that Al Gore dared to confront us with has become much more part of our twenty-first-century reality. Moreover the 2007 *Report of the UN* Inter-Governmental Panel on Climate Change spelled out the challenges and recommendations of urgent action. The report was lauded by all and sundry and was crowned by the award of the 2007 Nobel Peace Prize. We can no longer claim that 'the science is not yet in', as former President George Bush said; nor pretend that our part of the world is not likely to be affected. The tragedy of the poor is everywhere in evidence. But are we ready for a paradigm shift to reduce and mitigate risk and promote adaptive behaviour for the most vulnerable amongst us?

Copenhagen offers an opportunity for all countries regardless of level of development to have open strategic conversations about how they would each contribute to addressing this unfolding tragedy before it is too late. Finger pointing is not an option. We must recognise the greater responsibilities of the most advanced industrialised nations for the stock and flow of greenhouse gases and other environmentally damaging elements, as well as their impact on global sustainability. Large emerging economies such as India, China, Brazil and South Africa must engage in these conversations, ready to assume their own responsibilities for contributing to tackling both the stock and flow of undesirable emissions.

South Africa has a particular responsibility for taking the lead to help the African continent to tackle practices and challenges that put our fragile and water-scarce continent at risk. Africa's youthful population of about a billion people faces the greatest risks, given the continent's weak states, poor governance, conflicts and social instability, including displacements of large populations within and between national boundaries, low levels of education and health status. These risks and challenges can be turned into opportunities if leaders live up to the promise of the New Partnership for Africa's Development that now seems like a distant memory. South Africa's opportunity is to address its own climate-changing development practices that impact negatively on our environment as well as on our neighbours. SASOL has the opportunity to leverage its leadership position in the energy sector to use known technologies and pioneer new ways to reduce harmful emissions and enhance efficiencies in its operations across the country as well as in its international ones. The same applies to ESKOM.

But Africa as a whole has an opportunity to use the growing carbon trade and the risk-mitigation and adaptive proposed pooled resources to become a green continent. The Alliance for a Green Revolution in Africa (AGRA) is an example of what North–South collaborative efforts can achieve in the field of food security. AGRA is an African-led initiative facilitated by the Rockefeller

Foundation and Bill & Melinda Gates Foundation in response to African leaders' calls for support to help Africa feed itself. AGRA is an enabling platform that has attracted other donors and is supporting governments to live up to their own commitments to allocate 10 per cent of government expenditure to support their agricultural sectors of their countries. AGRA is active in fourteen countries, strengthening the development and preservation of seed varieties, promoting soil health, supporting agro-dealerships, promoting innovative water-management programmes and growing agro-science human resources. Africa should use this example to tackle the enhancement of forests, water management, soil erosion and many sectors that would both preserve the environment and provide jobs and sustainable development.

The link between local African challenges and global ones cannot be ignored. Simon Barber, a US country manager for the South African International Marketing Council, makes an interesting link between the African farmer and a super-sized Coke.[2] He argues persuasively that the USA's continuing subsidies to farmers, at huge cost to its taxpayers, are fuelling the inefficient use of corn to make sugar (high-fructose corn syrup – HFCS). The latter is heavily implicated in the growing obesity epidemic amongst those using Coke regularly. More than 35 per cent of US citizens are now officially obese compared to 15 per cent in 1980. High import tariffs are keeping out healthier cane sugar produced in the developing world. Obesity is also partly to blame for the high levels of health expenditures in the US at 16 per cent of GDP, with worse outcomes than smaller nations such as Sweden, who spend less on health care and get better outcomes. International trade barriers are not just costly for poor countries who miss out on opportunities to grow themselves out of poverty, but they degrade both the physical environment and the health of nations.

Enlightened self-interest and bold leadership are called for if we are to avoid the tragedy of the commons that has the potential to devastate our globe. There is only one world and we need to look after it as its citizens and stewards.

The social crisis

The global recession that has made itself felt across the world highlights once more the risks of a world with disproportionate levels of inequality. The 2006 *World Development Report* published by the World Bank, focused on equity and development, argued passionately that 'With imperfect markets, inequalities in power and wealth translate into unequal opportunities, leading to

---

[2] *Business Day*, 15/9/09.

wasted productive potential and to an inefficient allocation of resources.'[3] The world has thus not just a moral or ethical imperative to fight poverty and inequality, but enlightened self-interest calls for investments in outcomes that enable all to develop and use their potential to the full. Sustainable social stability can only be built on this basis.

South Africa is the poster child of how much inequality costs to nations and regions. The entire colonial and apartheid period, stretching over more than 300 years prior to 1994, were years of lost opportunity. The ideological focus on advantaging a minority of the population on the basis of racial engineering brought the country to ruin by the end of the twentieth century. The political settlement that has been much lauded by the global community ignored a key factor in the conditions for a free democratic and prosperous society. That key factor is the importance of mobilising and utilising the energy and creativity of poor people as essential elements of sustainable development. The Truth and Reconciliation Commission deliberately excluded violations of socio-economic rights in an attempt to secure an elite settlement that would then allow the new elites to control and command the redress of social and economic inequities.

The failure of both the reconstruction and development programme of the 1994–9 ANC government as well as the subsequent and continuing failure of 'delivery of social services by the government of the day' share a fatal flaw. Poor people's capacity for innovation, energetic engagement and leveraging of their long hard experiences has not been taken into account in the development framework of our post-apartheid governments. Poor people have been treated as objects of charity in the provision of free houses, basic services and social-welfare grants. Their voice in how these could be restructured has not been sought, nor listened to when expressed. A paternalistic-governance approach, with strong authoritarian elements by both government and the governing party, has characterised post-apartheid South Africa.

It is not surprising that so much unrest has broken out over the last decade, as poor people recognise how they have been marginalised in the new South Africa. Rampant corruption, nepotism and lack of accountability by public- and private-sector leaders have made poor people realise that they have been robbed of the fruits of freedom they were promised. After the April 2009 election, social instability is a reflection of the growing awareness that the elites are largely in the governing process for themselves. Passivity, which characterised much of the last decade, has turned into 'passive aggression'. The last few weeks have been witness to the sight of part of the military

[3] *World Development Report*, 2006, p. 7.

scaling the fence of the seat of government they are meant to defend. This says it all.

South Africa has a youth bulge – almost 60 per cent of our population is between eighteen and thirty-five years of age – that should be turned into an opportunity to develop them into a formidable workforce that can compete with their global peers. White males who are in the prime of their careers should be harnessed as mentors and trainers of the next generation of skilled people and leaders. We have severe skills shortages side by side with almost 70 per cent unemployment amongst young people of the same age group. A longer time horizon is needed to turn the imbalances in our society around. Leveraging existing skilled people – black, white, male and female – as strong branches to support young entrants into the workplace is essential to success.

Our short-term view on employment equity has created a lose–lose situation for our country. It has become a zero-sum game in which those with skills hoard them to ensure their indispensability, whilst new entrants struggle to find the support they need to grow into their full potential. A win–win situation requires leadership at the highest levels to ensure that growing the talents of all young South Africans that our economy so badly needs becomes everybody's job. Elevating veterans to become the champions of such an active programme would give them a stake in the transformation process for which they should be adequately rewarded and publicly recognised.

Trust is a scarce commodity in our society. Mistrust characterises relationships between citizens and the government at all levels, between customers and service providers and, within institutions, between employers and employees as well as among employees. The assets we built around the transition to democracy that allowed us to transcend our tragic history and come together as a united nation, have been steadily eroded over the last fifteen years.

The main contributor to the erosion of trust is the reassertion of politics of competition over scarce resources within both the public and private sectors. Differences are leveraged to ensure that those who are 'insiders' keep out the 'outsiders'. Ethnic differences have come to the fore in some areas of our society, especially in rural provinces, fuelled by the ambiguity towards traditional customary law entitlements alongside a human-rights national Constitution. The fear of women as competitors to black men is rearing its head too. There are subtleties to the complex process of addressing race and gender inequities at the same time. Black men who feel that it is their time to access power and privilege have difficulties acknowledging that white women too have to be included in the transformation of our workplaces, given past discrimination against them. The strengths of our diversity as a nation are being undermined by the focus on competition and neglect of collaboration as teams.

The reality is that trust building is the most important responsibility of leadership and top management in any institution and in society as a whole. Nelson Mandela's iconic status is due largely to his capacity not only to transcend differences between himself and his former captors, but also to enable the rest of South Africa to recognise the benefits of investing in trust building as a foundation for a prosperous democracy for us all. Some of our political leaders seem to have forgotten that this is a key role for them to play: to be the purveyors of hope and trust in a better future.

Private-sector companies have to invest senior-management time in building trust between staff in these difficult times. The economic downturn makes it harder to have opportunities for all who aspire to them as new recruits or as veterans looking for promotion. Transforming an organisation within such a constrained environment is a challenge. Successful companies globally are those that use downturns as periods during which to strengthen foundations and re-engineer their institutions to become more competitive when the tide turns.

The global downturn offers an opportunity for South Africa to review its approach to inclusive and sustainable growth. The tragedy of 50 per cent of our twenty- to twenty-four-year-olds not being in school, not in training and not employed can be turned into new beginnings for them and the country as a whole. The government's nearly R800 billion infrastructure investment should be used to mount a massive skills-development programme as a public–private partnership targeted at these young people. We should be able to create opportunities for them to become artisans in road building, fitting and other aspects of the construction industry. The housing and human-settlement arena also offers opportunities to involve poor people in the construction of their own homes as well as facilities such as schools and clinics in their residential areas. Turning our over 12 million welfare recipients into trainees for jobs that would see them climb out of poverty as well as supporting those with entrepreneurial talents would strengthen our social fabric and secure a more sustainable future.

South Africa's future prospects

South Africa is at a crossroads in 2009. Fifteen years of experimenting with democracy has been brought to an abrupt stop by the growing inequalities in our society, conflicts with the governing party and the global meltdown. We now need to confront the need for difficult dialogues. The 2009 Dinokeng Scenarios, sponsored by Old Mutual and Nedbank,[4] offer South Africa a choice between three futures: Walk Apart (continuing on a path of mistrust

4 See www.dinokengscenarios.co.za

and self-centredness), Walk Behind (following leaders comes easily to us, given our history) or Walk Together (the most demanding path that requires a change in mindset from all).

It has been remarkable to see how participants in all presentations of the Dinokeng Scenarios have opted for the Walk Together scenario despite clear appreciation of the radical shift it would entail. There seems to be a willingness by citizens to assume a more active role of asserting their rights and responsibilities and working to support the government to build a stronger and more efficient state machinery. Leadership at all levels is needed to make the Walk Together scenario work: at home, at school, in communities, in the private sector and in the government. The inspiration of the African proverb seems to have captured the imagination of many citizens: 'If you want to walk fast, walk alone; if you want to walk far, walk together.' South Africans seem to be ready for the long road to prosperity.

Conclusion

South Africa has much to contribute to the tackling of the triple crisis not least because it embodies all the contradictions, risks and opportunities characterising our global community today. It may be out of its position of weakness and youthful enthusiasm that South Africa may yet help the world to focus on the search for a truly human face that is so essential to sustainable development of our interconnected world.

The world faces the unprecedented threat of a global economic meltdown, rising prices for fossil fuels and the real-time impacts of climate change on the earth's ecosystems and, particularly, on agriculture and food production. We are at a turning point in the history of humanity.

What is missing is an economic vision and game plan that can bring the many concerns and priorities together with the goal of creating a new hi-tech infrastructure for a twenty-first-century economy.

We are on the cusp of a third industrial revolution that can address the triple challenge of global economic recovery, energy security and climate change. Today, the same design principles and smart technologies that made possible the World Wide Web, and vast global communication networks, are just beginning to be used to reconfigure the world's power grids so that people can produce their own renewable energy and share it peer-to-peer to power their homes and businesses and run their vehicles, just like they now produce and share information on the Internet, creating new, distributed forms of energy use.

By drawing together four coequal industrial pillars – renewable energies, buildings, hydrogen storage and a distributed electrical grid and plug-in vehicles – this revolution promises to change our relationship to energy as significantly as the first and second industrial revolutions in the nineteenth and twentieth centuries.

Renewable forms of energy – solar, wind, hydro, geothermal, ocean waves and biomass – make up the first of the four pillars of the third-industrial-revolution infrastructure. Although these sunrise energies still account for a small percentage of today's global energy mix, they are growing rapidly as cities, regions and national governments mandate targets and benchmarks for their widespread introduction into the market, and their falling costs – coupled with the prospect of a price on carbon – make them increasingly competitive.

While renewable energy is found everywhere and new technologies are allowing us to harness it more cheaply and efficiently, we need infrastructure to collect it. This is where the engineering, construction and building industries – the largest sectors of the world economy – step to the fore to lay down the second pillar of the third industrial revolution.

Buildings are the major contributor to human-induced global warming. Worldwide, buildings consume 30 to 40 per cent of all the energy produced and are responsible for equal percentages of all CO_2 emissions. Now, new technological breakthroughs make it possible, for the first time, not only to increase energy efficiency, but also to renovate existing buildings or construct new ones that may serve as both power plants and habitats. In the future, millions of homes, offices, shops and factories, will collect and generate energy locally from the sun, wind, garbage, agricultural and forestry waste, ocean waves and tides, hydro- and geothermal – enough energy to provide for their own power needs as well as enough surplus to be shared across national and continental power grids.

To maximise the potential of intermittent renewable energies, it will be necessary to develop the third pillar of the third-industrial-revolution infrastructure: energy storage. Hydrogen is the universal medium that stores all forms of intermittent renewable energy to assure that a stable and reliable supply is available for power generation and, equally important, for transport.

The fourth pillar, the reconfiguration of the American power grid along the lines of the Internet, allowing businesses and homeowners to produce their own energy and share it with each other, is just now being introduced by utility companies and IT companies in various parts of the world.

The electricity we produce in our buildings from renewable energy will also be used to power electric plug-in cars or to create hydrogen to power fuel-cell vehicles. The electric plug-in vehicles, in turn, will also serve as portable power plants that can sell electricity back to the main grid.

Just as second-generation grid IT allows businesses to connect thousands of desktop computers, creating far more distributed computing power than even the most powerful centralised computers that already exist, millions of local producers of renewable energy, with access to intelligent utility networks, can potentially produce and share far more distributed green power and help the world reach the goal of decarbonising the electricity supply by 2050.

The third industrial revolution will usher in a new era in which millions of existing and new businesses and homeowners become energy players. In the process, we will dramatically increase productivity, jump-start a new technology revolution, and create millions of green jobs, as well as mitigate climate change.

The most significant impact of the third industrial revolution is likely to be on developing nations. Thirty per cent of the human race has no access to electricity and an additional 20 per cent has only limited and sporadic access. Lack of access to electricity is a key factor in perpetuating poverty around the world. Conversely, access to energy means more economic opportunity.

If millions of individuals and communities around the world were to become producers of their own energy, the result would be a profound shift in the configuration of power. Local peoples would be less subject to the will of far-off centres of power. Communities would be able to produce goods and services locally and sell them globally. This is the essence of the politics of sustainable development and reglobalisation from the bottom up.

The developed nations, working with industries and civil-society organisations, can help facilitate the next phase of sustainable globalisation by reorienting development aid, leveraging macro- and microfinance and credit, and by providing favoured-nation trade status in order to help developing nations establish a third industrial revolution.

The shift from centralised fossil fuels and uranium-based energies to distributed renewable energies, takes the world out of the 'geopolitics' that characterised the twentieth century, and into the biosphere politics of the twenty-first century. Much of the geopolitical struggle of the last century centred on gaining military and political access to coal, oil, natural gas and uranium deposits. Wars were fought and countless lives lost, as nations vied with each other in the pursuit of fossil fuels and uranium security.

The ushering in of the third industrial revolution will go a long way towards diffusing the growing tensions over access to ever more limited supplies of fossil fuels and uranium and help facilitate biosphere politics based on a collective sense of responsibility for safeguarding the earth's ecosystems.

The democratisation of energy becomes a rallying point of a new social vision. Access to energy becomes an inalienable social right in the third-industrial-revolution era. Every human being should have the right and the opportunity to create their own energy locally and share it with others across regional, national and continental intergrids. For a younger generation that is growing up in a less hierarchical and more networked society, the ability to share and produce their own energy in an open-access intergrid will be regarded as a fundamental right and responsibility in a biosphere world.

ANDREW SENTANCE

In recent years, we have seen the potential for imbalances to develop within a highly integrated economic and financial system and for shocks to be transmitted rapidly and dramatically across national borders. In addition, the experience of the financial boom and bust of the last decade shows that the emergence of the new global economy has changed the way growth and inflation respond to demand conditions in national economies.

The financial excesses in the United States and some other countries did not lead to particularly strong GDP growth or rising inflationary pressures in the economies that were at the heart of the credit boom. Rather, strong growth was most noticeable in emerging market and developing economies, including energy and commodity producers. This was not just an Asian phenomenon, as strong growth was experienced in the mid-2000s by economies in the Middle East, Africa, Latin America and Eastern Europe as well.

The inflationary pressures created by the credit boom were also different in character from the past. Inflation was not experienced in its traditional form – through a general upward pressure on wages and prices. The downward competitive pressure exerted by low-cost producers such as China acted as a powerful disinflationary influence – in particular in the late 1990s and early 2000s. When we did eventually see inflation pick up in the mid-2000s, it was driven by rising energy and commodity prices. Property-price inflation was also very rapid in many economies, fuelled by credit growth.

One consequence of this pattern of growth and inflation was the emergence of global imbalances. In the United States and a number of other economies – including the UK and Spain – domestic spending growth outstripped the production of goods and services fairly consistently over the decade from the mid-90s to the mid-2000s. The consequence was large, widening deficits in economies where domestic demand was relatively strong, mirrored by surpluses in more export-oriented economies. The US developed a particularly large external deficit, with large surpluses accumulating in China and oil-producing economies. These imbalances have been eroded to some degree by the recession, but there is clearly a risk they will re-emerge once the world economic recovery gets into its stride.

Another important effect of globalisation was to dampen inflationary pressures – and hence the response of monetary policy to the growth of credit and domestic spending. In the new global economy, the close correspondence that used to link domestic demand conditions, national economic growth and inflation has been weakened through the tendency of spending to spill over and support growth overseas instead of in home markets. As a result, the normal channels through which demand generates inflationary pressure – with higher activity putting upward pressure on capacity and labour costs – do not necessarily operate in the same way as in the past. The warning signal to monetary authorities from potential or actual domestic inflationary pressures may be very muted as a result.

Challenges for Economic Policy

These changes have made the task of managing national economies more challenging in the new global economy. At the same time, we have seen heightened volatility in both growth and inflation at the national level driven by global developments – undermining the 'Great Stability' in macroeconomic performance that appeared to have taken root in the UK and many other economies from the 1990s onwards.

How should economic policy makers respond to the challenge of managing in the 'new global economy' of the twenty-first century? The solution is not to row back on globalisation and bow to protectionist pressures. There are clearly aspects of the global economy that need to be better regulated, including the financial sector. But an open world trading economy can deliver massive economic benefits. It offers poorer countries their best chance to raise living standards, improve health and life expectancy, and achieve a better quality of life. We should not turn our back on this potential but seek to develop the way in which we manage national economies and the global economy to take into account the process of globalisation.

In a highly integrated world economy, there is an increased need for effective international policy coordination across a range of policy areas – including global environmental issues. But achieving this coordination and making it effective is extraordinarily difficult. As we have seen recently at the G20 meetings, international policy coordination can be achieved on an ad hoc basis in a crisis situation when interests are well aligned. But it is much harder to achieve over the longer haul.

Effective institutions are critical to underpin international coordination over the longer term. On the economic front, there is a need to reform and adapt institutions that were put in place to respond to a post-war economic situation. We need to build these effective institutions to help us meet other global challenges, including climate change.

However, even if better frameworks for international cooperation can be developed, national monetary authorities will still face the challenge of dealing with volatility created by actual or potential global economic shocks. Indeed, almost all the shocks that the Monetary Policy Committee in the UK has had to deal with in its twelve-and-a-half-year history have been global in nature. We cannot isolate the UK – or any other national economy – from major international economic shocks or from price volatility in global markets for energy and other commodities. What we can do is ensure that policy interventions are in a stabilising direction and are consistent with the medium-term objective of economic growth underpinned by low inflation.

In this context, the current financial crisis has taught us a salutary lesson about what national monetary policies can and cannot achieve. It is realistic for monetary policy to maintain a reasonable degree of price stability, so the inflation-target framework within which the UK Monetary Policy Committee operates remains appropriate. But inflation can be buffeted around even under this framework and in the short term by global factors, as we have seen in the past couple of years.

Having a sound framework for monetary policy does not mean the economic cycle has been abolished – even though we should avoid the inflationary boom–bust cycles of the past. Nor can monetary policy alone guarantee the stability of the financial system. We have had to develop other policy instruments and mechanisms in the current crisis to do that. And the framework for providing financial stability is likely to need further development in the years ahead.

We should therefore be cautious about expecting a return to the apparent 'Great Stability' that characterised the period from the mid-90s to the mid-2000s. That period was shaped by the particular circumstances that helped create a period of strong and steady growth, as well as by improvements in policy frameworks that helped to stabilise inflation. But recent experience has reminded us that the new global economy of the twenty-first century is also a potentially volatile place.

Not only have we experienced a global financial boom and bust, but we have also seen increased volatility in energy and other commodity prices. Just as we saw in the 1970s, and as we have seen throughout our economic history, there is considerable potential for these energy- and other commodity-price swings to generate or reinforce economic cycles.

If we do embark on another long economic expansion in which prosperity rises and employment prospects become more secure, we should always remember that such sustained economic expansions do eventually come to an end. And – as we have seen in the current episode – they are normally brought to an end by behaviours that have been encouraged by the long expansion itself – as we also saw with the build-up in inflationary pressures in the 1950s and 1960s.

The new global economy of the twenty-first century offers the prospect of extending prosperity and facilitating the economic development of poorer nations. But it also brings with it the challenge of increased global volatility. So as we move into the coming recovery, we need to be looking ahead very carefully to see where the next big global shock might be coming from!

GUY VERHOFSTADT

Looking to what lies ahead, or what should be done to overcome the current crisis, I consider the European Union to hold the best hand for finding a way out of the crisis. If really united, the European Union should be the greatest economic, financial and commercial power on earth. At the same time the USA, actually the world's leading economy, does not have the means to be the forerunner of global recovery; instead, the Americans need to reinvent themselves and save many billions of dollars, as suggested by the Obama plan. Also Japan, still the world's second economy, is not in the economic and financial mood for global initiatives, as it as at the tail end of recovering from its own long-lasting recession of the 1990s, and needs all its means for its own sake. At the other end of the economic scale of powerhouses, the new emerging economies (the BRIC countries) are not yet capable of taking the lead; thus, only the European Union has both the means and the potential to do so. That's why I invest my greatest hopes for global recovery in the European Union.

My most recent book, *A Way out of the Crisis*, calls for a European recovery plan of the same magnitude as the separate American and Chinese plans. I call this 'an action-and-investment plan', for about €600 billion, 4.5 per cent of EU GDP, to be invested into a new (not fossil-fuel based) economy and at the same time to be used to fight climate change, saving our natural environment and developing renewable energy sources. It is a cross-border action-and-investment plan based on an integrated network of a wide variety of companies and enterprises to strengthen, invent or renew trans-European networks in transport, telecom and energy facilities, investing in European IT and ITC networks as yet confined within national borders. It takes into account the most massive challenge of the new decade for all industrialised nations: the greying of our population. Within a few decades one European citizen out of three will be of pensionable age. Combined with a qualified health service, more expensive for the elderly, enhanced pension costs will add a structural dimension to the current challenge to save our financial institutions.

In order to be effective, there is no alternative but for this action-and-investment 'Europlan' to be managed and supervised by the European institutions, not by the individual member states. In 2005, I strongly emphasised the need for a European social and economic governance. Today, this need is a must. Let me be clear: up to now such European social and economic governance does *not* exist. Yes, we have an economic and monetary union. Fortunately we have a European Central Bank, in Frankfurt, and a common European currency, the euro. But an economic and monetary union, a European Central Bank and a common currency do not yet make a supervising European economic and financial unified policy, first of all because the euro up to now has been accepted and introduced by only sixteen of the Union's twenty-seven member states, the countries of the eurozone. But there is more. Even within this eurozone, a common economic and financial policy has yet to be established. The European Central Bank does a good job of defending the euro and combating inflation, but a broader European approach to social, economic and even financial matters is left to the member states. Having seen what has happened during these past eight months since the outbreak of the global financial crisis, there can be no doubt that in dangerous times the twenty-seven member states fall back on their national constituencies and act alone. They save their *own* banks and insurance companies first of all, while preparing *national* recovery plans to combat great international upheaval. Coming to Europe in the midst of the crisis, in April 2009, President Obama was welcomed by twenty-seven European heads of state and government, not by a unified European front.

If we want the Union, or at least the eurozone, to develop a genuine European social, economic and financial policy, which is absolutely needed to combat the crisis, we should do more. Next to the European Central Bank, or within this existing institution, I suggest we create one financial regulator: the European Financial Supervisor (EFS) as a supreme and solitary european watchdog for the eurozone, not to defend the euro (this remains the job of the ECB) but to regulate financial markets and financial policies on a European scale. In close contact with national regulators, in a certain sense local chapters of the EFS, it would be a major task to clean up the eurozone financial infrastructure, to regulate and control the eurozone financial markets and to watch new financial products as they were introduced to the European market.

At the same time this European Financial Supervisor should co-define and follow the same guidelines and standards as put forward by the international financial institutions, first of all the IMF and the Basêl Committee of Banking Supervisors. Contrastingly, in the most globalised sector ever seen, globalised finance networks, national and even regional financial rules and standards are obsolete. On global financial markets only global rules and standards can effectively be applied. But, again, regional initiatives can be pioneers for strengthening global control on financial markets, particularly initiatives taken by one of those financial powerhouses most actively involved in global finance, global economics and global trade.

We have no time to waste, having seen the tremendous financial turmoil that has caused the deepest recession of our lifetime: the need for financial rules and standards is clear. Age-old rules should be revived and new rules considered, especially with regard to non-banking financial activities and dubious financial products. If we are able to agree on quality controls for milk, meat and cheese products, we should also be able to agree on quality control for financial products.

But most importantly and urgently, European banks and insurance companies must be saved. Recalling the 'Japanese winter' of the 1990s and the 'toxic' financial products that led our global finance institutions into a frightful nightmare, the financial bubble needs to be stopped. As we learned from the Japanese experience in the 1990s, no financial and economic recovery is thinkable as long as our banking systems fail to recover. Faltering banks must be recapitalised. Toxic financial products must be removed. Billions of dollars, or euros, must be found to heal the wounds of this great financial crisis. Likewise, our financial institutions must accept the new rules and standards put forward by public authorities. New financial products should be weighed and watched. And I repeat once more that financial and economic globalisation cannot hold without any form of political globalisation. Globalisation cannot be turned back, but should be completed by public control and regulation of its financial backbone.

I have not forgotten the major question yet to be answered. Where do we find such huge and necessary financial resources? My Europlan would not be funded by the taxpayers, with taxes still being the most nationalised and the most sensitive European matter. Nor can I imagine the member states paying more for the European institutions. Although the EU's annual budget only represents about 1 per cent (!) of the combined EU GDP, most member states want to pay less for European initiatives, not more. That's why I suggest the introduction of 'eurobonds' to be issued by the (existing) European Investment Bank or a new European Investment and Stability Fund on international capital markets. These eurobonds may find a wide and interested audience of investors far beyond our national borders. In order to save our financial institutions and to feed the aforementioned European recovery plans, we should find at least €1,000 billion, just to start with. This amount can be found, I expect, by the issue of eurobonds guaranteeing both saving stability and a fixed return, as well as a European Fund important enough, and similar to the American Treasury market, to make the difference for a truly European recovery.

NORBERT WALTER

The financial crisis has revealed problems in very many parts of the financial sector. Arguably the most important change as a result of the crisis is that banks will have to become better capitalised. But by how much should banks now deleverage? Ultimately, this will depend upon two main considerations: first, how much leverage investors in bank equity are willing to tolerate; and second, how much leverage is profitable.

Deleveraging will take place anyway – it is in fact happening already – as regulators and investors press banks to reduce risk. This results in shrinking balance sheets, given that the other option – raising more capital – has become much more expensive since the onset of the crisis. Hence, banks have started to reduce both their assets as well as their liabilities but are not treating all asset classes the same, focusing on trading assets instead of traditional loans to non-financial corporations.

In any case, in the end balance-sheet structures will revert to how they looked a few years ago, and banks will have lower total assets. Indeed, the largest European banks slashed the size of their balance sheets throughout 2009, while risk-weighted assets began to shrink for the first time in years in the second quarter of 2008, and have continued to do so into 2009. Lastly, an adjustment of banks' compensation mechanisms to better align bonus payments with banks' long-run interests is a topic with economic significance within the current emotional debate.

Adjusting these compensation schemes is in the interest of both banks and their supervisors. UBS became the first large European bank to start a comprehensive review of its compensation policy. The proposal to derive bonus payments from profits made over a period of several years and to retain part of them for some time as 'collateral' clearly points in the right direction. Such a bonus–malus system may better align the remuneration of staff with a bank's long-term sustainable profitability. On the other hand, setting absolute limits on bonuses as stipulated in some of the state rescue programmes may reflect the demands of politicians' constituencies but may be detrimental if it leads to banks losing some of their brightest staff.

While 2008 may have been one of the worst years in living memory, 2009 will go down in history as the year that reshaped the global financial system. Banks will need not only to restore their capital bases, but also to regain their clients' trust and confidence. They need to rethink their business models and the design of financial markets and products. The authorities will need to improve the functioning of the financial system by designing the building blocks of a regulatory and supervisory system that is commensurate with global, interdependent financial markets.

The financial industry is vigorously addressing all areas where deficiencies have been revealed by the crisis. A wide range of recommendations has been presented by the Institute of International Finance (IIF) and the Counter-party Risk Management Policy Group. These are now in the process of being implemented by banks worldwide.

Three issues stand out: first, much more attention must be given to the issue of liquidity, which is at the heart of the stability of any financial system, especially one that is market-based. Yet the crisis has revealed that the previously held assumption of continuously available liquidity is no longer tenable and that there is a gap in our understanding of market dynamics in times of illiquidity. Moreover, the repercussions for the valuation of illiquid assets in a mark-to-market accounting regime need to be addressed with urgency.

Second, transparency: we would thoroughly misunderstand the nature of this issue if we were to limit it to greater and more comparable transparency about banks' exposures. Greater transparency must extend to better disclosure of a bank's institutional arrangements for risk management, risk models and techniques used. Moreover, greater transparency must be achieved for financial products, especially the complex structured credit products that lie at the heart of this crisis. Investors will only return to these markets if originators disclose sufficient data about the underlying assets and enable investors to perform their own due diligence rather than rely passively on the judgement of originators and rating agencies. Realistically, even this will not save these markets from shrinking dramatically, as investors shift their preferences towards simpler products and business models.

Third, we need to strengthen the infrastructure (or 'plumbing') of financial markets. In order to increase price transparency, transaction data should be pooled and made available. In order to reduce settlement risk in the trade business and to enable netting in OTC markets, central counterparties should be established, as in the process for CDS. Greater automation in these markets will also reduce settlement risk, but will require a higher degree of standardisation.

While banks' individual and collective efforts will be sufficient and successful in many areas, others will require intervention by standard-setting bodies and authorities, especially regarding greater transparency on the distribution of risks in the financial system and the difficulty of coordinating a large number of diverse creditors in the event of a crisis. The same applies to valuation issues. Here, reform efforts must recognise that this is more than merely an accounting issue. Mark-to-market accounting imposes stricter discipline on banks' risk management and acts as an early-warning system, with losses appearing in banks' Profit and Loss accounts before they materialise in the real economy. Any changes must respect these benefits of fair-value accounting but at the same time address the issues of illiquid markets, procyclicality (i.e. higher equity capital requirements during a recession) and consistency between accounting standards.

Intensive international coordination is a *conditio sine qua non* for these efforts as well as for any state action aimed at stabilising financial markets. It is recognised that state action needs to be attuned to individual circumstances; nonetheless, uncoordinated action using a plethora of diverging instruments will only create more uncertainty, spread the virus and distort competition. It also limits the effectiveness of rescue measures.

This holds particularly true for the European Union, where member states are currently faced with a stark choice when responding to the crisis: either to act jointly and create a supervisory system that is commensurate with a truly integrated financial market or relapse into a system of essentially separate national financial markets. It is to be hoped that the choice is clear.

The financial crisis will cost us dearly and the financial industry bears as much responsibility for this as past mistakes in both macroeconomic and regulatory policies. Comprehensive yet targeted action, as outlined above, is needed to re-establish the foundations of the global system. More and louder calls for tighter regulation will continue to be heard in 2010. This is understandable in the light of the mounting fiscal burden stemming from the crisis. But this must not result in the blocking of financial-market integration or the stifling of financial innovation. Though it seems hard to believe these days, the market-based financial system has made a major contribution to global growth. While some of the structures created have not been sustainable, reverting to fragmented, nation-based and overregulated banking markets is not the answer. What we need is greater resilience in terms of more sophisticated market participants, more robust market infrastructure and supra-national structures for the regulation and supervision of the global financial system.

LINDA YUEH

There is a global shift in economic power and influence from West to East, but perhaps ever more, it is a growing recognition that the world is multipolar with more than one engine of growth. America, particularly its capitalist ideology and practices, has stumbled badly in this economic crisis. China, by contrast, on the surface appears to be a more sensible system.

Evident during the decade of the 'Great Moderation' and certainly so in the 2007–8 global financial crisis, China's importance in the global economy is ever-increasing. Indeed, the World Bank estimates that China has contributed as much to global incremental growth as the United States over the past couple of decades, leading them to be termed the 'twin engines' of growth.

But China's own institutional fragilities were more apparent with the economic slowdown. Under a weak legal system and regulatory structures, companies will irresponsibly close their doors and leave their workers with little recourse. Thus, there is a perennial concern over social unrest when there is a decline in output or exports. Riots replace the usual orderly process of claiming benefits and bankruptcy proceedings. Although both America and China appear to have recapitalised their banks and state ownership is now a trait alongside the private sector, the legacy of central planning makes China more vulnerable to an inefficiency-driven collapse of its financial sector, as with most transition economies, while the US still deals with its banks at arm's length, such that even the part-nationalised ones operate on a commercial basis. That being said, the depth of the US crisis is still unknown and it is sometimes said that there is nothing more permanent than a temporary government programme.

China's relationship with the United States, hitherto the leading economy in the world and likely to remain so for some time, is likewise changing. More than ever as tensions flare over trade/investment and exchange rates, there is a need to define how China, the United States other major economies relate to each other, i.e., as economic partners who coordinate and cooperate through various forums such as the G7, which encompasses the rich economies of the world (the United States, Japan, Germany, the United Kingdom, France,

Italy and Spain). The G7 meet regularly to discuss issues that affect the global economy. In the late 2000s, there has been a growing recognition that China was larger than most of the G7 and so meetings began to informally include the four large emerging economies of China, India, Mexico, South Africa and Brazil.

In this respect, the 2008 financial crisis has already reshaped the global economic power structure. The first international summit held to address the crisis in Washington DC in November 2008 was of the G20 group of major economies, and not just the G7. The G20 includes nineteen of the top twenty-five largest economies in the world plus the European Union (EU): Argentina, Australia, Brazil, Canada, China, France, Germany, India, Indonesia, Italy, Japan, Mexico, Russia, Saudi Arabia, South Africa, South Korea, Turkey, the United Kingdom and the United States. Spain is excluded except through its membership of the EU, while Thailand is also not a member, singly or via another entity. There is no definitive forum for global economic coordination, but the trend is certainly shifting to include China and other large emerging economies in recognition of the shift in global economic weight. The G8 (G7 plus Russia) is rumoured to be considering expanding to the G12, so that it is the G8 plus China, India, Mexico, South Africa and Brazil. Some have even argued for the Group of Two: the United States and China.

These forums are often criticised for not producing concrete results, but they serve an important function in facilitating discussions about global economic problems. Globalisation accelerating in the 1990s has led to more such forums, importantly between the United States and China in the semi-annual high-level Strategic Economic Dialogues that involved several members of the cabinets of both countries, which was started under US Treasury secretary Henry Paulson in the second Bush administration. The EU has followed suit, initiating its own high-level summits with China that also arranged for twice-a-year meetings, as well as bilateral summits between China and key European countries such as Britain.

These summits serve a useful purpose as the relations between the two engines of the world economy are crucial, usually not only for them but for other countries as well. But these informal meetings are not themselves enough to contend with the changed global economic structure. Instead, the United States and China are in a position to provide leadership to ensure that the international economic system is reformed to reflect the challenges of the global economy of the twenty-first century. These strictures can also serve to moderate US–China relations as international trade rules, for instance, can counter protectionist tendencies arising in either country. Protectionism in one of these countries of course affects many other economies, underscoring the importance of not only good bilateral but also multilateral efforts. In other words, the US–China relationship has global implications and should also operate on a multilateral basis.

The scale of the economic crisis has already led to discussions of forming Bretton Woods II – a new international economic system that would supplant the original Second World War institutions of the IMF and the World Bank. A relevant international economic system would be more beneficial than relying on forums that are useful in agreeing cooperative measures. It would be in the interests of China, the United States and indeed all countries to supervise international financial markets accordingly as well as agreeing to monitor the build-up of the next global imbalance, which could result in devastating asset bubbles with widespread consequences. Participating as an active member of the G20 seeking to reform the Bretton Woods institutions would be beneficial not only to the global economy but to the future of all economies, developing and developed.

A new set of Bretton Woods institutions that identified these global capital flows and assessed their consequences would help policy makers coordinate responses to try and lean against future asset bubbles. Indeed, the next one could be in emerging economies, as cheap currencies and high levels of domestic savings fuel housing bubbles even as interest rate cuts to stimulate the West promote global liquidity searching for the next investment opportunity, which could be in Asia. Changing the shareholding in the World Bank and IMF as well as the constituents of other supra-national bodies such as the Bank for International Settlements (BIS, known as 'the central banks' central bank') to better reflect shifting world economic power would allow for more representative policy making and bring countries such as China on board to play a more active role in the governance of the global economy. Strengthening the coverage of the World Trade Organization would also restrain protectionist tendencies as well. Thus, a reformed international economic system could be a positive legacy of the 2008 financial crisis. Certainly, leading the reform of the international economic system to better reflect the changed global economic structure will be advantageous and China and the US will be key to this process.

No country is immune from a global economic crisis, particularly China, with its high degree of global integration. Often criticised for the inward-looking nature of its economic policies, China is in a position to act to shape the governance of the global economy. Doing so would go a long way towards the position of China becoming an active stakeholder in the world economy as befits one-half of the twin engines of growth alongside the United States.

The year 2009 is the first in the post-war period in which China, and other emerging economies contributed to the bulk of the economic growth, while the rich economies were in rec— ——— undoubtedly arrived on the world stage and does so in an admirable way in many respects, particularly in the lifting of hundreds of millions out of poverty.

But perhaps the most important indicator of the future shape of global power is not the outward signs but the shifts in ideology and persuasiveness. America is still the 'shining city on the hill' for many in the world. China lags behind. But with this crisis, faith in the capitalist system and its liberal ideology has been shaken. China's phenomenal growth over thirty years is the best testament to its benefits. Will the follower now become the leader?

MUHAMMAD YUNUS

The recession of 2008–9 has well and truly shaken the foundations of global finance. Financial pundits and central banks are now analysing how they got here and how to prevent things from crashing through the floor. The stimulus packages announced in the richest economies of the world are being widely judged as being insufficient. Quarter-on-quarter output changes published in *The Economist* for the G7 countries paint a ghastly picture.

There is much concern that the developed world is not spending enough on stimulus packages (despite Obama's fiscal stimulus package of US $787 billion – the largest in US history – and China, which is spending 6.9 per cent of its GDP, which will in turn hurt the developing countries that sell goods and services to them. The developing countries are not expected to implement stimulus spending on these large scales mainly because they do not have the liquidity to borrow in the first place. Financial pundits in Bangladesh, for example, are in fact trying to explain the time lag between the global recessionary economy and Bangladesh's own economy, which is partially shielded from feeling the aftershocks.

They are, however, advising the government to take advantage of the time lag by designing stimulus packages for the banking system and government spending with the goals of creating new jobs and improving the long-term competitiveness of the economy. They are creating financial packages so that they can lend more to retail and business customers. All of this, no doubt, makes sound financial sense, but I would like to ask a few questions: What is the future of global capitalism when there is no financial package for the protection of the world's poorest? What is the goal of financial planning at a time of recession if no one talks about those who are too poor to even have a bank account? What kind of changes should we be looking for that protects the interests of people who have no access to food and nutrition even when the markets are bullish?

Capitalism and Poverty

Poverty is not created by the poor people. Rather it is created by the economic and social system that we have designed for the world. It is created by the institutions that we have built, by the concepts we have developed, by the policies borne out of our reasoning and theoretical framework. In order to overcome poverty, we have to go back to the drawing board and redesign our concepts and institutions of capitalism. There is something fundamentally wrong with an institution that leaves out more than half the population of the world, because they are considered not creditworthy. This is what my work with the Grameen Bank has been about: to design a banking method that can deliver the financial service to the people left out, particularly to the women, who are the most difficult to reach.

In the context of the global banking crisis of 2008–9, it is paramount that we redesign the way finance is handled globally. It has been described in the media as 'casino', or irresponsible, capitalism.

Credit markets were originally created to serve human needs – to provide business people with capital to start or expand companies, and to enable families to buy homes. In return for these services, bankers and other lenders earned a reasonable profit. Everyone benefited. In recent years, however, the credit markets have been distorted by a relative handful of individuals and companies with a different goal in mind: to earn unrealistically high rates of return through clever feats of financial engineering. They repackaged mortgages and other loans into sophisticated instruments whose risk level and other characteristics were hidden or disguised. Then they sold and resold these instruments, earning a slice of profit on every transaction.

All the while, investors eagerly bid up the prices, scrambling for unsustainable growth and gambling that the underlying weakness of the system would never come to light. The poor, as usual, will feel the worst effects. As economies falter, as government budgets collapse, and as contributions to charities and NGOs dwindle, efforts to help the poor will diminish. With the slowing down of economies everywhere, the poor will lose their jobs and income from self-employment.

Even if we can overcome the problem of financial crisis, we will still be left with some fundamental questions about the effectiveness of capitalism in tackling many other unresolved problems. In my view, the theoretical framework of capitalism that is in practice today is a half-done structure.

The theory of capitalism holds that the marketplace is only for those who are interested in making money, for the people who are interested in profit only. This theory treats people as one-dimensional beings. But people are multidimensional. While they have their selfish dimensions, at the same time they also have their self*less* dimensions. Capitalism, and the marketplace that has grown up around the theory, make no room for the selfless dimensions of the people. If some of the self-sacrificing drives and motivations that exist in people could be brought into the business world to make an impact on the problems that face the world, there would be very few problems that we could not solve.

The present structure of the economic theory does not allow these dimensions of people to play out in the marketplace. I argue that given the opportunity, people will come into the marketplace to express their selfless urges by running special types of businesses – let us call them social businesses, to make a change in the world. In the absence of such opportunities in the marketplace people express their selflessness through charities. Charitable efforts have been with us always, and they are noble, and they are needed. But we have seen that business is able to innovate, to expand, to reach more and more people through the power of the free market. Imagine what we could achieve if talented entrepreneurs and business executives around the world devoted themselves to ending, say, malnutrition, without any intention of making money for themselves or the investors.

The Banks vs the Grameen Model

Banks explain that poor people are not creditworthy. The Grameen Bank model challenges that, and continues to do so during the worst recession in recent memory. In the Grameen Bank there are no legal instruments between lender and borrower, no guarantees, no collateral. You cannot get riskier than that, and yet our money comes back while the prestigious banks all over the world are going down with all their intelligent paperwork, all their collateral, all the lawyers and legal systems to back up their lending.

When people ask me, 'How did you figure out all the rules and procedures that are now known as the Grameen system?' my answer is: 'That was very simple and easy. Whenever I needed a rule or a procedure in our work, I just looked at the conventional banks to see what they did in a similar situation. Once I learned what they did, I just did the opposite.' That's how I got our rules. Conventional banks go to the rich, we go to the poor; their rule is 'The more you have, the more you get', so our rule became 'The less you have, the higher the attention you get. If you have nothing, you get the highest priority.' They ask for collateral, we abandoned it as if we had never heard of it.

They need lawyers in their business. We do not. No lawyer is involved in any of our loan transactions. The rich own them; our bank is owned by the poorest, the poorest women to boot. I can go on adding more to this list to show how the Grameen does things quite the opposite way.

Was it really a systematic policy – to do it the opposite way? No, it was not. But that is how it turned out ultimately, because our objective was different. I had not even noticed it until a senior banker admonished me by saying: 'Dr Yunus, you are trying to put the banking system upside down.'

I quickly agreed with him. I said: 'Yes, because the banking system is standing on its head.'

Social Business from the Grameen Bank

Corporate social responsibility (CSR) is considered to be a part of company policy nowadays in many developed and developing countries. CSR usually means: 'Let us make money and then use part of that wealth to help society.'

This is an important development in the business world. But this still does not allow business people to express their selfless urges within the framework of the market. Just as an individual person who makes money in business may then give away a part of his income to charity, similarly now a company, a legal person, may do the same – make money and give part of it to charity. I am proposing a different structure of the market itself; I am proposing a second type of business to operate in the same market along with the existing kind of profit-maximising business. I am not opposed to the existing type of business (although I call for many improvements in it, like many others do.) I am proposing a new business in addition to the existing one. This new type of business I am calling 'social business', because it is for the collective benefit of others.

This is a business whose purpose is to address and solve social problems among the poorest people, not to make money for its investors. It is a non-loss non-dividend company. Investors can recoup their investment capital. Beyond that there are no profits to be taken out as dividends by the investors. These profits remain with the company and are used to expand its reach, improve the quality of the product or service it provides and design methods to bring down the cost of the product or service. If the efficiency, the competitiveness, the dynamism of business could be harnessed to deal with specific social problems, the world would be a much better place.

Birth of the Social Business

The concept of a social business crystallised in my mind through my experience with Grameen companies. Over the years, Grameen created a series of companies to address different problems faced by the poor in Bangladesh.

Whether it was a company to provide renewable energy or a company to provide health care or yet another company to provide information technology to the poor, we were always motivated by the desire to address the social need. We always designed them as profitable companies, but only to ensure their sustainability so that the product or service could reach more and more of the poor – and on an ongoing basis. In all these cases the social need was the only consideration, making personal money was no consideration at all.

That is how I realised that businesses could be built that way, from the ground up, around a specific social need, without motive for personal gain.

Social Business in Motion

The idea of social business took wings when we launched a joint venture with Danone (known as Dannon in the USA). Together we formed Grameen Danone Foods Ltd and we produce nutritious fortified yogurt for the undernourished children of rural Bangladesh. The yogurt, called Shakti Doi, is made with full-cream milk that contains protein, vitamins, iron, calcium, zinc and other micronutrients that the poor people might not get in their regular diet. Each pot is sold at *taka* 5 (about 5 pence) in Bangladeshi villages, so it is easily affordable. Grameen Danone Foods is a prime example of social business because it sources raw materials locally and employs local people. But more importantly, neither we nor Danone will make money from this venture beyond recouping the initial investment money.

The bottom line for the company is to see how many children overcome their nutrition deficiency each year. We have one plant operating in Bangladesh, and we hope to have fifty such plants throughout the country.

In 2006 we set up the Grameen Health Care Services Ltd with the idea of contributing to the health-care sector in Bangladesh. Under that initiative in 2007, we started an eye-care hospital in Bogra, Bangladesh, targeting about 3.5 million poor Bangladeshis. The Grameen eye hospital is charging patients based on their ability to pay, wealthier patients are charged at a normal rate, while poor patients pay a subsidised rate. The fee for an eye exam is *taka* 50 (about 50 pence). A second eye hospital is being built, while two more are in the pipeline.

We have created a joint-venture with Veolia of France to deliver safe drinking water in the villages of Bangladesh. Under the company we are building a small water-treatment plant in a rural part of Bangladesh to bring clean water to 100,000 villagers, in an area where the existing supply of water is highly arsenic-contaminated. We will sell the water at a very affordable price to the villagers to make the company sustainable, but no financial gain will come to Grameen or Veolia. This social-business water company will be a prototype for supplying safe drinking water in a sustainable and affordable way to people who are faced with a water crisis. Once it is perfected, it can be replicated in other villages, within Bangladesh and outside.

Our next initiative came from Crédit Agricole of France. We created the Grameen Crédit Agricole Microfinance Foundation to provide financial support to microfinance organisations and social-businesses. We have signed a joint-venture agreement with Intel Corporation, to create a social business company called Grameen-Intel to bring information-technology-based services to the poor. These services pertain to the fields of in health care, marketing, education and remittances. We also signed a social-business joint venture agreement with the Saudi–German Hospital Group to set up a series of hospitals in Bangladesh. In March 2009 BASF SE and the Grameen Health Care Trust have announced the establishment of a joint social-business venture to supply, at reasonable cost, dietary-supplement sachets containing vitamins and trace elements, and impregnated mosquito nets that offer protection against insect-borne disease. BASF Grameen Ltd is not a charity. It combines business sense with social needs.

Many more companies from around the world are showing interest in such social-business joint ventures. A leading shoe company wants to create a social business to make sure that nobody goes without shoes. One leading pharmaceutical company wishes to set up a joint-venture social-business company to produce nutritional supplements appropriate for Bangladeshi pregnant mothers and young women, at the cheapest possible price.

Some people are sceptical. Who will create these businesses? Who will run these businesses? I always say that, to begin with, there is no dearth of philanthropists in the world. People give away billions of dollars. Imagine if those billions could be used in a social-business way to help people.

These billions will be recycled again and again, and the social impact could be all that much more powerful. The CSR money of the companies could easily go into social businesses. Each company can create its own range of social businesses.

Once the concept of social business is included in economic theory, millions of people will come forward to invest in social business because they all have those social dreams in their hearts. We will need to create social stock markets to channel these funds to appropriate social businesses.

The Social Stock Market

To connect investors with social businesses, we need to create a social stock market where only the shares of social businesses will be traded. An investor will come to this stock exchange with the clear intention of finding a social business that has a mission of his or her liking. Anyone who wants to make money will go to the existing stock market. To enable a social stock exchange to perform properly, we will need to create rating agencies, standardisation of terminology, definitions, impact-measurement tools, reporting formats and new financial publications, such as the 'Social Wall Street Journal'. Business schools will offer courses and business-management degrees on social businesses to train young managers how to manage social-business enterprises in the most efficient manner, and, most of all, to inspire them to become social-business entrepreneurs themselves.

Once social business is recognised in law, many existing companies will come forward to create social businesses in addition to their foundation activities. Many activists from the non-profit sector will also find this an attractive option. Unlike the non-profit sector, where one needs to collect donations to keep activities going, a social business will be self-sustaining and create surplus for expansion since it is a non-loss enterprise. Social business will go into a new type of capital market of its own, to raise capital.

How to Begin Change

I have talked a lot about how the current financial crisis brings new risks to the world's poor. It is time to change. The thought that always energises me is that poverty is not created by the poor people. Poverty is an artificial imposition on the people. Poor people are endowed with the same unlimited potential of creativity and energy as any human being in any station of life, anywhere in the world. It is a question of removing the barrier in front of the poor people to unleash their creativity to solve their problems. They can change their lives only if we give them the same opportunity as we get. Creatively designed social businesses in all sectors can make this unleashing happen in the fastest way. To make a start all that each one of you has to do is to design a business plan for a social business. Each prototype of a social business can be a cute little business. But if it works out, the whole world can be changed by replicating it in thousands of locations.

Three basic interventions will make a big difference in the existing system: a) broadening the concept of business by including social business in the framework of the marketplace, b) creating inclusive financial and health-care services that can reach out to every person on the planet, c) designing appropriate information-technology devices and services for the bottom-most people and making them easily available to them.

I always insist that poverty does not belong in civilised society. Poverty belongs only in a museum where our children and grandchildren can go to see what inhumanity people had to suffer, and where they will ask themselves how their ancestors allowed such a condition to persist for so long. We overcame slavery, we overcame apartheid. Together if we face the recession of 2008–9 through changing capitalism and its institutions, we can change the way people think. Social businesses can be an important part of that vision.

MARVIN ZONIS [1]

With so many people acting as though the complete globalisation of business is hard upon us, students of history might reflect on the 1920s and 1930s. That was the last time when barriers to international business were disappearing as fast as they are in today's Internet-driven world. The results weren't pretty. Businesses helped cause the worldwide depression, creating massive upheaval that led to a nationalistic backlash against globalisation and helped create the environment that produced the Second World War.

Now, I'm not predicting another depression. Nor am I suggesting that another world war is in the offing. I'm actually optimistic that the emphasis the US and some other countries are placing on free trade will ultimately distribute economic benefits widely and increase personal freedoms around the world. But the history of the twenties and thirties is still worth noting because so many people seem to have forgotten that globalisation is inherently destabilising. It causes cultural crises in many countries, leads to discomfort among workers in a wide array of jobs, and usually produces a dangerous backlash.

Companies that want to take advantage of today's wealth of international opportunities while protecting themselves against the risks need to focus on three issues. Let's look at each:

Regional Risks

Governments pose the greatest risks. Government actions may sometimes be aimed at a particular company – as when Yugoslav President Slobodan Milosevic ordered the seizure of American-owned ICN Pharmaceuticals in Belgrade. But companies generally face greater liabilities from broadly targeted changes in government policies affecting areas such as taxes, profit repatriation and currency conversion. In a prime example, the United Kingdom recently imposed a 'gas moratorium' to support its ailing coal industry. It thus began denying approvals for new gas-fired power plants. Several gas

[1] This entry was previously published in *Context* magazine, August/September 2000.

plants being developed by foreign owners face a highly uncertain future.

Even more damaging than fickle economic policy is poor public policy. Unwise governments can debase their currencies, drive inflation up and stimulate political unrest. Investors in Indonesia and Pakistan recently rediscovered that truth. Because of the economic crises there, foreign companies are finding that their contracts with local companies are being unilaterally rewritten, and companies are facing corruption investigations by officials looking for scapegoats.

Weak political institutions create another set of risks. In India, one foreign investor was hit with contract renegotiations, nuisance lawsuits, and bureaucratic hassles that eventually added up to $27 million. The company finally abandoned the project. Countries that once were communist usually welcome foreign firms, but their political institutions are often too ineffective to protect those companies.

Even more menacingly, corrupt government institutions may make local competitors nearly invincible. In China, for instance, counterfeiting has devastated major global packaged-goods companies. As much as half of the goods sold there under their brand names are actually knock-offs by Chinese companies. In Russia, where 'gangster capitalism' prevails, an investor negotiated a deal to develop a Siberian diamond mine. Once development was under way, though, the firm's local partner claimed exclusive control, with the tacit blessing of the Russian government.

Cultural Political Crises

Globalisation inevitably produces a 'sense-making crisis' in each new country it touches. The conventional expectations of the way the world works are upset by American or other foreign culture. Young people are likely to adopt the new, foreign ideas. They change the most. But the loss of a 'sensible' world generates alienation, anomie, rootlessness and boredom among those who resist the change. The responses can be violence, alcohol and drugs, crime, divorce, even suicide. Indeed, these cultural crises can lead to political instability and revolution.

Despite the social costs, few countries actually try to wall themselves off from globalisation. Most political leaders seem willing to tolerate some decline of cultural vitality and political stability. Remarkably, hostility to Americanisation has actually decreased. Nowhere is this more true than in Latin America, where the fear of 'Yankee imperialism' has diminished – witness the dramatically greater commitment to free trade. Latin states also seem confident of their ability to preserve the distinctiveness of their own cultures.

Still, globalisation disrupts modes of production and consumption. Cheaper imports undercut domestic production, which leads to factories moving across national boundaries. The disruptions are not equally distributed. Different regions suffer differently. So do various groups within the population, with workers usually being hit particularly hard. The difficulties can lead to resentment and unrest.

New Global Groups

Anti-globalisation groups have arisen and, through sophisticated use of the Internet, are forming alliances across national boundaries. The power of these non-governmental groups, or NGOs, has been seen on the streets of Seattle and Washington, DC, and in Ching Mai, Thailand, where some 4,000 demonstrators recently protested the policies of the Asian Development Bank.

Some NGOs, such as the International Chamber of Commerce, work to counter the broad protests seen in Seattle. But the opponents of global business have also begun a guerrilla public-relations war, choosing to target the operations of specific companies with attacks that can hit their stock prices. Nike and Reebok, for instance, find themselves on the defensive concerning sweatshop labour. Monsanto has to defend itself against charges that it is making food dangerous through genetic engineering. Canada's Talisman Oil was crippled by NGOs critical of its operations in Sudan.

NGOs will continue to batter companies to get them to 'protect' the environment, adopt 'fair' labour practices and hire local people. NGOs have become powerful arbiters of reputation at a time when any company wanting to do business globally absolutely must have a strong brand. They have a lot of leverage.

None of the barriers to globalisation will stop it. Even the mullahs of Iran are beginning to acknowledge the inevitability of globalisation. So, few countries will go the route of the Taliban in Afghanistan, who recently ordered the destruction of all television sets in their country.

Still, as NGOs spur the backlash to globalisation, governments will follow. Thus, we can expect legislation against companies believed to be despoilers of the environment or exploiters of labour in emerging markets. France will continue to pass laws to preserve its language and culture. So will countries that see themselves as models for the rest of the world. These include Russia, the Islamic countries, Israel and Malaysia.

The efforts to limit the effects of globalisation may indeed lessen cultural upheaval, but they will also slow needed economic development and create a tricky environment for businesses that operate on a global basis.

GLOSSARY

AAA ratings – known as 'Triple A', the highest form of rating awarded to investment products by rating agencies, who are private-sector watchdogs for quality in financial activities.

amortization – the gradual repayment of a loan, such as a mortgage, over a set period of time, accounting for the amount due in interest as well as the capital sum.

APEC – Asia-Pacific Economic Cooperation. A forum supporting sustainable economic growth , cooperation, trade and investment in the Asia-Pacific Region. http://apec.org

ASEAN – Association of South East Asian Nations. A group made up of ten nations from South East Asia with the aim of accelerating economic growth, social progress and cultural development to strengthen the foundation for a prosperous and peaceful community. www.aseansec.org

ASEM – Asia-Europe Meeting. An informal meeting between Asia and Europe aiming to strengthen the partnership between the two regions by facilitating the discussion of political, economic and cultural issues. www.aseminforboard.org

basis point – used to calculate minute changes in interest rates and other financial variables. One basis point equals 1/100th of 1 per cent.

bonus-malus system – implemented in the wake of the recent financial crisis as a way to regulate and moderate the payment of bonuses, particularly within the banking industry. The bonus-malus system is similar to a share scheme, whereby the money is paid into account but cannot be accessed until a later date and according to the company's future performance.

Bretton Woods Agreement – the result of a meeting between 43 countries in Bretton Woods, New Hampshire in July 1944. The aim was to help rebuild the shattered post-war economy and to promote international economic cooperation. The Bretton Woods Institutions are the World Bank and the International Monetary Fund (IMF).

BRIC – a term coined by Jim O'Neill to denote the fast-growing developing economies of Brazil, Russia, India and China.

carry trade – a form of exchange whereby a commodity, such as currency, is borrowed at a low interest rate in order to finance investment in a product that may yield a high interest rate.

CDO – Collateralised Debt Obligation. A CDO is the final step of the low-volatility process that adds opacity by allowing the products to be managed before they are sold so that the investor never knows exactly what collateral is behind the structure.

CDS – Credit Default Swaps

community reinvestment act – enacted by US Congress in 1977 with the aim of encouraging depository institutions to help meet the credit needs of the communities in which they operate. www.ffiec.gov/CRA

counterparty – the other person (or party) involved in a contractual agreement.

ESKOM – Electricity Supply Commission. A South African electricity supply company with an aim to encourage the sustainability of their business by focusing on economic, social and environmental decision making. www.eskom.co.za

EURATOM – The European Atomic Energy Community. A community coordinating the member states' research programmes into peaceful use of nuclear energy. They combine their knowledge, infrastructure and funding of nuclear energy to ensure the security of an atomic energy supply within a centralised monitoring system. http://ec.europa.eu/energy/nuclear/euratom/euratom_en.htm

FOMC – Federal Open Market Committee. Part of the Federal Reserve in the United States that meets regularly to review economic and financial conditions to assess the risks to its goal of price stability and sustainable economic growth in the country. www.federalreserve.gov/monetarypolicy/fomc.htm

FSB – Financial Stability Board. Established in April 2009 following the G20 London summit, the FSB aims to address vulnerabilities affecting the financial system to increase financial stability within international financial markets. www.financialstabilityboard.org

fair-value accounting – the value of an asset or liability bought or sold in a current transaction between two willing parties, other than in a liquidation.

Glass-Steagall Act (1933) – passed by the United States Congress in the wake of the Great Depression to limit the scope of commercial banking activities and remits and, crucially, preventing commercial banks from becoming involved with commercial banks or brokers. The act was repealed in 1999 in an effort to enable American banks to compete with their English counterparts.

gold standard – a way to set the value of currency by measuring its worth against an agreed value in gold, for which it may be exchanged.

green-field investments – projects that companies undertake in foreign, often developing countries, whereby they build new, satellite-company facilities on virgin land.

G7 – The Group of Seven is the predecessor to the G8. It is made up of seven leading industrialised nations: Canada; France; Germany; Italy; Japan; United Kingdom; United States.

G8 – The Group of Eight. The group is made up of the members of the G7 plus Russia. The European Union is also represented but does not take part in political discussions.

G20 – The Group of Twenty is a group of finance ministers and central bank governors from key industrialised and developing economies whose target is to strengthen the international financial architecture and to encourage sustainable economic growth and development. www.g20.org

G77 – Named after the seventy-seven founding countries, the Group of Seventy-Seven has expanded to consist of 130 developing nations. The organisation's objective is to promote their collective economic interests and enhance their joint negotiating capacity within the United Nations. www.g77.org

ICBC – Industrial and Commercial Bank of China.

IFC – International Finance Corporation. IFC encourages sustainable economic growth in developing countries by financing private-sector investment, mobilising capital in the international financial markets, and providing advisory services to businesses and governments. www.ifc.org

LIBOR – London Inter Offered Rate. The agreed rate that London banks charge each other for loans. (See also **three-month LIBOR**).

IMF – International Monetary Fund. An organisation working to foster global monetary cooperation, secure financial stability, facilitate international trade, promote high employment and sustainable economic growth, and reduce poverty around the world. www.imf.org

leverage – to use a relatively small amount of money to fund (and hopefully produce) a high yield or return.

liquidity – represents the ability to meet financial obligations as they become due by drawing on a ready source of funds.
www.fdic.gov/regulations/safety/manual/section6-1.html

M1 & M2 money supply – M1 refers to the total amount of money in circulation; M2 to the money in circulation combined with the money on deposit in banks and building societies.

mark-to-market accounting – a way of valuing a commodity based on speculative future realisations of its worth. Made famous by the Enron scandal.

MDG – Millennium Development Goals.

national champions – smaller companies that are provided with financial and other support by their home countries to help them compete on a global scale, in larger economic markets.

NEPAD – New Partnership for Africa's Development. Established in 2001 as a programme of the Organisation of African Unity, the NEPAD's primary objectives are to eradicate poverty, promote sustainable growth and development, halt the marginalisation of Africa in the globalisation process, and enhance its integration into the global economy. www.nepad.org

non-recourse loans – in the event of non-repayment of this type of loan, the lender is able only to recoup the amount laid down as collateral, or assets in lieu, and only the assets or collateral paid by the person who took out the loan; thus, this type of loan is low risk for the borrower, high-risk for the lender.

NPL – Non-Performing Loan. A loan where the principle or interest payments are ninety days overdue.
www.imf.org/external/pubs/ft/fsi/guide/2008/pdf/071408.pdf

OECD – Organisation for Economic Cooperation and Development. An international organisation that brings together the governments of countries committed to democracy and the market economy to support sustainable economic growth, boost employment and living standards and to maintain financial stability. www.oecd.org

OTC – Over-the-counter (markets).

peak oil (production) – refers to the point in time when half of the world's oil will be depleted.

Ponzi scheme – a fraudulent investment scheme that promises regular and extraordinarily high returns; however, all payouts are generated from the revenue from new investors to the scheme, rather than from actual profits. Named after Charles Ponzi, who was prosecuted for operating such a scheme in the 1920s.

price volatility – the record of price changes or values of a commodity over a set period of time. The more change, the more volatile; thus the higher the risk and vice versa.

Sarbanes-Oxley Act (2002) – passed by the United States Congress and aimed at refining the standards of regulation and protecting investors from the possibility of fraudulent accounting activities by corporations.

SASOL – South African Synthetic Oils. An integrated energy and chemical company. Using coal, oil and gas they produce liquid fuels, fuel components and chemicals. www.sasol.com

securitisation – a method of finance whereby various assets are grouped together to then divide and sell off separately, with the purchaser liable for the risk but also the recipient of any potential gain.

SME – Small and Medium-sized Entreprises.

Smoot-Hawley Tariff Act (the Tariff Act) – US protectionist legislation passed in 1930 to raise tariffs. Initially aimed at helping farmers in the midst of the Depression, the legislation was then applied to other sectors. In turn, foreign trade retaliated by enacting their own set of high tariffs and as a result of both US and foreign measures, international trade was stifled, and the Depression possibly worsened.

SOE – State Owned Enterprise.

TALF – Term Asset-Backed Securities Loan Facility. A facility created by the Federal Reserve in the United States in November 2008 to help participants meet the credit needs of households and small businesses. It supports the issuance of asset-backed securities collateralised by student loans, auto loans, credit-card loans and loans guaranteed by the Small Business Administration.

TARP – Troubled Asset Relief Programme. A voluntary capital-purchase programme created by the Federal Reserve in the United States to encourage financial institutions to build capital to increase the flow of financing to businesses and consumers and to support the economy.

Taylor rule – Introduced by John Taylor, a Stanford University economist. The Taylor rule aims to adjust interest rates in order to stabilise the economy and at the same time encourage growth.

teaser rate – loss-making introductory interest rate used to entice customers. After a set and usually short period of time the rate is hiked to a more standard, if not higher, charge.

three-month LIBOR – the average, calculated over a period of 90 days, of the interest rates used between banks to lend to one another.

tier-one capital base – one measure of a bank's financial position. Used by regulators to assess the ability of a bank to meet its own financial obligations at short notice.

Tobin tax – Proposed by James Tobin, a Harvard economist who suggested taxing speculative foreign currency transactions to prevent destabilising the currencies involved and to raise revenue that could be funnelled in to worthy projects.

toxic assets – a financial asset with a value that has fallen significantly and in a market that has ceased to function (such as a house bought at peak price prior to the collapse of a real-estate market which then becomes stagnant).

wholesale-funding model – an alternative way for banks to satisfy liquidity needs, which may be met through sources other than core deposits. Sources include, but are not limited to, Federal funds, public funds, Federal Home Loan Bank advances, the Federal Reserve's primary credit program, foreign deposits, brokered deposits, and deposits obtained through the Internet or CD listing services.

CONTRIBUTORS

James Alexander, co-founder of Zopa and CEO Green Thing
James was co-founder of Zopa (Zopa.com), the marketplace where people meet to lend and borrow money, and was UK CEO through to August 2007 and a board director until September 2009. Prior to Zopa, James was Strategy Director at Egg (egg.com), a world leader in digital banking. James is currently a trustee and CEO of Green Thing (dothegreenthing.com), a public service that inspires people to lead a greener life.

Dr Jacques Attali, Special Economic Adviser to President Sarkozy
Jacques Attali was the founder and first president of the European Bank for Reconstruction and Development. He is now CEO of PlaNet Finance, an international non-profit organisation whose mission is to alleviate poverty through the development of microfinance. In 2007, President Sarkozy appointed Jacques Attali to head a commission to examine the obstacles to French economic growth and propose reforms.

Professor Jagdish Bhagwati, University Professor at Columbia University and Senior Fellow in International Economics at the Council on Foreign Relations
Jagdish Bhagwati has been Economic Policy Adviser to Arthur Dunkel, Director General of GATT, Special Adviser to the UN on Globalization, and External Adviser to the WTO. He has served on the Expert Group appointed by the Director General of the WTO on the Future of the WTO and the advisory committee to Secretary General Kofi Annan on the NEPAD process in Africa. He is a Director of the National Bureau of Economic Research and was adviser to India's Finance Minister, now Prime Minister, on India's economic reforms.

Professor David Blanchflower, former Monetary Policy Committee member at the Bank of England
David Blanchflower was appointed as an external member of the Monetary Policy Committee with effect from 1 June 2006. David is the Bruce V. Rauner

Professor of Economics at Dartmouth College and a research associate at the National Bureau of Economic Research. In addition he is also a research fellow at the Centre for Economic Studies at the University of Munich and a research fellow at the Institute for the Study of Labour at the University of Bonn.

Ambassador John Bruton, former Taoiseach (Prime Minister) of Ireland and immediate former ambassador of the European Union to the United States

John Bruton is the former EU ambassador to the United States. He is a former Irish Prime Minister (Taoiseach), who helped transform the Irish economy into the 'Celtic Tiger', one of the fastest-growing economies in the world. While Prime Minister, Ambassador Bruton presided over a successful Irish EU presidency in 1996 and helped finalise the Stability and Growth Pact, which governs the management of the single European currency, the euro.

Todd Buchholz, former Director of Economic Policy at the White House

Todd Buchholz is a former Director of Economic Policy at the White House, a managing director of the $15 billion Tiger hedge fund and an award-winning economics teacher at Harvard. Buchholz advised President Bush and is a frequent commentator on ABC News, PBS and CBS and recently hosted his own show on CNBC. He is co-founder and Managing Director of Two Oceans Management, LLC, and served as a fellow at Cambridge University in 2009.

Dr Vince Cable, Deputy Leader and Shadow Chancellor, Liberal Democrats

Vince Cable worked as Treasury Finance Officer for the Kenyan Government between 1966 and 1968. After lecturing at Glasgow University in Economics he worked as a first secretary in the Diplomatic Service in the Foreign and Commonwealth Office (1974–76). From 1983 to 1990 Vince worked as Special Adviser on Economic Affairs for the Commonwealth Secretary General, Sir Sonny Ramphal. From 1990 he worked for Shell International and in 1995 became Shell's Chief Economist. He was made head of the economics programme at Chatham House and, since becoming an MP, has been appointed a fellow of Nuffield College, Oxford and a visiting research fellow at the Centre for the Study of Global Governance at the LSE.

Hon Peter Costello, Australia's longest serving Treasurer of the Commonwealth of Australia

Peter Costello was a member of the House of Representatives (Parliament of Australia) from 1990 to 2009. He was Treasurer of the Commonwealth of

Australia from 11 March 1996 to 3 December 2007, the longest serving Treasurer in Australia's history. Peter Costello currently serves on an Independent Advisory Board to the World Bank and has served as Chair of the OECD Ministerial in 2000, Chair of the APEC Finance Ministers in 2007 and Chair of the G20 in 2006. The G20 is the group of 20 countries considered systemically important to the International Financial System.

F W de Klerk, former President of South Africa

In 1989 F W de Klerk became President of South Africa and began to dismantle the provisions of apartheid. He lifted a thirty-year ban on the African National Congress and freed ANC leader Nelson Mandela, setting the stage for the 1994 election. When Mandela was elected President, de Klerk became Executive Deputy President. Together they led the process of transition and shared the Nobel Peace Prize.

Hernando de Soto, President of the Institute for Liberty and Democracy

Mr de Soto is currently President of the ILD – headquartered in Lima, Peru – considered by *The Economist* as one of the two most important think tanks in the world. *Time* magazine chose him as one of the five leading Latin American innovators of the century in its special issue 'Leaders for the New Millennium', and included him among the hundred most influential people in the world in 2004. Mr de Soto has served as an economist for the General Agreement on Tariffs and Trade, as President of the Executive Committee of the Intergovernmental Council of Copper Exporting Countries (CIPEC), as CEO of Universal Engineering Corporation (Continental Europe's largest consulting engineering firm), as a principal of the Swiss Bank Corporation Consultant Group and as a governor of Peru's Central Reserve Bank. Mr de Soto has published two books about economic and political development: *The Other Path*, in the mid–1980s, and at the end of 2000, *The Mystery of Capital: Why Capitalism Triumphs in the West and Fails Everywhere Else*. Both books have been international best-sellers – translated into some twenty languages.

Professor Martin Feldstein, Professor of Economics at Harvard University

Martin Feldstein is the George F. Baker Professor of Economics at Harvard University and President Emeritus of the National Bureau of Economic Research. He served as President and CEO of the NBER from 1977 to 1982 and from 1984 to 2008. The NBER is a private, non-profit research organisation that has specialised for more than eighty years in producing non-partisan studies of the American economy. From 1982 through 1984, Martin Feldstein was Chairman of the Council of Economic Advisers and President Reagan's Chief Economic Adviser. He served as President of the American Economic Association in 2004. In 2006, President Bush appointed him to be a member of the President's Foreign Intelligence Advisory Board. In 2009, President Obama appointed him to be a member of the President's Economic Recovery Advisory Board.

Tony Fernandes, founder and CEO of AirAsia

Tony Fernandes and three friends took over an ailing, debt-ridden airline in Malaysia in December 2001 and relaunched it as a low-cost carrier. In the process, they unleashed a revolution in air travel in the region. AirAsia began with two aircraft, one destination and 250 staff. In its first year of operations, it transported 250,000 guests. Eight short years later, Asia's largest low-cost carrier operates eighty-five spanking new Airbus A-320 aircraft, flies to more than sixty destinations from hubs in Malaysia, Indonesia and Thailand and employs a staff of almost 7,000. AirAsia carried 24 million passengers in 2008. Its tagline, 'Now Everyone Can Fly', animates its determination to democratise air travel and free it from the clutches of the elite.

Professor Dr Wolfgang Franz, President of the Centre for European Economic Research and Chairman of the German Council of Economic Experts

In March 2009 Franz became Chairman of the German Council of Economic Experts, which advises the German Government and Parliament on economic-policy issues. Franz had already been a member of this advisory body from 1994 till 1999 and was reappointed in 2003. Franz is a member of the Heidelberg Academy of Sciences and Humanities and also heads the Economics and Empirical Social Sciences section at the Leopoldina, the German Academy of Sciences. He is a member of the Scientific Advisory Board of the Federal Ministry of Economics and Technology. He was key adviser for economics at the German Research Foundation (DFG) and co-editor of several magazines on economics. He is also President of the Centre for European Economic Research in Mannheim and Chair of Economics at the University of Mannheim.

Professor Stephane Garelli, World Authority on Competitiveness

Stephane Garelli is a professor at both the International Institute for Management Development (IMD), one of the world's leading business schools, and at the University of Lausanne. He is also the director of IMD's World Competitiveness Center and an authority on World Competitiveness: his research focuses particularly on how nations and enterprises compete in international markets.

Dr Fred Hu, Chairman of Greater China at Goldman Sachs

Dr Fred Hu is Chairman of Greater China at Goldman Sachs. Before joining Goldman Sachs as Chief Economist for China in 1997, Mr Hu was a staff member at the International Monetary Fund (IMF) in Washington, DC. He has advised the Chinese Government on financial reform, state-owned-enterprise restructuring and macroeconomic policies, and has worked closely with China's leading companies and financial institutions on business strategy, capital raising, domestic and cross-border mergers and acquisitions.

Will Hutton, Executive Vice Chair of the Work Foundation

Will Hutton is executive vice chair of the Work Foundation, the most influential voice on work, employment and organisation issues in the UK. Regularly called on to advise senior political and business figures and comment in the national and international media, Will Hutton is today one of the pre-eminent economics commentators in the country.

Andrew Keen, expert on the Future of Media, Culture and Technology

Andrew Keen is one of the world's most influential thinkers about twenty-first-century business, technology and media. Andrew is author of *Cult of the Amateur: How the Internet is Killing our Culture*, and is widely regarded as the leading contemporary critic of the Internet.

Vaclav Klaus, President of the Czech Republic

Vaclav Klaus is the second President of the Czech Republic. He was first elected in 2003 and re-elected in 2008. He is recognised as one of the most influential post-communist leaders in Eastern Europe.

Richard Koo, Chief Economist of Nomura Research Institute

Richard C Koo joined Nomura in 1984 and is now the Chief Economist of Nomura Research Institute, the research arm of Nomura Securities. Prior to that, he was an economist with the Federal Reserve Bank of New York and a doctoral fellow of the board of governors of the Federal Reserve System. Consistently voted as one of the most reliable economists by Japanese capital and financial market participants for nearly a decade, he has also advised successive prime ministers on how best to deal with Japan's economic and banking problems.

Lord Norman Lamont, former Chancellor of the Exchequer

Norman Lamont was Chancellor of the Exchequer during the last recession, presiding over the withdrawal of sterling from the Exchange Rate Mechanism and what quickly became known as Black Monday. He has since been described by the economist Sir Alan Walters as 'not only the most effective, but also the bravest Chancellor since the war'. Originally an investment banker with N M Rothschild, Lamont spent twenty-five years in the Commons, serving in the Cabinet under both Margaret Thatcher and John Major.

Maurice Levy, Chairman and Chief Executive Officer of Publicis Groupe

Mr Levy joined Publicis, one of the world's largest advertising and media-services conglomerates, in 1971. He was given responsibility for its data-processing and information-technology systems. However, he moved swiftly up the organisation, being appointed Corporate Secretary in 1973, Managing Director in 1976 and Chair and CEO of Publicis Conseil in 1981. He then became Vice Chair of Publicis Groupe in 1986 and was appointed Chairman and CEO of the management board in November 1987. Maurice Levy also sits on the board of the World Economic Forum and Deutsche Bank.

Augusto Lopez-Claros, director and founder, EFD – Global Consulting Network

Augusto Lopez-Claros is a former professor at the University of Chile at Santiago, a resident representative at the International Monetary Fund in Russia, a senior international economist at Lehman Brothers in London and a former Chief Economist and Director of the Global Competitiveness Programme at the World Economic Forum.

Dr Gerard Lyons, Chief Economist and Group Head of Global Research at Standard Chartered Bank

Dr Gerard Lyons is an expert on the world economy, international financial system, macroeconomic policy and global markets in his role as Chief Economist and Group Head of Global Research at Standard Chartered. Lyons is also an economic adviser to the board and is a member of the bank's Executive Forum. He has over twenty years experience in the City in senior positions, and previous roles include Chief Economist at DKB International and consultant to the Dai-Ichi Kangyo Bank, Chief UK Economist at Swiss Bank Corporation, beginning his career with Chase Manhattan.

George Magnus, Senior Economic Adviser at UBS

George Magnus is the Senior Economic Adviser at UBS Investment Bank, one of the world's leading financial-services institutions, having previously been the Chief Economist for ten years. In almost thirty years of working experience in the City, he has held senior positions at S G Warburg, Chase Manhattan Bank and Bank of America. He is a well-known and highly regarded economist in the financial community and has won many accolades in professional surveys as one of the top global economists. He was one of few analysts to predict in early 2007 the financial meltdown and global recession. He has a major interest and reputation in demographics, and is the author of *The Age of Aging: How Demographics are Changing the Global Economy and Our World* (John Wiley, 2008).

Hamish McRae, Principal Economic Commentator at the *Independent*

An outstanding journalist, Hamish McRae is the Principal Economic Commentator of the *Independent* and the *Independent on Sunday*. He is also the author of the acclaimed work on the future, *The World in 2020: Power, Culture and Prosperity*, first published in 1994 and translated into more than a dozen languages.

Thierry Malleret, senior partner, Head of Research and Networks at IJ Partners

Thierry Malleret is a senior partner, Head of Research and Networks at IJ Partners – an investment company based in Geneva ('IJ' stands for 'Informed Judgement'). He was until April 2009 managing partner at Rainbow Insight, an advisory boutique which he founded and that provided tailor-made intelligence to investors. Previously, Thierry headed the Global Risk Network at the World Economic Forum. Prior to that, he worked in investment banking (as a chief economist and strategist of a major Russian investment bank, and previously as an economist at EBRD in London), think tanks and academia (both in New York and Oxford) and in government (with a three-year spell in the Prime Minister's office in Paris).

Hon Mike Moore, former Prime Minister of New Zealand

Mike Moore is a former Director General of the World Trade Organization and Prime Minister of New Zealand, and a leading voice on globalisation. An active participant in discussions on trade liberalisation, he helped launch the Uruguay Round of GATT negotiations. Moore's term at the helm of the WTO coincided with momentous changes in the global economy as well as the launch of the Doha Round and the inclusion of China in the WTO.

Jim O'Neill, Head of Global Economics, Commodities and Strategy Research at Goldman Sachs

Jim O'Neill is Head of Global Economics, Commodities and Strategy Research for Goldman Sachs, which he became in 2008. In this role, Jim manages the firm's economics, strategy and commodity research and the output of these teams around the world. Jim O'Neill joined Goldman Sachs in October 1995 as a partner, co-Head of Global Economics and Chief Currency Economist. Jim has spent much of his twenty-eight-year career analysing the world's foreign-exchange market and is also the creator of the acronym 'BRICs', and together with his colleagues he has published much research about BRICs which has become synonymous with the emergence of Brazil, Russia India and China as the growth opportunities of the future.

Michael O'Sullivan, author of *Ireland and the Global Question* and *What Did We Do Right?*

Michael O'Sullivan is Head of UK Research and Global Asset Allocation at Credit Suisse Private Bank. He previously worked as a strategist for Goldman Sachs International, UBS Warburg and Commerzbank Securities and State Street Global Markets. He has taught finance and economics at Oxford and Princeton Universities. Michael O'Sullivan is the author of *Ireland and the Global Question* and *What Did We Do Right?*, two books that examine the economic, social and foreign-policy aspects of how Ireland became one of the world's most globalised countries and the challenges that lie ahead of it in a post-credit-crisis world.

Nenad Pacek, founder and President of Global Success Advisers

Nenad Pacek is founder and President of Global Success Advisers, a boutique consultancy dedicated to assisting companies outperform competition in international markets. He is an acclaimed international economist and business strategist who authored the best-selling book *Emerging Markets: Lessons for Business Success and Outlooks for Different Markets*. Previously he was Vice President of the Economist Group's economic intelligence and corporate advisory division, where he worked for almost two decades advising more than 300 multinational companies. He is an adjunct professor of International Economics and International Business at two private business schools in Vienna.

Professor Edmund Phelps, winner of the Nobel Prize in Economics, 2006

Edmund Phelps earned his BA from Amherst (1955) and his PhD from Yale (1959). He is McVickar Professor of Political Economy at Columbia University, Director of Columbia's Center on Capitalism and Society, and winner of the 2006 Nobel Prize in Economics. His career began at the RAND Corporation. From 1960 to 1966 he held appointments at Yale and its Cowles Foundation, then a professorship at Penn.

Jonathon Porritt CBE, founder director of Forum for the Future
Jonathon Porritt is a founder director of Forum for the Future, and an eminent writer, broadcaster and commentator on sustainable development. He was formerly Chairman of the UK Sustainable Development Commission (2000–9); director of Friends of the Earth; co-Chair of the Green Party, of which he is still a member; chairman of UNED-UK, Chairman of Sustainability South-West, the South-West Round Table for Sustainable Development; and a trustee of WWF UK.

Dr Mamphela Ramphele, former Managing Director of the World Bank
Mamphela Ramphele, a South African national, is the Chair of Circle Capital Ventures, a Cape Town based black economic-empowerment company focusing on growing companies and investing in people. She served as a Managing Director of the World Bank from May 2000 to July 2004. Prior to joining the World Bank, Mamphela Ramphele was Vice Chancellor of the University of Cape Town, becoming the first black woman to hold this position at a South African university.

Jeremy Rifkin, founder and President of the Foundation on Economic Trends
Jeremy Rifkin is President of the Foundation on Economic Trends and the author of seventeen best-selling books on the impact of scientific and technological changes on the economy, the workforce, society and the environment. Mr Rifkin advised the government of France during its presidency of the European Union (1 July to 31 December, 2008). Mr Rifkin also served as an adviser to Chancellor Angela Merkel of Germany, Prime Minister José Sócrates of Portugal and Prime Minister Janez Janša of Slovenia, during their respective European Council presidencies, on issues related to the economy, climate change and energy security. He currently advises the European Commission, the European Parliament and several EU heads of state, including Prime Minister José Luis Rodriguez Zapatero of Spain and Chancellor Angela Merkel of Germany.

Dr Andrew Sentance, external member, Bank of England Monetary Policy Committee
Dr Andrew Sentance is an external member of the Monetary Policy Committee of the Bank of England, appointed by the Chancellor of the Exchequer in 2006. The Monetary Policy Committee is responsible for setting interest rates in the UK to meet the Government's inflation target. Before joining the Bank of England, Andrew was Chief Economist and Head of

Environmental Affairs at British Airways. He is also a part-time Professor of Sustainable Business at the University of Warwick.

Guy Verhofstadt, former Prime Minster of Belgium
Guy Verhofstadt won the 1999 Belgian elections, becoming their first liberal prime minister in more than sixty years. He presided over two governments with the Belgian socialist parties, following the longest formation crisis in Belgium's political history. Confirming his European beliefs, he wrote *The United States of Europe* in 2005, which was translated into a dozen European languages and won 2007 European Book of the Year.

Professor Dr Norbert Walter, Chief Economist of Deutsche Bank
Norbert Walter is Chief Economist of the Deutsche Bank Group and CEO of Deutsche Bank Research. Prior to this position, he was a professor and director at the renowned Kiel Institute for World Economics and was the John J. McCloy Distinguished Research Fellow at the American Institute for Contemporary Studies at the Johns Hopkins University in Washington, DC. Professor Walter is a member of the Committee of Wise Men on the Regulation of European Securities Markets and, since 2007, a member of the Business and Industry Advisory Committee of the OECD (BIAC).

Dr Linda Yueh, Professor of Economics at Oxford University
Linda Yueh is a fellow in economics at St Edmund Hall, Oxford University, a visiting professor at the London Business School and an economics commentator on global economic, financial and business issues, regularly contributing to broadcasters such as the BBC, Channel 4 News, CNBC, CNN and ITV News, among others. She is Director of the China Growth Centre at Oxford University, which focuses on researching economic issues of relevance to China and the global economy, and is considered one of the world's foremost experts on the Chinese economy.

Professor Muhammad Yunus, founder of Grameen Bank and Nobel Peace Prize winner, 2006
Professor Muhammad Yunus is the founder and Managing Director of Grameen Bank, which provides microcredit to millions of poor people in Bangladesh. In 2006 he was awarded the Nobel Peace Prize. As founder of Grameen Bank, Yunus pioneered microcredit, the innovative banking programme that provides the poor – mainly women – with small loans they use to launch businesses and lift their families out of poverty.

Dr Marvin Zonis, Professor at the Graduate School of Business at the University of Chicago

At Chicago's Business School, Marvin Zonis teaches courses on International Political Economy, Leadership, and E-Commerce. He was the first professor at the business school to teach a course on the effects of digital technologies on global business. He also consults to corporations and professional asset-management firms throughout the world, helping them to identify, assess and manage their political risks in the changing global environment.

ACKNOWLEDGEMENTS

I would like to thank Louisa Joyner, Editorial Director at Virgin Books, for opening the door to a world of new opportunity and believing in me as a new author. This book would not have been possible without the tireless energy, enthusiasm, professionalism and support of Kelly Falconer, Senior Editor at Virgin Books. Thanks also to Richard Cable, MD Random House, Dame Gail Rebuck, Chair and CEO of Random House, Sophia Brown, Davina Russell, Will Francis at Janklow & Nesbitt, Reetu Kabra and Keith Egerton for his thoughtful copy-edit.

Special thanks to Tom Kenyon-Slaney, co-founder and CEO of The London Speaker Bureau and to all those who work in our offices around the world.

Personal thanks to Vince Cable, Ambassador John Bruton, Dr Bernard Kouchner, Lord Lamont, Jonathan Porritt, Dr Linda Yueh, Augusto Lopez-Claros, Professor Norbert Walter, Martin Feldstein, Hon Mike Moore, F W de Klerk, Marvin Zonis and Professor Jagdish Bhagwati for their advice, interest and input despite punishing schedules of their own. My sincere thanks also to all those contributors and their offices around the world for delivering these invaluable essays which give the book such wide appeal.

To Professor Niall Ferguson, Professor Joseph Stiglitz, Mikhail Gorbachev, Professor Nouriel Roubini, Gerard Shroeder, James Wolfensohn, Jeffrey Sachs and Gary Kasparov who despite wanting to contribute were unable to do so due to current literary commitments.

I would like to acknowledge: Columbia University in New York; Heldref Publications; the French Foreign Office; Lingoleaf Language Services; Grameen Bank in Bangladesh; the Delegation of the European Commission to the United States; the Office of The President of the Czech Republic; F W de Klerk Foundation; House of Representatives in the Australian Parliament; National Bureau of Economic Research in the US; Kansas City Federal Reserve; Harvard University; Oxford University; The Work Foundation; Forum for the Future.

Should you require further information on any of the contributors featured in this book please contact:

The London Speaker Bureau
Elsinore House
77 Fulham Palace Road
London W6 8JA
United Kingdom
+44 (0)208 748 9595
enquiries@londonspeakerbureau.co.uk
www.londonspeakerbureau.co.uk

Copyright Acknowledgements

INDEX